No Other Way Out

No Other Way Out: States and Revolutionary Movements, 1945–1991 provides a powerful explanation for the emergence of popular revolutionary movements, and the occurrence of actual revolutions, during the Cold War era. This sweeping study ranges from Southeast Asia in the 1940s and 1950s to Central America in the 1970s and 1980s and Eastern Europe in 1989. Following in the "state-centered" tradition of Theda Skocpol's *States and Social Revolutions*, Goodwin demonstrates how the actions of specific types of authoritarian regimes unwittingly channeled popular resistance into radical and often violent directions. Revolution became the "only way out," to use Trotsky's formulation, for the opponents of these intransigent regimes. By comparing the historical trajectories of more than a dozen countries, Goodwin also shows how revolutionaries were sometimes able to create, and not simply exploit, opportunities for seizing state power.

Jeff Goodwin is associate professor and director of graduate studies in the Department of Sociology at New York University. He has published numerous papers on revolutions and collective action in such journals as the *American Journal of Sociology*, *American Sociological Review*, *Social Science History*, *Sociological Forum*, *Theory and Society*, and *Politics and Society*. His articles have been awarded prizes by two sections of the American Sociological Association, including the Barrington Moore Prize of the Comparative-Historical section. Professor Goodwin has also edited three forthcoming volumes: *Paths to Protest*, *Passionate Politics: Emotions and Social Movements* (with James M. Jasper and Francesca Polletta), and *Social Movements: Readings, Cases, and Concepts* (with James M. Jasper). He has conducted research in Central America, the Philippines, and Ireland.

Cambridge Studies in Comparative Politics

General Editor
Margaret Levi *University of Washington, Seattle*

Associate Editors
Robert H. Bates *Harvard University*
Peter Hall *Harvard University*
Stephen E. Hansen *University of Washington, Seattle*
Peter Lange *University of Duke*
Helen Milner *Columbia University*
Frances M. Rosenbluth *Yale University*
Susan Stokes *University of Chicago*
Sidney Tarrow *Cornell University*

Other Books in the Series

Continued on page following index

No Other Way Out

STATES AND REVOLUTIONARY MOVEMENTS, 1945–1991

JEFF GOODWIN

New York University

CAMBRIDGE
UNIVERSITY PRESS

PUBLISHED BY THE PRESS SYNDICATE OF THE UNIVERSITY OF CAMBRIDGE
The Pitt Building, Trumpington Street, Cambridge, United Kingdom

CAMBRIDGE UNIVERSITY PRESS
The Edinburgh Building, Cambridge CB2 2RU, UK
40 West 20th Street, New York, NY 10011-4211, USA
10 Stamford Road, Oakleigh, VIC 3166, Australia
Ruiz de Alarcón 13, 28014 Madrid, Spain
Dock House, The Waterfront, Cape Town 8001, South Africa

http://www.cambridge.org

First published 2001

Printed in the United States of America

Typeface Janson Text 10/13 pt.   *System* QuarkXPress [BTS]

A catalog record for this book is available from the British Library.

Library of Congress Cataloging in Publication Data
Goodwin, Jeff.
        States and revolutionary movements, 1945–1991 / Jeff Goodwin.
            p.   cm. – (Cambridge studies in comparative politics)
        ISBN 0-521-62069-4 – ISBN 0-521-62948-9 (pb)
        1. Revolutions.   2. World politics – 1945–   I. Title.   II. Series.

    JC491 .G64 2001
    322.4′2 – dc21   00-058585

ISBN   0 521 62069 4   hardback
ISBN   0 521 62948 9   paperback

Contents

Figures, Tables, and Maps

Figures

Tables

Maps

Abbreviations and Acronyms

Abbreviation, Acronym, or Name	Nation/Region	Organization
AD	Venezuela	Democratic Action
ALN	Brazil	National Liberating Action
ARENA	El Salvador	Nationalist Republican Alliance
ARVN	Vietnam	Army of the Republic of Vietnam
ATC	Nicaragua	Association of Rural Workers
AVC	Ecuador	¡Alfaro Lives, Damn It!
BRP	El Salvador	Popular Revolutionary Bloc
CD	El Salvador	Democratic Convergence
CGUP	Guatemala	Guatemalan Committee of Popular Unity
CMEA	Soviet bloc	Council for Mutual Economic Assistance
CNT	Guatemala	National Confederation of Workers
CNUS	Guatemala	National Committee for Trade Union Unity
Comecon		(see CMEA)
CONDECA	Central America	Central American Defense Council
CPRs	Guatemala	Communities of People in Resistance
CUC	Guatemala	Committee of Peasant Unity
DA	Philippines	Democratic Alliance
DCG	Guatemala	Christian Democratic Party of Guatemala
DIT	Guatemala	Department of Technical Investigations
DRV	Vietnam	Democratic Republic of Vietnam
EDCOR	Philippines	Economic Development Corps
EGP	Guatemala	Guerrilla Army of the Poor
ELN	Bolivia	National Liberation Army
ELN	Colombia	National Liberation Army
ELN	Peru	National Liberation Army
EPL	Colombia	Popular Army of Liberation
EPR	Mexico	Popular Revolutionary Army
ERP	Argentina	People's Revolutionary Army
ERP	El Salvador	Popular Revolutionary Army

EZLN	Mexico	Zapatista National Liberation Army
FALN	Venezuela	Armed Forces of National Liberation
FAO	Nicaragua	Broad Opposition Front
FAPU	El Salvador	United Popular Action Front
FAR	Guatemala	Rebel Armed Forces
FARC	Colombia	Revolutionary Armed Forces of Colombia
FARN	El Salvador	Armed Forces of National Resistance
FDNG	Guatemala	New Guatemala Democratic Front
FDR	El Salvador	Democratic Revolutionary Front
FDRC	Guatemala	Democratic Front Against Repression
FECCAS	El Salvador	Christian Federation of Salvadoran Peasants
FENASTRAS	El Salvador	National Union Federation of Salvadoran Workers
FFF	Philippines	Federation of Free Farmers
FMLN	El Salvador	Farabundo Marti Front for National Liberation
FNO	Guatemala	National Opposition Front
FP-31	Guatemala	January Thirty-First Popular Front
FPL	El Salvador	Popular Forces of Liberation
FPR	Honduras	Lorenzo Zelaya Popular Revolutionary Forces
FPMR	Chile	Manuel Rodríguez Patriotic Front
FPN	Nicaragua	National Patriotic Front
FSLN	Nicaragua	Sandinista National Liberation Front
FSN	Romania	National Salvation Front
FUR	Guatemala	United Front of the Revolution
GN	Nicaragua	National Guard
HMB	Philippines	People's Liberation Army
Hukbalahap	Philippines	People's Anti-Japanese Army
ICP	Vietnam	Indochinese Communist Party
KOR	Poland	Committee for the Defense of Workers
L-23	Mexico	September Twenty-Third Communist League
LP-28	El Salvador	February Twenty-Eighth Popular Leagues
JUSMAG	Philippines	Joint U.S. Military Advisory Group
M-14	Dominican Republic	June Fourteenth Movement
M-19	Colombia	April Nineteenth Movement
M-26-7	Cuba	July Twenty-Sixth Movement
MAAG	Vietnam	Military Assistance Advisory Group
MASAKA	Philippines	Free Farmers' Union
MCA	Malaya	Malayan Chinese Association
MCP	Malaya	Malayan Communist Party
MDN	Nicaragua	Nicaraguan Democratic Movement
MIC	Malaya	Malayan Indian Congress
MIPTES	El Salvador	Independent Movement of Professionals and Technicians of El Salvador
MIR	Chile	Movement of the Revolutionary Left
MIR	Peru	Movement of the Revolutionary Left

Abbreviations and Acronyms

MLN	Guatemala	National Liberation Movement
MLN	Uruguay	National Liberation Movement (Tupamaros)
MLP	El Salvador	Popular Liberation Movement
MNR	El Salvador	Revolutionary National Movement
MPAJA	Malaya	Malayan People's Anti-Japanese Army
MPL	Honduras	Cinchonero Popular Liberation Movement
MPN	Argentina	Montonero Peronist Movement
MPSC	El Salvador	Popular Social Christian Movement
MPU	Nicaragua	United People's Movement
MRLA	Malaya	Malayan Races Liberation Army
MRTA	Peru	Tupac Amaru Revolutionary Movement
OAS	Americas	Organization of American States
ORDEN	El Salvador	Nationalist Democratic Organization
ORPA	Guatemala	Revolutionary Organization of People in Arms
PAC	Guatemala	Civilian Self-Defense Patrol
Partindo	Indonesia	Indonesian Party
PCN	El Salvador	National Conciliation Party
PCS	El Salvador	Salvadoran Communist Party
PCV	Venezuela	Venezuelan Communist Party
PGT	Guatemala	Guatemalan Labor Party (Communist)
PKI	Indonesia	Indonesian Communist Party
PKKI	Indonesia	Indonesian Independence Preparatory Committee
PKP	Philippines	Philippine Communist Party
PLI	Nicaragua	Independent Liberal Party
PNI	Indonesia	Indonesian Nationalist Party
PPL	El Salvador	Local Popular Power
PPSC	Nicaragua	People's Social Christian Party
PRTC	El Salvador	Revolutionary Party of Central American Workers
PRTC-H	Honduras	Revolutionary Party of Central American Workers–Honduras
PSD	Guatemala	Democratic Socialist Party
PSN	Nicaragua	Nicaraguan Socialist Party (Communist)
RCP	Romania	Romanian Communist Party
ROTC	U.S.	Reserve Officer Training Corps
UDEL	Nicaragua	Democratic Union of Liberation
UDN	El Salvador	Nationalist Democratic Union
UMNO	Malaya	United Malays National Organization
UNO	El Salvador	National Opposition Union
UNTS	El Salvador	National Unity of Salvadoran Workers
UPD	El Salvador	Popular Democratic Union
URNG	Guatemala	Guatemalan National Revolutionary Unity
USAFFE	Philippines	U.S. Armed Forces in the Far East
VNQDD	Vietnam	Vietnamese Nationalist Party
VPR	Brazil	Popular Revolutionary Vanguard

Preface and Acknowledgments

The various chapters and ideas in this book have been presented on so many occasions and before so many colleagues, peers, and students that any list of the people who have kindly (and sometimes impatiently) responded to its arguments would no doubt consume several pages. I would like to thank, however, a rather smaller circle of friends and colleagues who have been especially helpful, directly or indirectly, in my continuing efforts to understand revolutions, social movements, and political conflict more generally.

I have been most privileged – perhaps uniquely privileged – to know and to have worked with the two most influential contemporary scholars of revolutions, Theda Skocpol and Charles Tilly. I want to thank them for their inspiration and encouragement, both that which they have expressed personally and that embodied in their own exemplary scholarship. I also want to recognize several other important scholars of revolutions who have also greatly influenced my thinking, albeit often from a somewhat greater distance, including John Foran, Jack Goldstone, Tim McDaniel, Eric Selbin, and Timothy Wickham-Crowley. And I would like to thank Mustafa Emirbayer and Jim Jasper, intellectual collaborators who have continually engaged and challenged my thinking about a host of issues.

A number of people at Harvard, Northwestern, and New York Universities (many of whom have since moved on to other institutions) have also helped me, more than they may realize, to think more clearly about revolutions and not-so-related issues. Thanks, then, to J. Samuel Valenzuela, Stephen Cornell, Orlando Patterson, Murray Milgate, Peter Bearman, David Brain, Debra Satz, Daniel Goldhagen, Joseph Schwartz, Richard Snyder, John A. Hall, John D. Stephens, Evelyne Huber, Charles Ragin, Edwin Amenta, and Edward Lehman. Finally, I would like to thank a number of research assistants who have helped me over the years (although not all of their diligent efforts are reflected in this book): Loren Bough (at Harvard) and Ellen Bienstock, Liena Gurevich, Miliann Kang, Meenoo Kohli, and Miranda Martinez (all at NYU).

Chapter 2 draws heavily upon a paper that appeared in *Theorizing Revolutions* (1997), edited by John Foran, reprinted here with the permission of Routledge; and an earlier version of Chapter 8 appeared in *Social Science History* 18 (1994). I would like to thank Roy Wiemann for his help with the figures in this book.

I should note at the outset that this book is based upon, for all intents and purposes, widely available secondary sources. I have managed over the years to visit all of the Central American countries that I write about, and I have spoken with various intellectuals as well as ordinary folk there; these travels certainly shaped my understanding of that region in subtle and not-so-subtle ways, but they did not result in the production of any new data, other than that of a strictly subjective and impressionistic variety. I have also researched primary materials in the Philippines that pertain to the Huk rebellion, but the results of that inquiry, in which I deploy an altogether different theoretical framework from the one found in this book, are published elsewhere (see Goodwin 1997). In fact, like many first books too long in the making, this one reflects a theoretical standpoint that I have largely moved beyond, as the discussion in Chapter 2 may suggest.

There is, in short, no "new" historical data in the pages that follow. What *is* new, I think, is my juxtaposition within a single analytic framework of data that has generally remained compartmentalized by academic divisions of labor, particularly those that separate "area experts" from one another and from theorists. I can only hope that I have juxtaposed this data in interesting ways and drawn the right conclusions therefrom. My plea to historians and area specialists, who are certain to lament my chutzpah in this vast undertaking, is to note that comparative sociologists, as T. H. Marshall once put it,

must inevitably rely extensively on secondary authorities, without going back to the original sources. [We] do this partly because life is too short to do anything else when using the comparative method, and [we] need data assembled from a wide historical field, and partly because original sources are very tricky things to use. . . . It is the business of historians to sift this miscellaneous collection of dubious authorities and to give others the results of their careful professional assessment. And surely they will not rebuke the sociologists for putting faith in what historians write. (1964: 38)

Of course, I have tried not to read what anyone writes, even historians, uncritically!

This book also prioritizes analysis over historical narrative, although I have tried to write for the proverbial general reader who has little if any knowledge of the various regions and countries that I discuss. Accordingly, I have tried to include just enough narrative and background information (including several chronologies) to make my analyses accessible and, I hope, persuasive to such readers as well as to specialists. However, this book does not offer anything like comprehensive historical narratives of the revolutionary movements, revolutions, or time periods that it examines. For those who seek such narratives, or who wish to explore issues that this book touches upon only lightly, I offer an old and increasingly rare device, the annotated bibliography, which I hope will help light the way.

I was once told that before I could write sensibly about revolutions, I would need to decide for myself whether they were morally good or just. Are they? As is so often the case with the big questions about revolutions, this one has no simple or invariant answer. Certainly, after Stalin and Pol Pot, it is impossible to believe in the inherent goodness or progressive character of revolutions. Yet I have come to believe that revolutions are generally necessary or, more accurately, perceived as necessary by most of their ordinary protagonists – politically, morally, and even existentially necessary in the fact of extreme duress and hardship. "Prudence, indeed, will dictate," an American revolutionary once wrote, "that Governments long established should not be changed for light and transient causes; and accordingly all experience hath shewn, that mankind are more disposed to suffer, while evils are sufferable, than to right themselves by abolishing the forms to which they are accustomed." These words from the Declaration of Independence capture an important truth: Revolutions do not usually happen – for good or ill – until the status quo becomes truly insufferable for masses of ordinary folk. It hardly follows from this that revolutions are necessarily good and just, although I find equally wanting the idea that they are invariably evil in their consequences. What seems invariably evil are not revolutions per se, but the circumstances that give rise to them. This said, those who are looking for a moral interpretation of Revolution (with a capital R) will find this book deeply disappointing; my goal is to provide a plausible causal account of a subset of revolutions.

Although this book is analytic in nature (perhaps excessively so for some readers), I have attempted to write it with a modicum of academic jargon and precious neologisms. Not to sound too self-righteous, but I share Gerrge Orwell's suspicion that opaque language usually masks (and reflects) bad ideas as well as bad politics. Given my subject matter, certainly, it would be all too easy to lapse into talk of "transgression," "post-coloniality," "subalternity," "subject positions," and the like. Suffice it to say that "ordinary" words like "revolution" and "the state" pose enough conceptual difficulties for the analyst, at least for this one; heaping on still more verbiage rarely removes those difficulties, and it typically creates additional ones. Accordingly, I offer up in the pages that follow precisely one "new" concept, if I am not mistaken, namely, "state constructionism" – although the term refers to an idea that has survived in various forms at least since the work of Tocqueville. I am not sure, in the end, that all of the arguments that I advance in this book are either correct or interesting, but the reader should not have to struggle to figure out what those arguments are.

Attentive readers will notice that I have toyed with the title of Walter LaFeber's (1993) excellent book on Central America in the title of my own Chapter 6. I hope Professor LaFeber (whom I have never met) appreciates that, under the circumstances, some such riposte was, well, inevitable. Finally, I have played with the title of both a wonderful article by Eldon Kenworthy (1973) and Werner Sombart's classic *Why Is There No Socialism in the United States?* (1976 [1906]) in my section on Honduras in Chapter 5. Sombart's is a leading question, to be sure, as any lawyer would point out. And yet I believe, like Sombart, not only that counterfactual questions are worth raising, but also that comparative analysis can go a long way towards answering them.

I would like, finally, to thank my parents, Dorothy and Roger Goodwin; my brothers, Ron and Don; and my parents-in-law, Lucy and Gerhard Steinhagen, for their affection and support. I dedicate this book to my wife, Renée Steinhagen, who has herself challenged my thinking for the better on so many issues, and to our wonderful daughter, Naomi. They're the best thing that's ever happened to me.

PART ONE

Introduction

1

Comparing Revolutionary Movements

Scholars have offered some interesting theories on how revolution develops and why it develops, but they have generally failed to explain how similar elements have produced revolutions in some cases and not in others. Research in the field should begin to examine "failed revolutions" and "revolutions that never took place" as well as successful ones to determine the revolutionary element or elements.

– William E. Lipsky (1976: 508)

Revolutionary movements are not simply or exclusively a response to economic exploitation or inequality, but also and more directly a response to political oppression and violence, typically brutal and indiscriminate. This is the principal thesis of this book, one that I reach through an examination of revolutionary movements that emerged during the second half of what has been called the "short" twentieth century (1914–91), a period characterized by the Cold War between the United States and the former Soviet Union.

The Cold War era (1945–91) was truly an "age of revolution," even more so, arguably, than the great revolutionary age of 1789–1848 (see Hobsbawm 1962). Dozens of powerful revolutionary movements emerged across the globe during this period, mainly in the Third World, and a number of them successfully overthrew existing political authorities. In the process, some movements also radically restructured, destroyed, or replaced key institutions, social relationships, and shared beliefs. In fact, many more radical, or "social," revolutions occurred during the Cold War era than had occurred in all previous history prior to the Second World War (see Table 1.1).

This book is but the latest installment in a long line of studies that have compared revolutions and revolutionary movements in order to

Table 1.1. *Major social revolutions, 1789–1989.*

Country (or region)	Year
France	1789
Mexico	1910
Russia	1917
Yugoslavia	1945
Vietnam	1945
China	1949
Bolivia	1952
Cuba	1959
Algeria	1962
Ethiopia	1974
Angola	1975
Mozambique	1975
Cambodia	1975
South Vietnam	1975
Iran	1979
Nicaragua	1979
Grenada	1979
Eastern Europe	1989

Note: The listed dates are conventional markers, usually referring to the year in which revolutionaries overthrew extant political regimes. Revolutions, however, are best conceptualized not as events, but as processes that typically span many years or even decades.

understand better both the similarities and differences in their causes, processes, and achievements. Like other authors who have compared revolutionary movements, I begin from the assumption that understanding them better is eminently worthwhile not only because of the enormous importance of these movements for the national societies in which they occurred, but also for their effects on the configuration of power and beliefs in other societies (including, not least, the United States) and thus on the international balance of power as well. One simply cannot understand the twentieth century histories of, for example, Mexico, Russia, China, Vietnam, Indonesia, Cuba, Iran, Nicaragua, El Salvador, Guatemala, or many other countries without understanding the revolutionary conflicts that occurred there; and understanding these conflicts is also crucial for comprehending a variety of important and contemporaneous transnational processes, including, for example, the demise of colonial empires and the history of the Cold War itself. In fact, with the possible exception of international wars, revolutions have been the most consequential form of political conflict in the twentieth century and, indeed, in human history.

Social scientists in the United States, myself included, have been particularly fascinated with revolutions and revolutionary movements and in particular with the comparative analysis of these phenomena – not least, one suspects, because of the sometimes strenuous efforts by our own government to prevent or reverse revolutions abroad. Crane Brinton, Barrington Moore, Chalmers Johnson, Ted Robert Gurr, Samuel Huntington, Eric Wolf, James Scott, Jeffery Paige, and Ellen Kay Trimberger are just a few of the scholars who have made important contributions to this tradition. Following the ground-breaking work of Charles Tilly (1978) and Theda Skocpol (1979), moreover, a veritable explosion of comparative studies of revolutions has occurred. Recent works by John Walton, Terence Ranger, Jack Goldstone, John Mason Hart, Charles Brockett, Tim McDaniel, Timothy Wickham-Crowley, John Foran, Farideh Farhi, Fred Halliday, Carlos Vilas, and Eric Selbin, among others, have further enriched our understanding of revolutions. And these works are just the tip of an intellectual iceberg that includes innumerable case studies of particular revolutions and revolutionary movements.

The idea for this particular study germinated at a time when the U.S. government was attempting to destroy – brutally and largely ineffectually – revolutionary movements in Central America. Why were (some) Central Americans rebelling, and would they succeed? I began to read about and travel through the region. To get a better handle on these issues, I also plunged into the literature on previous rebellions in Southeast Asia, another region of generalized conflict and U.S. intervention (in this case, following World War II). And before I was through, popular protests in Eastern Europe necessarily forced themselves upon my thinking.

But why, the reader may be asking, do we need yet *another* comparative study of revolutions? For two reasons. First, the particular set of revolutionary movements and revolutions that I analyze here is somewhat different from that which most other scholars have examined – and different, I believe, in an interesting and instructive way. In one sense, my sample of revolutions is drawn from a quite delimited universe of cases. I am interested in revolutions and revolutionary movements that occurred exclusively during the Cold War era – the period between the dropping of atomic bombs on Japan and the disintegration of the Soviet Union. All the cases that I examine, moreover, occurred in so-called peripheral or dependent societies of one type or another. Presumably, if revolutions share any common causes or dynamics (which can by no means be assumed), these are likely to be found among a relatively homogeneous pool of cases such as this one.

Unfortunately, there have simply been *too many* revolutionary movements, even in peripheral societies during the Cold War era alone, for one scholar or even a whole team of scholars to examine them all in more than a cursory fashion. Accordingly, a comparative study of such movements that has any historical complexity or nuance must necessarily limit itself to an examination of a sample of these movements. At the same time, such a sample should itself be as *heterogeneous* as possible to ensure a more or less adequate representation of the larger universe of cases, because, again, the opportunity to generalize about what might be called "peripheral revolutions" is certainly one which the analyst should seize if possible. (However, I reject the a priori assumption that there must be "general laws" that cover all cases of revolutions or even of peripheral revolutions of the Cold War era.)

Accordingly, this book examines instances of revolutionary movements and revolutions in three vastly different peripheral *world regions* during specific periods within the larger Cold War era: Southeast Asia from World War II to the mid-1950s (specifically, Vietnam, Indonesia, the Philippines, and Malaya), Central America from 1970 through the 1980s (focusing on Nicaragua, El Salvador, Guatemala, and Honduras), and Eastern Europe in 1989. In each of these regions, transnational "cycles of protest" (Tarrow 1994: ch. 9) or "revolutionary waves" (Katz 1997) occurred during the periods that I examine, although national revolutionary movements followed quite distinctive trajectories, which I hope to explain. So if this book, unlike some comparative studies of revolutions, does not traverse centuries, it at least traverses continents and the domains of various "area experts."

A second way in which this book differs from most comparative studies of revolutionary movements or of revolutions is its refusal to compare only "successful" revolutions with one another (in statistical terms, this is known as "selecting" or "sampling on the dependent variable"). Such a strategy, in fact, can be dangerously misleading, confusing causal processes that are in fact found in a very wide range of societies with the actual (and much rarer) causes of revolutions. Accordingly, this book also examines several types of nonrevolutions or "negative" cases, as comparativists

6

refer to them. I consider, for example, some important revolutionary movements that, however successful in mobilizing substantial numbers of people (in some cases, for many years or even decades), ultimately failed to topple extant political regimes, let alone to transform radically the societies from which they sprang. These "failed" revolutionary movements are not only important and interesting in their own right, but their failure also sheds considerable light on why successful revolutionary movements do in fact succeed. I also examine a case of a successful revolutionary movement (the Indonesian nationalist movement) that was not especially "radical" in terms of the broader socioeconomic changes that its dominant leaders sought to bring about. (I explain the distinction between "revolutionary" and "radical" in the next section.) Finally, I look at one national society (Honduras) in which a strong revolutionary movement, radical or otherwise, did not emerge at all, despite socio-economic conditions that were every bit as unpleasant as (and in some ways worse than) those of neighboring countries in which strong revolutionary movements *did* emerge.

This comparative strategy is driven by a belief that "counterfactual" cases in which powerful radical movements fail to take power, or fail to emerge at all – despite what various theories might lead us to expect – have not received sufficient attention in the social-scientific literature on revolutions and social movements. This neglect is somewhat surprising, moreover, since counterfactual cases are actually a major preoccupation of many social and labor historians who study the advanced capitalist "core" societies. For these scholars, the weakness or failure of radical working-class movements – despite the expectations of Karl Marx – has been an important and longstanding concern. In addition, there certainly has been no shortage of failed or "missing" revolutions in peripheral societies; scholars do not lack for data then, on this matter.

My comparative strategy is also driven by a concern with discovering those causal processes that *differentiate* cases from one another. This concern springs from the explicitly *comparative* questions that I hope to answer in this book: Why have radical groups mobilized large followings in *some* peripheral societies, but not in others? Why have *some* revolutions involved prolonged popular mobilization and extensive violence and bloodshed, but not others? And why have *some* revolutionary movements successfully toppled extant states, but not others? I have chosen to focus in this book on *world regions*, in fact, because doing so makes it relatively easier to discern (at least in principle) those causal factors that account

7

for these distinctive types of outcomes. Logically, that is, any historical, social-structural, political or cultural traits that are *shared* by the national societies that comprise such regions cannot explain these societies' divergent historical trajectories. At any rate, the attempt to discover these differentiating causal factors (and to understand how they work) is a primary goal of this book. I certainly do not presume to develop exhaustive or "total" explanations for the many revolutions and revolutionary movements that I examine in the following pages, and I have concluded, moreover, that there can be no such thing as a general theory of peripheral revolutions, let alone a general theory of revolutions as such.[1] My goal in this book, however, is still ambitious: to discover the general causal mechanisms that do the most to explain the origins and trajectory of several important revolutionary movements.

This is a book, in sum, that is centrally concerned with why radical revolutionary movements became important forces in some peripheral societies but not in others during the Cold War era, and why some but not all of these movements successfully toppled the states that they confronted. My wager is that the diverse political fortunes of revolutionary movements in peripheral societies during this era were not fortuitous nor randomly distributed, but were the result of general (if not universal) causal mechanisms.

Defining Terms

These introductory remarks beg for clarification. Accordingly, before proceeding to a discussion of the major theoretical approaches to revolutions and to the analytic framework that animates this particular book, I want to define formally some of the basic concepts that I employ – most of which I have already used in the preceding discussion. Defining these concepts clearly is not simply a formal, "academic" exercise in hair splitting, but a necessary effort to spell out as clearly as possible just what this book is, and is not, attempting to explain. Getting that right, in fact, is half the battle.

An initial ambiguity that all studies of revolution must invariably confront is that the word *revolution* has at least two general meanings, neither of which is inherently more correct or accurate than the other. (Concepts

---

[1] On the logics of comparative analysis, see Paige 1999, Mahoney 1999, Lieberson 1991, Ragin 1987, Skocpol 1984, Tilly 1984, Skocpol and Somers 1980, and Eckstein 1975.

as such are not more or less true, but more or less *useful* for generating falsifiable explanations of interesting phenomena.) According to one (broader) definition, *revolution* (or *political revolution*) refers to any and all instances in which a state or political regime is overthrown and thereby transformed by a popular movement in an irregular, extraconstitutional, and/or violent fashion; this definition assumes that revolutions, at least those truly worthy of the name, necessarily require the mobilization of large numbers of people against the existing state. (Some scholars, however, have analyzed so-called "revolutions from above" that involve little if any popular mobilization prior to the overthrow of the state [see, e.g., Trimberger 1978].) As Leon Trotsky (1961 [1932]: xvii) once wrote,

The most indubitable feature of a revolution is the direct interference of the masses in historic events. In ordinary times the state, be it monarchical or democratic, elevates itself above the nation, and history is made by specialists in that line of business – kings, ministers, bureaucrats, parliamentarians, journalists. But at those crucial moments when the old order becomes no longer endurable to the masses, they break over the barriers excluding them from the political arena, sweep aside their traditional representatives, and create by their own interference the initial groundwork for a new regime.

According to the other (more restrictive) definition, revolutions entail not only mass mobilization and regime change, but also more or less rapid and fundamental social, economic, and/or cultural change during or soon after the struggle for state power. (What counts as "rapid and fundamental" change, however, is a matter of degree, and the line between it and slower and less basic change can be difficult to draw in practice.) Revolutions in this latter sense – revolutions "involving . . . the refashioning of the lives of tens of millions of people" (Lenin 1997 [1917]: 80–1) – are sometimes referred to as "great" or "social" revolutions, and I shall use the term *social revolution* after this fashion (Huntington 1968; Skocpol 1979).[2]

In the chapters that follow, I generally employ the concept of revolution in the first and more general sense described above. This is primarily a study, that is, of revolutions in the sense of irregular, extraconstitutional, and sometimes violent changes of political regime and

---

[2] According to a third (and extremely broad) definition, revolutions include *any* instance of relatively rapid and significant change – hence, the industrial revolution, the academic revolution, the feminist revolution, the computer revolution, the revolution of rising expectations, etc.

control of state power brought about by popular movements. More specifically, this book mainly attempts to explain why and how such revolutions occur – why they "succeed" in this specific sense – and why they occur in some peripheral societies but not in others.

By this definition, the revolutions examined in this book were the result, to a greater or lesser extent, of the actions of revolutionary movements, which are a special type of social movement. A *social movement* has been defined as a "collective challenge" to "elites, authorities, other groups or cultural codes" by some significant number of "people with common purposes and solidarity in sustained interaction with elites, opponents and authorities" (Tarrow 1994: 3–4). A revolutionary social movement, or what I shall simply call a *revolutionary movement*, is a social movement "advancing exclusive competing claims to control of the state, or some segment of it" (Tilly 1993: 10). Few social movements attempt to gain control of the state as such, but this is a necessary (and sometimes exclusive) goal of that subset of social movements that are revolutionary. There is no hard and fast line, furthermore, that separates revolutionary movements from reform-oriented social movements. Under certain circumstances (which I hope this book will illuminate), social movements may become revolutionary, and revolutionary movements may become social movements (or political parties). I am primarily concerned in this book, then, with understanding why revolutionary movements sometimes become powerful forces and sometimes gain control of state power in peripheral societies.

Not all social movements, revolutionary or otherwise, are necessarily, or equally, "radical." Most social movements, including some revolutionary movements, seek directly or indirectly to reform the state or to utilize state power in order to reform existing economic, social, or cultural arrangements. Most social movements, that is, do not attempt to restructure national societies in truly fundamental ways. (Although, again, the distinction between reform and "fundamental" change can be difficult to draw.) A radical social movement, on the other hand, seeks the destruction or fundamental transformation of (at least) several important institutions. A *radical revolutionary movement*, as I use the term, not only seeks to control the state, but also aims (among other things) to transform more or less fundamentally the national society or some segment thereof, ruled by that state. To speak of radical revolutionaries, then, is not redundant. Of course, whether and under what conditions a radical revolutionary movement can actually bring about

10

such a social revolution is another question altogether, and one that lies largely beyond the scope of this book (but see Foran and Goodwin 1993). In any event, while the term "conservative social revolution" would clearly be an oxymoron, based on my definition of terms, it is certainly possible to speak of a conservative or reformist revolutionary movement, that is, a movement that seeks state power but which also wishes (or whose dominant leaders desire) to preserve or at most to modestly reform existing economic, social, and cultural arrangements, without changing them fundamentally. (For example, many leaders of the American War of Independence, sometimes called the American Revolution, and of the Mexican Revolution may be accurately described as "conservative revolutionaries.") This book focuses on the trajectory of radical revolutionary movements.

A significant change in the control and organization of state power is a sine qua non of both revolutions and social revolutions, as I am using those terms. By *state* I mean those core administrative, policing, and military organizations, more or less coordinated by an executive authority, that extract resources from and administer and rule (through violence if necessary) a territorially defined national society (the term *national society* is defined later in this section). As Lenin put it, by "state" or "apparatus of government is meant, first of all, the standing army, police and officialdom" (1997 [1917]: 38). (I make no assumption, however, that states are unitary actors that are not themselves potentially riven by conflicts of interest, identity, and vision.) Generally, states claim the right to exercise final and absolute authority (i.e., *sovereignty*) within national societies. By *state power* or *infrastructural power* I mean the capacity of these core organizations to carry out their projects, and to enforce extant laws, throughout the territories that they claim to govern, even in the face of opposition from the population that they rule or from other states (see also Chapter 7, Appendix 2, for more on this concept).

Generally, modern states are organized in either a bureaucratic or patrimonial fashion, to use Max Weber's terms, with many combinations of these ideal-types in between. A *bureaucratic* or "rationalized" state organization is characterized by the appointment of officials, based upon achievement in a course of appropriately specialized training, to positions (or "offices") with clearly defined responsibilities. A *patrimonial* state, by contrast, is staffed by officials who have been appointed on the basis of political loyalty to a leader or party, kinship, ethnicity, and/or some other characteristic, ascribed or achieved, that has no specific connection to the responsibilities of office; the latter responsibilities, in any event, are generally not clearly defined in patrimonial organizations, being either quite general or ad hoc in nature, and tend to overlap across offices. Needless to say, a bureaucratic state tends to expend resources, and to attain its declared goals, other things being equal much more efficiently than a patrimonial state.

Following Weber, the state is often defined as that institution that monopolizes the means of coercion in a society – or monopolizes the legitimate use of coercion in a society.[3] Yet this definition is clearly problematic. A state does not cease being a state, certainly, when some other organization – such as an invading army or, indeed, a revolutionary movement – also possesses significant coercive powers within the territories that state claims to rule. A *revolutionary situation*, in fact, is characterized precisely by "dual power" or "multiple sovereignty" – the existence, that is, of two or more political blocs (including, typically, extant state officials and their allies), both or all of which *claim* to be the legitimate state, and both or all of which may possess significant means of coercion (see Tilly 1978, 1993). Nor does a state cease being a state when its use of violence is *not* viewed as legitimate by large numbers of people; indeed, the existence of a strong revolutionary movement (hence also a revolutionary situation) presumably indicates that such legitimacy is not in fact widespread. (It is an open question, furthermore, whether particular authoritarian states have been considered legitimate by most or even many of the people whom they have claimed to rule.)

Based on the foregoing, a state is perhaps best defined as an organization, or set of organizations, that attempts, and claims the right, to monopolize the legitimate use of violence in an extended territory. It follows that armed revolutionary movements are a type of state-in-formation or, put differently, a type of state-building, since armed revolutionaries are attempting to construct an organization that can monopolize the principal means of coercion in a territory. The statelike character of revolutionary movements is especially evident when they are able to control and govern "liberated territories" within a national society.

States, as I use that term, are not quite the same thing as political regimes. By *political regime*, or simply *regime*, I mean the formal and informal organizations, relationships, and rules that determine who can employ state power for what ends, as well as

---

[3] Weber adopted this formulation from Leon Trotsky, the Russian Marxist revolutionary.

how those who are in power deal with those who are not. The distinction between democracy, totalitarianism, and authoritarianism thus deals with the question of *regime type*. . . . Regimes are more permanent forms of political organization than specific governments [or rulers], but they are typically less permanent than the state. (Fishman 1990: 428; see also Young 1994: 40–2; Linz 1975.)

A crucial dimension of any political regime is its relative inclusiveness or exclusivity – or, to put it another way, the extent of its "embeddedness" in or connections to the national society that it governs. Very inclusive regimes, including but not limited to *democratic* regimes, have multiple mechanisms for incorporating into decision-making processes the preferences or claims of citizens and social groups, including elections, political parties, interest groups, and even social movements. By contrast, *authoritarian* regimes have greater autonomy from society, though not necessarily from economic elites, and they sometimes forcibly exclude certain mobilized groups from any role in political decision making. An extreme form of authoritarianism – and one that will make more than one appearance in this book – is what Weber termed *sultanism* or sultanistic dictatorship. Such dictatorships, which entail the concentration of more or less unchecked power in the person of the dictator, may be extremely, and violently, exclusionary, denying political influence even to wealthy elites.

The distinction between state and regime can become quite blurred in the real world. This happens the more that states and regimes interpenetrate one another, as when the armed forces (a key component of the state) directly wield executive power, or when a one-party regime penetrates key state organizations, or when important state officials are the personal clients of a powerful monarch or dictator, sultanistic or otherwise. In these instances, the fate of both the state and regime tend to become fused; if for whatever reason the regime collapses, it may bring the state down with it or, at least, result in a fundamental transformation of the state (and vice versa). This point, needless to say, is of obvious importance for the question of why revolutions occur where they do. As we shall see, moreover, the distinction between state and economy may also become blurred, with revolutionary consequences should the state break down in such circumstances.

By *national state* I mean a state "governing multiple contiguous regions and their cities by means of centralized, differentiated, and autonomous structures" (Tilly 1992: 2). (My use of the term "state" in this book implies "national state," because all the states that I am examining are of this

13

type.) By *national society*, or simply *society*, I mean the people and social relations within those contiguous regions.[4] (Of course, national states not only govern their societies, but often attempt to impose themselves upon – and sometimes fight – other states in the international *state system*.) A *world region* or *region*, as I use these terms, refers to geographically concentrated and/or contiguous national societies that share important political, economic, or cultural characteristics.

By *political context*, I refer to the ways in which a national society, or some component of it, is governed and regulated by, has access to, and otherwise relates to the national state as well as to the larger state system. (As I use the term, then, *political context* encompasses *geo*political context.) This book emphasizes how the influence and effects upon populations of many social and economic institutions and relationships (including class relations) are mediated or refracted, as in a "force field," by the political context in which the latter are embedded.[5]

In other words, state structures and policies are not only important in their own right, but they also powerfully shape how other factors alternately encourage or discourage collective action of various types. More specifically, for our purposes, political context is of crucial importance for understanding the variable capacity of radical revolutionaries both to mobilize masses of people and to seize state power. For example, whether economic grievances or cultural beliefs (e.g., nationalism) find expression in specifically revolutionary movements is largely determined by political context.

I make no assumption, I should add, that national states are true *nation-states*, that is, states that rule a people with a common ethnicity, language, and/or religion – in other words, a *nation*. As Tilly (1992) reminds us, there are and have been very few nation-states in this sense;

---

[4] Norbert Elias (1978: chs. 5–6) refers to what I am calling national societies as *state-societies*, as distinct from such other forms of "attack-and-defense units" (as he terms them) as tribes and city-states.

[5] This notion of *political context* is similar to that of *political opportunities* or *political opportunity structures*, which is found in much recent social-movement research (see, e.g., Tarrow 1994). I prefer the term *political context*, however, because (1) not all the state structures and practices that influence societies, including social movements, are "structural" (in the sense of relatively fixed or permanent) and (2) such structures and practices typically create constraints upon, as well as opportunities for, collective action. This idea of political context is similar to the notion of *political mediation* employed by Edwin Amenta and his colleagues (e.g., Amenta, Carruthers, and Zylan 1992).

most states, and most societies, are multinational. National societies, in other words, are not necessarily equivalent to nations – a fact that lies behind much ethnic violence – and the borders and territories of such societies are neither fixed nor impenetrable. National societies, in short, are not "naturally" bounded, hermetic, or independent entities shut off from external forces – and revolutions simply cannot be understood if we assume that they are.

By *peripheral state* (a term that encompasses colonial states as well as many post- or "neocolonial" states) I mean a state whose power and projects are more or less strictly determined or at least very tightly constrained by a much more powerful "core" or "metropolitan" state (or states) within the state system (see, e.g., Triska 1986). *Colonial states* are de jure administrative and military extensions or branches of specific metropolitan states, although the *colonial regimes* that attach to them are almost invariably more exclusive and autonomous from the peripheral societies that they govern compared to the metropolitan regimes that oversee and more or less direct them. While colonial states thus lack true sovereignty, which is invariably a claim of the metropolitan states of which they are extensions (Young 1994: 43–5), many colonial regimes are characterized by a certain degree of autonomy from metropolitan regimes. As a result, conflicts of interest, identity, and vision may occur *between* colonial and metropolitan states and regimes, just as such conflicts may occur *within* states and regimes.

A *peripheral society*, finally, is a national society governed by a peripheral state. By *Third World* I mean those peripheral societies whose economic institutions are predominantly capitalist, as distinguished from the former "socialist periphery" of Soviet-dominated societies in Eastern Europe. Generally, peripheral states are much weaker than and thus subordinate to core states precisely because peripheral societies are much poorer (in per capita if not always in gross terms), smaller, and/or more socially disorganized than are the national societies governed by these more powerful states.[6] ("Peripherality," therefore, is a relational concept; some states – variously designated as "semiperipheral" or "subimperialist" – are subordinate to core states even as they dominate still

[6] In other words, there is a close – but certainly not an automatic – relationship between the size, wealth, and cohesion of a national society and the power of the state that governs it.

15

less powerful states.) All the revolutionary movements whose formation and political fortunes I attempt to explain in this book sought to overthrow and to reorganize what were clearly peripheral states – colonial or neocolonial states in Southeast Asia, "client states" of the United States in Central America (see, e.g., Coatsworth 1994), and Soviet "satellite states" in Eastern Europe.[7]

These definitions should help to identify more clearly the object of study in this book: *the formation (or absence) and subsequent fate of radical revolutionary movements in peripheral societies during the Cold War era.* My goal, again, is not to provide a complete or invariant theory of such movements, or of their historical trajectories (which in any case is simply not possible), but rather to provide a parsimonious explanation of the emergence and fate of these movements that highlights the key causal mechanisms that operate across the cases I examine.

Theoretical Approaches to Revolutionary Movements

Before adumbrating the state-centered perspective on revolutionary movements that I employ in this book, I want to review briefly the two general theoretical approaches that have shaped most profoundly both popular and scholarly understandings of revolutions, at least in the English-speaking world. These approaches are the modernization and Marxist perspectives. The theoretical literature on revolutions and revolutionary movements has grown quite complex, and it encompasses much more than these dominant paradigms.[8] Scholars of revolutions have been sensitized by a variety of theoretical perspectives to a vast range of factors that may potentially contribute to the mobilization of revolutionary movements. Instead of reviewing this entire literature, however, which simply cannot be done adequately in a chapter, I will limit myself to a brief examination of these

---

[7] I do not use the concepts of core and periphery in this book in precisely the same technical sense as world-system theorists (e.g., Wallerstein 1979). What I call the periphery, for example, also encompasses what those theorists would term the semiperiphery. Peripheral societies, moreover, are not exclusively capitalist in nature; they may also be economically organized along socialist or precapitalist lines.

[8] A comprehensive survey of theories of revolutions could (and has) filled volumes. This is one theoretical literature, in fact, that has largely outrun empirical research. Guides to this literature include Eckstein 1965, Kramnick 1972, Hagopian 1974, Cohan 1975, Lipsky 1976, Goldstone 1980, Zimmermann 1983: ch. 8, Aya 1990, Kimmel 1990, Collins 1993, Foran 1993, Goodwin 1994b, and McAdam, Tarrow, and Tilly 1997.

two influential approaches, partly as a means of setting my own theoretical approach in bolder relief. (I do comment briefly on much of the theoretical literature on revolutions in my annotated bibliography.) I should state at the outset that I do not think that these two approaches (or certain others) are altogether wrong in emphasizing the various factors that they do. These factors – in fact, a very wide range of factors – do in fact play an important role in many (although not all) revolutions and revolutionary movements. I am mainly critical of these perspectives, rather, for their tendency to abstract these factors from, to neglect, or simply to analyze inadequately the *political context* in which they are embedded. The absolutely crucial importance of political context, in fact, shall be a major refrain – indeed, *the* major refrain – of the comparative analyses in this book.

How exactly do the modernization and Marxist perspectives explain revolutions? Modernization theory links revolutions to the *transition* from traditional to modern societies, that is, to the very process of modernization itself.[9] "Traditional" societies, in this view, are characterized by fixed, inherited statuses and roles; simple divisions of labor; social relations regulated by custom; local and particularistic attachments to the family, clan, tribe, village, ethnic, or religious community; and thus very limited and localized forms of political participation. "Modern" societies, by contrast, are distinguished by social mobility and achieved statuses and roles; complex divisions of labor; social relations regulated by legally enacted rules; broader collective identifications with the nation; and mass political participation in national states.

Most modernization theorists argue that revolutions are especially likely to occur in transitional societies undergoing very *rapid* (albeit uneven) modernization; revolutions themselves, moreover, serve to push forward the modernization process. "Revolution," suggests Samuel Huntington, "is thus an aspect of modernization. . . . It will not occur in highly traditional societies with very low levels of social and economic complexity. Nor will it occur in highly modern societies" (Huntington 1968: 265). In Walter Rostow's evocative phrase, revolutionaries are "the scavengers of the modernization process," and Communism in particular "is best understood as a disease of the transition to modernization" (Rostow 1967 [1961]: 110).

---

[9] Useful surveys and/or critiques of the massive literature on modernization include Gusfield 1967, Portes 1976, Bendix 1977 (1964), Valenzuela and Valenzuela 1978, Wallerstein 1979, and Taylor 1979.

Why is this so? Modernization theorists have developed a number of explanations that link rapid modernization to the development of revolutionary movements. These explanations usually hinge on some sort of "lag" or lack of fit between different components of society, which are "modernizing" at different rates. Thus, Huntington argues that revolution, like "other forms of violence and instability, . . . is most likely to occur in societies which have experienced some social and economic development [but] where the processes of political modernization and development have lagged behind the processes of social and economic change" (Huntington 1968: 265). More psychologically inclined theorists suggest that rapid modernization unleashes a "revolution of rising expectations" – expectations that a suddenly stagnant or depressed economy may prove unable to meet, thereby creating the widespread anger and sense of "relative deprivation" of which revolutions are allegedly made (see, e.g., Gurr 1970; Newton 1983). Others have argued that rapid modernization may "dis-synchronize" a society's values and social structure. Accordingly, revolutionaries who offer an alternative set of values that better "fits" the social structure will become influential (see, e.g., Johnson 1982; Smelser 1962). And for still others, rapid modernization destroys the "integrative" institutions that held traditional societies together, creating a sense of meaninglessness (or "anomie") or uncertainty about one's place in society (or "status anxiety"). Revolutionaries, in this view, may become influential in transitional societies because they are able to replace the institutions that modernization undermines. As Harry Benda (1966: 12–13), an analyst of Asian Communism, has written,

it is not inconceivable that in Asia (as elsewhere) Communist movements as such provide a substitute for decayed or vanishing institutions – the family, the clan, the tribe, or the village community – that have suffered most heavily under the eroding onslaught of the new economic and political systems carried to Asia by the West in the course of the past century or so. . . . If iron discipline, rigid hierarchies, and unquestioning obedience are among Communism's most detestable features in the eyes of truly free men everywhere, they may yet spell security, order, and a meaningful place in the world for the social splinters of contemporary Asia.

During the 1950s, a large literature explained the "appeals of Communism" and radical nationalism in much the same terms as Benda's (see, e.g., Almond et al. 1954).

Modernization theorists, however, generally do recognize that even very rapid modernization does not produce successful revolutions *everywhere*. It is at this point that many point to the role of politics: The success or failure of revolutionary movements, they rightly claim, depends in large part upon how incumbent governments *respond to* revolutionary movements and to the broader social problems created by rapid modernization. More specifically, if a "modernizing elite" controls the government and responds flexibly and creatively to such problems – by "resynchronizing" values and the social structure, for example, through "conservative change" – then revolution can be avoided. On the other hand, "elite intransigence," as Chalmers Johnson puts it, "always serves as an underlying cause of revolution" (Johnson 1982: 97). Huntington similarly argues that revolutions "are unlikely in political systems which have the capacity to expand their power and to broaden participation within the system. . . . Ascending or aspiring groups," he concludes, "and rigid or inflexible institutions are the stuff of which revolutions are made" (Huntington 1968: 275).

Having come this far, one might expect modernization theorists to discuss at some length the factors that explain the flexibility (or lack thereof) of different types or configurations of states or political regimes. Curiously, however, one finds little such analysis. Even Huntington, the most "state-centered" of modernization theorists, offers only a vague generalization in this regard:

The great revolutions of history have taken place either in highly centralized traditional monarchies (France, China, Russia), or in narrowly based military dictatorships (Mexico, Bolivia, Guatemala, Cuba), or in colonial regimes (Vietnam, Algeria). All these political systems demonstrated little if any capacity to expand their power and to provide channels for the participation of new groups in politics. (Huntington 1968: 275)

Unfortunately, this formula is not altogether helpful. Not *all* colonial regimes, after all – in fact, relatively few – have been overthrown by revolutions (as we shall see in Part 2 of this book). Moreover, if those colonial regimes that were so overthrown did indeed collapse because they lacked the capacity to incorporate new groups, what might explain this? Similarly, not *all* military dictatorships – even "narrowly based" military dictatorships – have been toppled by revolutionaries (as we shall see in Part 3). Again, if those that were so toppled actually fell because they lacked the capacity to incorporate new groups, how can we explain this? Answering these questions requires a more thorough analysis of state structures and policies than the modernization perspective offers.

Like modernization theorists, Marxists also view revolutions as occurring in "transitional" societies – only in this case the transition,

19

which is seen as the result of class struggle, is from one economic mode of production to another. Class struggles may become particularly acute, in this view, when the existing mode of production has exhausted its potential for further growth and development and has entered a period of crisis. This said, it must be noted that the specific character of recent revolutions in peripheral societies has come as something of a surprise to traditional Marxists. Specifically, the socialist orientation of many revolutions in the capitalist periphery (including Southeast Asia and Central America) has virtually "stood Marx on his head." As Ernest Mandel (1979: 11) notes,

In general, traditional Marxism looked upon relatively backward countries – those of Eastern and Southern Europe, and even more those of Asia and Latin America – in the light of Marx's well-known formula: the more advanced countries show the more backward ones the image of their future development as in a looking glass. This led to the conclusion that socialist revolutions would first occur in the most advanced countries, that the proletariat would take power there long before it would be able to do so in more backward countries.

In fact, not only have a series of avowedly socialist revolutions occurred in the capitalist periphery, but the industrialized capitalist societies of the core have proven surprisingly immune to this form of social change. One notable aspect of this historic "reversal" of Marxist expectations is that recent Third World revolutions have relied heavily on classes deemed secondary (at best) to the classic socialist project, particularly the peasantry, rather than on the industrial proletariat or working class. Instead of being built on the technological foundations of advanced capitalism, moreover, socialism has been one of the means by which certain "backward" countries have attempted to "catch up" with the advanced capitalist core. In short, rather than being a *successor* to capitalism, socialism has been something of a historical *substitute* for it in many developing societies (see, e.g., White, Murray, and White 1983: 3).

Recent events in the erstwhile socialist periphery of Eastern Europe have also taken Marxists – and most everyone else – by surprise. Marxists have ably pondered, probed, and theorized a variety of sweeping historical changes, but the transition from socialism to capitalism is not one of them. Indeed, such a transition was virtually unthinkable to Marxists only a few years ago. Even anti-Communist Marxists and socialists who were harsh critics of authoritarian state socialism in the Soviet bloc did not anticipate such a transition to capitalism. On the contrary, many expected, or at least hoped, that state socialism would be democratized by popular movements; the Communist elite that had expropriated capitalist property following World War II would itself be expropriated, in this scenario, by the people. Instead, Communism is now widely viewed, as the Eastern European joke goes, as the longest and most painful route from capitalism to . . . capitalism.

How exactly have Marxists attempted to explain revolutions in peripheral societies? For the capitalist Third World, many (following the lead of Lenin, Trotsky, and Mao) begin by pointing to the weakness of the capitalist or bourgeois class. Peripheral bourgeoisies – or "lumpenbourgeoisies," as Andre Gunder Frank has termed them – are small, only partially differentiated from feudal landowning elites (if at all), and, partly for these reasons, heavily dependent on the existing state apparatus for economic opportunities and protection. Consequently, capitalist classes in the Third World have proven unwilling or unable to play their "historic role" of leading antifeudal, democratic revolutions in the manner of their European counterparts (see, e.g., Paige 1997). Ironically, "bourgeois" revolutions in Third World societies must thus be made by the working class – guided by vanguard parties – in a strategic alliance with the peasant majority in such societies. But because such antifeudal revolutions are made by worker-peasant alliances, they may, unlike Europe's bourgeois revolutions, more or less quickly initiate a transition to socialism. Third World revolutions, to use Trotsky's phrase, thus assume the form of "permanent" or "uninterrupted" revolutions that undertake socialist as well as antifeudal policies or "tasks" (Trotsky 1969 [1930]; see also Löwy 1981). A similar line of argument about socialist revolutions has been introduced into academic social science by Barrington Moore's *Social Origins of Dictatorship and Democracy* (1966). —> Communists

Marxists do recognize, however, that significant revolutionary movements have not developed in *all* peripheral societies. This has been variously attributed to "unusually" strong peripheral bourgeoisies, to a lack of revolutionary leadership, or to the fact that not all *types* of peasants are inclined to support revolutionary movements – although just what sort of peasants are revolutionary, and why, have been the subjects of much debate.

For many Marxists, rural producers whose mode of life most closely approximates that of urban workers are, not surprisingly, the most likely stratum to ally with workers. Consequently, landless rural workers and, to a lesser degree, poor peasants (especially tenants) have usually been considered by Marxists as the most revolutionary strata in the

21

countryside. These groups are seen as having irreconcilable conflicts of interest with landowners as well as an "objective" interest in socialism, understood as the collective self-management of production. These groups are revolutionary, in other words, or will eventually become so, by virtue of their economic class position. Landowning "middle" peasants, by contrast, are thought to waiver in their political allegiances, while rich peasants (not to mention landlords themselves), who hire wage labor, have usually been regarded as counterrevolutionary. Peripheral societies with large middle and rich peasantries, then, are not likely to generate radical social movements, revolutionary or otherwise.

More recently, however, this general picture has been questioned in various ways by neo-Marxist or Marxist-influenced students of peasant politics. Eric Wolf (1969), for example, has argued that landowning middle peasants, not rural workers or poor peasants, are in fact *most* likely to be revolutionary. Wolf, who examines peasant involvement in the Mexican, Russian, Chinese, Vietnamese, Algerian, and Cuban revolutions, views peasant rebelliousness as a reaction to the disintegrative effects produced by "North Atlantic capitalism" as it penetrates traditional societies (1969: 276–82). He argues that landowning middle peasants, as well as "free" peasants (e.g., squatters) who are outside landlord and state control, are most likely to rebel, both because their way of life is more threatened by capitalism compared to other social groups *and* because they are better able to act collectively to preserve their traditional ways.[10] As Wolf puts it, "it is the very attempt of the middle and free peasant to remain traditional which makes him revolutionary" (1969: 292). Wolf does however recognize that poor and landless peasants have also become involved in revolutions when they can be mobilized by "external" political parties and military organizations – organizations, moreover, that typically seek to do much more than preserve "traditional" ways of life (Wolf 1969: 290).

Wolf's arguments have been contested by Jeffery Paige (1975, 1997), who argues that sharecropping tenants and migratory "semiproletarians," not middle peasants, are the most revolutionary rural strata. Like Wolf, however, Paige also links "agrarian revolution" to the penetration of world capitalism into preindustrial societies and, more specifically, to the creation of "export enclaves"; his first book, in fact, is subtitled *Social Move-*

---

[10] Craig Calhoun has argued that urban artisans have been more revolutionary than the urban proletariat for similar reasons (1982: ch. 6).

ments and Export Agriculture in the Underdeveloped World. And Paige also agrees with Wolf – as against the traditional Marxist view – that landless rural workers are unlikely revolutionaries, being more inclined to support merely reformist political movements. Unlike Wolf, however, Paige argues that revolutionary movements develop because sharecroppers and semi-proletarians are *wage-earning* cultivators who face a noncultivating class that derives its income from more or less fixed landholdings (as opposed to capital investments), the control of which is nonnegotiable. And Paige, unlike Wolf, argues that revolutionary socialist movements in particular are "internally generated, not introduced by outside urban-based parties" (1975: 62).

Thus, whereas modernization theorists view the development of Third World revolutionary movements as a consequence of very rapid modernization, and their success as a consequence of intransigent elites, Marxists tend to explain revolutions in peripheral societies as a reaction to the incorporation of such societies – or at least those with the "right" kinds of peasants – into the capitalist world economy.

Are the Marxists right? Or rather, *which* Marxists are right in their search for the "really" revolutionary peasantry? All and none, I shall argue. More exactly, I will show in the following chapters that a wide variety of rural *and* urban strata – including but certainly not limited to middle peasants and wage earners – can and have played important roles in particular peripheral revolutionary movements. They have done so, however, not simply or even mainly as economically exploited classes, but also and more immediately as excluded and often violently repressed state subjects. There is thus something askew in the Marxist search for the class or economic "roots" of revolutions. Class and economic grievances do usually play an important role in revolutions, but the roots of revolutionary movements are found in the political context in which class relationships and economic institutions (among other factors) are embedded.

Marxists (and others) have also said too little about the conditions that determine whether revolutionary movements, *whatever* their class composition, will succeed or fail in actually overthrowing the state. (Some Marxists once implied that the triumph of socialism in the Third World was no less inevitable than its triumph in advanced capitalist societies was once thought to be – although those days have largely passed.) The failure of any particular revolution presumably indicates that class contradictions have not yet fully "matured" or that the revolutionary class or class alliance has not yet attained a critical mass.[11] In my own view, however, which I discuss next, the success or failure of revolutionary movements depends more fundamentally upon the nature of the specific states that revolutionaries have sought to overthrow.

The State-Centered Perspective

The following chapter discusses in considerable detail both the strengths and limitations of the state-centered perspective (which actually encompasses several distinct analytic strategies) that I employ in this book. Here I simply wish to summarize in very broad strokes why this approach is so important for understanding both the formation and success or failure of revolutionary movements.

Why, indeed, place the state at the center of an analysis of revolutions? Why "privilege" the state in this way when revolutions are obviously complex historical processes that involve multifarious economic, social, cultural, organizational, social-psychological, and voluntarist factors (Goodwin 1994b; Emirbayer and Goodwin 1996)? For two general reasons. First, successful revolutions necessarily involve the breakdown or incapacitation of states. Of course, revolutions obviously involve much more than this, and no claim is made here that all states break down in precisely the same way, or independently of pressure from revolutionaries. Still, there would be no revolutions to study (or to emulate, or to denounce) if states did not at least occasionally break down or were otherwise incapacitated, whether from the efforts of revolutionaries themselves or for some other reason(s) (e.g., economic crisis or war). This "state-centered" idea is now widely if not universally accepted not only among scholars of revolutions but also among large numbers of social scientists more generally (see, e.g., Collins 1993).

The importance of state breakdown or incapacitation for revolutions, which is implicit in the very definition of revolution, needs to be differentiated from the claim that "expanding political opportunities" are necessary for the mobilization of social movements (see, e.g., McAdam 1982; Tarrow 1994; McAdam, Tarrow, and Tilly 1997). While the latter claim is often true, movements – and perhaps especially revolutionary

---

[11] Many Marxists, in fact, have exhibited a "Third Worldist" orientation, according to which the Third World as a whole is viewed as "ripe" for revolution because of its imperialist exploitation by the more advanced capitalist countries.

movements – also emerge when political opportunities are negligible or even contracting. State breakdowns, then, do not always precede the emergence of powerful revolutionary movements, just as expanding political opportunities do not always precede the mobilization of social movements. In fact, state breakdowns are often brought about by revolutionary movements; in this sense, revolutionaries sometimes create their own opportunities. There is, in any event, a second and perhaps more interesting reason for centering the state in a study of revolutions: Strong revolutionary movements, even if they ultimately fail to seize state power, will emerge only in opposition to states that are configured and that act in certain ways. As I discuss in greater detail in the following chapter, there is a sense in which certain state structures and practices actively form or "construct" revolutionary movements as effectively as the best professional revolutionaries, by channeling and organizing political dissent along radical lines. I refer to this idea as "state constructionism," which I model after the notion of "cultural constructionism" – that is, the claim that certain ideas or ideologies (e.g., about gender or race) are not "natural," or representative of the objective world, but rather historically contingent constructs or artifacts of specific cultures. My claim is that revolutionary movements are largely artifacts or products of historically contingent political contexts. To be sure, the state itself does not literally or intentionally construct revolutionary movements (any more than cultures self-construct ideas or ideologies); revolutionaries do that. But they do so, and can only do so, in particular political contexts. To paraphrase Marx, people make their own revolutions, but not just where or when they please; people do not make revolutions under circumstances chosen by themselves, but within specific political contexts directly encountered, given, and transmitted from the past. State structures and practices invariably matter, in other words, for the very *formation* of revolutionary movements, not just for their success or failure – and they generally do so in quite unintended ways. This, at any rate, is a major contention of this book.

Why is the development of revolutionary movements dependent upon particular state structures and practices? This book will provide several answers to this question, but two in particular might be noted at the outset. First, people do not tend to join or support revolutionary movements when they believe that the central state has little if anything to do with their everyday problems, however severe those problems may be. Not surprisingly, few people – even when they are extremely poor and palpably exploited – seek to overthrow states (perhaps risking their lives in the process) that seem peripheral to their most pressing concerns. Second, few people join or support revolutionaries – even when they are more or less in agreement with their demands or ideology – if they feel that doing so will make them more vulnerable to state violence or if they believe that they can obtain much or even some modicum of what they want, in political terms, through some routine, institutionalized, and therefore low-risk channel for political claim making (e.g., voting, demonstrating, or petitioning). Other things being equal, people, like electric currents, take the path of least resistance. As Trotsky once put it, "People do not make revolution eagerly any more than they do war. . . . A revolution takes place only when there is no other way out" (1961 [1932], III: 167). And people sometimes conclude that revolution is the only "way out" of their predicament, this book suggests, when they confront certain types of states that respond to political dissent with repression, typically of a violent and indiscriminate nature.

Social scientists, in sum, need to examine what Nicos Mouzelis (1986) has termed "modes of political domination" in order to understand how and why revolutionary mobilization and the seizure of state power occur or do not occur in different social contexts. Especially important in this regard is the way in which the state relates to voluntary associations or informal networks of people who seek some sort of redress of their grievances – grievances that may themselves originate in any number of state or social practices. Whether the state tolerates, represses, or sponsors such organizations – and which *sort* of organizations – is crucial for understanding why specifically revolutionary movements are able (or unable) to mobilize mass followings and even seize state power.

This book concludes, more specifically, that the formation of revolutionary movements in the periphery has been unintentionally facilitated and even encouraged by that subset of violent and exclusionary authoritarian states that are also organizationally incoherent and militarily weak, especially in those outlying areas of the national society – the periphery of the periphery, so to speak. Other things being equal, the political context that is most conducive to the formation of strong revolutionary movements is found in peripheral societies in which especially repressive *and* disorganized states possess geographically and socially delimited power. Such repressive states, I should emphasize, may at times be linked to regimes that hold regular, competitive elections in which a wide spectrum of political parties participates (although this is fairly rare). It is quite possible, that is, for a regime that has been freely elected to repress brutally and indiscriminately certain social sectors, usually those suspected of supporting regime opponents – or to lack the means for preventing military officers or private parties from doing so. Such states – which should not be confused with democracies, which are characterized by the rule of law and by civilian control of the armed forces – may also unintentionally facilitate the formation of revolutionary movements.

I also conclude that revolutionary movements have become especially powerful actors in peripheral societies when they have been able to build broad multiclass (and, if necessary, multiethnic) coalitions with strong international support. The formation of such coalitions, moreover, has been encouraged and facilitated (again, quite unintentionally) by especially autonomous – or socially "disembedded" (Evans 1995) – authoritarian states that exclude and repress not only lower classes (i.e., peasants and workers), but also middle and even upper or "dominant" classes. In fact, such autonomous, exclusionary, disorganized, and weak states are particularly vulnerable to actual *overthrow* by revolutionary movements – and not necessarily by the largest or best organized revolutionary movements. As we shall see, moreover, this vulnerability derives in part from the fact that such states tend to preclude the sort of political "openings" that have elsewhere incorporated important social groups into institutional politics and thereby limited the appeal of revolutionaries. Revolutions are unlikely, in fact, where the state has institutional linkages with nonelite groups, is organized in a rational-bureaucratic fashion, and effectively governs throughout the entire territory of the national society. In other words, revolutions are unlikely in societies with democratic regimes, especially longstanding or "consolidated" ones.

The preceding ideas can be figuratively represented, drawing upon some of the concepts that I have defined. Figures 1.1 and 1.2 describe conceptual spaces in which empirical states may be located. Figure 1.1 provides a conceptual map of states as a function of their *organization* (from bureaucratic to patrimonial), on the one hand, and of the relative inclusiveness or exclusivity of the *political regimes* to which they are attached, on the other – ranging from liberal and inclusive democratic regimes at one extreme to exclusionary and repressive dictatorships at the other. Figure 1.2 adds an additional variable: the extent of the state's infrastructural power (from weak to strong).

My basic claims about the relationship between states and revolutionary movements are represented in Figures 1.3 and 1.4. Briefly, the shaded

27

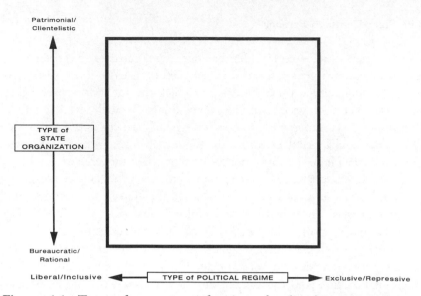

Figure 1.1 Types of states as a function of political regime and state organization.

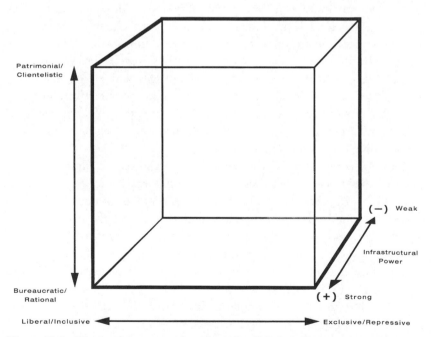

Figure 1.2 Types of states as a function of political regime, state organization, and infrastructural power.

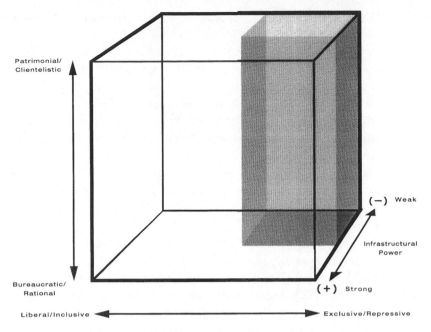

Figure 1.3 States most likely to "incubate" revolutionary movements (shaded area).

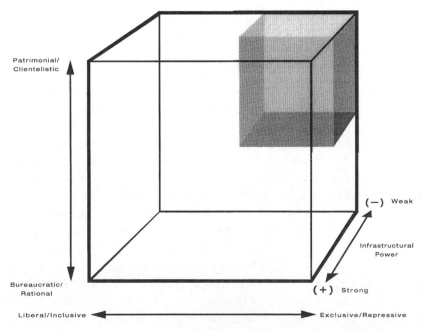

Figure 1.4 States most likely to be overthrown by revolutionary movements (shaded area).

area in Figure 1.3 indicates the type of states that tend unintentionally to "incubate," or encourage the formation of, revolutionary movements – namely, those states that are especially exclusionary and/or repressive and yet infrastructurally weak. Exclusion, especially violent exclusion or repression of certain social groups, tends to "push" these oppressed groups into revolutionary movements, and the state's weakness prevents the state from destroying such movements. By contrast, more liberal and inclusionary regimes may confront considerable opposition, but it tends to be less radical in its ends and means; and especially powerful states are generally able to repress their opponents, even if political repression provides them with an incentive to rebel.

Not all states that "incubate" or encourage revolutionary movements, however, are necessarily vulnerable to actual overthrow by such movements. As Figure 1.4 indicates, only a subset of states that unintentionally nurture revolutionary movements is especially vulnerable to being overthrown, namely, those especially repressive yet weak states that are also organized patrimonially rather than bureaucratically. The key idea here is that patrimonial states do not easily allow for the implementation of the type of initiatives that can successfully counter a popular revolutionary movement. Patrimonial states cannot easily jettison unpopular leaders, incorporate new groups into decision-making processes (or state offices), or prosecute a counterrevolutionary war rationally or efficiently.

I do *not* claim that revolutionary movements only or automatically form or seize power (or not) when there exists a specific type of state – although I will argue that certain types of states tend to be much more vulnerable to revolution than others. The preceding claims, in fact, are about general tendencies or probabilities, not lawlike regularities; these claims have an "other things being equal" character. Clearly, states are not the *only* thing that matters for the formation of revolutionary movements; a very broad array of factors can contribute the development of such movements and influence their political fortunes. Still, I do want to challenge the tendency among some scholars to view revolutionary movements as the products of rapid social change, intense grievances or poverty, certain class structures or land-tenure systems, economic dependence, imperialist domination, the actions of vanguard parties, etc., or some combination of these factors, abstracted from the political context in which all of these factors are embedded. Although it is not a major subject of this book, I also want to challenge the tendency to treat political context as a simple reflex of one or more of these factors. I want to suggest, instead, that a close examination of states as a reality sui generis, to use Emile Durkheim's expression, is crucial for understanding the formation and fate of revolutionary movements. Political context is not simply one more variable to be examined by the conscientious scholar of revolutions (on the order, for example, of educational attainment or median income), but a "force field" that mediates and powerfully refracts the effects of a wide range of factors that typically impinge upon the development and trajectory of revolutionary movements. Political context, in short, is not the only factor that explains the formation and fate of revolutionary movements, but it is generally the most important factor.

The Analysis to Come

As noted, Chapter 2 discusses in much greater detail the strengths *and* limitations of the state-centered perspective that I employ in this book. I examine a number of reasons that this perspective, despite several serious limitations, remains, generally, the single most powerful lens for examining revolutions. The discussion in Chapter 2 is admittedly quite abstract, although I attempt to illustrate some of my remarks with evidence from the Cuban Revolution. Readers who wish to get straight to the empirical meat of this book may wish to skip this appetizer.

Part 2 examines the revolutionary movements that challenged Western colonial (or neocolonial) regimes in Southeast Asia after World War II. I focus here on four societies: Vietnam, which was part of French Indochina; Indonesia, the former Dutch East Indies; British Malaya, now peninsular or Western Malaysia; and the Philippines, which was a colony of the United States following a much longer period of Spanish rule. Chapter 3 discusses the formation of the revolutionary movements in these countries, which have their roots in the period of Japan's occupation of Southeast Asia during World War II. This chapter makes two key points. First, the conditions that encouraged the formation of strong Communist-led movements in several, but not all, of the societies in this region were more political (and geopolitical) than socioeconomic in nature. In fact, the variable nature of Japanese rule in Southeast Asia emerges as a crucial explanatory factor in this respect. This point is made particularly well by the case of Indonesia, where *non*-Communist nationalists dominated the postwar movement against Dutch colonial rule, despite a social structure that was hardly inimical to Communism. (The

Communist Party, in fact, was quite powerful in Indonesia during the 1920s and would later become the single most powerful party in that country after the anticolonial struggle was won.)

Second, no simple or homogeneous "social base" was behind the revolutionary movements in Southeast Asia, whether these were Communist-led or not. A more general claim of this book, in fact, is that attempts to identify a single "revolutionary class" in peripheral societies (or in the Third World in particular) have foundered on the shoals of empirical reality – and will no doubt continue to do so.[12] This is not to say that all social classes and groups are equally drawn to revolutionary movements (or to socialism or Communism in particular). (For obvious reasons, a movement hostile to private property is unlikely to consist mainly of landlords and factory owners.) As we shall see, however, revolutionaries – socialists and Communists in particular – have sometimes proven adept at attracting the support of a variety of laboring classes, middle strata, and even, in some cases, economic elites.

Chapter 4 then tries to explain why the Communist-led movement in Vietnam was the only such movement in Southeast Asia to attain state power during the first postwar decade. (The Communist-led insurgencies in Malaya and the Philippines, by contrast, were decisively defeated.) Here again, I suggest that political context – more specifically, the variable nature of Western colonial rule in Southeast Asia, including the character of the colonialists' response to insurgency – is the key to solving this puzzle.

In Part 3, I turn to an analysis of four Central American countries during the 1970s and 1980s: Nicaragua, El Salvador, Guatemala, and Honduras. Chapter 5 parallels Chapter 3, focusing on the formation of revolutionary movements. Here again, I suggest that socioeconomic factors do not provide an adequate explanation of these movements. Such factors cannot explain why a strong revolutionary movement failed to emerge in Honduras, nor can they explain why the revolutionary movement in Nicaragua, alone among those in the region, was able to seize state power.

[12] Many of these attempts, it should be noted, seem to be motivated by an interest in discovering the functional equivalent in peripheral societies of Marx's putatively revolutionary working class of the advanced capitalist core. The fact that this working class has only rarely exhibited revolutionary aspirations, and only in some core societies, under peculiar *political* conditions, immediately suggests the chimerical nature of this quest (see, e.g., Katznelson and Zolberg 1986; Mann 1995).

Chapter 6 focuses more directly on the latter issue: the relative success of the revolutionary movements that did emerge in Nicaragua, El Salvador, and Guatemala. I argue that the success of the Sandinistas in Nicaragua was due to the peculiarities of the Somoza dictatorship, which was more autonomous or socially disembedded, organizationally incoherent, and infrastructurally weaker than the institutional forms of military domination that revolutionaries confronted in El Salvador and Guatemala. Throughout Parts 2 and 3, in fact, I emphasize the importance of both crossnational differences in states and regimes *and* how these differences shaped and constrained the dynamic responses of these states and regimes to revolutionaries and political challengers generally. My focus is on both state structures and practices – structure *and* process – not one or the other.

In the last part of this book, I attempt to extend and refine the state-centered perspective on revolutions employed in Parts 2 and 3. If Part 3 emphasizes the failure of revolutionary movements in El Salvador and Guatemala to overthrow extant states, Chapter 7 examines the other side of the coin: the failure of the Salvadoran and Guatemalan states to defeat the revolutionaries. I also briefly consider a third case of persistent insurgency, that of the Sendero Luminoso (Shining Path) revolutionary movement in Peru. I compare all three of these persistent insurgencies with major rebellions that were decisively defeated in the Philippines and Malaya (for reasons explored in Chapter 4) as well as in Venezuela. I suggest in this chapter that popularly supported insurgencies have persisted when and where the armed forces of weak states have committed massive and indiscriminate abuses against civilians suspected of collaborating with the insurgents.

The penultimate chapter of this book compares and contrasts the popular rebellions and "refolutions" of 1989 in Eastern Europe with the Third World revolutions and revolutionary movements discussed in previous chapters. Although my analysis of Eastern Europe is less extensive than that of Southeast Asia or Central America, comparing Second and Third World revolutions illuminates several interesting facets of the colossal events of 1989, including their nonviolent character. I suggest in this chapter that a state-centered approach is a particularly powerful perspective on those events – notwithstanding the popularity of economic and "civil society" explanations for the fall of Communism – given the specific character of the Eastern European states as Soviet satellites. I conclude that what collapsed in Eastern Europe in 1989 was not socialism as such, but a type of dependent and authoritarian state socialism – just as what Third World revolutionaries have overturned was not capitalism, or even "backward" capitalism, but authoritarian modes of colonial and oligarchic (or "crony") capitalism. More generally, revolutions should not be viewed as upheavals, grounded primarily in economic conflicts, that are necessary to propel most or even all national societies along the tracks of history, but as political struggles that are mainly the result of historically contingent, and relatively rare, types of state structures and practices.

2

The State-Centered Perspective on
Revolutions: Strengths and Limitations

> *The basic question of every revolution is that of state power. . . . [T]hat "power"*
> *which is termed the state [is] . . . a power arising from society, but placing itself*
> *above it and becoming more and more separated from it. What does this power*
> *mainly consist of? It consists of special bodies of armed men who have at their dis-*
> *posal prisons, etc. . . . A standing army and police are the chief instruments of state*
> *power. But can this be otherwise?*
> – V. I. Lenin (1974 [1917]: 370; 1943 [1917]: 10)

This chapter analyzes the strengths and limitations of the state-centered
perspective on revolutions, which I briefly introduced in the previous
chapter and which I deploy in the chapters that follow. As I noted earlier,
the discussion here is primarily theoretical and somewhat abstract,
although I do try to ground this discussion in a short case study of the
Cuban Revolution, itself one of the major revolutionary conflicts of
the Cold War era. Nonetheless, some readers may wish to forge straight
ahead into the more empirical chapters on revolutionary movements in
Southeast Asia and Central America in Parts 2 and 3, respectively.

I argue in this chapter that state-centered theoretical approaches
comprise some of the most powerful analytic tools that are currently available to analysts of revolutions – more powerful (as I argued in the previous chapter) than the modernization and Marxist perspectives. Compared
to state-centered approaches, furthermore, "poststructuralist" conceptions
of power that are currently fashionable among some scholars simply beg
too many fundamental questions. Certain types of cultural analysis as well
as the recent turn to "civil society" are somewhat more helpful. But state-
centered approaches are even more powerful for resolving the key puzzles
that are distinctive to the study of revolutions. (Throughout, I refer to
state-centered *approaches* in the plural, because – as I detail in this chapter

35

– there is no single statist perspective or argument, but several overlapping ones.) State-centered analysis, like any theoretical tradition, has its blindspots and limitations, which I will also address. Fortunately, these limitations point the way toward a more powerful synthetic perspective on revolutions and political conflict more generally – a perspective, however, that I do not believe we have yet fully attained.

What is the statist theoretical tradition all about? All the state-centered approaches that I shall review emphasize or "center" a particular set of *causal mechanisms* – namely, those processes whereby states (foreign as well as domestic) shape, enable, or constrain economic, associational, cultural, and even social-psychological phenomena. State-centered theorists argue that these mechanisms are, for certain purposes, more powerful or causally important than (or at least complementary to) a range of alternative causal processes – for example, those emphasizing class conflict, civil society, culture, or social psychology. Statist perspectives, then, are intentionally one-sided.

And yet partly *because* of this very one-sidedness, state-centered approaches are exceptionally valuable for understanding revolutions. This follows, at least in part, from the fact that revolutions themselves are unusually state-centered phenomena, at least as most social scientists have conceptualized them. As Charles Tilly notes, "whatever else they involve, revolutions include forcible transfers of power over states, and therefore any useful account of revolutions must concern, among other things, how states and uses of force vary in time, space and social setting" (1993: 5).

I should emphasize that I do not write as an unbiased observer. My own previous empirical investigations into insurgencies and revolutions have found this state-centered perspective to be extremely illuminating (see Goodwin 1989, 1994a; Goodwin and Skocpol 1989; Foran and Goodwin 1993). At the same time, I will try to clarify the various limitations of this perspective (see also Goodwin 1994b; Emirbayer and Goodwin 1996). After discussing the considerable strengths of state-centered approaches to revolutions, accordingly, I will review the main weaknesses of statist analysis and suggest some of the theoretical resources that are available for redressing them.[1] I also examine how certain strengths and limitations of

---

[1] This chapter discusses the relevance of state-centered analysis exclusively for understanding the origins or causes of revolutions, including the formation of strong revolutionary movements. I should note, however, that statist perspectives have also been employed to explain the long-term *outcomes* or achievements of revolutions. See, e.g., Skocpol 1979: part 2; Foran and Goodwin 1993.

36

state-centered approaches are exemplified in a recent scholarly study of the Cuban Revolution (Pérez-Stable 1993).

Before discussing the analytic strengths of state-centered approaches to revolutions, let me begin by distinguishing the distinctive forms of state-centered analysis. Understanding the *variety* of statist perspectives is important for appreciating both the strengths and limitations of this theoretical tradition.

Four Types of State-Centered Analysis

A good deal of confusion has resulted from the failure of proponents and critics alike to distinguish among – or even to note the existence of – four quite distinctive versions of statist analysis: the state-autonomy, state-capacity, political-opportunity, and "state-constructionist" approaches. Because individual states exist within an international state system, furthermore, each of these approaches has geopolitical or transnational as well as domestic dimensions.

The *state-autonomy perspective*, with which the other statist approaches are most often conflated, emphasizes the variable autonomy of state officials or "state managers" from the dominant social class, civil society more generally, or other states (see, e.g., Mann 1993, 1984; Skocpol 1979; Chorley 1943). According to this perspective – which derives in part from Max Weber's political sociology – politicians, bureaucrats, and military officers may develop identities, interests, ideologies, and (ultimately) lines of action that are very different from those of organized groups in civil society or the officials of other states; state officials may not be usefully conceptualized, accordingly, as representatives of powerful capitalists, interest groups, the "popular will," or foreign potentates. In fact, the interests of state officials in accumulating resources (through taxes, for example) and mobilizing the population (for wars against other states, for example) may sometimes conflict with the interests of powerful social groups (including the dominant class), not to mention powerful foreign states. Overt conflicts between state officials, on the one hand, and economic elites, mobilized groups, and foreign officials, on the other, are typically adduced as evidence for this perspective.

A second statist approach – which may also be traced to Weber – emphasizes the actual material and organizational capacity (or lack thereof) of state officials to implement successfully their political agenda, even in the face of opposition from powerful actors in civil society or from other states. This perspective focuses on variations in states' fiscal resources, military power, and organizational reach (or "penetration") into civil society – what I referred to in the previous chapter, following Michael Mann, as the "infrastructural power" of states. Infrastructural power refers, more specifically, to "the institutional capacity of a central state, despotic or not, to penetrate its territories and logistically implement decisions" (Mann 1993: 59; see also Evans 1995; Migdal 1988). Key determinants of such variations include the organizational or bureaucratic rationality of state institutions as well as the extent to which states confront threats, real or perceived, from other states that require war preparation. Some states also receive large infusions of resources from other states; a state's position in the international state system, in other words, may strongly shape its capacities (see, e.g., Collins 1995; Tilly 1992). While this second, *state-capacity approach* is typically utilized alongside the state-autonomy perspective, the two are analytically distinct; state officials, after all, may have very different aims than economic elites or other states and yet lack the capacity to actually implement their preferred policies. State autonomy, in other words, does not necessarily imply state capacity, or vice versa.

A third state-centered approach emphasizes how the apparent tolerance, permeability, or responsiveness of states or "polities" influences the ability of mobilized social groups to act collectively and/or to influence state policies.[2] More specifically, "political opportunities" have been deemed necessary – in addition to (for example) grievances and organization – for people to act collectively or to shape the agenda of state officials. Such opportunities, according to Sidney Tarrow (1994: 85), refer to "consistent – but not necessarily formal or permanent – dimensions of the political environment that provide incentives for people to undertake collective action by affecting their expectations for success and failure." At the very least, according to this *political-opportunity perspective*, the state must either lack the means (infrastructurally) or simply be unwilling to suppress such groups violently; it also helps if these groups can find

---

[2] This approach rests upon two important distinctions made by Charles Tilly: the distinction between "states," on the one hand (i.e., organizations that attempt to monopolize the principal means of coercion within a bounded population) and "polities," on the other (i.e., the state plus those "member" groups with routine access to it), and the distinction between the capacity to act collectively, which Tilly terms "mobilization" (i.e., the quantity of resources, including labor and skills, collectively controlled by a group) and actual collective action. See Tilly 1978: ch. 3.

powerful allies within a divided state or polity (see, e.g., Tarrow 1994; Kitschelt 1986). And geopolitics is again important here. Some social groups, for example, may form alliances with, and receive significant resources from, foreign states; and international wars and imperial overextension have often produced political crises that have created unprecedented opportunities for political mobilization (see, e.g., Tilly 1992; Kennedy 1987; Collins 1993). In this sense, one may speak of "transnational political opportunities" (McCarthy 1997).

There exists, finally, what Theda Skocpol (1985: 21) calls a "Tocquevillian" approach, which emphasizes how states shape the very identities, goals, strategies, social ties, ideas, and even emotions of actors in civil society. This approach is so named because of Alexis de Tocqueville's masterful employment of it in *The Old Régime and the French Revolution* (1955) and in *Democracy in America* (1981). This is perhaps the most interesting and important statist approach of all, yet it is often elided in discussions of state-centered theory or else conflated with the political-opportunity perspective. I propose that we label this approach the *state-constructionist perspective*,[3] because it examines the ways in which states help to construct or constitute various social forces and institutions that are (falsely) conceptualized as wholly exterior to states.[4] In other words, the focus here – as against a political-opportunity approach – is not so much on whether a state or polity provides incentives or opportunities to act for *already existing* networks of like-minded people; rather, state constructionism emphasizes how the actions of foreign as well as domestic states help to make cognitively plausible and morally justifiable certain types of collective grievances, emotions, identities, ideologies, associational ties,

[3] As noted in Chapter 1, this label is modeled on the well-known idea of "cultural" or "social constructionism," that is, the notion that certain social phenomena – e.g., cultural assumptions, political grievances, and collective identities – are recognized, defined, or even produced (in whole or in part) through cultural and discursive practices. I do not limit the idea of state constructionism, however, to the cultural or discursive work of states; as I have suggested, the organization and practices of states – which are only partially discursive in nature – are equally if not more consequential for social life. See also Lieberman 1995 on "political construction."

[4] For example, a "private" corporation cannot logically or temporally exist outside of a state-enforced legal order; the corporate form itself is legally defined and enforced, as are the property rights that attach to it. More generally, it makes little sense to view states as the dependent "superstructures" of economies, given that economic relations themselves are constituted through de jure or de facto legal orders and, standing behind these, coercive state power. In some contexts, it would be more nearly correct to describe economies as the superstructures of states.

and actions (but not others) in the first place (see, e.g., Birnbaum 1988; Wuthnow 1985).

A major thesis of this book is that states largely "construct" (in this specific sense) the revolutionary movements that challenge and sometimes overthrow them. Of course, this "construction" is never accomplished by states alone, or ex nihilo. Nor is state constructionism intended to slight the agency of revolutionaries themselves. The point is simply that revolutionaries cannot will revolutionary movements, let alone revolutions, into existence. Rather, as I suggested in the previous chapter, revolutionaries have been most successful when they have confronted states, and the populations ruled in certain ways by those states, that exhibit certain determinate features and characteristic practices. But this claim stands or falls according to the adequacy of the empirical studies in subsequent chapters.

Analytic Strengths of State-Centered Approaches to Revolutions

Before turning to the weaknesses of the statist theoretical tradition, and of my state-constructionist thesis in particular, I want to emphasize how statist approaches help to resolve a series of key problems that are distinctive to the study of revolutions as a specific form of collective action and political conflict.

The Centrality of State Power and State Breakdowns

To begin with, consider this puzzle: *Why is revolution, unlike many other forms of social and political conflict, a peculiarly modern phenomenon?* Why, in other words, did revolutions occur with increasing frequency during the twentieth century, yet do not seem to have occurred at all before the seventeenth? This puzzle concerns the "conditions of existence" of revolutions – that is, the background conditions (which have only widely existed, evidently, for the past century or two) that are necessary for revolutions to occur. A state-centered perspective offers a compelling solution to this puzzle: the existence of the international state system itself. In other words, *no states, no revolutions*. This proposition follows tautologically, in fact, from the very definition of revolutions as involving, at the very least, the overthrow of national states or political regimes. Thus, there could be no revolutions, in the modern sense of the word, before there were states, and it follows that there cannot be revolutions if and when the international state system is replaced by some other mode (or modes) of governance. This simple yet profound proposition, frequently reiterated by Charles Tilly, is usually overlooked by analysts of revolutions; it is taken for granted by virtually all scholars of revolutions, including Marxists, cultural analysts, and many state-centered analysts themselves.

From a state-centered approach, it is much more than a convention or mere matter of convenience that scholars write books and articles about, for example, the "French," "Russian," and "Cuban" revolutions. In fact (as a state-capacity approach would suggest), prior to the emergence of modern national states,[5] revolutions as we now understand them – whether as radically transformative processes, a distinctive repertoire of contention, or a moral ideal – were simply impossible and generally unthinkable. Until the modern era, that is, no institution had sufficient infrastructural power – with the possible exception of the Catholic Church – to reform extensive social arrangements in more or less fundamental ways; the national state, however, made it possible to do – and to think of doing – just that. (Radical revolutionaries, in fact, have themselves often sought to consolidate national states precisely in order to remake societies.) Thus, while wars and political conflict may be old as humanity itself, the reality and ideal of reshaping a "political order," "society," "nation," or "people" – the political, economic, and/or cultural arrangements of a large population – are coeval with the modern state system as it originated in Europe and was then transported, imposed, and emulated around the globe.

This line of argument immediately suggests a solution to another puzzle: *Why are radical movements, unlike reformist movements and other forms of political conflict, typically concerned with "seizing" or "smashing" state power?* If the preceding analysis is correct, those who would "radically" transform modern societies must obviously concern themselves with the state. (If they don't, the state will certainly concern itself with them!) In other words, because the state enforces (through violence if necessary) the most fundamental "rules" of a society (whether these are codified as laws or exist as traditions or conventions) by virtue of its control of the

---

[5] Tilly differentiates modern "consolidated" national states ("large, differentiated, [and] ruling heterogeneous territories directly, claiming to impose a unitary fiscal, monetary, judicial, legislative, military and cultural system on its citizens") from "segmented" states (for example, "a city-based bishopric and its immediate hinterland, or . . . a composite of different sorts of unit, each enjoying considerable distinctness and autonomy"). See Tilly 1993: 31, 35. Note that "national" states in this sense are *not* necessarily "nation-states," which rule peoples who share a homogeneous ethnic or religious identity. See Tilly 1992: 2–3.

principal means of coercion, any fundamental recasting of these rules requires access to, and indeed a thorough reorganization of, state power itself. Because of their actual and potential infrastructural power, in other words, states are necessarily the target (although not always the *only* target) of revolutionary movements.

This view of revolutions, I should note, is shared by state-centered and Marxist analysts alike, even though the latter are otherwise keen to emphasize how class struggles are supposedly the driving force behind revolutions. "The basic question of every revolution," wrote Lenin, "is that of state power. . . . The question of power cannot be evaded or brushed aside, because it is the key question determining *everything* in a revolution's development" (1974 [1917]: 370; emphasis in original). The task of revolutionaries, in Lenin's view, was not simply to change laws or to replace government officials, but rather to change the structural characteristics of the state – to bring about "a gigantic replacement of one type of institution with others of a fundamentally different order" (1943 [1917]: 37) by means of which the social order as a whole could be radically reshaped. Perry Anderson (1974: 11; emphasis in original) similarly notes that

one of the basic axioms of historical materialism [is] that secular struggle between classes is ultimately resolved at the *political* – not at the economic or cultural – level of society. In other words, it is the construction and destruction of States which seal the basic shifts in the relations of production, so long as classes subsist.

It follows that successful revolutionary movements must, at the very least, secure or seize state power. And this implies, by definition, that the old state (especially its army) must collapse or surrender; for if it persists in the face of a revolutionary challenge, then the revolutionaries have obviously failed to attain the type of power that they need in order to change the political and/or social order as a whole in a more or less fundamental fashion.[6]

We now possess the solution to yet another conundrum: *Why must the state break down, collapse, or capitulate for a revolutionary movement, unlike many other forms of social protest, to succeed?* The fact that "state breakdowns," particularly the incapacitation of armies, create the possibility for full-fledged revolutionary change is one of the best-known ideas to emerge

[6] This does not rule out the possibility, of course, that revolutionaries may institute radical changes in those territories of a national society that they effectively control or rule, even if the central government has not been toppled.

42

from statist analyses of revolution; it is a point that is central, for example, to Theda Skocpol's influential state-centered study, *States and Social Revolutions* (1979).[7] In fact, Skocpol not only implicitly utilizes a political-opportunity approach in order to explain why transformative, class-based revolts from below could occur in France, Russia, and China; she also employs a state-autonomy perspective in order to explain the political crises that created such opportunities in the first place. Indeed, one of the more interesting claims of Skocpol's study is that the political crises that made revolutions possible in France, Russia, and China were *not* brought about by revolutionaries; rather, conflicts between dominant classes and autonomous state officials – conflicts, Skocpol emphasizes, that were produced or exacerbated by geopolitical competition – directly or indirectly brought about such crises, thereby opening up opportunities that rebellious lower classes and self-conscious revolutionaries seized, sometimes years later.

By illuminating the origins of, and the political opportunities created by, these sorts of state crises and breakdowns, state-centered approaches help to resolve yet another classic puzzle: *Why do revolutions occur when and where they do?* It has become virtually obligatory for scholars to note that people are not often rebellious in the poorest of societies or during the hardest of times; and even where and when people are rebellious, and strong revolutionary movements form, they may not always be able to seize state power – *unless*, that is, they are able to exploit the political opportunities opened up by state breakdowns. "It is the state of the army, of competing armies," Barrington Moore, Jr., has noted, "not of the working class, that has determined the fate of twentieth-century revolutions" (1978: 375). Of course, revolutionaries need not wait for political opportunities to appear. They often topple states, especially infrastructurally weak states, through their own efforts.

The limited utility of poststructuralist conceptions of power (e.g., Foucault 1990), at least for the analysis of revolutions, follows from what has been said thus far. In fact, any view of power as "decentered," largely nonviolent, local, mobile, and ubiquitous fails to grasp the crucial

---

[7] See also Skocpol 1994. State breakdowns are also emphasized in Goldstone 1991. Although Goldstone presents an explanation of these breakdowns that is very different from Skocpol's (one that emphasizes demographic pressures), he shares her view that revolts from below cannot succeed so long as states remain fiscally and militarily strong. See Collins 1993 and Chorley's (1943) classic study.

difference that centralized state power (and its breakdown) makes for a variety of social processes, including but not limited to revolutions. Furthermore, the notion that the state itself is simply the "institutional crystallization" or "institutional integration of power relationships" that are fundamentally "local" in nature (Foucault 1990: 93, 96) fails to grasp the potential autonomy and distinctive capacities of states; it also underestimates the role of state power in constructing, or reconstructing, localized power relationships in the first place. It is precisely because not all forms of domination are "local" that revolutions are sometimes desired and even possible.

The Formation of Revolutionary Movements

And yet, state power and its breakdown cannot alone explain (or predict) revolutions; analysts also need to explain why and how specifically revolutionary movements are able to take advantage of these crises – or *create* such crises – and actually seize power.[8] After all, an organized revolutionary movement simply may not exist or possess the sufficient leverage or "hegemony" within civil society that is necessary to take advantage of (or create its own) political opportunities. In such cases, state power will be reconsolidated – if it is reconsolidated at all – by surviving factions of the old regime or by political forces that eschew any significant transformation of the state or society.

Here again, a state-centered perspective provides us with some indispensable analytic tools. For although statist approaches (as we shall see) do not completely or adequately theorize collective action as such, they *are* particularly helpful in resolving the following puzzle: *Why are groups with a specifically revolutionary agenda or ideology, as well as a militant or "high-risk" strategy, sometimes able to attract broad popular support?*[9] State-centered approaches point to at least five distinctive state practices or characteristics that help to engender or "construct" hegemonic revolutionary movements; these practices and traits, moreover, are causally "cumulative," in

---

[8] I thus disagree with Randall Collins to the extent that his writings sometimes seem to imply that state breakdowns themselves automatically induce revolutionary movements or popular mobilizations. See, e.g., Collins 1995: 1561; 1993: 119. To add to the confusion, Collins (following Goldstone) sometimes suggests that popular mobilization is a defining element of state breakdowns.

[9] The concept of "high-risk" activism is borrowed from McAdam 1986.

the sense that a hegemonic revolutionary movement is more likely to develop the more they characterize a given state:

1. *State sponsorship or protection of unpopular economic and social arrangements or cultural institutions.* In certain societies, economic and social arrangements – particularly those involving people's work or livelihood or important cultural institutions – may be widely viewed as unjust (that is, as not simply unfortunate or inevitable). Yet unless state officials are seen to sponsor or protect those institutions – through legal codes, surveillance, taxation, conscription, and, ultimately, force – specifically *revolutionary* movements are unlikely to emerge. People may blame their particular bosses or superiors for their plight, for example, or even whole classes of bosses, yet the state itself may not be challenged (even when the aggrieved are well organized and the political context is opportune) unless there exists a widely perceived symbiotic or dependent relationship between the state and these elites. Indeed, the fact that a despised state must actively protect certain institutions and groups will itself serve, in many instances, to delegitimate and stigmatize those institutions and groups.

For this reason, "ruling classes" that do not directly rule may be safer from revolutionaries than those which do; other things being equal, that is, some measure of state autonomy from the dominant economic class may act as a bulwark against revolution. In such contexts, contentious, anti-elite actions may be chronic, in such forms as pilfering, malingering, sabotage, riots, strikes, and demonstrations. Yet such actions are unlikely to escalate beyond a local or, at most, regional level in a way that would seriously and directly threaten a strong state.[10] But rebels are not revolutionaries, we have seen, unless they seriously contend for state power. Thus, if and when domination is widely perceived to be purely local and "decentered" (i.e., as poststructuralists conceptualize it), then revolution is unlikely, no matter how oppressive that domination is felt to be.

It follows that states that regulate, reform, or even abolish perceived economic and social injustices are less likely to become the target of political demands (revolutionary or otherwise) than those that are seen to cause or perpetuate such injustices. On the other hand, a state that

---

[10] As James C. Scott (1990) has emphasized, class struggles "from below" only very rarely break out of their localistic and necessarily disguised forms, even when inequalities, class identities, and oppositional subcultures are quite salient.

suddenly attempts to reform unpopular institutions that it has long protected may not be able to preempt a revolutionary challenge; on the contrary, such reforms, or even attempted reforms, may be perceived as signs of the state's weakness and, accordingly, will simply serve to accelerate revolutionary mobilization. We might term this the "too-little-too-late syndrome." As Tocqueville argued, "the most perilous moment for a bad government is one when it seeks to mend its ways. . . . Patiently endured so long as it seemed beyond redress, a grievance comes to appear intolerable once the possibility of removing it crosses men's minds" (1955: 177).

In sum, economic grievances and cultural resentments may only become "politicized" (that is, framed as resolvable only at the level of the state), and thereby a basis for specifically revolutionary movements, when the state sponsors or protects economic, social, or cultural arrangements that are widely viewed as grievous. Note that this is a "state-constructionist" argument: State practices, in this case, help to constitute both a distinctive *target* and *goal* for aggrieved groups in civil society – namely, the state itself and its overthrow (and reorganization), respectively.

2. *Repression and/or exclusion of mobilized groups from state power or resources.* Even if aggrieved groups direct their claims at the state, they are unlikely to seek its overthrow (or radical reorganization) if they manage to attain some significant share – or believe they *can* attain such a share – of state power or influence. Indeed, even if such groups view their political influence as unfairly limited, their access to state resources or inclusion in policy-making deliberations – unless palpably cosmetic – will likely prevent any radicalization of their guiding ideology or strategic repertoire. In fact, the political "incorporation" of mobilized groups – including the putatively revolutionary proletariat – has typically served to *deradicalize* them (see, e.g., Mann 1993: ch. 18; Bendix 1977 [1964]). Such groups often view this sort of inclusion as the first step in the accumulation of greater influence and resources; in any event, they are unlikely to jeopardize their relatively low-cost access to the state – unless that state itself is in deep crisis – by engaging in "disloyal" or illegal activities.

Political inclusion also discourages the sense that the state is unreformable or an instrument of a narrow class or clique and, accordingly, needs to be fundamentally overhauled. Tocqueville emphasized how the exclusionary nature of French absolutism bred, by contrast, a political culture characterized by a utopian longing for total revolution – even though French social conditions were comparatively benign by European standards of the time (1955: pt. 3, ch. 1).[11]

Accordingly, neither liberal democratic polities nor authoritarian yet inclusionary (for example, "populist") regimes have generally been challenged by powerful revolutionary movements. By contrast, chronic repression and/or exclusion of mobilized groups from access to state power is likely to push them toward a specifically revolutionary strategy – that is, militant, extralegal, and even armed struggle aimed at overthrowing the state. Such repression, after all, serves as an object lesson in the futility of legalistic or constitutional politics (i.e., "playing by the rules"). A major claim of this book is that repressive and exclusionary authoritarian regimes – even those that stage competitive elections – tend to "incubate" or "construct" radical collective action: Those who specialize in revolution tend to prosper under such regimes, because they come to be viewed by politically repressed groups as more realistic and potentially effective than political moderates, who themselves come to be viewed as hopelessly ineffectual. Partly for this reason, virtually every powerful revolutionary movement of the present century – including those examined in this book – developed under a repressive and exclusionary regime, including the Bolsheviks in Russia, the Communists in China and in Southeast Asia (see Chapter 3), Castro's July Twenty-Sixth Movement in Cuba, the broad coalition that opposed the Shah in Iran, and the guerrilla movements of Central America (see Chapter 5).

Note that this argument has both political-opportunity and state-constructionist aspects. In the former sense, it emphasizes how the *lack* of routine opportunities to influence state policy (or the contraction of such opportunities) tends to push certain groups and individuals toward radical politics; in the latter sense, emphasis falls on the ways in which repressive state practices reinforce the plausibility and justifiability of a radical political orientation or collective identity.

3. *Indiscriminate, but not overwhelming, state violence against mobilized groups and oppositional political figures.* Indiscriminate state violence against mobilized groups and oppositional figures is likely to reinforce

---

[11] I argue in Chapter 8 that Tocqueville sheds considerable light on the gradual rejection by Eastern European dissidents of a reformed socialism or a "socialism with a human face"; by 1989 these dissidents generally rejected Communism in toto and were, with some exceptions, proponents of a Western-style, democratic capitalism.

the plausibility, justifiability, and (hence) diffusion of the idea that the state needs to be violently "smashed" and radically reorganized. For reasons of simple self-defense, in fact, people who are literally targeted by the state may arm themselves or join or support groups that have access to arms. Unless state violence is simply overwhelming, then, indiscriminate coercion tends to backfire, producing an ever-growing popular mobilization by armed movements and an even larger body of sympathizers (see, e.g., Mason and Krane 1989; Gurr 1986). Revolutionary groups may thus prosper not so much because of their ideology per se, but simply because they can offer people some protection from violent states. Many studies of revolutions (including this one) emphasize that groups have turned to militant strategies or armed struggle only after their previous efforts to secure change through legal means were violently repressed (see, e.g., Booth and Walker 1993; Walton 1984; Kerkvliet 1977).

Like political exclusion, indiscriminate state violence also reinforces the plausibility and diffusion of specifically revolutionary ideologies – that is, ideologies that envisage a radical reorganization not only of the state, but of society as well. After all, a society in which aggrieved people are routinely denied an opportunity to redress perceived injustices, and even murdered on the mere suspicion of political disloyalty, is unlikely to be viewed as requiring a few minor reforms; those people are more likely to view such a society as in need of a fundamental reorganization. In other words, violent, exclusionary regimes tend to foster unintentionally the hegemony or dominance of their most radical social critics – religious zealots, virtuous ascetics, socialist militants, and radical nationalists, for example, who view society as more or less totally corrupted, incapable of reform, and thus requiring a thorough and perhaps violent reconstruction (see McDaniel 1991: ch. 7).

Revolutionaries themselves, it must be noted, sometimes use violence against civilians and their political competitors, not just the state (see, e.g., Kriger 1992; Stoll 1993, 1999). Some revolutionaries coerce civilians or attack political moderates to ensure that they are seen as the only viable alternative to the state; some employ violence purposely to incite or provoke the state repression that will presumably expand their ranks. But this can easily become a self-defeating strategy since the targets of such violence are likely to blame the revolutionaries as much as the state for their travails. Indiscriminate counterstate violence can produce a popular backlash as easily as state violence. Perhaps the best example of this is

48

the Shining Path insurgency in Peru, which I discuss in Chapter 7. Not surprisingly, the violence and abuses of the most popular and successful revolutionary movements pale in comparison to the crimes perpetrated by the states that they confront.

4. *Weak policing capacities and infrastructural power.* As the political-opportunity approach emphasizes, no matter how iniquitous or authoritarian a state may be – or the society that it rules – it can always retain power so long as it is capable of ruthlessly repressing its enemies. Such a state may in fact have many enemies (including revolutionaries), yet they will prove quite ineffective so long as the state's coercive might remains overwhelming.

Long before a state breakdown, however, revolutionaries may become numerous and well organized if the state's policing capacities and infra-structural power more generally are chronically weak or geographically uneven. Guerrilla movements, for example, have typically prospered in peripheral and especially mountainous areas where state control is weak or nonexistent: The Communist movement in China grew strong in the northwest periphery, Castro's movement in Cuba's Sierra Maestra, and El Salvador's guerrilla armies in that country's mountainous northern departments (see, e.g., Wolf 1969: ch. 6, on Cuba; Pearce 1986 on El Salvador). And revolutionaries are doubly fortunate if they confront states and armies that are ineffectual due to corruption or bureaucratic incoherence – traits that are often purposively fostered by ruling cliques or autocrats who fear palace coups. In such situations, revolutionaries themselves may bring about or accelerate state breakdowns not only through direct military pressure, but also by exacerbating conflicts between states (especially personalistic dictatorships) and dominant classes, and between states and their foreign sponsors. These types of conflicts, in addition to creating the general insecurity associated with revolutionary situations, may accelerate state breakdowns by creating economic downturns that bring on fiscal crises for states (see Foran 1992, 1997).

5. *Corrupt and arbitrary personalistic rule that alienates, weakens, or divides counterrevolutionary elites.* As these last remarks suggest, autocratic and so-called neopatrimonial (or "sultanistic") dictatorships are especially vulnerable to revolution (see, e.g., Dix 1984; Goldstone 1986; Goodwin and Skocpol 1989; Wickham-Crowley 1992; Foran 1992; Snyder 1992; Chehabi and Linz 1998). In fact, such regimes not only tend to facilitate the formation of hegemonic revolutionary movements, but they also

cannot easily defeat such movements once they have formed; examples of such regimes include the dictatorships of Díaz in Mexico, Chiang in China, Batista in Cuba (discussed later in this chapter), the Shah of Iran, Somoza in Nicaragua (see Chapter 6), and Ceauşescu in Romania (see Chapter 8). As especially narrow and autonomous regimes, such dictatorships tend to have few fervid supporters; they also possess the discretionary power that may alienate certain state officials and military officers as well as vast sectors of society – including middle strata and even elites in addition to lower classes. In fact, because dictators often view economic and military elites as their chief foes, they may attempt to weaken and divide them in various ways, even though such groups share with dictators a counterrevolutionary orientation. By weakening counterrevolutionary elites, however, dictators may unwittingly play into the hands of revolutionaries, since such elites may thereby become too weak either to oppose revolutionaries effectively or to oust the dictator and reform the regime, thereby preempting revolution. Some dictators have even driven elites, or segments thereof, into the camp of the revolutionaries.

Of course, not all dictators are equally adept at controlling their armed forces and rival elites; their incompetence or incapacity in this regard does not bode well for them personally, but it may prove decisive in preempting revolution. For if civilian and military elites can remove corrupt and repressive dictators, and perhaps institute democratic reforms, they thereby undermine much of the appeal of revolutionaries. In fact, this is precisely what happened in the Philippines in 1986 with the ouster of Ferdinand Marcos (Snyder 1992).

In sum, certain types of states are not only liable to break down and thereby to create the sort of political opportunities that strong revolutionary movements can exploit; certain states also unintentionally foster the very formation, and indeed "construct" the hegemony or dominance, of radical movements by politicizing popular grievances, foreclosing possibilities for peaceful reform, compelling people to take up arms in order to defend themselves, making radical ideologies and identities plausible, providing the minimal political space that revolutionaries require to organize disgruntled people, and weakening counterrevolutionary elites, including their own officer corps.

By thus illuminating both state breakdowns *and* processes of revolutionary mobilization, state-centered approaches provide us with some very powerful tools for explaining revolutions.

Some Common Criticisms of State-Centered Approaches

Like any theoretical tradition, the statist perspective has its share of critics. However, the various complaints that have been directed against this tradition are very uneven in their persuasiveness. Before turning to some of the more potent criticisms of statist analysis, I want to examine several that either rest upon unfounded assumptions or are simply unconvincing. Four such criticisms merit a brief response:

1. *"Societies affect states as much as, or possibly more than, states affect societies"* (Migdal, Kohli, and Shue 1994: 2). This broad generalization challenges one combination of the state-autonomy and state-capacity approaches: the view that all states are autonomous from civil society and actually have the capacity to impose their preferred policies.[12] This is certainly a view worth challenging, but it is not clear that many state-centered theorists would defend it. In fact, state-centered theorists have generally emphasized that state autonomy and capacities are *potential* and *variable* rather than "given" a priori. As we have seen, moreover, statist analysts have emphasized precisely how state *breakdowns*, as well as infra-structurally *weak* states, have encouraged or made possible important social processes, including the formation of revolutionary movements.

This criticism also seems to confuse state-centered analysis with a sort of sweeping *political determinism* that robs "society" of any analytic auton-omy whatsoever.[13] But a perspective that "centers" the state hardly implies that states are the *only* institutions that matter or that states themselves are not potentially shaped and constrained by a variety of socioeconomic and cultural forces. In fact, it is possible and sometimes desirable to combine or complement a state-centered analysis with, for example, class analysis (see, e.g., Skocpol 1979; Wickham-Crowley 1992).

2. *State officials are usually not autonomous actors; instead, they typically respond to the demands of the dominant class or (occasionally) of militant lower classes.* This criticism – the principal one expressed by Marxists (see, e.g., Cammack 1989) – is a narrower version of the preceding one,

---

[12] Migdal, for example, emphasizes how state-centered theories "encounter . . . difficulties when they assume that the state organization is powerful and cohesive enough to drive society." This assumption, he notes, is especially problematic for students of African soci-eties, such as Senegal, which has a conspicuously "weak" state (Migdal 1992: 20).

[13] To be sure, a few state-centered theorists (e.g., Birnbaum 1988; Kitschelt 1986) sometimes lapse into a sort of political determinism, but this is hardly inherent to statist analysis as such.

emphasizing how specifically *class*-based demands determine state policies. Like the previous criticism, this one also challenges one extreme version of the state-autonomy approach – namely, the idea that all states are autonomous from the demands of social classes (and, accordingly, are never influenced by such classes). Again, this is a claim that few if any statists would wish to make; it seems more reasonable, in fact, to assume that the relationship between states and classes is in fact quite variable over space and time.

Two other points about this criticism also need to be made. First, it has usually been raised in the context of complex, detailed debates about the relative importance of class and state actors in formulating specific state policies (e.g., Goldfield 1989; Skocpol and Finegold 1990). These debates, whichever side one finds most convincing, hinge upon the marshaling and interpretation of particular facts and sequences of events. Neither side, including that which emphasizes the importance of class actors, has suggested that its opponents *must* be wrong a priori, irrespective of the actual historical record. The *theoretical* grounds for believing that states *may* be autonomous from class forces, in other words, have not been convincingly challenged – or seriously challenged at all – in these debates; what is disputed is the relative autonomy of *particular* state actors in *specific* times and places (e.g., Democratic politicians in the U.S. Congress during the 1930s).

Second, even in those cases in which the class-biased character of state policies has been convincingly established, it would be quite unfortunate to dismiss or ignore state-centered perspectives on that account. In fact, state autonomy may very well explain why such policies were adopted in the first place. (For example, certain state officials may be in a better position than particular capitalists to assess the interests of the capitalist class as a whole.[14]) The state-capacity approach, furthermore, may be helpful for understanding which, if any, class-based policies can actually be implemented. The political-opportunity perspective, furthermore, may be helpful for understanding whether other classes or groups can successfully mobilize *against* such policies. (In this regard, it may make a great deal of difference whether individual capitalists are simply acting in similar ways or the state is enforcing – with violence, if necessary – certain laws or policies at their behest.) And a state-constructionist analysis may be helpful for understanding why specifically *class*-based actors are politically organized and influential in the first place.

---

[14] This was Nicos Poulantzas's position in his famous debate with Ralph Miliband.

Some Common Criticisms of State-Centered Approaches

3. *As a type of "structuralism," state-centered analysis necessarily neglects the purposive (including strategic) and cultural dimensions of social action.* The conflation of state-centered analysis with the sort of "structuralism" that denies the importance of purposive human agency would seem to rest upon an elementary confusion.[15] In fact, statist analysis may emphasize the actions and policies of state actors just as much as the impersonal "structural" characteristics of states (and both are undoubtedly important). For example, rationally calculating and acting state officials are the analytic pivot in some types of state-centered studies (see, e.g., Levi 1988).

The criticism that state-centered analysis fails to treat culture seriously is only partially correct (see, e.g., Friedland and Alford 1991). (I discuss the sense in which it *is* accurate in the next section.) While most statist analyses have in fact been "structuralist" or "instrumentalist" in the sense of neglecting the shared beliefs of politicians and state officials, this quality seems contingent rather than inherent to this perspective. So, for example, one important state-centered study, James M. Jasper's *Nuclear Politics: Energy and the State in the United States, Sweden, and France* (1990), emphasizes precisely the ways in which the ideologies and "policy styles" of state officials shape state policies. Jasper's study is no less state-centered for treating such officials as cultural actors rather than as rational calculators or as puppets of external forces. As Jasper's study emphasizes, moreover, state practices are "always already" cultural practices.

It is also possible, as Robert Wuthnow (1985) has convincingly shown, to explain the diffusion and institutionalization of ideologies from a state-centered perspective. As we have seen, in fact, a state-constructionist approach is indispensable for understanding how radical ideologies and strategic repertoires sometimes resonate with and diffuse among broad masses of people.

4. *Because they interpenetrate one another, the very distinction between "states" and "societies" is untenable and should be scrapped.* This criticism,

---

[15] See, e.g., Cohen 1994: chs. 2–3. The confusion probably derives from Skocpol's polemic against "voluntaristic" accounts of revolutionary political crises. See Skocpol 1979: ch. 1. But this polemic was clearly directed against the view that such crises – as they arose in France, Russia, and China – were caused by the actions of self-conscious revolutionaries and/or revolts from below; for Skocpol, that argument stood the actual historical record on its head. Nowhere, in any event, did she question the potential importance of human agency as such. This simply is not what the statist perspective is all about.

which is perhaps the most radical that has been raised against statist approaches, has been elaborated most fully in a much-discussed article by Timothy Mitchell (1991). Mitchell notes that "the edges of the state are uncertain; social elements seem to penetrate it on all sides, and the resulting boundary between state and society is difficult to determine" (1991: 88). Mitchell terms this the "boundary problem." He points out, for example, that upper classes have sometimes controlled certain state institutions, making it difficult if not impossible to distinguish state power from the class or economic power of such groups. Mitchell concludes that, "The state should not be taken as . . . an agent, instrument, organization or structure, located apart from and opposed to another entity called society" (1991: 95). But he goes even further, questioning the *analytic* utility of the conceptual distinction between states and societies.

This is a problematic argument. To begin with, upper-class control of certain state institutions does not remove the "statist" character of those institutions – the fact, that is, that they are buttressed (unlike most other organizations) by substantial means of violence. Indeed, this situation would seem to be precisely one in which state institutions are a virtual "instrument" of the upper classes.

The rejection of the state-society distinction exemplifies what Margaret Archer (1988) has termed, in a different context, the fallacy of "central conflation." Archer uses the term to characterize studies that, striving mightily to avoid either cultural or "structural" determinism, posit that ideas and social structures are so closely connected that "there is no way of 'untying' the constitutive elements. The intimacy of their interconnection denies even relative autonomy to the components involved" (1988: 80). Mitchell, analogously, seems to assume that because states and societies are so closely bound together, it is impossible to speak of their interaction.

The "boundary problem" that Mitchell discusses is real enough, and social analysts do often reify the concepts of state and society in problematic ways (Goodwin 1994b). Yet it seems more helpful to recognize that concrete institutions and social forces (including, not least, revolutionary movements) may sometimes *share* certain analytic characteristics of both states *and* societies rather than to jettison these concepts completely. Throughout his article, in fact, Mitchell himself refers quite un-self-consciously to such things as "the French state," "state practices," and "state-society relations." His own language, in other words, would seem to testify to the unavoidable importance of the *conceptual* distinction

54

between states and societies.[16] In sum, while states and societies can often (although certainly not always) become quite intertwined in the real world, the conceptual distinction between them is still worth preserving.

Limitations of State-Centered Approaches

Although these general criticisms of state-centered perspectives are ultimately unhelpful, statist approaches do have their limitations. In this section, I examine some of the more serious theoretical gaps in state-centered analysis and point to some theoretical resources than can help to bridge them. A proper recognition of these gaps not only reveals the limits of what state-centered analyses can reasonably hope to explain, including the present study, but also helps to highlight more clearly what statist approaches to revolutions *can* explain.

For analysts of revolutionary movements (or collective action in any of its forms), the fundamental weakness of statist analysis is that it does not theorize the nonstate or nonpolitical sources – or the *independent* explanatory weight – of three general factors: (1) *associational networks* (including class formations and "civil society" more generally), (2) *material resources*, and (3) *collective beliefs, assumptions, and emotions* (including grievances, strategies and tactics, moral convictions, and identities). Needless to say, this is a significant problem indeed given the potentially crucial connection between social networks, resources, and culture, on the one hand, and collective action (revolutionary or otherwise), on the other. Fortunately, there are some powerful theoretical resources at hand that can help to make that connection.

For example, the role of social networks and interpersonal ties in mobilization processes has been powerfully addressed in recent years by so-called social-network analysts (see, e.g., Gould 1995; Bearman 1993; McAdam 1986). These scholars emphasize the crucial role of networks of social ties in recruiting people into, and then sustaining their collective identification with and commitment to, social movements

---

[16] Mitchell would have us focus on "disciplinary power," which he argues has produced the state-society distinction as a "metaphysical effect" (1991: 94). Yet this would simply re-create the "boundary problem" in a new form, since it is often difficult to distinguish disciplinary from other practices. (Is resistance to discipline itself disciplinary?) Here again, Mitchell seems to be talking about an *analytic* distinction that is often blurred in the real world, but should not be jettisoned for that reason.

and perhaps even larger political communities (thereby obviating a need, in some cases, for substantial material resources). Network analysts also stress how such social ties, sometimes in the shape of formal organizations, provide the "relational infrastructure" of actual collective actions. These insights have also been underscored by those who emphasize the importance of "civil society" – that is, voluntary associational activities – as a mechanism for democratic dialogue and as a bulwark against state oppression; these insights may also be found in the work of Marxists who emphasize the importance of class-based collective action in particular.[17]

From all these perspectives, in fact, individuals with a strong inclination to pursue reformist or even revolutionary change, and who also find themselves in a political context that allows or even encourages such pursuits, will still be unable to act effectively unless they are connected to a sufficiently large social network of like-minded people. Seemingly "appropriate" political opportunity structures, in other words, will not give rise to collective action if such networks do not exist.

State-centered analysts can justly counter, on the other hand, that these associational networks are often politicized and radicalized, and even constructed in the first place, as a result of specific state structures and policies. Social networks, after all, do not simply fall from the sky. Network analysts, proponents of "civil society," and Marxists, unfortunately, often neglect the ways in which state actions shape the very formation (or prevent the formation) of voluntary organizations and revolutionary movements in particular. Still, these associations are also typically rooted in class or ethnic relations, extended kinship networks, religious communities, urban neighborhoods, or rural villages – still other social networks, that is, that do not derive wholly or even in part from state practices. And associational networks and practices have their own dynamics and emergent properties that need to be taken seriously and analyzed in their own right. Revolutionaries themselves, for example, may act in ways that expand or corrode their ties to other people. For these reasons, a state-centered perspective on the associational networks of civil society is inherently limited.

---

[17] Recent works on civil society include Putnam 1993 and Cohen and Arato 1992. The Marxist and class-analytic literature on revolutions and collective action is of course vast. Among the more influential recent studies are Paige 1975, 1997; Wolf 1969; and Moore 1966.

Limitations of State-Centered Approaches

The potentially autonomous influence of material resources on collective action, for its part, has been most carefully theorized by resource-mobilization and political-process theorists (e.g., McCarthy and Zald 1977; Tarrow 1994; McAdam 1982; Tilly 1978), as well as by certain rational-choice theorists (e.g., Popkin 1979; Olson 1965). All of these analysts point out (albeit in somewhat different ways) that even tightly knit groups may not be able to act collectively – at least not for long or with much effectiveness – if they do not have steady access to the resources, including infrastructure and technology (means of communication and transportation, weapons, safehouses, etc.) that are necessary to sustain their activities and (perhaps) motivate people to contribute to their cause. In other words, even tightly knit groups that would seem to have the opportunity as well as an interest in acting collectively may not be able to do so effectively without substantial material resources. So again, collective action (whether revolutionary or not) may depend on much more than the extant political context.

A group's access to material resources generally depends on how it is inserted into specific social networks and institutions; the class composition of such groups is of particular importance in this regard. Nonetheless, access to specifically *state* resources may also be quite important for political mobilization – even for would-be revolutionaries who are violently excluded from the state. Defectors from the state's armed forces, for example, often bring along their guns. Guerrilla armies, furthermore, usually build up their arsenals through raids on peripheral army garrisons or ambushes of government troops. And some revolutionary groups have access to the resources of *foreign* states – which is one of the ways in which the international state system (and geopolitical competition in particular) matters for revolutionary conflicts. While the extent of external aid to revolutionaries has often been exaggerated by their opponents (Wickham-Crowley 1992: ch. 5), such aid figured prominently (but not necessarily decisively) in the revolutionary conflicts in Mexico, Vietnam (see Chapter 4), Algeria, and Afghanistan.

Finally, the potentially independent role of beliefs, identities, and repertoires of contention in collective action has been powerfully underscored recently by theorists of "framing processes" and culture more generally (see, e.g., Jasper 1997; Selbin 1993, 1997a, 1997b; Snow and Benford 1992; Sewell 1985). Framing theorists, for example, drawing on Goffman's (1974) important study, argue that "objective" reality is recognized (or indeed recognizable) as unjust *and* alterable only when it is interpreted or "framed" as such by means of specific cultural systems or discourses. When extant collective frames do not allow such an interpretation – even of a reality that an external observer might find both unconscionable and easily rectified – then collective action aimed at altering that reality is obviously impossible. In fact, even resourceful groups that would seem to have the opportunity as well as a rational interest in changing their predicament will not (indeed, cannot) do so in the absence of an appropriate cognitive frame.[18]

As we have seen, a state-centered perspective would emphasize that specific state practices can strongly shape the plausibility, justifiability, and diffusion of a militant collective-action repertoire or a specifically revolutionary ideology or identity. In other words, revolutionary "frames," ideologies, strategies, and cultures no more drop from the sky than do social networks or material resources. Unfortunately, framing theory and other forms of cultural analysis often overlook the ways in which states shape the processes by which collective beliefs and norms are formulated and broadly diffused – typically as quite unintended outcomes of states' practices.

Still, like associational networks, revolutionary ideologies and strategic repertoires are also rooted in a variety of social relations and cultural systems that are not shaped wholly or much at all by state practices. Such ideologies have their own substantive properties that demand to be taken seriously and analyzed in their own right, and this has rightly become the focus of much recent scholarship on social movements and revolutions. (Revolutionary Marxism and Islamic "fundamentalism," for example, envisage the radical reconstruction of societies in very different and distinctive ways.) For these reasons, a state-centered perspective on culture and ideology – like that on social ties and resources – is inherently limited. Again, however, my goal in this book is not to present an exhaustive explanation of the revolutionary movements that I examine, if that were even possible, but a powerfully parsimonious one. And for that task a state-centered perspective is appropriate, or so I shall argue, despite its theoretical limitations.

[18] The "cultural turn" in studies of political conflict remains overwhelmingly ideational or cognitive; emotions and affect, in other words, remain largely neglected. But see Jasper 1997; Goodwin 1997.

The Case of the Cuban Revolution

The strengths and limitations of the statist approaches discussed in the preceding section are evident in several recent comparative studies of Latin American revolutions, including important works by Robert Dix (1984), Timothy Wickham-Crowley (1992), and John Booth and Thomas Walker (1993). All of these studies engage, if only implicitly, and often endorse different strands of state-centered theory (and sometimes other theoretical lenses) in their attempt to explain why radical revolutionary movements in the region have seized power only in Cuba and Nicaragua in recent decades. The strengths and limitations of statism are also evident in a recent case study of the Cuban Revolution – an exceptional historical study that does not explicitly draw upon or attempt to criticize a state-centered (or any other) theoretical perspective. I shall use Marifeli Pérez-Stable's *The Cuban Revolution: Origins, Course, and Legacy* (1993) to ground my main theoretical points about the strengths and weaknesses of state-centered analysis. (Pérez-Stable notes that while she has been influenced by both Theda Skocpol and Charles Tilly, she has "refrained from engaging the literature on revolutions" [1993: 184–5, fn16].) The Cuban Revolution is also interesting to examine in this context because of its intrinsic importance as well as its enormous influence on the revolutionary movements in Central America, which I analyze in Part 3.

Pérez-Stable develops a persuasive multicausal account of the Cuban Revolution, albeit one that especially "highlights the importance of social classes in the breakdown of the old Cuba and the making of the revolution" (1993: 8). In fact, two of the factors that, according to Pérez-Stable, "interacted to render Cuba susceptible to radical revolution" were the weakness of Cuba's *clases económicas* (i.e., the bourgeoisie) and the relative strength of the *clases populares*, or popular sectors, influenced in part by the ideology of radical nationalism (1993: 7).[19] Thus far, Pérez-Stable's account might seem like a purely Marxist or class-analytic interpretation of the Cuban Revolution. However, Pérez-Stable also draws attention to two other causal factors that implicate characteristics of the Cuban state: what she terms "mediated sovereignty" (i.e., the Cuban state's lack

---

[19] Although it reappears throughout her text, and she might have treated it as an analytically independent factor, Pérez-Stable does not consider radical nationalism an independent cause of the revolution.

of autonomy from the U.S. government and U.S. corporations) and a near-chronic "crisis of political authority" that deepened with the dictatorship of General Fulgencio Batista during the 1950s (1993: 7).[20]

Pérez-Stable's account thus demonstrates both the necessity and the insufficiency of treating the prerevolutionary Cuban state as an independent causal factor in the revolution. She implies that the geopolitical subservience and weakness of that state, as well as the serious legitimation crisis that developed following Batista's coup of 1952, created a structural potential for some type of popular movement against the dictatorship; at the same time, she suggests that analysts also need to take into account the strength (and ideology) of Cuba's social classes in order to understand why a radical revolution actually occurred. Indeed, Pérez-Stable strongly suggests that the political crisis of the 1950s would not have resulted in revolution were it not for the weakness of the Cuban bourgeoisie and the strength of the radicalized popular sectors.

And yet the story that Pérez-Stable tells is even more interesting than this. For her account also suggests that the very weakness of conservative and moderate political forces in Cuba on the eve of the revolution, as well as the gradual attachment of the popular sectors to Fidel Castro, the July Twenty-Sixth Movement, and its Rebel Army, were themselves primarily a result of actions taken by the Batista dictatorship. In other words, Pérez-Stable makes a number of state-constructionist arguments, in my terminology, in her account of the fidelistas' rise to power: The dictatorship itself simultaneously created and pushed its opposition in a revolutionary direction.

Pérez-Stable repeatedly suggests, for example, that "Batista's resistance to calling elections undermined the moderate opposition and bolstered the July 26th Movement," and, more generally, "bolstered those who argued that armed struggle was the only way to challenge his rule" (1993: 9, 56; see also 57). Indeed, both the moderate opposition to Batista and Cuba's Communist Party – which at first viewed Castro as a "putschist" and

---

[20] Pérez-Stable also includes two other factors in her list of the causes of the revolution: "sugar-centered development" and "uneven development." These particular factors, however, seem only indirectly related to the revolution. They powerfully influenced both class and state formation in Cuba, to be sure, but because they characterized the island since the nineteenth century (at least), they do not tell us all that much about why a revolution occurred there in 1959. "Uneven development," furthermore, is a characteristic of virtually every capitalist country, including many that have never had anything remotely resembling a revolution.

"adventurist" – positively "endorsed armed rebellion when other avenues of struggle against Batista had all but disappeared" (1993: 69). Pérez-Stable further notes how broad sectors of the popular classes and even members of the clases económicas were disgusted by the harsh repression and undisguised corruption of the batistato. She notes that many wealthy Cubans supported the insurrection, contributing 5 to 10 million pesos to the rebels; indeed, Pérez-Stable suggests that "virtually all Cubans" backed Castro and the Rebel Army by January 1, 1959, when Batista fled the country: "the *clases económicas* ... joined in celebrating the revolution" (1993: 62–3).

At the same time, Pérez-Stable emphasizes that Batista might have preempted the revolution had he simply been less intransigent: "The general might have consented to free and honest elections and ushered in a provisional government in late 1955 when Cosme de la Torriente led the civic dialogue movement or early in 1958 when the Catholic church revived it" (1993: 58). Unfortunately, "Batista became more intransigent as momentum gathered against his rule" (1993: 57).

Revolution might also have been averted had the Cuban military replaced Batista with some sort of provisional government – as the United States government came to hope and scheme (see, e.g., Benjamin 1990: ch. 6) – or had the armed forces simply contained the guerrillas in the Sierra Maestra. But the corruption and politicization of the Cuban military under Batista divided and fatally weakened that institution. Pérez-Stable notes the unsuccessful coup attempt led by Colonel Ramón Barquín and the much more serious naval uprising against Batista at Cienfuegos (1993: 56).[21] She also refers to the failed government offensive against the rebels during the summer of 1958 – an offensive that clearly demonstrated that the Cuban armed forces as a whole had neither the political will nor the capacity to fight an effective counterinsurgency war, thereby sealing Batista's fate. The commanding officer in northern Oriente province – a political appointee whose promotion rankled many professional officers – simply refused to engage the rebels (Bonachea and San Martín 1974: 231, 262). "By the end of the summer," Luis Pérez (1988: 309) has noted,

---

[21] See also Bonachea and San Martín 1974: 63–4, 147–52. The Cienfuegos revolt, they note, was led by "naval officers [who] felt frustrated at Batista's appointments of men who had not graduated from the Mariel Naval Academy to the highest ranks in the service" (1974: 147).

The army simply ceased to fight. Desertions and defections reached epidemic proportions. Retreating units became easy prey for advancing guerrilla columns. . . . Local military commands surrendered, often without firing a shot. Some defected and joined the opposition.

"Military prowess," Pérez-Stable concludes, "did not ultimately defeat Batista" (1993: 57).

In sum, the facts that the army could not geographically contain the rebels and the state could not preempt popular support for them were primarily a consequence of the character and decisions of the Cuban armed forces and of the Batista dictatorship.

Pérez-Stable's analysis thus clearly demonstrates the utility of a state-centered perspective for understanding the Cuban Revolution. The Batista regime, she shows, was not only an ideal target for some type of mass movement in Cuba, but it also positively weakened the civilian and military enemies of a radical revolution and unwittingly enhanced the popular appeal of the fidelistas. In other words, the alignment (and ideology) of class forces in Cuba that Pérez-Stable highlights was itself very strongly shaped by the nature of the batistato. Thus, a state-centered perspective greatly illuminates the Cuban Revolution, although this is a case in which the regime and armed forces did not break down until they were beset by a powerful mass movement. For the most part, that is, Cuban revolutionaries made their own political opportunities.

On the other hand, Pérez-Stable's account of the causes of the Cuban Revolution also points to some of the limitations of a purely statist perspective. The weakness of the Cuban bourgeoisie, for example, was not simply a result of state policies, but was also rooted in (among other factors) the historic division of interests between nascent industrialists and the sugar industry (1993: ch. 1). The oppositional hegemony of the fidelistas, moreover, while certainly bolstered by the character of the batistato, was also a result of the astute political maneuvering of the rebels themselves and of their unswerving commitment to armed struggle and Cuban self-determination (1993: 58–9). Castro himself first "captured the popular imagination," as Pérez-Stable puts it, with his "integrity, compassion, and dignity, and . . . a political program of nationalist reform" (1993: 53). Radical nationalism itself, in fact, appealed to many Cubans not simply because their state was historically subservient to the United States, but also because the Cuban economy and class relations – which were strongly but not wholly shaped by that state – were widely viewed as exploitative and unjust (1993: 3–5). Pérez-Stable's study suggests, in sum,

Conclusion

that an adequate explanation of the Cuban Revolution requires an examination not only of the prerevolutionary Cuban state and its effects on civil society; it also demands an analysis of the independent role of class relations, popular culture, and the nature and actions of the revolutionaries themselves as they built a vast network of active supporters and sympathizers.

Conclusion

Due to its various theoretical shortcomings, a state-centered perspective alone will not completely explain (nor accurately predict) the emergence or character of collective action, including the revolutionary movements discussed in this book. No theory can do this. These very shortcomings, however, point the way toward a more powerful synthetic perspective on revolutions and collective action. Clearly, such a perspective will necessarily highlight the role of social ties, resource mobilization, and culture in addition to state structures and practices. Of course, these factors cannot simply be "tacked on" to a state-centered analysis in the guise of "independent variables." For, as the state-constructionist approach in particular emphasizes, all these factors are themselves more or less strongly shaped, influenced, or even induced by state-centered processes.

We still await the formulation of the sort of synthetic perspective on revolutions and collective action that we clearly need.[22] Until that theory materializes, however, state-centered approaches will remain perhaps our single most powerful theoretical perspective on revolutions, and any superior perspective will need to incorporate the insights of this theoretical tradition. Indeed, this tradition's insights into both state breakdowns and revolutionary mobilization tell us much that we need to know about revolutions, and they help to resolve some of the key puzzles that revolutions have raised for social analysts.

In adopting a state-centered perspective, however, including what I have called a "state-constructionist" standpoint, this book certainly does

---

[22] Tarrow's much-discussed *Power in Movement* (1994) certainly approaches such a synthesis (see also McAdam, Tarrow, and Tilly 1997), although I believe that it exaggerates the importance of political opportunities, on the one hand, and says too little about the cultural and social-psychological dynamics of collective action, on the other (see Goodwin and Jasper 1999). For rather different sketches of what such a theory might look like – ones that try to incorporate culture, social psychology, and biography – see Jasper 1997 and Emirbayer and Goodwin 1996.

not pretend to offer a complete or fully adequate account of the complex and multifaceted revolutionary movements that it examines. There are many interesting and important questions about these movements that I shall not even attempt to address (including questions about, for example, their "gendered" character). Still, I want to push the statist perspective on revolutions as far as it can go, which I believe is quite far. And I shall make some bold claims in subsequent chapters about the power of the state-centered perspective to illuminate the revolutionary movements of the Cold War era. In particular, I shall argue that the statist approach goes a long way toward explaining both the emergence and differing ideological character of revolutionary movements in postwar Southeast Asia (Chapter 3); why those movements either succeeded or failed to seize state power (Chapter 4); the emergence (or reemergence) of popular revolutionary movements in some but not all of the countries of Central America during the 1970s and 1980s (Chapter 5); why those movements either succeeded or failed to seize state power (Chapter 6); why certain states failed to defeat revolutionary movements over the course of many years or even decades (Chapter 7); and, finally, the patterns of popular protest and revolutionary change in Eastern Europe in 1989 (Chapter 8). These are complex and multifaceted (as well as important) issues, but I believe that a state-centered perspective shines the brightest light on them. In the end, however, the latter claim must be proven, not merely asserted, and that is the goal of the following chapters.

PART TWO

Southeast Asia

Chronology for Southeast Asia

Vietnam

1858–83	consolidation of French colonial rule; Vietnam divided into three political units: Tonkin, Annam, Cochinchina (north, center, south)
1917	Constitutionalist Party founded
1927	Socialist Governor-General Varenne recalled; Vietnamese Nationalist Party (VNQDD) founded
1930	Communist Party founded by Ho Chi Minh in Hong Kong; Nationalist-led Yen Bai uprising suppressed, VNQDD leadership flees to China; Communist-led Nghe-Tinh soviets brutally suppressed
1936–9	Popular Front government in France allows Communists and Trotskyists to function openly
1940	fall of France and establishment of Vichy regime; Japanese troops occupy Vietnam with French approval; French administration remains; abortive Communist uprising
1941	Viet Minh (League for the Independence of Vietnam) founded by Communists
1944	France liberated; widespread famine in Vietnam results in two million deaths
1945	Japanese coup disarms the French; Japan surrenders to the Allies; Viet Minh seizes power in August Revolution; Emperor Bao Dai abdicates; Ho Chi Minh declares independence of the Democratic Republic of Vietnam (DRV); Vietnam occupied by Chinese Nationalist forces in the north and British forces in the south; French troops begin to return, driving Viet Minh and allied forces out of Saigon; the Viet Minh eliminates the Trotskyist movement
1946	French-DRV negotiations break down; the French bomb Haiphong; the First Indochina War, or Nine-Year National Resistance War, begins
1949	Chinese Communist forces enter Peking; the French-backed State of Vietnam proclaimed by Emperor Bao Dai

1950	the People's Republic of China and the Soviet Union recognize the DRV; the United States recognizes the Bao Dai regime; the French suffer major losses along the Sino-Vietnamese border; Korean War begins
1953	the DRV launches agrarian reform
1954	the fall of Dienbienphu to Viet Minh forces; the Geneva Accords partition Vietnam at the seventeenth parallel into north and south regroupment zones pending reunification elections (scheduled for 1956, but never held); the United States does not accept the agreement
1955	French troops leave northern Vietnam; Premier Ngo Dinh Diem defeats Bao Dai in a rigged election and proclaims the Republic of [South] Vietnam
1956	the last French troops leave Vietnam; the U.S. Military Assistance Advisor Group (MAAG) begins training South Vietnamese troops

Malaya

1874–1919	consolidation of British colonial rule over the Malay peninsula
1930	Malayan Communist Party (MCP) founded in Singapore
1939	MCP calls for united front against fascism; Loi Teck named party leader
1941	MCP decides to support the British war effort; British officers and MCP establish guerrilla training schools
1942	Japan occupies the Malayan peninsula; Malayan People's Anti-Japanese Army (MPAJA) founded by MCP
1945	Japan surrenders to the Allies; clashes between MPAJA guerrillas and ethnic Malays; MPAJA dissolved by MCP
1946	MCP sets moderate course; Loi Teck reelected party leader; the British Malayan Union proposals stir Malay nationalism; United Malays National Organization (UMNO) founded
1947	Loi Teck disappears shortly prior to his denunciation by the MCP; Chin Peng assumes party leadership
1948	Federation of Malaya inaugurated; the British declare "Emergency" following the murder of three British planters by MCP
1949	Malayan Races Liberation Army (MRLA) founded by MCP; formation of the Malayan Chinese Association (MCA) by businessmen
1950	the Korean War leads to an economic upswing
1951	the Briggs Plan results in forcible resettlement of Chinese squatters into "New Villages"; Sir Henry Gurney, British high commissioner, killed in a guerrilla ambush; MCP, increasingly isolated, reorients efforts toward greater political, as opposed to military, activity
1952	the Alliance of UMNO and MCA dominates the Kuala Lumpur municipal council election
1955	the Alliance dominates legislative elections; talks between government and Communists aborted
1957	independence of Malaya declared
1960	"Emergency" formally ended

The Philippines

1898–1902	the United States intervenes in Philippine war of independence against Spain; the U.S. Senate votes to annex Philippines; Philippine-American war
1907	Nationalist Party founded; elections for first Philippine assembly and provincial governors
1916	the Jones Law promises eventual independence for the Philippines
1930	Communist Party of the Philippines (PKP) founded
1932	Socialist Party founded; PKP declared illegal (to 1938)
1935	Sakdalista peasant revolt; Philippine Commonwealth established with Manuel Quezon as president
1938	the Communist and Socialist parties merge
1940	eight members of the merged Communist and Socialist parties are elected mayors in Pampanga province, Central Luzon
1941	Japan attacks the Philippines and Pearl Harbor
1942	Japanese troops enter Manila; People's Anti-Japanese Army (Hukbalahap ng Bayan Laban sa Hapon), better known as Huks, founded by PKP; Corregidor falls to the Japanese
1943	the Japanese grant nominal independence to the Philippine Republic with Jose Laurel as president
1944–5	U.S. troops land on Leyte; Commonwealth officially restored; Manila liberated after fierce fighting; Japan surrenders to Allies
1946	Manuel Roxas elected president; Democratic Alliance candidates denied seats in the legislature; the Philippine Trade Act (Bell Trade Act) enacted; the Philippines becomes formally independent; PKP peasant leader Juan Feleo murdered
1947	"Parity" amendment to the constitution ratified in a plebiscite; military bases agreement signed with the United States for a 99-year term
1948	collaborators with the Japanese pardoned; President Roxas dies in office, succeeded by Elpidio Quirino; Huk veterans form the People's Liberation Army (Hukbong Mapagpalaya ng Bayan or HMB), also known as Huks; PKP decides that armed struggle should be its main form of struggle
1949	Quirino elected president in an election marred by widespread violence and fraud
1950	PKP declares that a "revolutionary situation" is at hand and calls for the armed overthrow of the government; Ramon Magsaysay named minister of defense; successful PKP raids on towns in Central and Southern Luzon; PKP Politburo members in Manila arrested
1951	the U.S.-Philippine Mutual Defense Treaty signed; Huk rebels on defensive
1953	Luis Taruc suspended from PKP for violating democratic centralism; Magsaysay defeats Quirino for the presidency
1954	Taruc surrenders to the Philippine government; a "surrender epidemic" ensues

1957	PKP decides to implement gradually a new strategy based on legal and parliamentary struggle

Indonesia

1602–1798	the Dutch East India Company consolidates control over much of Java and the "outer islands"
1798	the area dominated by the East India Company placed under the control of the Netherlands government; colonial authority continues to expand
1912	Sarekat Islam, the first major nationalist organization, founded
1920	Communist Party of Indonesia (PKI), the first Communist party in East Asia, founded
1926–7	Communist-led revolts in Java and Sumatra brutally suppressed; PKI decimated
1927	Indonesian Nationalist Party (PNI) founded by Sukarno
1929	Sukarno and other PNI leaders arrested
1931	Sukarno, released from prison, joins leadership of Partindo (Indonesian Party), a successor party to the PNI
1933	Sukarno and other nationalist leaders rearrested and sent into "internal exile"
1935	"Illegal PKI" founded
1942	Japan occupies Indonesia; Sukarno and other nationalist leaders freed by the Japanese
1943	the Japanese organize an Indonesian army, the "Defenders of the Fatherland," better known as the Peta
1945	the Japanese establish the Indonesian Independence Preparatory Committee (PKKI), with Sukarno as chairman; Sukarno proclaims the independent Republic of Indonesia (August 17) shortly after Japan surrenders to the Allies; British Indian troops arrive; the battle of Surabaya results in fifteen thousand Indonesian deaths
1946	the Linggajati Agreement between Dutch and Republican officials calls for establishment of an independent Indonesian federation, with the Republic as one of the member states
1947	Dutch troops occupy the wealthiest parts of Java and Sumatra in the first "police action"
1948	the Renville accord reaffirms the principle of an independent Indonesian federation; a PKI-supported military revolt at Madiun crushed by Republican forces; PKI leaders executed; the Dutch occupy the Republican capital of Yogyakarta, arresting major Republican leaders, and occupy all other major cities of Java in the second "police action"; anti-Dutch guerrilla activity expands
1949	under pressure from the United States and the United Nations, the Dutch reinstate Republican leaders in Yogyakarta; the Round Table Conference between Dutch and Republican officials results in the formal transfer of

Indonesia

	sovereignty from the Netherlands to the federal Republic of the United States of Indonesia (December 27), not including Irian Jaya (West New Guinea)
1950	unitary Republic of Indonesia proclaimed (August 17)
1955	conference of nonaligned nations held in Bandung

3

The Formation of Revolutionary Movements in Southeast Asia

> *The Pacific War created an entirely new pattern in Southeast Asian politics – so much so that the observer who was fairly closely in touch with the situation in 1940 would, if he did not return to Southeast Asia until 1948 and had not kept himself up to date with a close study of reports, find himself unable to recognise what he saw.*
>
> – Victor Purcell (1965: 551)

This chapter presents a state-centered explanation of the uneven development of armed, Communist-led revolutionary movements in Southeast Asia in the aftermath of the Second World War. More specifically, it attempts to explain why Communist movements became formidable threats to incumbent regimes in Vietnam, Malaya, and the Philippines during the decade or so following World War II, but not in Indonesia.[1] The following chapter attempts to explain why only the Vietnamese Communist insurgency was subsequently able to seize state power (at least, during the period under examination, in northern Vietnam), while the other two Communist insurgencies that developed in the region were defeated.

After noting some of the common characteristics of Southeast Asian societies at midcentury, I examine two hypotheses about "Indonesian exceptionalism" (i.e., the absence of a Communist-led national liberation movement in that country), and present my own solution to this puzzle. I then attempt to explain the emergence of radical revolutionary movements

---

[1] I do not examine here the important Communist movement that also developed in Burma during this period, nor the strong Communist insurgencies that subsequently emerged (or reemerged) in Laos, Cambodia, and (again, during the 1970s) the Philippines (the last under the leadership of a new and "rectified" Communist Party).

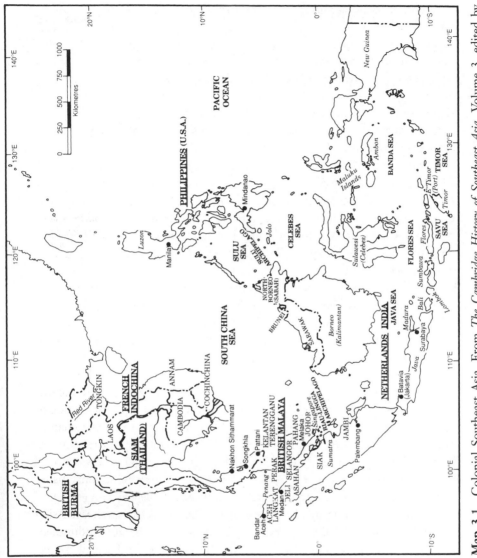

Map 3.1 Colonial Southeast Asia. From *The Cambridge History of Southeast Asia*, Volume 3, edited by Nicholas Tarling. Copyright © 1999 Cambridge University Press. Reprinted with permission.

in Vietnam, Malaya, and the Philippines. These insurgencies, I suggest, are not well explained simply as reactions to the incorporation of Southeast Asia into the global capitalist economy or to the rapid and disruptive "modernization" associated with this process; nor do the interests, grievances, and actions of any particular social class (or class alliance) adequately explain the formation and trajectory of these movements. At best, these theories illuminate certain limited, albeit important, aspects of these insurgencies; at worst, they provide quite misleading general explanations of their development and ultimate fate.

I argue in this and the following chapter that it was the political institutions and actions of Western and Japanese imperialists in Southeast Asia that were decisive not only for creating a political context in which revolutionaries could build armed movements without simply being crushed by those powers, but also for inducing or constructing a disposition among large numbers of ordinary people to join or support these movements. The possibilities for both revolutionary mobilization and the actual seizure of power – given socioeconomic and cultural conditions that were, I shall suggest, potentially conducive to revolution throughout the region – were fundamentally determined by the Japanese occupation of the region and by the general type of colonial rule (either politically and racially inclusionary or exclusionary) practiced by Western and Japanese imperialists in each colony.

This state-centered approach, it should be emphasized, differs sharply from the "new" conventional wisdom on insurgencies in Southeast Asia, which is heavily influenced by neo-Marxist writings on capitalist imperialism and the capitalist world-system (see Wallerstein 1979). Much recent work, following Eric Wolf (1969) and Jeffery Paige (1975), attempts to explain Southeast Asian protest movements – if not Southeast Asian history as a whole – in terms of the larger transnational dynamics of the global capitalist economy. This emphasis is hardly surprising, given the undeniably "peripheral" and economically dependent character of Southeast Asia vis-à-vis Western Europe, the United States, and Japan. These theorists argue that the rapid and often violent "incorporation" of Third World societies into the global capitalist division of labor has generated resistance from those classes and strata adversely affected (and in some cases created) by this process.[2]

---

[2] In addition to Wolf 1969 and Paige 1975, see, e.g., Migdal 1974, Scott 1976, and Petras 1978a.

But not all peripheral societies that have been incorporated into the capitalist world economy, however rapid and violent this process has been, have undergone revolutions or even witnessed the development of significant revolutionary movements. Most theorists in the world-systems tradition have turned to more traditional Marxist ideas about class formation and class struggle in order to resolve this puzzle. They suggest that it is the specific nature of the class structure of peripheral societies that determines whether or not protest movements will take on a social-revolutionary character (or even arise at all) – although just what sort of classes or class structures will produce revolutionary movements, as I noted in Chapter 1, is the subject of much debate among Marxist and neo-Marxist writers. As noted, Wolf argues that the landowning "middle" peasantry is "the most instrumental in dynamiting the peasant social order" (Wolf 1969: 292), whereas Paige (1975: 59–66) suggests that landless sharecroppers are most likely to support socialist "agrarian revolutions." As we shall see, neither is altogether correct; more importantly, their shared class-analytic approach is simply inadequate for the explanatory tasks at hand.

Southeast Asia Circa 1950

Southeast Asia circa 1950 appears in many ways quite strange and extra-ordinary from the perspective of the present. Stalinist Communists and Western colonialists – actors who have now almost completely vanished from the world stage[3] – were enormously important forces, sometimes engaged in life-and-death struggles, in many of the countries in the region. Indeed, a regionwide cycle of protest or revolutionary wave was at its height at about this time. In Vietnam, France's most important Asian colony, the Communist-dominated Democratic Republic of Vietnam (DRV), was officially recognized in early 1950 by the new People's Republic of China and the Soviet Union. The DRV had been proclaimed by Ho Chi Minh and his comrades in the wake of the August Revolution of 1945, following the surrender of Japan in World War II, in which Communist-led forces had managed to secure local authority in Hanoi and much of the countryside, particularly in northern and central Vietnam. Vietnamese Communists had organized an anti-Japanese and anti-French movement,

[3] This is not to imply that either socialist ideals or noncolonial forms of imperialism are now exhausted.

75

the Viet Minh, after Japan occupied Indochina – with the grudging approval of the Vichy regime in France – in 1940. (Viet Minh is short for Viet Nam Doc Lap Dong Minh, or League for the Independence of Vietnam.) It was this movement that was the principal force behind the August Revolution and that later led the fight against French and pro-French forces in the First Indochina War (1946–54), or what Vietnamese Communists call the Nine-Year National Resistance.[4]

To say that the Vietnamese revolutionary movement was a threat to French rule in 1950 would be a gross understatement. The Viet Minh included about two hundred and fifty thousand armed soldiers at this time, and the Communist Party had nearly half a million members (Duiker 1981: 135, 141). A Vietnamese offensive in the fall of 1950 overran a chain of French garrisons in northern Vietnam, killing six thousand French troops in the process. According to Bernard Fall, "When the smoke had cleared, the French had suffered their greatest colonial defeat since Mont-calm had died at Quebec" (Fall 1967a: 111).

Although not as powerful as the Vietnamese movement – for reasons I explore in Chapter 4 – strong Communist insurgencies also developed in Malaya and the Philippines after World War II. In Malaya, Communists confronted a restored British colonial regime. This regime declared a state of emergency in June 1948 after three British planters were killed in guerrilla attacks by what would become known as the Malayan Races Liberation Army (MRLA), organized and led by the Malayan Communist Party (MCP). The MRLA, like the Viet Minh, grew out of an anti-Japanese resistance movement, the Malayan People's Anti-Japanese Army (MPAJA), which was formed by the MCP in 1942, following Japan's invasion of Malaya. The MCP returned to a strategy of armed struggle following the war, after the colonial regime attempted to break up the strong organized labor movement led by the Communists. By early 1950, the colonial government feared that it was rapidly losing ground to the Communists, who had armed about eight thousand guerrillas and claimed about half a million active supporters. The following year, the high commissioner of the colony, Sir Henry Gurney, was killed in a guerrilla ambush.

---

[4] It has been customary to refer to the Communist-led movement in Vietnam during the entire 1941–54 period as the Viet Minh, although this front was officially dissolved, and its membership merged into the so-called Lien Viet Front, in 1951. Lien Viet is short for Hoi Lien Hiep Quoc Dan Viet Nam, or the League for the National Union of Vietnam.

A serious Communist-led insurgency also emerged in the Philippines after the war. The Hukbong Mapagpalaya ng Bayan (HMB), or People's Liberation Army, took on the U.S.-backed regime to which formal independence (with many strings attached) had been ceded in 1946. The HMB was also an outgrowth of an anti-Japanese resistance movement, in this case the PKP-led People's Anti-Japanese Army, or Hukbalahap. The Communist Party of the Philippines (PKP) returned to armed struggle after the war in the face of physical attacks on Huk veterans and the Communist-led peasant movement. A number of victorious Huk-supported candidates in the first postwar elections, in April 1946, were also denied their seats in the Philippine Congress on spurious charges that they had employed terror and intimidation in order to be elected. In March and August of 1950, the Huks – who had as many as fifteen thousand armed guerrillas and one hundred thousand active supporters (Scaff 1955: 28; Kerkvliet 1977: 210) – launched coordinated and generally successful raids on fifteen and eleven towns, respectively. Huk leaders were confident that a relatively quick seizure of power was possible, perhaps within as little as two years.

I should note, in this context, that there was also a formidable Communist movement in Burma following the war. And the seriousness of all these Southeast Asian insurgencies was undoubtedly compounded, in the eyes of their foes, by the stunning Communist victory in China in 1949 and by the outbreak of the Korean War in June 1950. Among Western political leaders and their local collaborators, the notion that the whole of Southeast Asia might possibly fall like dominoes to Communism seems to have been widespread and can hardly be regarded, under the circumstances, as delusional. U.S. leaders in particular, who had generally ignored Southeast Asia after the war, acquiescing to the reimposition of colonial rule by their European allies, became increasingly obsessed with the very real strength of Communist movements in the region after 1949 (see, e.g., Kahin 1977; Rotter 1987).

But then there is the case of Indonesia. Although armed nationalists fought for, and won, independence from the Netherlands during the late 1940s, Communists were not central to this struggle. Indeed, while the Indonesian Communist Party (PKI) was extremely influential during the early 1920s and then again after independence, it was quite weak during the 1930s and 1940s. (The PKI eventually became the largest nonruling Communist party in the world; but it did so, significantly, as an aboveground and unarmed movement, and the party was all but destroyed by

77

the Indonesian army in a veritable bloodbath in 1965, in which a half million to one million people were killed.) Forces of the Indonesian Republic rather easily suppressed a Communist-backed rebellion in 1948, while the nationalist struggle against the Dutch was still in progress. This helped to consolidate the anti-Communist credentials of the Republic in the eyes of Western leaders, and convinced the U.S. government (and many Dutch businesspeople with interests in Indonesia) that decolonization was imperative. The "populist" nationalist leaders who ruled Indonesia after independence were not, to be sure, the same sort of unambiguously pro-Western, neocolonial elites to whom power was transferred in the Philippines and (eventually) in Malaya, but neither did they envision, like the Vietnamese Communists, a fundamental reordering of society and redistribution of property.

Postwar Communist movements, then, were not powerful everywhere in Southeast Asia, nor in colonial or newly independent countries more generally, during this period.[5] What explains this pattern? Why did formidable Communist challenges to colonial (and neocolonial) rulers develop in Vietnam, Malaya, and the Philippines following World War II, but not in Indonesia? Why was the Communist bid for power in Indonesia so weak, comparatively speaking, during the postwar struggle against the Dutch?

Regional Similarities

Fortunately, postwar Southeast Asia provides something like a "natural laboratory" for exploring various hypotheses about Third World revolutions or, at least, their anticolonial variant. Indeed, the value of the sort of regional approach adopted in this book is precisely that it allows one to "control" for a variety, although certainly not all, of the factors and processes that may potentially account for the insurgencies in each of the regions that I examine. Logically, the various socioeconomic, political, and geopolitical processes that are *common* to the national societies in each region cannot in themselves explain the quite different political fortunes of national revolutionary movements.

---

[5] In fact, Communists were relatively weak at this time not only within the nationalist movement in Indonesia, but also in South Asia and most of colonial Africa and the Caribbean. Communists were also quite weak in Thailand, the only Southeast Asian country that was never colonized.

Regional Similarities

With this in mind, seven regional similarities are especially worthy of note in the case of Southeast Asia:

1. Western conquest and colonial rule of the region (with the exception of Siam or Thailand), along with the more or less broad range of authoritarian and racist practices inherently associated with them.
2. The integration of local economies into the capitalist world system and concomitant socioeconomic changes (including the development of export agriculture, increasing tenancy and indebtedness, proletarianization, urbanization, the development of small professional and middle classes, etc.).
3. The development, due principally to the two preceding factors, of widespread social grievances and incipient forms of proactive social protest (especially among the producing classes and in rural as well as urban areas).
4. The formation of reformist as well as revolutionary parties and movements (including Soviet-aligned Communist parties), both of which eventually adopted political programs emphasizing the goal of independence or national liberation.
5. The Japanese occupation and privations of World War II.
6. The formation of anti-Japanese resistance movements – all of which employed the strategy or "repertoire" of guerrilla warfare – by what were, at the time, relatively weak Communist parties.
7. The attempt by the Western colonial powers and their collaborators to reassert their hegemony over Southeast Asia after the war.[6]

Each of these shared regional characteristics may have been potentially conducive to revolution in Southeast Asia, but, again, they cannot logically explain the very diverse outcomes of the postwar revolutionary struggles in the region. Nonetheless, many analysts of the various Communist movements in Southeast Asia – and of the successful Vietnamese Revolution in particular – have cited one or more of these processes when "explaining" events in a particular country, failing to note that these same factors were also operative in Indonesia, where no mass-based Commu-

---

[6] These and other regional similarities are discussed in four excellent comparative histories of Southeast Asia: Pluvier 1974, Williams 1976, Osborne 1983, and Steinberg 1987.

nist insurgency, let alone a successful one, developed after the war. The Vietnamese Revolution, for example, is often simply explained as a the work of a dedicated Leninist organization (the infamous "organizational weapon") or, more typically, as a nationalist reaction to Western colonialism. But these interpretations obviously beg the most important questions that arise from a comparative perspective: Why did Leninist parties fail to attain substantial popular support, let alone state power, throughout the entire region? And why did Communists, of all groups, assume such commanding leadership of the nationalist movement in Vietnam?

National *variations* among some of these regional similarities, by contrast, are more dispositive. I shall argue that it was the precise nature of Japanese *political* rule during World War II (i.e., variations of the fifth factor) as well as the particular type of Western colonial domination in each country (i.e., variations of the first factor) that were the crucial determinants of both the incidence and outcome of revolutionary situations in the region. Especially important in this regard is whether the Western powers and Japan employed generally inclusionary or exclusionary forms of rule – that is, whether or not they allowed indigenous leaders or parties to play a relatively autonomous role in colonial government and decision making as part of a process leading to local self-government, even if this occurred within a framework of continuing imperial hegemony.[7] To be sure, all the Western powers, as well as Japan, utilized indigenous elements to staff the lower ranks of their administrations; in this particular sense, virtually all forms of colonial rule are "inclusionary." As I use the term, however, inclusionary colonial rule characterizes those situations in which indigenous political leaders play an independent, claim-making role *within* the polity and policy-making process.

To anticipate my conclusions, I will argue that the one successful radical revolutionary movement in the region, the Vietnamese, triumphed largely because of the racially exclusionary and broadly repressive nature of

[7] This distinction between (racially) inclusionary and exclusionary forms of colonialism is closely related to, but not equivalent to, the traditional distinction between "indirect" and "direct" forms of colonial rule (see, e.g., Emerson 1937; Benda 1967; Robinson 1972). Some forms of "indirect" colonialism, as in Indonesia, do not allow indigenous elites (or aspiring elites), let alone popular groups, to make political claims against the state or, in fact, to play anything more than a purely administrative role; this sort of indirect rule, accordingly, represents a form of *exclusionary* colonialism in my terms. In an earlier article, alas, I tended to conflate "indirect" rule with inclusionary colonialism (Goodwin 1989).

80

French colonial politics *and* because of Japan's decision not to sponsor a popular non-Communist nationalist leadership in Vietnam during its occupation of Indochina, but rather to allow the French to remain in power until the war was virtually over. Geopolitics also favored Vietnamese Communists, who had unique access to assistance from foreign states (see Chapter 4). Elsewhere in the region, by contrast, where Western colonial regimes *or* the Japanese allowed or even encouraged various types of non-Communist political leaders to participate in imperial rule and decision making as part of a transition toward local self-government, revolutionary movements were unable to seize power, even where they had become quite strong. This analysis rests on the view that revolutionary movements in Southeast Asia were by no means "spontaneous" class or nationalist struggles; rather, they are more accurately seen as attempts by armed revolutionary organizations – drawing on *both* class-based grievances and nationalist sentiments, among other motives – to establish not only popularly supported movements but also what have been called "guerrilla governments" in opposition to colonial or neocolonial regimes.[8]

Before turning to an examination of the Communist insurgencies that emerged in Southeast Asia, however, let us turn to the exceptional or "negative" case of Indonesia, where Communists were comparatively weak. Given its broad similarities to the other colonies in the region, why were Communists in Indonesia unable to make a serious bid for state power after the war?

Why Was There No Communist Insurgency in Indonesia?

By 1950, when mass-based Communist movements were challenging colonial and neocolonial regimes in Vietnam, Malaya, and the Philippines, the Indonesian struggle for national liberation against the Dutch had already been won by non-Communist "populist" nationalists, following five years of protest, armed conflict, and diplomatic negotiations. The Indonesian "National Revolution" of 1945–9, in other words, was a political, not a social, revolution (see, e.g., Reid 1981, 1974: 170–2). The Indonesian Communist Party (PKI), I have noted, was largely peripheral to this struggle, although it did muster a small rebellion against the nationalist forces – not against the Dutch – in and around the Javanese city of

[8] The term "guerrilla government" is taken from Wickham-Crowley 1987.

Madiun in 1948. This rebellion was quickly and decisively put down, however, and the Communists – who appeared to many to be traitors to the nationalist cause – would not reemerge as a significant political force in Indonesia for a number of years. How, then, did non-Communist nationalists come to dominate the armed national liberation struggle in Indonesia? And why were the Communists, by contrast, so weak at this time?

In many ways, it is quite surprising that Indonesian Communists did not lead the struggle for independence. The PKI was the first Communist party to be established in East Asia, preceding even the founding of the Chinese party; moreover, it very quickly developed into a formidable mass-based movement during the early 1920s, although it was decimated by the Dutch following an abortive uprising in 1926–7 (see McVey 1965; Williams 1990). Furthermore, the PKI later became the single most influential political party in Indonesia during the postindependence period, although it was violently destroyed by the Indonesian army in 1965 (see, e.g., Brackman 1969; Tornquist 1984).

Were Communists relatively weak in Indonesia during the independence struggle because the Dutch were less intrusive or because their economic exploitation of the archipelago was somehow less extreme than that of the other colonies in the region? The fact that the PKI was comparatively strong during the 1920s immediately suggests that this hypothesis is misleading. In fact, a number of statistical indicators suggest that Indonesia was among the most exploited Western colonies in Asia in the decades prior to World War II. In demographic terms, the European population of Indonesia (as a percentage of total population) was surpassed only by that of Malaya and Singapore during this period (although no Asian colony was a true "settler colony") (see Table 3.1). In terms of foreign capital investment, only Malaya ($164 per capita) ranked higher than Indonesia ($35) in the late 1930s, followed by the Philippines ($18) and Indochina ($17) (Maddison 1990: 331). While balance-of-payments data are not available for all the colonies in the region, one crude measure of the payments burden – the ratio of exports to imports – indicates that the Indonesian capital "drain" was the largest in Asia: During the period 1913–38, exports exceeded imports in Indonesia by an average of 75 percent per annum; this is significantly higher than Indochina (22.9 percent), the Philippines (18.6 percent), and Malaya (15.7 percent) (Maddison 1990: 327). "This . . . reflects the drain to the Netherlands on Dutch account (residents' home remittances, remittances to non-residential

Table 3.1. *European presence in Asian colonies.*

Colony	European population*	Percentage of total population
Indonesia, 1930 (Dutch)	240,162	0.40
India, 1931 (British)	168,134	0.05
Burma, 1931 (British)	34,000	0.23
Malaya and Singapore, 1931 (British)	33,811	0.77
Indochina, 1937 (French)	42,345	0.18
Philippines, 1939 (U.S.)	36,000	0.15

* Includes metropolitan nationals, those of assimilated status, and Eurasians in Indonesia, Malaya, and Indochina. The Philippines figure includes 10,500 Japanese, but excludes U.S. military personnel and Hispano-Filipino mestizos.
Source: Maddison 1990: 324 (Table 14.1).

commercial interests, and government transfers) and much smaller remittances on Chinese account" (Maddison 1990: 326). There obviously is no clear connection between these various indicators and the strength of postwar Communist insurgencies.

Another possible answer to the puzzle of Indonesian exceptionalism is suggested in the work of Jeffery Paige, who argues that socialist and nationalist movements in the Third World have distinctive class bases (1975: 58–71). Paige suggests that socialist movements in developing countries have largely been movements of landless sharecroppers, whereas nationalist movements find their principal base among semiproletarian migratory laborers who work seasonally on settler estates. Such laborers are supposedly more conservative than sharecroppers since they own at least some property; moreover, a nationalist ideology is more conducive than socialism to forming an alliance between such laborers and traditional rural elites – an alliance that Paige implicitly suggests is necessary to challenge or overthrow colonial regimes based on settler estates (1975: 66–70).

The logic of Paige's arguments about peasant behavior has been subjected to telling criticisms elsewhere (see Somers and Goldfrank 1979; Skocpol 1982). For present purposes, it is enough to note that his analysis simply does not fit the Southeast Asian cases very well. To be sure, sharecroppers *did* constitute the principal social basis of the Huk rebellion in the Philippines, although peasant smallholders as well as elements of Manila's working class also supported the Huks (see, e.g., Kerkvliet 1977:

83

33; Pomeroy 1978: 510–1). However, the Communist insurgency in Malaya was not based on that country's sharecroppers (most of whom were ethnic Malay), but rather on the Chinese (and to a lesser extent Indian) urban working class, laborers on British rubber plantations, and especially squatters – again, mainly ethnic Chinese – on the fringes of Malaya's jungles (see, e.g., Stenson 1974; Short 1975).

In Vietnam and Indonesia, moreover, the Communist and Republican leaderships, respectively, formed very broad multiclass (and multiethnic) alliances. The Viet Minh mobilized sharecroppers, to be sure, but also middle and rich peasants (and even some "patriotic landlords"), agricultural estate workers, a number of ethnic minority communities in the highlands, and elements from the urban working and middle classes, including many sons and daughters of the traditional Confucian scholar-gentry, who came to hold many important leadership positions within the Communist party (see, e.g., Wolf 1969: ch. 4; White 1974: 94–5, 1983a, 1983b; Elliott 1974). For a number of reasons, in fact, the Viet Minh was comparatively weak in the southern part of Vietnam, where sharecropping was most prevalent (see Wolf 1969: 176–7, 192–5). Indonesian nationalists, for their part, did mobilize migratory workers, as Paige's theory would predict, but they were also supported by permanent estate laborers and by the urban working and middle classes, particularly students and youth (the *pemuda*) (see, e.g., Anderson 1972; Stoler 1988; and the essays in A. Kahin 1985). It is quite misleading, in short, to suggest that Southeast Asian Communism was primarily a movement of sharecroppers – or any other single class – and Indonesian nationalism a movement of migratory laborers.

In fact, as Tony Smith has suggested, "communism in Indonesia was not so much defeated by the predispositions of the country's social structure, which rather encouraged its development, as by a series of fortuitous political developments" (Smith 1981: 127; see also Dunn 1972: 128–30). The proximate cause of the hegemony of non-Communist nationalists in Indonesia's national liberation struggle lies, in fact, in the particular nature of Japanese rule in that country during World War II. When the Japanese first arrived in Indonesia, notes George Kahin, "they were generally enthusiastically received. The popular feeling [was] that they came as liberators" (G. Kahin 1952: 102). Dutch colonial rule was so oppressive that the "Indonesian masses, hardly surprisingly, gave little support to the beleaguered colonial forces and sometimes gladly turned against Dutch civilians and soldiers" (Ricklefs 1993: 195). The Dutch had long practiced a racially and politically exclusionary form of colonial rule, rejecting demands for even modest reforms, let alone independence. Governor-General B. C. de Jonge (1931–6) famously announced at the start of his term that Holland had been in the East Indies for 300 years and would remain there for another 300 years.

Unlike Vietnam, moreover, where the Japanese permitted Western colonialists to remain in office, the Japanese interned virtually all Europeans in Indonesia – some 170,000 in all, including women and children. The Japanese subsequently relied on Indonesians to fill the middle- and upper-level administrative positions vacated by the Dutch. Even more significantly, the Japanese released a number of popular non-Communist nationalist leaders who had been incarcerated by the Dutch – Sukarno and Mohammad Hatta in particular – and sponsored a number of nationalist political organizations in an attempt (ultimately unsuccessful) to rally public sentiment for the Japanese war effort. (The Japanese also sponsored amenable Muslim leaders and organizations [Benda 1958].) As the course of the war turned against Japan, moreover, the Japanese began to make intimations that Indonesian independence might be forthcoming. Many prominent Indonesian nationalists decided to play along with the Japanese, calculating that the nationalist cause could be best served by working above- as well as underground. Sukarno, who founded the Indonesian Nationalist Party (PNI) in 1927, decided to collaborate openly with the Japanese, while Sutan Sjahrir, another prominent nationalist, would maintain contact with Sukarno and the above-ground movement while organizing an underground resistance (see G. Kahin 1952: ch. 4).

The so-called "Illegal PKI," established in 1935 after the Communist Party had been virtually destroyed in the wake of the abortive insurrection of 1926–7, also participated in the underground, although it was not as large as Sjahrir's organization. "As a separate force in the resistance movement," in fact, "the PKI – in contrast to Ho Chi Minh's organization in Indochina – appears to have been singularly ineffective" (McLane 1966: 279). Given Japan's sponsorship of popular nationalist leaders and nationalist organizations, moreover, the underground as a whole did not recruit a particularly large popular following. As Rex Mortimer has argued,

[T]he main thing that worked against the development of a popular resistance movement was the Japanese policy of catering to nationalist sentiment in Indonesia. By sponsoring a myriad of organizations that were designed to rally the population to their side but at the same time held out the ultimate promise of independence, the Japanese managed to co-opt most of the actual or potential nationalist leadership. (Mortimer 1974: 107)

In September 1943, the Japanese even established a military organization, officered by Indonesians, to help the Japanese defend Indonesia against an expected Allied invasion. The Pembela Tanah Air (Defenders of the Fatherland), better known as the Peta, numbered some 120,000 armed men by the middle of 1945. "It was the Peta," Kahin notes, "which was to become the backbone of the Indonesian Republic's army" that fought against the returning Dutch (G. Kahin 1952: 109). The Japanese also organized a number of paramilitary groups comprised of Indonesian students and youth, or *pemuda*; these pemuda groups came to play an important role during the postwar liberation struggle (see Anderson 1972; Frederick 1989).

The Japanese surrendered to the Allies, as it turned out, before the latter were able to launch an invasion of Indonesia. The resulting "power vacuum" – which, as we shall see, was also crucial for the Viet Minh's initial seizure of power in Vietnam – was eventually filled by Sukarno and non-Communist nationalist or Republican forces. Sukarno, pressed by *pemuda* leaders – who briefly kidnapped him to force the issue – declared the independence of the Republic of Indonesia on August 17, 1945, three days after Japan's surrender. "The absence of a significant Communist underground in Indonesia during the war," notes one commentator, "meant that the PKI played no part in the dramatic events leading to the establishment of the Indonesian Republic after the war" (McLane 1966: 281). In fact, Communist activists did not officially "reestablish" the PKI until October 1945.

Leftists did play a role in many of the local "social revolutions" that broke out across the archipelago following the surrender of Japan (see Anderson 1972; Reid 1979; A. Kahin 1985; Frederick 1989; Cribb 1991). These "revolutions," however, sought mainly to remove village headmen and other officials who had collaborated with the Japanese; although they involved popular mobilizations, they did not attempt to seize land, factories, or other property. Moreover, as Anthony Reid (1981: 145) notes,

in none of these revolutionary outbursts did the Left stay in power for more than a few weeks. The reasons were that their enemies – the Republican army apparatus, sometimes assisted by modernist Muslim forces – were too strong, that their presumed friends in the central Government failed to support them and that they lacked any organised popular base.

86

The most influential leftists within the Republican movement, including Sjahrir and Amir Sjarifuddin, opposed these revolts, fearing that they would disturb the Western powers, whose support Indonesia presumably required to achieve independence: "The needs of the national revolution," they concluded, "must take precedence over those of the social revolution" (Reid 1974: 61).

While the Communist Party remained quite small during the conflict with the Dutch – recruiting no more than three thousand members by 1948 (G. Kahin 1952: 277) – it did win some influence among certain officers in the Republic's armed forces. When an effort was made to curb the influence of these officers, in fact, local Communist leaders (without the knowledge of the top leadership of the PKI) decided to seize the city of Madiun and to launch a revolt in self-defense against the Republican government. The PKI's national leadership, presented with this fait accompli, apparently attempted to transform this defensive revolt into a full-scale rebellion against Republican authority as such. The Madiun revolt, however, failed to spark a popular uprising as the party leadership had hoped. In the next few days, Communists seized several other towns in the vicinity of Madiun, but these initial successes "were the products of *pronunciamento*'s [sic] by local military commanders rather of any popular uprising" (Pluvier 1974: 479; see also Swift 1989). Indeed, in the eyes of many Indonesians, according to Kahin, "the Communists were attacking leaders who had become the very symbol of the Republic and of Indonesian independence." Sukarno, "in particular, had for an undoubted majority of the Indonesian rank and file come to symbolize the Republic" (G. Kahin 1952: 301). Within two weeks, Republican armies had put an end to the "Madiun affair." Most PKI leaders were arrested or killed, including Musso, the top official of the party. "Inadequately prepared, militarily as well as psychologically, and inefficiently carried out, the 'Commune of Madiun' could not result in anything but a dismal failure" (Pluvier 1974: 481). The "PKI was removed as a threat to the established Republican leaders until the 1950s, and was tainted forever with treachery against the Revolution" (Ricklefs 1993: 229).

The failure of the Communist revolt at Madiun had even broader political ramifications. "More than any other single event in post–Second World War Indonesia," Jan Pluvier has noted, "the suppression of the Madiun rebellion by the republican government jeopardized the Dutch chances of restoring their colonial rule" (Pluvier 1974: 482):

[T]he Republic's defeat of a Communist rebellion turned vague American sympathy based upon anti-colonial sentiments into diplomatic support based upon global strategy. . . . American strategic thinking was now dominated by the idea that a "cold war" was under way between an American-led "free world" and a Soviet-led bloc. Within this framework, the Indonesian Republic had shown itself to be anti-Communist and hence worthy of American support. When the Dutch . . . made their last bid for conquest [in December 1948], they found the weight of the United States thrown onto the diplomatic scales against them. (Ricklefs 1981: 218)

The Dutch government, under intense pressure from both the United States – which threatened to suspend Marshall Plan economic aid (van der Eng 1988) – and businesspeople who feared for their investments in Indonesia (see G. Kahin 1963: 563), formally recognized Indonesian independence on December 27, 1949; a unitary republic was proclaimed the following August. (Indonesia, it should be noted, was "saddled with nearly $1,130,000,000 of the colonial regime's obligations, much of which had been incurred since 1945 in financing the effort to suppress the Republic" [G. Kahin 1963: 563].) Sukarno and Hatta were elected president and prime minister, respectively, prior to the transfer of sovereignty. "[T]he vigor of Republican guerrilla resistance and pressure from the international community ultimately forced the Netherlands toward accommodation" (A. Kahin 1985: 10).

In sum, nationalist domination of the postwar independence struggle is best explained by Indonesia's changing political context, from racially exclusionary colony to Japanese occupation and defeat to the Netherlands' doomed attempt at recolonization. Non-Communist nationalists in Indonesia were best positioned to seize the political opportunity for popular mobilization afforded by the breakdown of political authority that resulted from the defeat of Japan. However, the subsequent closing down of political space during the Netherlands' attempt to reimpose colonial rule proved no less beneficial to the nationalist cause, effectively driving a broad array of Indonesians behind the Republican banner. The populist, yet eclectic nature of the nationalist movement is well expressed by the "Pancasila," or five principles, a vague, quasi-official doctrine first developed by Sukarno to undergird the Republic by attracting the largest possible popular following. These principles, which are encoded in the Republic's constitution, are (1) belief in God, (2) national unity, (3) humanitarianism, (4) people's sovereignty, and (5) social justice and prosperity. Nationalists generally avoided talk of class struggle, land reform, or the redistribution of wealth.

The Formation of Communist Movements

The failure of the Communist Party or other left groups to lead and/or radicalize the independence struggle in Indonesia was not due to any fundamental economic, class, or cultural factors, but to circumstances, in John Dunn's words, "of a highly contingent character":

By the time that the Japanese control of Indonesia could be broken, a very broad nationalist movement, large sections of which had been organized under Japanese tutelage had come into existence. Dutch colonial social control had been disrupted for years. Hence when a war of colonial reconquest could at last be undertaken, the broadly-based and highly syncretistic nationalist government enjoyed too wide support for it to be crushed by military means at any level acceptable to the Dutch. (Dunn 1972: 129)

Due to the harshness and racially exclusionary character of Dutch rule, there was no influential pro-Western elite to whom sovereignty could be "safely" entrusted, as in the Philippines and Malaya (which I discuss in the next section). For this reason, Indonesia's non-Communist nationalists were also suspicious of the West and would become leading proponents of the movement of "nonaligned" countries during the Cold War; in 1955, in fact, Indonesia hosted the first prominent meeting of nonaligned nations in the city of Bandung (see Wright 1994 [1956]). Japanese sponsorship of non-Communist nationalists, furthermore, effectively preempted the formation of a strong anti-Japanese resistance movement – the initial vehicle of the Communist insurgencies that emerged elsewhere in the region.

The Formation of Communist Movements in Vietnam, Malaya, and the Philippines

The postwar Communist insurgencies in Southeast Asia – like the nationalist struggle in Indonesia – are also intimately connected to the period of Japanese rule; in fact, these insurgencies grew directly out of the anti-Japanese resistance movements formed by Communist parties during World War II. The Japanese occupation was primarily responsible – quite unintentionally, of course – for transforming small or relatively ineffectual Communist parties into much more powerful, legitimate, and well-armed forces in Vietnam, Malaya, and the Philippines. After Japan's defeat, the armed revolutionary movements led by these parties came to oppose – sooner or later, as the case may be – the reimposition of Western colonial rule (or, in the case of the Philippines, the attempt by the Philippine oligarchic elite – with substantial backing from the United States – to restore the old social order). National sovereignty, in other words, as well as the elimination of class oppression, was a fundamental objective of these radical movements.

Indeed, despite Japan's defeat in the war, its effort to destroy Western colonialism in Asia was not totally ineffectual; Japanese rule "had unloosed a political avalanche that could not be forced back into the artificiality of the old colonial order" (Bastin and Benda 1968: 152). The Japanese had themselves wished to substitute their own hegemony for Western influence in Asia – under the slogan "Asia for Asians" – and to incorporate the whole of the *Nampō* (the "southern regions") into a "Greater East Asia Co-Prosperity Sphere." The aim of this scheme was both to eliminate Western imperialism and to establish in its place a form of neocolonialism based on nominally independent regimes headed by the same sort of compliant, collaborating elites that the British and Americans had sponsored in Malaya and the Philippines; the Japanese also seem to have planned to relocate a huge number of permanent settlers in "Japan-towns" throughout the region (see Pluvier 1974: pt. 3; Dower 1986: ch. 10).

The Communist parties of Southeast Asia, despite the enormous hardships wrought by Western colonialism, remained small and/or generally ineffective organizations prior to the war. The reasons for this had less to do with social structure or culture than with the severe repression of Communism by colonial authorities. Communist-led uprisings in Indonesia in 1926–7, as noted previously, as well as in Vietnam in 1930–1, were ruthlessly put down, with thousands killed and many party activists incarcerated; political conditions were only somewhat less harsh for Communists in Malaya and the Philippines. The Communists' turn to a "popular front" orientation after 1935, moreover, which called for support of the Western "democracies" in their fight against fascism and for a consequent deemphasis of the goal of national liberation, also contributed to their unpopularity in many Western colonies. In this context, the Japanese occupation was something of a godsend for Communists in Southeast Asia; they could now fight fascism without conspicuously collaborating with Western imperialists. As Harry Benda has suggested, "The height of the Communist alliance with the West during the war led to a complete, if temporary, break between nationalism and Communism . . . in India; a similar effect on the Southeast Asian scene was only prevented by the Japanese invasion of the area" (Benda 1956: 425).

The Japanese occupied Vietnam and the rest of French Indochina in the fall of 1940, well before the other Southeast Asian colonies. This occupation was based on a most consequential agreement with the collaborationist Vichy regime in France (which was invaded by Japan's German allies earlier in the year) – an agreement that permitted the French, alone among the western imperialists in Southeast Asia, to retain the trappings of power. According to Huynh Kim Khanh,

> By common agreement, there was little visible change in the manner of governing Indochina. The Japanese forces, well disciplined and tough, rarely ventured outside of their bases, nor did their leaders attempt to influence directly the administration of internal Indochinese politics. French administration, armed forces, and police continued to function exactly as before. (1971: 763)

The Japanese did not sponsor non-Communist nationalists (such as they were), as they had in Indonesia, until very late in the war, an effort that proved too little, too late. In any event, by far the most popular nationalists proved to be Communists (Vu Ngu Cheiu 1986).

In May 1941, in response to the Japanese occupation, the Vietnamese-dominated Indochinese Communist Party (ICP) – founded in 1930 by Ho Chi Minh – established the Viet Minh, or League for the Independence of Vietnam.[9] The Viet Minh adopted a strategy of armed resistance to both the Japanese and French and began to plan for a popular insurrection that would seize power at some "opportune moment." Shortly before the Japanese occupation, significantly, "the Central Committee [of the Communist Party] withdrew the slogan 'To confiscate landlords' land and distribute it to the tillers,' and by May 1941 the theme of 'national liberation' held the center of the stage" (Modelski 1964: 189). The Viet Minh strove, in Ho Chi Minh's words, to "unite all patriots, without distinction of wealth, age, sex, religion, or political outlook" (quoted in Hodgkin 1981: 302).

The Viet Minh established bases in the isolated and mountainous province of Cao Bang, situated along the border with Nationalist China, where guerrillas could find sanctuary when pursued by the French or Japanese. The border region was inhabited primarily by ethnic minority groups, especially the Tay (or Tho) and Nung, and these were in fact the first groups organized by the Viet Minh. (By 1954, Tay constituted

---

[9] Good accounts of the Viet Minh from its founding to the August Revolution of 1945 may be found in McAlister 1969, Hodgkin 1981, Harrison 1982, and especially Khanh 1982.

approximately 20 percent of Viet Minh troops [Elliott 1974: 26].) In addition to a small guerrilla force, the Viet Minh also came to establish a number of mass organizations – known as "national salvation associations" – for youth, women, old people, and other social sectors. By early 1945, the Viet Minh was in fact the only significant anti-Japanese movement in Vietnam, although it only had about five thousand members at that time; the Vietnamese Liberation Army, moreover, formally organized by Vo Nguyen Giap in December 1944, had only about one thousand armed troops. However, between the early months of 1945 and the landing of Allied forces in Vietnam in late September (Japan surrendered on August 14), the Viet Minh grew very rapidly and expanded its influence widely in the countryside.

How did this come about? The Japanese, fearing that elements within the French colonial regime might support an Allied invasion, executed a coup d'etat against the French administration on March 9, 1945, imprisoning nearly all the French civil and military leaders that they could round up. If the Japanese occupation prompted the Viet Minh to adopt a strategy of armed struggle, the Japanese coup against the French opened up unprecedented, albeit short-lived, political opportunities for political and military organization – opportunities that the Viet Minh was willing and able to exploit far better than any other political grouping in the country. The Viet Minh obtained weapons and ammunition from French troops fleeing to China and, given the general breakdown of political authority in the countryside after March, was able to establish "People's Revolutionary Committees" in many towns and villages, particularly in northern and central Vietnam. The Vietnamese countryside, in fact, was gradually abandoned by the Japanese, who were directing all their resources at the Allied advance in the Pacific. Ironically, the Viet Minh, which rescued a number of American fighter pilots who were shot down over Vietnam, also received small amounts of arms and ammunition from the Office of Strategic Services (OSS), the forerunner of the Central Intelligence Agency (see Patti 1980).

The Japanese coup against the French, coincidentally, occurred during the peak of a terrible famine in north and north-central Vietnam that was brought on by Japan's decision to divert all rice paddy to Japan. This famine is estimated to have killed some two million people, about one quarter of the population of northern Vietnam (Long 1991b: 19). "Communist activists therefore declared 'the central task for mobilizing the masses' to be to 'seize paddy stocks to save the people from starvation,' with a view to 'launching a powerful movement of struggle against the Japanese fascists for national salvation'" (Harrison 1982: 93). Thomas Hodgkin notes that "'National salvation' and 'seize paddy stocks to save the people from starvation' became, like 'Peace, bread and land' in the Russian October Revolution, the slogans around which the people were mobilised" (Hodgkin 1981: 329).

Shortly after Japan's surrender to the Allies, the Viet Minh launched the August Revolution, seizing control of Hanoi, capturing the imperial capital of Hue (and obtaining the abdication of Emperor Bao Dai), and leading a coalition of nationalist forces in capturing Saigon. Ho Chi Minh proclaimed the independence of the Democratic Republic of Vietnam (DRV) at a huge rally in Ba Dinh Square in Hanoi on September 2, 1945. "The transfer of power was accomplished smoothly and with practically no bloodshed" (Huynh Kim Khanh 1971: 761–2; see also McAlister 1969 and especially Marr 1995 for detailed analyses of this period).

None of this, however, swayed the determination of the French to reconquer Vietnam. Following their arrival in September 1945, General Douglas Gracey's British troops – which, according to the terms of the Potsdam Conference held earlier in the year, were to occupy Vietnam south of the sixteenth parallel – attempted to disarm the Viet Minh and other nationalist groups in the south. French troops began to arrive the following month, and they gradually drove the Viet Minh out of the major southern cities. Chinese Nationalist forces, on the other hand, which occupied Vietnam north of the sixteenth parallel, tolerated the DRV government as a counterweight to French influence in the south. Reasonably free and fair elections to a national assembly were held in January 1946, and the Viet Minh formed a coalition government with two small, Chinese-backed political parties.

The developing civil war in China, however, eventually led to the withdrawal of Chinese forces from northern Vietnam and their replacement by the French. But negotiations between the French and the DRV over the issue of independence eventually broke down, and in November the French, following a disagreement over the control of customs authority, indiscriminately shelled the city of Haiphong, killing six thousand Vietnamese by their own estimates, three times that many according to the DRV. Convinced that war was unavoidable, the Viet Minh launched a surprise attack on French forces in Hanoi on December 19, 1946, allowing their main forces to withdraw to the mountain bases whence they could wage guerrilla warfare. The "First Indochina War" – or the Nine-Year National Resistance – had begun.[10]

The postwar revolutionary movement in Malaya, as in Vietnam, was an attempt to resist imperialist efforts, in this case British, to restore the status quo ante following the Japanese "interregnum." The Malayan insurgency also grew directly out of the Communist-led anti-Japanese resistance movement of World War II; the Japanese occupation of Malaya, as in Vietnam, not only led local Communists to adopt a strategy of armed struggle, but also created a political context in which Communists were able to expand their influence and legitimacy on an unprecedented scale.

In March 1942, following Japan's surprisingly swift occupation of Malaya and Singapore, the Malayan Communist Party (MCP) – whose membership, significantly, consisted almost entirely of ethnic Chinese – established the Malayan People's Anti-Japanese Union (MPAJU) and its armed wing, the Malayan People's Anti-Japanese Army (MPAJA).[11] The MPAJA, which grew to about seven thousand armed guerrillas by early 1945, was the largest anti-Japanese force, as a percentage of total population, in Southeast Asia. Indeed, noting how the Viet Minh was relatively inactive militarily prior to the Japanese coup against the French, one author has called the MPAJA "the one significant resistance movement which operated against the Japanese" (Osborne 1970: 84) – although this seems dubious if one includes the resistance movement in the Philippines discussed later in this section. The MPAJA, however, remained an overwhelmingly ethnic Chinese organization. Large numbers of impoverished Tamil workers on British rubber plantations were more attracted to the Japanese-sponsored Indian Independence League and the Indian National Army, led by Subhas Chandra Bose, a former president of the Indian Congress Party (see Ghosh 1997; Fay 1993).[12] (With Japanese assistance, the Indian National Army intended to liberate India from British rule by force of arms.)

The MCP, moreover, unlike the nationalists in Indonesia and the Viet Minh, made a serious political blunder: It failed to declare the independence of Malaya or to establish an independent government during the

[10] The complex unfolding of events in Vietnam between August 1945 and December 1946 is recounted in McAlister 1969, Giap 1975, Patti 1980, and Marr 1995.

[11] Good histories of the MPAJA may be found in O'Ballance 1966, Short 1975, and Lee 1977.

[12] Leaders of the Indian National Army later helped to found the anti-Communist Malayan Indian Congress (see Chapter 4).

94

crucial interval between Japan's surrender and the return of the British in September 1945. Indeed, the Communists decided to cooperate fully with the British military command, calculating that postwar conditions would not necessitate armed struggle, especially with a new Labor Party government in power in London (see, e.g., Cheah Boon Kheng 1977). The British formally dissolved the MPAJA in December 1945, "without . . . any formal protest by the Communist leadership" (McLane 1966: 307), paying 350 Malayan dollars to guerrillas who turned in their arms (although considerable caches of weapons remained hidden in the jungle) and awarding the guerrillas assorted ribbons and medals for services rendered. Admiral Mountbatten himself, Supreme Allied Commander in Southeast Asia, awarded a campaign medal to Chin Peng, future leader of the Communist insurgency. The MCP turned its efforts, as it had before the war, to labor organizing, especially among urban workers and laborers on British rubber estates; the party established the powerful Pan-Malayan Federation of Trade Unions (PMFTU) and engaged in considerable strike activity in the immediate postwar period, which was characterized by severe economic dislocations and hardships.

By 1948, however, the Malayan Communists had returned to Malaya's jungles and adopted a strategy of armed struggle for national liberation from British rule. Two factors seem to have led the MCP in this direction. On the one hand, the British administration in Malaya, responding to intense pressure from rubber planters and other businesspeople, cracked down hard on the Communist-led labor movement (see Stenson 1970). In May 1946 the government banned federations of labor unions except by trade, thereby making the PMFTU illegal. The government also decreed that trade union officials must have three years' experience in labor organizations; since most Communist activists had served in the MPAJA until the end of 1945, they were consequently ineligible. "About the same time the government began systematically to use its powers of banishment and deported many undesirable Chinese, most of them suspected Communists, who did not hold citizenship" (McLane 1966: 387).

About this same time, furthermore, the developing Cold War between the Soviet Union and the United States led the Soviets to press Communist parties to adopt a more militant stand against the "imperialist, antidemocratic camp." To this end, the Communist Information Bureau, or Cominform, was established in September 1947. A Southeast Asian Youth Conference held by Communist and leftist groups in Calcutta, India, in February 1948 also pressed this more militant line, although it stopped short of endorsing armed struggle. Lawrence Sharkey, an Australian Communist leader, addressed the Fourth Plenum of the MCP in Singapore in March 1948 en route home from Calcutta. According to Charles McLane, Sharkey "is said to have delivered a scathing criticism of the MCP's past policies, especially the decision to dissolve the MPAJA after the war" (McLane 1966: 385). The Plenum resolved that independence would ultimately require a "people's revolutionary war."

In this context of domestic repression and the leftward turn of Soviet-aligned Communist parties, the MCP initiated a campaign of assassinations of British colonial officials and businesspeople. The British declared a state of emergency in Malaya following the murder of three British planters on June 16, 1948. The following February, the MCP announced the formation of the Malayan Races Liberation Army (MRLA), calling for national independence through armed struggle waged by an alliance of all the ethnic communities in Malaya. The Malayan "Emergency," which would result in some eleven thousand deaths (Milne and Mauzy 1986: 24), would not be officially terminated until July 31, 1960.

The MRLA eventually grew to include about eight to ten thousand armed guerrillas, and the affiliated Min Yuen, or People's Movement, had at least another twenty thousand members. This latter organization was a clandestine group set up by the MCP in cities and towns in order to recruit volunteers for the MRLA, supply the guerrillas, and spread propaganda. Popular support for the insurgency, as noted earlier, seems to have come primarily from rubber estate workers (including some Indians), the Chinese urban working class, and especially rural Chinese squatters (see Short 1970a, 1975; Stenson 1974, 1980). This last group "had a long-standing distrust of the [Colonial] Government and . . . generally saw the MCP as a legitimate alternative" (Stubbs 1989: 6). Squatter communities had supported the MPAJA during the Japanese occupation, which was particularly onerous for Malaya's Chinese population since it was regarded with suspicion by the Japanese for its longstanding sympathies for both the Chinese Nationalists and the Chinese Communist Party. (Many Chinese squatters, in fact, had fled Singapore and other urban areas in order to escape Japanese persecution and surveillance.) The MCP also earned considerable legitimacy among this group due to the party's militant opposition to British attempts to evict squatters after the war.

The MPAJA, however, was unable to exploit the cause of nationalism as effectively as the Viet Minh. During the Japanese occupation, this was a result, at least in part, of the refusal of local British authorities to collaborate with the Japanese in the manner of the French in Vietnam. Prior to the Japanese invasion, in fact, the British released leftist political prisoners and cooperated with the MCP in establishing a guerrilla training school from which the MPAJA's original cadre emerged. The MPAJA later developed contacts with a Ceylon-based British military organization known as Force 136 – which attempted to coordinate anti-Japanese activities in occupied British colonies – and in January 1944 the MPAJA agreed to accept "instructions" from the Allied command in exchange for arms and assistance. It is quite revealing, in fact, that the Malayan Communists formed an "anti-Japanese" army and *not* an "independence" movement like the Viet Minh.

Neither the MPAJA nor the MRLA, moreover, had much success in mobilizing the ethnic Malay population against the Japanese or British.[13] This is mainly attributable to the *character* of British rule in Malaya. The British had long pursued policies aimed at the separation of the various ethnic communities in Malaya – Malay, Chinese, and Indian – including the reservation of civil service positions for Malays as against the two other "foreign" communities (see Stenson 1980; Hua Wu Yin 1983). Much of the traditional Malay elite, moreover, decided to collaborate with the Japanese, as with the British before them; indeed, while vigorously persecuting the Chinese, the Japanese went out of their way to accommodate this elite. "As a result," notes Jan Pluvier, "the overwhelming majority of Malay politicians and civil servants was not inclined to be drawn into any illegal activity, and even less to participate in the anti-Japanese resistance movement" (Pluvier 1974: 299). For reasons I explain in Chapter 4, this attitude was also widespread among Malay peasants both during and after the war.

The so-called Huk rebellion in the Philippines, like the rebellions in Vietnam and Malaya, also grew out of the Communist-led anti-Japanese resistance movement in that country. In this case, the postwar insurgency was primarily a response to efforts by the Philippine oligarchic elite, in close collaboration with the United States, to restore the prewar social order in the archipelago.[14] The Huk rebellion, then, differs from the other

[13] In 1947, ethnic Chinese comprised 44.7 percent of Malaya's population, while Malays comprised 43.5 percent. Most of the rest (about 10 percent) were Indian, primarily Tamil (see Stenson 1974: 331; Fairbairn 1974: 160).
[14] The war-time history of the Huks is recounted in Abaya 1946, Taruc 1953, Kerkvliet 1977, and Pomeroy 1978.

97

social-revolutionary movements in the region in that it was directed not against a returning colonial power, as in Vietnam and Malaya, but against a Philippine government that had become at least formally independent in July 1946.

Following the Japanese attack on the Philippines in December 1941, the Communist Party of the Philippines (PKP) established the Hukbong Bayan Laban sa Hapon (Tagalog for People's Anti-Japanese Army), better known as the Hukbalahap, in March 1942. The Huks, as they were called, were led by long-time activists in the prewar peasant movement in Central and Southern Luzon, especially activists from the Communist and Socialist parties, which had merged in 1938 (Kerkvliet 1977).

Although much of the Philippine elite, like their counterparts in Malaya, chose to collaborate with the Japanese (see Abaya 1946; Steinberg 1967), the anti-Japanese resistance movement grew to be quite large and influential, although it was extremely fragmented. According to one estimate, about three hundred thousand resistance fighters were active in one way or another, including about one hundred thousand who were led by American officers who were unable or unwilling to be evacuated in the wake of the Japanese invasion; in fact, the Philippines was the only country occupied by Japan in which the colonial army played a significant role in the resistance (see Pluvier 1974: 305–7). However, by all accounts the Huks were the most bold and effective guerrilla force, growing to include some ten to twelve thousand armed troops and seventy-six squadrons by late 1944.[15]

In addition to waging guerrilla warfare against the Japanese, "the Hukbalahap unchained an agrarian revolution in Central Luzon which aimed at breaking the economic power of the great landlords" (Pluvier 1974: 308). Unlike the USAFFE units, which eschewed political organizing, "the Huks claimed that military warfare was inseparable from political warfare and was, in fact, subordinate to it" (U.S. Department of State 1987 [1950]: 75). The Huks established a rudimentary system of local self-government in Central Luzon, and because most landlords in the region abandoned their estates and fled to the cities during the war years, much

---

[15] A confidential U.S. Department of State report noted that the non-Huk forces – which "were led by men of the *cacique* [landowning] class who had taken ROTC training in the universities or had served in the United States Armed Forces in the Far East [USAFFE] ... favored a 'lie-low' policy and concentrated on getting intelligence information for the Americans until such time as they would be aided by the return of American forces" (U.S. Department of State 1987 [1950]: 74–5).

land was freed up, releasing many tenants – the principal social base of the movement – from the burden of high rents. This contrasts sharply with the wartime situation in Vietnam, where, prior to the Japanese coup, French and Japanese repression severely limited Communist activities. In the Philippines, by contrast, not only were the Huks busy "making propaganda for their cause, influencing the population, building up an effective organization, committing acts of sabotage, killing Japanese and liquidating collaborators, [but] the Huks were successful, from the beginning, in carrying out their social and political programme" (Pluvier 1974: 307–8).

Unlike Indonesia, Vietnam, and Malaya, however, the Philippines experienced no interval between Japan's surrender and the return of Allied forces. On the contrary, American forces invaded the Philippines in October 1944, well before Japan's surrender, encountering heavy resistance. Manila was not taken from the Japanese until February 1945. In any event, the Huks, like the Malayan Communists, developed no plans to declare the independence of the Philippines or to establish their own alternative government. On the contrary, the PKP, like their Malayan counterparts, looked forward to a period in which it could organize legally and above-ground in a soon-to-be independent Philippines.[16]

Within a year and a half after liberation from the Japanese, however, the Huks would take up arms once again, this time against the newly independent government of the Philippines. This decision was the result of the policy of the United States and its elite Philippine allies, including many who collaborated with the Japanese, to dismember the Huks and the peasant movement in Luzon. Even before the Japanese surrendered, in fact, American forces harassed and arrested Huk fighters, who were ordered to turn over their weapons:

[General] MacArthur, in a manner the State Department found irritating and egocentric, implemented Washington's policy by speedily restoring the Old Order. He pressed the Filipino collaborationist police into the service of the United States, and the United States military authorities arrested and held the two major Huk leaders [Luis Taruc and Casto Alejandrino] for seven months as security risks. During 1945 MacArthur increasingly used United States troops to break up Huk meetings, and the landlords then successfully agitated for the legal recognition of their former holdings. (Kolko 1990 [1968]: 606)

---

[16] The Tydings-McDuffie Act of 1934 provided for Philippine independence after a ten-year transitional period, a promise renewed in a joint resolution of the U.S. Congress in 1944.

This was followed by blatant fraud against Huk-supported candidates in the first postwar elections. The PKP and a number of labor and peasant organizations formed the Democratic Alliance (DA) after the war, and six DA candidates were elected in the April 1946 congressional elections. However, the DA victors were denied their seats in the Congress by newly elected President Manuel Roxas for supposedly using terror and intimidation in order to win their elections. The DA candidates, not coincidentally, opposed the Bell Trade Act, signed by President Truman and delivered to the Philippine Congress, which extended "free trade" (thereby making protection of infant industries impossible) and which provided for "parity" for U.S. investors (nullifying an amendment in the Philippine constitution that limited foreign participation to 40 percent ownership of corporations). Also included in the Act's terms was the retention of ninety-nine-year leases on twenty-three U.S. military bases in the Philippines, including the huge Subic Bay naval station and Clark Air Base. With the DA representatives conveniently excluded, the Bell Act was passed in the Philippine Congress by a single vote (Kerkvliet 1977: 143–55; see also Shalom 1986 [1981]; Walton 1984).

In addition to political exclusion, moreover, growing intimidation of labor and peasant organizations also characterized the Philippine scene after independence, capped by the murder of Juan Feleo, a long-time peasant activist and PKP member, in August 1946. It was in this context of *shrinking* political opportunities – so similar to that in postwar Malaya – that the Hukbong Mapagpalaya ng Bayan (HMB), or People's Liberation Army, was formed in the summer of 1946 by former activists of the Hukbalahap. At first the PKP as a whole did not support the HMB's strategy of armed resistance, although many individual Communists were actively involved in the struggle, including Luis Taruc, the most famous Huk commander during the war and one of the DA representatives excluded from Congress.

At the PKP's central committee meeting of May 1948, however, the Communists reversed direction, following the general leftward direction of pro-Soviet Communist parties. The PKP called for an "anti-imperialist war" against the United States and its "tools" in the Philippines. The party believed that a "revolutionary situation" was at hand because the Philippine government and economy were thought to be on the verge of collapse, with the United States, its own economy supposedly crumbling, unable to offer any assistance. At its height, between 1949 and early 1951, armed Huks numbered somewhere between eleven and fifteen thousand,

Conclusion

roughly equal to the armed strength of the wartime Hukbalahap movement (Kerkvliet 1977: 210).

Thus, in Vietnam, Malaya, and the Philippines alike, the determination of Western colonial powers (or a neocolonial elite, in the case of the Philippines) to restore their rule after the war (through violence if necessary), coupled with a leftward shift in the Soviet camp after 1947, prompted Communist-led movements in these countries to take up arms in an effort to seize state power. In all three countries – in sharp contrast to Indonesia – Communist-led movements accumulated supporters, weaponry, and substantial legitimacy as a result of the train of events set in motion by the invasion of, and struggle against, Japanese forces. Against the backdrop of the regional similarities discussed previously, it was this shifting political and geopolitical context that best explains the emergence (and timing) of the Communist insurgencies in Southeast Asia.

Conclusion

We have seen that the colonial and neocolonial elites who attempted to reassert their political domination of Southeast Asia following World War II were confronted by armed national liberation movements throughout the region; however, not all of these movements were led by Communist parties nor were they all equally successful (as I shall attempt to explain in the following chapter) in resisting the reimposition of colonial or neocolonial rule. What, then, explains the emergence of mass-based Communist insurgencies in many, but not all, of the countries in the region in reaction to the attempted restoration of Western domination?

The principal hypotheses of modernization and Marxist perspectives on Third World revolutions seem clearly inadequate to account for the incidence of mass-based Communist insurgencies in Southeast Asia during the period that I have examined. The disruptive social change and imperialist economic exploitation associated with Western colonialism were clearly insufficient, as the Indonesian case perhaps best demonstrates, for generating powerful radical movements. Nor were the strong Communist insurgencies that *did* emerge after the war the vehicles of any particular social class or class alliance. The wrenching social changes and new class relations brought about by colonialism certainly rendered particular social classes and groups especially "available" for political mobilization by leaders who claimed to represent best the interests of the nation, but these factors did not evidently determine just what *type* of political leaders would be most effective in this regard. Nor, it must be added, did the mere presence of Leninist revolutionaries, with their "organizational weapon" of the disciplined vanguard party (Selznick 1979 [1952]), invariably channel these "available" social groups into Communist-led revolutionary movements.

The formation – and the specific *timing* of the formation – of mass-based Communist insurgencies in Southeast Asia is best explained as a result of factors, some of them fortuitous, of a specifically *political* nature. It was above all the character of Japanese rule in each colony during the war that determined whether or not Communists would be in a position to organize a significant armed insurgency during and after the war. Communists obtained substantial popular support and legitimacy where the Japanese allowed colonial or indigenous collaborating elites to retain the formal trappings of state power and administration and continued to exclude and repress popular nationalist organizations – as occurred in Vietnam, Malaya, and the Philippines. However, where the Japanese sponsored genuinely popular nationalists as well as nationalist organizations, as in Indonesia, Communists found it extremely difficult to mobilize popular support for armed struggle against these nationalists (or against the Japanese themselves) during or after the war.

The Japanese invasion of Southeast Asia, furthermore, not only led Communist parties to adopt a strategy of armed struggle, but also created unprecedented political opportunities for mobilizing and arming those "available" sectors of the population (which were not difficult to locate nor confined to any single social class) that had longstanding grievances against colonialists and their collaborators – grievances that were often reinforced and multiplied by Japanese policies. Most importantly, the Japanese occupation and internment of Western officials invariably led to some degree of breakdown in the administration and policing of the colonies, especially near the end of the war, which provided the requisite "political space" for the building of revolutionary movements. This political breakdown was perhaps most evident in Malaya and the Philippines, where the Japanese encountered the heaviest opposition from Communist-led resistance movements; it was less evident in Vietnam, ironically, at least until the Japanese coup against the French late in the war created the "opportune moment" that the Communists were expecting (see Marr 1995: ch. 6). This combination of administrative weakness and repression of organized dissent proved explosive, inadvertently producing an expanding counter-mobilization by the targets of repression, as it has in other contexts (see, e.g., Muller 1985). In Indonesia, by contrast, Communists and other overtly anti-Japanese forces found it extremely difficult to take advantage of the political space opened up by the Japanese occupation and its immediate aftermath, given Japan's support for popular anticolonial nationalists in that country.

This said, the emergence of the revolutionary movements discussed in this chapter – Communist and non-Communist alike – was not simply a result of the political opportunities or state breakdowns associated with the Japanese occupation and defeat. (These opportunities, in any event, more or less quickly evaporated after the fall of 1945.) Even more, these movements were a product of and response to the repressive and exclusionary character of Western and/or Japanese imperialism. By leaving masses of people "no other way out" of their various economic and political predicaments, to use Trotsky's phrase, political authorities focused and channeled popular grievances in a revolutionary direction. These authorities unwittingly helped to organize or construct popular revolutionary movements, movements that were able to prosper despite and even because of brutal repression and the contraction of political space. "Political opportunities," in short, do not exhaust the more general importance of political context for understanding the revolutionary movements that formed in the region.

The analysis of this chapter raises an important question: If the Japanese "interregnum" was so crucial in determining whether or not Communists would later be capable of organizing significant opposition to the reimposition of Western domination, what then accounts for the variable character of Japanese rule in Southeast Asia? Two factors seem especially important.[17] First, Japan's larger geopolitical needs and international alliances played a major role in shaping its policies in specific countries. Nowhere in Southeast Asia, significantly, did the Japanese feel that they had the capacity, given the demands of the war, to govern the region completely and directly by themselves; hence their sponsorship of nationalist organizations or reliance on indigenous

---

[17] On the local political ramifications of the Japanese "interregnum," see Elsbree 1953; Anderson 1966; Benda 1967; Bastin and Benda 1968: pt. 2, ch. 3; and the essays in McCoy 1980. For a fascinating discussion of Japanese imperialists' self-understanding of the Greater East Asia Co-Prosperity Sphere, see Dower 1986: ch. 10.

collaborators of one sort or another. In Vietnam, the character of the Japanese occupation was determined principally by exogenous events in the European, and then Pacific, theaters of war. Japan's decision both to allow the French to remain in power and then to oust them rapidly very late in the war reflected its perception of its broader, and shifting, geostrategic interests.

An equally crucial factor that shaped the character and impact of the Japanese occupation was the exact type of indigenous leaders who were *available* as collaborators, owing to the nature of Western rule in Southeast Asia before the war. Where powerful neocolonial elites already existed due to inclusionary forms of Western colonialism, as in Malaya and the Philippines, the Japanese immediately sought out such elites (and vice versa) as junior partners in their imperialist project; where, by contrast, racially exclusive forms of Western colonialism had largely preempted the formation of such elites, as in Indonesia, the Japanese necessarily turned to what they regarded as their next best option: non-Communist "populist" nationalists.[18]

It is important to note that Japanese policies in Southeast Asia were shaped by specific cultural beliefs and assumptions. As John Dower has argued, the concept of an "Asia for Asians" was not incompatible with the widespread and fundamentally racist view among Japanese that they were inherently superior to other Asian people as well as to whites (Dower 1986: 264). However, Japan did enact a number of "liberal" policies in Southeast Asia – including the sponsorship of nationalist organizations, the promotion of indigenous languages, the advancement of native civil servants, the waging of vast propaganda campaigns against Western racism and colonialism (including attacks on Britain's continuing rule of India), and, ultimately, steps toward the formal independence of the colonies – that cannot be dismissed as simple ruses aimed at attaining the compliance of conquered peoples. These policies also reflected the widespread Japanese belief that they were engaged, above all, in a sacred struggle to free and protect the morally superior civilization of Asia from the bankrupt materialism of the West (see, e.g., Thorne 1986: 113–19, 144–61).

[18] The Dutch practiced "indirect rule" in Indonesia (see, e.g., Emerson 1937; Furnivall 1948), with elites occupying important administrative posts at the local level; these elites, however, lacked the independent political influence of their counterparts in the Philippines and Malaya.

Conclusion

If the specific character of prewar Western rule and of the Japanese occupation of each Southeast Asian colony determined where Communist parties would be able to mobilize mass followings in the postwar period, these factors are certainly not sufficient to explain whether these mass-based insurgencies would succeed in actually seizing state power. The following chapter, accordingly, attempts to explain the distinctive outcomes of the three postwar Communist insurgencies in the region.

4

The Only Domino: The Vietnamese
Revolution in Comparative Perspective

*A measured response to the convulsion in Viet Nam could have been devised by the
French; they could have created institutions granting power to indigenous citizens and
permitting them opportunities for political mobilization on French terms, but this
appeared to be unnecessary and the institutions seemed difficult beyond comprehension to
construct. For this miscalculation France was to pay a dear price.*
– John T. McAlister, Jr. (1969: 274)

*Indochina under the French was a prison, and there was nothing to do but unite against
the jailer.*
– Ngo Van, Trotskyist militant (quoted in Goldner 1997: 140)

This chapter, building on the previous one, attempts to explain the different *outcomes* of the transnational cycle of protest that erupted across
colonial Southeast Asia during the decade following World War II. I claim,
once again, that a state-centered approach best explains these outcomes. I
argue, more specifically, that the success or failure of Communist movements in actually seizing state power in this region was determined by the
specific characteristics of colonial (or neocolonial) rule in each national
society, particularly policies toward moderate nationalists. This chapter,
then, takes the existence of the Communist-led national liberation movements that emerged during and immediately after the Japanese occupation
of World War II as "given" for present purposes.

The analysis of this chapter reflects two growing concerns in recent
analyses of social movements. First, it shares with a number of recent
studies the goal of theorizing the outcomes or consequences of social
movements in addition to their origins or causes (see, e.g., Gamson 1975;
Giugni, McAdam, and Tilly 1999); since I am concerned in this book with
specifically revolutionary movements, I am particularly interested in why

106

only some of them – in fact, relatively few – actually seize state power. Second, it is assumed here that social movements are components of larger, perhaps transnational, "cycles of protest" (Tarrow 1994: ch. 9); in fact, all of the movements that I examine in this chapter emerged out the generalized crisis in Southeast Asia that was brought on by World War II. I have adopted a comparative perspective in order to contextualize the manner in which political contexts shape, and are shaped by, social movements. Such a perspective is also useful for detecting, and debunking, overgeneralized explanations of movement outcomes.

What are the outcomes that this chapter attempts to explain? During the 1940s, as we have seen, Communist parties organized strong, mass-based national liberation movements in opposition to Western colonial or neocolonial regimes in Vietnam, Malaya, and the Philippines. In fact, Western leaders feared that these countries (and others beyond) would fall like dominoes to Communists if decisive actions of one sort or another were not taken. Because Communists were quite powerful in all three countries, these fears cannot be dismissed as symptoms of Cold War paranoia. As we now know, however, Communists would successfully seize state power only in Vietnam, and only in the northern part of that country, during the decade following World War II.[1] The Communist insurgencies in Malaya and the Philippines, by contrast, were largely defeated by government-organized counterrevolutions by the mid-1950s. Why?

One simple "explanation" for the unique success of the Communist movement in Vietnam and the contrasting failure of those in Malaya and the Philippines is that the former movement grew to become a much larger and popular force than the latter two. Success or failure, in this view, was a simple function of the size or popularity of each movement. But there are two problems with this view. First, it simply reframes the question that we need to answer: *why* the Communist movement in Vietnam became so much larger and more popular than those in Malaya and the Philippines. In fact, from the perspective of 1944, for example, the subsequent success of the Vietnamese Communists would have been rather surprising. At that time, the movement in Vietnam was not substantially larger or more influential than that in Malaya or the Philippines. Second, this thesis overlooks

---

[1] Communist-led movements would eventually seize power in 1975 in South Vietnam, Cambodia, and Laos, but this is another story altogether. There would be no Communist "dominoes" in Southeast (or South) Asia outside of what was once French Indochina.

the fact that the success of social movements is determined by the nature of their foes as much as by their own popularity. A relatively powerful revolutionary movement, for example, may not be able to topple a strong state (witness El Salvador, which I discuss in later chapters), and even a tiny movement may be able to overthrow a weak one (witness the revolution in Grenada in 1979). More than this, the very *popularity* of revolutionaries – as this chapter, like the last, will argue – is strongly shaped by the structure and practices of the states that they confront.

The Communist movement in Vietnam, most analysts agree, was able to oust the French both because it expanded very rapidly following the war, forging a broad multiclass (and multiethnic) alliance, and because French political leaders eventually decided that the resulting costs of remaining in this distant colony – costs that were as much political as military or economic – far outweighed the benefits. Of course, French withdrawal from Vietnam may not have resulted in Communist rule, even in the northern half of that country, if a strong, non-Communist force had been able to step into the breach; but no such force existed. Analysts disagree, however, in their explanations of these facts. I shall argue here that both the popularity of Communists and the weakness of their non-Communist rivals resulted primarily from the French failure to initiate a reformist process of decolonization "from above" – such as occurred in Malaya and the Philippines – either before or after the war.

By contrast, the Communist movements in Malaya and the Philippines *failed* to expand their influence significantly beyond certain lower classes and/or ethnic groups; the costs of counterrevolution in these countries were therefore much lower than in Vietnam, and they were borne to a much larger extent by collaborating sectors of the indigenous population, which were much stronger than in Vietnam. In my view, the containment of the Communist movements in Malaya and the Philippines resulted primarily from the fact that British and American colonial (or successor neocolonial) regimes initiated a process of decolonization that devolved political power to moderate nationalists, beginning either before (as in the Philippines) or after the war (as in Malaya); in this process, these regimes introduced key reforms that weakened the appeal of revolutionaries, especially democratic elections and a more discriminate use of military force against the insurgents.

One can only speculate as to whether a similar process of decolonization "from above" – particularly *after* the war, when Communists emerged as an especially powerful force – would have prevented a Communist revolution in Vietnam. Still, a more concerted French effort to strengthen non-Communist nationalists might have created a more pluralistic civil society (and significantly reduced the costs of counterrevolution in the process). The Communist Party would undoubtedly have remained a powerful force in Vietnam, but it might not have remained virtually the only one that could realistically claim to represent the interests of the Vietnamese people.

I will develop this state-centered explanation of the success and failure of Southeast Asian insurgencies in more detail after reviewing the history of these insurgencies through the mid-1950s. I also offer some speculation as to the causes of those variations in colonial rule in Southeast Asia that my account of movement outcomes emphasizes. Again, my intent here is not to propose a single-factor "statist" theory of revolutions, but to rethink the process by which a variety of factors (and *combinations* of factors) – including economic grievances, nationalist aspirations, and vanguard parties – may potentially cause revolutions when embedded in conducive political contexts (see Tilly 1993: 7–9). I spell out this view of revolutionary causation more fully in the conclusion to this chapter.

Vietnam

After a series of complex maneuvers and abortive negotiations in the year following the Second World War, what would become a bloody, nine-year struggle began in earnest in Vietnam between the French and the Viet Minh, the Communist-led national liberation front. After pulling out of Hanoi in late 1946, the Viet Minh concentrated its efforts over the following two years on building up popular support in "liberated areas" in the countryside, avoiding, whenever possible, major military engagements with the French.[2] In the immediate postwar period, the Viet Minh also attempted to eliminate rival nationalist and leftist groups, such as they were, that refused to cooperate with them, including Trotskyists, who had been influential in Saigon during the late 1930s (Goldner 1997). A rebellion in the French colony of Madagascar, significantly, prevented the French from reinforcing their own troops in early 1947, when the Viet Minh was most vulnerable.

---

[2] Good accounts of the First Indochina War may be found in Hammer 1955, Lancaster 1974 (1961), Buttinger 1967 (vol. 2), Duiker 1981, Dunn 1985, and Lockhart 1989.

Until 1953, the Viet Minh adhered to a "national liberation" program that explicitly deemphasized class struggle: "there was to be no redistribution of land to any great extent," notes one observer, "and agricultural collectivization was entirely out of the question" (Pluvier 1974: 463–4). In areas that it controlled, the Viet Minh seized land owned by French colonists or Vietnamese collaborators, but the Viet Minh focused its agrarian program on modest rent and interest reductions so as not to alienate rich peasants and even "patriotic landlords," who played a surprisingly large role in the movement.

France, meanwhile, struggled to reestablish a stable form of political rule in Vietnam with at least some indigenous support. The United States, while strongly backing the French war effort, encouraged the French to transfer power to a formally independent, anti-Communist regime so as to undermine the nationalist appeal of the Viet Minh. The result of this pressure was the notorious "Bao Dai solution." After several years of negotiations, the French announced, in December 1949, the creation of an "Associated State of Vietnam," headed by Emperor Bao Dai. (Bao Dai had actually abdicated during the August Revolution of 1945, and he briefly served as an "adviser" to the Communist-dominated Democratic Republic of Vietnam [DRV].) The United States recognized the State of Vietnam on February 7, 1950, just weeks after the new Communist regime in China – soon followed by the Soviet Union – recognized the DRV.

The French, however, never intended the Bao Dai regime to be a genuinely independent government (much to the disgruntlement of certain U.S. officials), and it had strictly limited powers, primarily within the areas of education, social services, and local police matters. Military and economic policy remained the exclusive preserve of the French. In 1953, a French parliamentary commission went so far as to describe the colonial regime in Vietnam as a "veritable dictatorship . . . without limit and without control" (quoted in O'Neill 1968: 31). The municipal elections that were held in early 1953 were a fiasco – residents of less than 10 percent of the villages in the northern Red River delta were allowed or able to vote – and the provincial and national elections scheduled for late 1953 were simply aborted. "The 'Bao Dai solution' did provide an alternative to Ho Chi Minh's government," notes William Duiker, "but most nationalists viewed it as simply a creation of French colonialism" (Duiker 1983: 43). Even the French referred to Bao Dai's ministers as "puppets" (Lockhart 1989: 212).

French military operations against the Viet Minh during this time were indiscriminately brutal and heavy-handed in the extreme:

Thanks to the fantastic amounts of U.S. aid that came pouring in [after 1950], air raids of the liberated areas became more frequent and destructive. Irrigation works and dikes were intentionally destroyed in order to create famine in the liberated areas. "Sweep-and-clean" operations by re-equipped mobile units were launched more often, causing widespread devastation and deaths to the civilian population. (Long 1991b: 24–5.)

As a result of such actions, not only were anti-French sentiments reinforced among the Vietnamese, but opposition to the "dirty war" in Vietnam also began to build in France, particularly after 1948, when the strong Communist Party there adopted a more radical political line (it had originally supported the reimposition of French rule in Indochina). In fact, while French forces in Vietnam were extraordinarily (and counterproductively) violent, a succession of governments in Paris proved "unwilling to provide adequate support to [the] military commanders in Indochina and, in consequence, French military policy continued to be caught between an offensive and defensive posture" (Duiker 1981: 150). Popular opposition to an expanded conscription in France prompted French authorities to create, in 1950, an indigenous Vietnamese "national army," the Army of the Republic of Vietnam (ARVN).

The Viet Minh scored its first major military victories in the summer of 1950, driving the French out of many of their bases on a route along the Chinese border – the "street without joy," as the French called it. (Martial law was promptly imposed in Hanoi as a result.) These victories, however, were followed by a number of defeats in 1951 and 1952, as the French expeditionary force in Vietnam was expanded to some one hundred ninety thousand troops (only sixty thousand of whom were native Frenchmen), in addition to the ARVN's muster of one hundred thousand.

Although the conflict was apparently stalemated in the early 1950s, two events tipped the balance of power in Vietnam toward the Communist side. First, the Communist leadership decided to organize a mass-mobilization campaign with the goal of implementing existing decrees on rent and interest reductions much more vigorously. (Substantial land redistribution, however, did not occur until after 1954.) This campaign, organized according to the Chinese Communist model, generated much popular enthusiasm for the Viet Minh, especially among poor and landless peasants (see White 1983a; Kolko 1985: ch. 4). For its part, "the Bao Dai government had no interest in reducing the power of the landlords"; on the contrary, military operations by French or ARVN forces "to 'clear and hold' Viet Minh villages would secure the villages for the return of the landlords or their agents" (White 1983a: 208–9).

The second event that worked to the advantage of the Viet Minh was the armistice in Korea in 1953. This made it possible for China, which had intervened in the Korean conflict, to double the amount of arms it was sending to Vietnam and to send heavier weaponry (and more instructors) as well. By 1953, in fact, the Viet Minh had developed a well-equipped regular army of some one hundred and twenty-five thousand troops, "territorial units" with another seventy-five thousand members, and village militias with between two hundred thousand and three hundred and fifty thousand members. As a result of the Viet Minh's popularity and armed might, the French/Bao Dai forces were never able to control more than a third of Vietnam's territory (mainly urban areas), and they were completely unable to dislodge the Viet Minh from the countryside. "[T]he French command just did not have sufficient men to keep most of the country pacified *and* defeat Giap's army" (Fairbairn 1974: 195; emphasis in original). The map prepared in May 1953 for General Henri Navarre, commander in chief of French forces in Vietnam, reveals the difficult situation of the French in the northern, central, and southern regions of the country alike (see Map 4.1). "Under Secretary of State Walter Bedell Smith informed Congress [in 1954] that the Viet Minh already controlled three-quarters of the country and, had elections been held, Ho Chi Minh would have won 80 percent of the vote" (Kahin 1987: 53). When Ho Chi Minh – who had no illusions about the possibility of defeating militarily the much wealthier and better-armed French – proposed peace talks in late 1953, the French soon accepted.

On May 7, 1954, the day before the peace talks on Indochina were to begin in Geneva, the Viet Minh inflicted a monumental defeat on the French at the battle of Dien Bien Phu. After a bloody six-week siege, the Vietnamese captured French positions with a mass assault; in all, some fifteen hundred French troops were killed at Dien Bien Phu, four thousand wounded, and another eleven thousand taken prisoner. An estimated twenty thousand to twenty-five thousand Vietnamese were killed or wounded.[3] This stunning victory was a result both of the Viet Minh's domestic popularity and external support. On the one hand, over two

---

[3] During the entire war, more than seventy thousand French troops were killed (including approximately twenty-one thousand Frenchmen). Vietnamese casualties are estimated at a half million killed and one million wounded (Harrison 1982: 124).

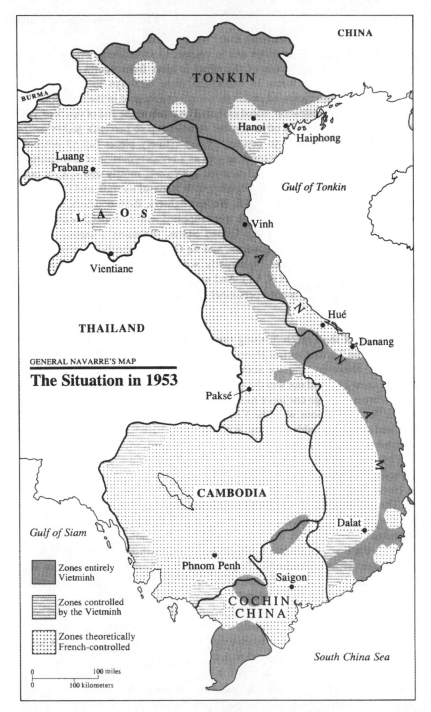

CHINA

TONKIN

BURMA

Hanoi

Haiphong

Gulf of Tonkin

Luang
Prabang

L A O S

Vinh

Vientiane

THAILAND

Hué

Danang

GENERAL NAVARRE'S MAP

The Situation in 1953

Paksé

CAMBODIA

Dalat

Gulf of Siam

Zones entirely
Vietminh

Phnom Penh

Saigon

Zones controlled
by the Vietminh

COCHIN
CHINA

Zones theoretically
French-controlled

South China Sea

0   100 miles
0   100 kilometers

Map 4.1 General Navarre's map, May 1953. From *Intervention* by George McT. Kahin. Copyright © 1986 Knopf. Reprinted with permission.

hundred thousand peasants were mobilized by the Viet Minh to build roads, carry supplies, or actually fight at Dien Bien Phu:

All through the North, women and men mobilized to transport dismantled how-itzers and mortars (American in the main, captured by the Chinese in Korea), tons of ammunition, and rice by bicycle and shoulder pole. . . . Roped to the heaviest artillery pieces, men dragged the guns through the last 50-mile stretch of jungle where no roads could be built. (Young 1991: 32–3)

On the other hand (as the preceding quote makes clear), "The Vietminh attack had been made possible by massive shipments of arms from China" (Duiker 1983: 46).

At Geneva, French and DRV representatives agreed to a cease-fire and to the division of the country into two "regroupment" zones pending national elections in 1956 (which were never held due to U.S. opposition). The Viet Minh and their supporters regrouped in the northern part of the country, above the seventeenth parallel, while the French and supporters of the Bao Dai government regrouped in the south, including most Catholics living in the north. (The accord also called for all foreign forces to quit the country, and restricted both zones from joining a military alliance or allowing the establishing foreign military bases within their territory.)

While the agreement to partition Vietnam temporarily at the seven-teenth parallel was an enormous compromise for the Viet Minh – given its strength in the central and southern regions of the country as well as in the north[4] – it obviously represented a substantial victory as well: After eight decades of brutal colonial rule, the French finally pulled out of Vietnam, and the Viet Minh became the de facto sovereign power in the northern part of the country.[5] Try as it might, moreover, the United States was never able to establish a southern state with significant popular support. Indeed, the subsequent defeat of the United States and its local allies (in what Americans came to call the "Vietnam War" and Vietnamese the "American War") was prepared to a significant extent by the Viet Minh in the period prior to 1954 (see, e.g., Race 1972; Kiernan 1992).

---

[4] After Dien Bien Phu, "it was generally accepted that the DRV controlled 80% of the population and 75% of the country" (Lockhart 1989: 264).

[5] The Viet Minh was under a great deal of Soviet and especially Chinese pressure to accept the compromise at Geneva. The Chinese, fearful of an American invasion, were anxious to see an internationally recognized state in at least northern Vietnam that would serve – like the North Korean regime – as a "buffer" against the United States.

Malaya

The Malayan rebellion – or "Emergency," as it was officially known – contrasts sharply with the Vietnamese in that the Communist-led Malayan Races Liberation Army (MRLA), from its founding in 1949, encountered much greater difficulties than the Viet Minh in mobilizing popular support and external assistance for its armed struggle against the British colonial regime.[6] The MRLA was certainly a mass-based movement, and its sizable constituency "seemed to offer a fair chance of a successful insurrection" (Short 1975: 254). The MRLA grew to include perhaps ten thousand armed guerrillas at is peak, and the affiliated Min Yuen, or "People's Movement" – a clandestine organization established by the Malayan Communist Party in cities and towns to recruit volunteers, supply the guerrillas, and spread propaganda – had a membership of at least twenty thousand and perhaps as many as sixty thousand. In addition, it has been estimated that more than half a million people (out of a total population of five million) may have supported the guerrillas in one way or another (Caldwell 1977b: 231).

The insurgents, however, found it extremely difficult to obtain support outside the ethnic Chinese population in Malaya. As a result, and because of the Communist Party's decision in 1948 to relocate to the countryside in order to fight a rural guerrilla insurgency, the MRLA became increasingly dependent upon communities of Chinese squatters settled near the jungles. These communities had supported the Communist-led Malayan People's Anti-Japanese Army (MPAJA) during the war, and the Communist Party vigorously opposed subsequent British efforts to evict them.

The British, consequently, implemented the Briggs Plan in 1950 (named after the British high commissioner, General Sir Harold Briggs), which eventually resulted in the forced resettlement of more than half a million Chinese squatters into approximately four hundred "new villages" (see Short 1975: chs. 7–9). The British also resettled many plantation and mine workers, ordering that "all workers and their families who were living on land owned by the mines and estates ... be moved and assembled within barbed wire compounds" (Renick 1965: 12). Official internment camps eventually housed another eleven thousand known or suspected collaborators of the MRLA. In July 1951, moreover, the British initiated

---

[6] Useful accounts of the Malayan "Emergency" may be found in O'Ballance 1966, Short 1975, Caldwell 1977b, and Stubbs 1989.

Operation Starvation, intensifying their inspection of rice transports in order to prevent food from being smuggled to the guerrillas from the cities. In implementing these various policies, the British could count on a forty-thousand-man colonial army (which included Australians, Fijians, Africans, and Gurkhas), a police force of some seventy thousand (mainly ethnic Malay), and a paramilitary "home guard" of another two hundred and twenty-five thousand. The British also received arms and helicopters from the United States (Caldwell 1977b: 233, 246).

The MRLA was thus gradually cut off from its main source of recruits, supplies, and information. The MRLA also failed to receive significant foreign assistance; unlike the Viet Minh, it did not enjoy access to a border with China or any other sympathetic state. Morale and discipline gradually became serious problems, and insurgents began to surrender. Moreover, "the occasional execution of Party members and supporters suspected of being 'politically unreliable' eroded people's confidence in the MCP and its cause" (Stubbs 1989: 189). The British even paid one member of the MCP Politburo nearly half a million dollars to surrender; he provided authorities with information that led to the arrest of 183 rebels, which "all but broke the back of all MRLA activity in southern Malaya" (O'Ballance 1966: 161). All told, 6,710 rebels were killed during the Emergency, 2,810 were wounded, and another 3,989 were captured or surrendered; on the government side, 1,865 were killed and 2,560 wounded (O'Ballance 1966: 177).

Despite its primarily ethnic Chinese composition, moreover, the insurgency failed to win the support of the larger Chinese population in Malaya. In February 1949, the same month as the MRLA was formed, Chinese businesspeople, strongly encouraged by the British, formed the Malayan Chinese Association (MCA). The creation of the MCA "was the outcome of the realization that the communist victory in China forced the Malayan Chinese to focus their loyalty upon Malaya and that a political structure was needed to take care of them" (Pluvier 1974: 533). In March 1953, the MCA, again encouraged by the British administration, agreed to form the Alliance with the United Malays National Organization (UMNO), the dominant political force in the ethnic Malay community, to pursue independence through peaceful means. "The Alliance was certainly not revolutionary or anti-British; it was very moderate, politically, and conservative, socially, and in its heart not disloyal to the colonial authorities" (Pluvier 1974: 541).

British sponsorship of the Alliance, in fact, was part of a larger counterrevolutionary strategy of transferring formal political power to "responsible" Malayan elites in order to deprive the Communists of the nationalist issue. As early as 1948, self-rule was held to be the eventual goal of the newly created Federation of Malaya.[7] In 1951, a system of local government through elected bodies was established, and municipal elections were held in Kuala Lumpur in February 1952. And in July 1953 elections were held for a Legislative Council, with the Alliance of the UMNO, MCA, and MIC (the predominantly petit-bourgeois Malayan Indian Congress) winning fifty-one of the fifty-two contested seats (another forty-six seats were appointed by the British). The small but powerful British settler community did not vigorously oppose the gradual transfer of power to this conservative alliance.

The colonial state, furthermore, became much less abusive of civilians after Sir Gerald Templer – who introduced the notion of "winning the hearts and minds" of ordinary folk – was appointed high commissioner in early 1952. Following Templer's arrival, "the essentially military approach to counter-insurgency was replaced by more of a political approach which sought to address many of the grievances of the population, thereby depriving the communist guerrillas of their base of support" (Stubbs 1997: 59). Indeed, it was at this time that the Briggs Plan "really began to bear fruit" (Stubbs 1997: 61):

Templer ordered that the new villages should be provided with services and amenities such as agricultural land, schools, roads, drains, public health facilities, places of public worship and community centres. . . . Templer's strategy, which stressed addressing the grievances of the rural Malay-Chinese so that their interest in supporting the communist guerrillas waned, proved successful. (Stubbs 1997: 61)

Templer also implemented Operation Service, an attempt to reform the colonial police that "exceeded initial expectations. Because of better training, and the new equipment sent from Britain . . . the police gained confidence in their own abilities, were less ill-disposed towards the general public, and less inclined to treat all Chinese as suspects" (Stubbs 1989: 157, 166; see also Short 1975: 160–6). Despite opposition from sectors of the armed forces, a series of well-publicized amnesties for guerrillas were also proclaimed (O'Ballance 1966: 150–9, 174).

The precariousness of the Communist insurgency was strikingly revealed at the December 1955 meetings between the MCP leader Chin

[7] This federation was itself created largely in response to ethnic Malay agitation against Britain's attempt to impose a more centralized and exclusionary "union" on Malaya after the war (see, e.g., Stockwell 1977; Lau 1991; Stubbs 1997).

Peng and Malayan and British officials. The Communists, whose ranks had been depleted by death and desertion, offered to put down their arms if the MCP were legalized. (The offer was turned down.) During the late 1950s, the rebels were forced to look for support among Malaya's sparse aboriginal population, which lived in exceedingly isolated jungle areas, a move that only further marginalized the movement (Leary 1995). The Emergency was not officially terminated until 1960, but the Communist insurgency was all but defeated when Malaya attained formal independence on August 31, 1957. From the British perspective, notes Malcolm Caldwell, "The expense and ferocity of the 'Emergency' had paid off": "at independence, 75 per cent of all rubber plantation acreage was in European (mostly British) hands, along with 61 per cent of all tin production, and 75 per cent of all services and trade" (Caldwell 1977b: 251).

The Philippines

Like their Malayan comrades, Philippine Communists also found it difficult to exploit the nationalist issue during the postwar Huk rebellion, in part because the United States granted formal independence to the archipelago very shortly after the war. The Communist Party did not have a great deal of success in politicizing the existence of vast U.S. economic assets or extensive U.S. military bases in the islands. In fact, although American advisers from the Joint U.S. Military Advisory Group (JUSMAG) played an important role in conceiving and implementing the government's counterinsurgency, American troops were never introduced into the conflict.

The Huk rebellion fared particularly poorly after Ramon Magsaysay – a protégé of the American CIA – was named minister of defense in September 1950. The following month, the Philippine government arrested most of the Communist Party leadership in Manila, including party leader Jose Lava. (One observer has called this "probably the greatest Intelligence success in the history of counter-insurgency" [Fairbairn 1974: 171].) With massive U.S. aid, Magsaysay reorganized and retrained the Philippine armed forces during the early 1950s, resulting in a more discriminate use of force against the Huk insurgents. (The Huks, for their part, received no significant external assistance.) Magsaysay merged the twenty-two-thousand-man Philippine Constabulary with the army, which included another thirty-three thousand troops, thereby creating a single chain of command. In addition, special "Battalion Combat Teams" were formed that were more mobile than traditional military companies and that American advisers trained in counterguerrilla warfare (see Kerkvliet 1977: 192–3, 240–1).

The regular pay and feeding of troops were also instituted under Magsaysay, and the "civilian guards" – essentially the private armies of large landowners who were notorious for their mistreatment of villagers – were disbanded. Magsaysay described his policy toward the guerrillas as one of "all-out force and all-out fellowship" in order to underline the leniency that would be shown to those Huks who surrendered. These reforms seem to have been particularly effective: "The great majority of Huks," as Jesus Lava later noted, took up arms in the first place "because of repression by the Philippine government, American soldiers, and civilian guards. Many felt it was either join or be killed without at least putting up a fight" (quoted in Kerkvliet 1977: 227).

Philippine elections of the early 1950s were also marked by less fraud and violence than those of the immediate postwar period. Both the local elections of 1951 and the presidential election of 1953 were relatively peaceful. Magsaysay himself, whom Geoffrey Fairbairn has called "the only counter-insurgent to acquire the status of hero in the eyes of large numbers of people" (Fairbairn 1974: 170), was elected president in 1953, obtaining more than 70 percent of the vote in Central Luzon, the Huk heartland. Huk leaders themselves later acknowledged that peasants had come to see "elections as alternatives to rebellion" (Kerkvliet 1977: 238).

The Philippine government also began to implement at this time a number of modest yet symbolically important economic reforms, many aimed specifically at the sharecropping peasants of Luzon, the principal social base of the Huk rebellion:

They included agricultural extension services, cash credit for peasants, barrio health clinics, agrarian courts to hear grievances between tenants and landlords, new bridges and roads, several hundred "liberty wells," and irrigation canals. Between 1952 and 1955 the government devoted far more attention and money to rural public works and agrarian reform than it had during the previous six years. (Kerkvliet 1977: 238–9)

While minister of defense, moreover, Magsaysay promised homestead lands to Huks who surrendered to the government. The Economic Development Corps (EDCOR) program that he established actually resettled less than two hundred and fifty guerrillas and their families onto lands on the southern island of Mindanao. Still, the program stole from the Huks "the idea of 'land for the landless' with a well-publicized experiment that was more than the Huk movement itself had been able to do" (Kerkvliet 1977: 239; see also Scaff 1955). Magsaysay's reforms, in sum, while stopping well short of a major land reform in Luzon – in fact, no land at all was redistributed there – and while not disturbing the neocolonial relationship with the United States, nevertheless "played on the peasantry's hope that revolt was no longer necessary" (Kerkvliet 1977: 240).

With the implementation of these economic, military, and political reforms, the Huk insurgency was not only unable to break out of its traditional stronghold in Central Luzon, but also began to disintegrate there after 1951. The Philippine military claimed that between 1950 and 1955 it killed over six thousand Huks and captured forty-seven hundred; another ninety-five hundred took advantage of its amnesty offers (Kerkvliet 1977: 245):

By 1953, the movement's remaining leaders were powerless to prevent even larger numbers of armed peasants from leaving. And few peasants now joined the Huks, unlike in the past, to replace those who lay dead in the rice fields and on the mountain slopes. By 1955–1956, only widely scattered handfuls of desperate rebels remained. (Kerkvliet 1977: 234)

As the insurgency dwindled, a split developed within the Communist Party over the issue of negotiations to end the rebellion. Luis Taruc, the best-known guerrilla commander, openly favored negotiations, and he was suspended from the party in November 1953 for allegedly violating "democratic centralism" (Saulo 1990: ch. 11). The following May – ironically, the same month as the battle of Dien Bien Phu – Taruc voluntarily surrendered to Philippine government officials. (A young journalist by the name of Benigno Aquino, Jr., acted as mediator between Taruc and the government.) A "surrender epidemic" then ensued, with even "top-ranking party cadres and Huk commanders [giving] up without a struggle" (Saulo 1990: 181).

Accounting for Movement Outcomes: Variations in Colonial Rule

What accounts for the radically different outcomes of the postwar Communist insurgencies in Southeast Asia? Why did a Communist-led national liberation movement successfully seize power in Vietnam, but fail in Malaya and the Philippines? After all, as Brian Crozier has noted, the Communist insurgencies in Malaya and the Philippines, "at the outset at least, had a very real chance of success" (Crozier 1968: 73). In this section, I develop the argument that the uneven success of revolutionary movements in Southeast Asia was primarily determined by the specific character of Western colonial rule (and of succeeding neocolonial regimes) in the region.

It cannot be argued that Vietnamese Communists faced opponents who were any less formidable or ruthless than those that their counterparts elsewhere confronted. On the contrary, the French had many more troops at their disposal in Vietnam than the British in Malaya or the Philippine government. Conversely, the defeat of the insurgencies in Malaya and the Philippines would not appear easily attributable – as some have suggested[8] – to British or American intervention. After all, the French also intervened, and intervened massively, in Vietnam, but with considerably less success. Why?

Most analysts, not surprisingly, attribute the success of the Viet Minh to its greater popularity compared to the other Communist-led movements in Southeast Asia (see, e.g., Caldwell 1970: 83). Vietnamese Communists certainly succeeded in organizing a much larger and more broadly based insurgent coalition than Malayan or Filipino Communists, who were unable to expand beyond their traditional ethnic and/or class constituencies (i.e., the Chinese working class and squatters in Malaya and the sharecropping peasants of Luzon in the Philippines). Moreover, many observers correctly attribute this greater popularity of Vietnamese Communists (at least in part) to their more thorough domination of the nationalist cause compared to the other Communist movements in the region. Milton Osborne, for example, suggests that "if one is seeking to gain some understanding of why Communist-led revolts failed in the Philippines and Malaya but in part succeeded . . . in Viet-Nam, close attention must be given to the way in which neither the Huks nor Malaya's Chinese insurgents could convincingly claim the nationalist mantle" (Osborne 1970: 110). The crucial issue, however, which has received much less analysis, is exactly *why* this was the case. *Why* were Communists in Vietnam so much more successful than their counterparts in Malaya and the Philippines in mobilizing – and *arming* – masses of people for the cause of national liberation?

[8] For example, both Jesus Lava (1979: 77) and William Pomeroy (1978: 515), an American Communist who fought with the Huks, attribute the Huk defeat primarily to U.S. intervention in the Philippines.

121

In attempting to answer this question, one might begin with the common observation that the Vietnamese people (especially compared to the more ethnically heterogeneous populations of most other Southeast Asian countries) have a particularly well-developed national identity, shaped in large part through their historic conflicts not only with the French, but also with China – conflicts that stretch back over many centuries. But while the strong national identity of the Vietnamese may partly explain the strength of anti-French feeling in that country, it does not explain why *Communists* in particular (indeed, *armed* Communists), and not some other type of political leadership, came to lead the anticolonial struggle there.

As we have seen, moreover, ethnic minorities, and not just ethnic Vietnamese, were actually a very important component of the Viet Minh coalition (see McAlister 1967); this suggests that "resentment of French intrusion and abuses was so great that it could outweigh any feelings of mistrust that these minorities might have had against the Vietnamese" (Elliott 1974: 30). What needs to be explained, then, is not so much the strong sense of Vietnamese national identity as the specifically (and intensely) anti-French grievances among a variety of ethnic groups *and* the ability of Communists, in particular, to harness these grievances (among others) to an armed and radical, as opposed to conservative or reformist, movement.

Might the availability of external material assistance account for the variable success of the insurgencies in Southeast Asia? In part, yes. After all, the unsuccessful insurgencies in Malaya and the Philippines received little if any such aid. And foreign aid was very important, as we have seen, in contributing to the victory of the Communists in Vietnam – at Dien Bien Phu in particular. Thanks to the Communist triumph in China (and to Vietnam's long border with that country), large amounts of foreign arms and matériel began to flow into Vietnam after 1950 and especially after the Korean armistice in 1953. (It bears emphasizing, however, that this aid did not nearly approach the levels of external assistance to the Viet Minh's adversaries.)

External aid to the Viet Minh, however, would have been ineffectual or even useless (and probably not proffered in the first place) had it been unable to mobilize so many people so effectively against the French – and so many more people than their non-Communist rivals. (In fact, the much less popular postwar Communist movement in Burma, which also received significant aid from neighboring China, was effectively contained by non-Communist nationalists [see Bagley 1974; Smith 1991: pt. 2].) It is also far from certain (although here we must speculate) that the Viet Minh, given its broad popular backing, would have proven unable to wage an effective protracted guerrilla struggle against the French *without* external aid. Kahin and Lewis (1967: 30) point out that the Viet Minh "had gained the military initiative well before the communists came to power in China. Their military strength against the French was already clearly established before they were able to secure even modest military assistance from Communist China."

My own thesis is that Vietnamese Communists were able to expand the ranks of their followers quite dramatically during the postwar decade, more or less dominating the nationalist cause in Vietnam, primarily because of the counterproductive policies of the French imperialists whom they confronted. Neither before nor after the war did France introduce the sort of political reforms, including steps toward decolonization or "home rule," that might have undermined the appeal of armed revolutionaries or bolstered the power and influence of more conservative political forces. On the contrary, France's authoritarian and often brutally repressive policies unintentionally encouraged the further growth of the Viet Minh and rendered more moderate leaders – at least those who were not themselves radicalized by French policies – largely irrelevant or illegitimate.

Eventually, confronted by the expansion of the Viet Minh, growing military losses, domestic opposition to the war, and international pressures to decolonize, France abandoned its colonial project in Southeast Asia at Geneva. The only popular indigenous political force capable of filling the vacuum – in either northern or southern Vietnam – was the Viet Minh. As we have seen, in fact, the Geneva accords effectively ratified the Viet Minh's hegemony north of the seventeenth parallel. The United States – which was not a party to the Geneva accords – proceeded to underwrite a separate southern state with massive financial and military assistance, but that state's rule was never popular and always dependent on U.S. largesse (see, e.g., Kolko 1985; Young 1991).

In retrospect, it would appear that the historic "mistake" of French imperialists (and of the Dutch in Indonesia), and the source of their vulnerability in Vietnam following World War II, was their failure (unlike the Americans in the Philippines and the British in Malaya) to preserve or to create a moderate, anti-Communist political leadership to whom they could transfer state power without jeopardizing imperial economic or strategic interests. This failure, however, was implicit in the authoritarian and repressive form of colonial rule that France exercised in Vietnam. Perhaps Ho Chi Minh put it best: "If the French colonialists are unskillful in developing colonial resources, they are masters in the art of savage repression. . . . The Gandhis and the De Valeras would have long since entered heaven had they been born in one of the French colonies" (quoted in Fall 1967c: 27).[9] In fact, by failing to tolerate (or to sponsor proactively) moderate nationalist political parties, French colonialism quite inadvertently produced its own gravediggers in Southeast Asia. "[T]he pitiless suppression of [moderate] Vietnamese political parties by the French," notes one author, favored "clandestine organizations totally dedicated to the forceful overthrow of colonial authority" (Duiker 1976: 184).

In fact, in the political context of colonial Vietnam, even an ideologically moderate political party could feel compelled to take up arms against the French. The Viet Nam Quoc Dan Dang (VNQDD) or Vietnamese Nationalist Party, loosely modeled on the Chinese Kuomintang, attempted to incite an armed rebellion by Vietnamese soldiers at Yen Bay in northern Vietnam in February 1930. They were quickly defeated, however, and survivors were forced to flee to China. The Nationalists were never again a significant political force in Vietnam – or a viable alternative to the Communists.

Soon after the Yen Bay fiasco, the French parliament debated colonial policy in Vietnam:

The Socialist Party argued for gradual decolonisation, with practical emphasis on identifying and nurturing those native elements most committed to "modern civilization" and most likely to participate voluntarily in some post-colonial relationship with France. The right-wing coalition then in government called instead for a revitalisation of colonial institutions, so that the rural Indochinese economy would prosper, peasants would turn a deaf ear to Communist propaganda and all anticolonial malcontents would be either silenced or eliminated. (Marr 1981: 164–5)

The right-wing position was supported by leading colonial officials, who argued that "the government should be looking to recent Dutch success in crushing the Indonesian Communist Party [in 1926–7] rather than

---

[9] Ho may be exaggerating the comparatively benign nature of British imperialism. The Irish nationalist leader Eamon de Valera would almost certainly have been executed by the British – along with most of the other leaders of the Easter Rising of 1916 – were it not for his American citizenship.

being led astray by reference to the British dominions" (Marr 1981: 165). The Socialist proposal was defeated, and there would not be a similar debate in the French parliament until after World War II. By then, however, thanks in large part to the Japanese occupation, France confronted a formidable revolutionary movement in Vietnam.

Coopted or suppressed, then, "nationalist reformists had almost disappeared as a political force in Vietnam" as early as the 1930s (Duiker 1976: 178). The Viet Minh's domination of the nationalist movement was greatly facilitated by this absence of any alternative non-Communist political leadership with a nationwide organization.[10] (George Modelski has suggested that "the major element in [the Viet Minh's] success was the weakness of their opponents" [Modelski 1964: 201].) In the Vietnamese political context, in sum, *only* an armed and clandestine revolutionary movement such as the Viet Minh could possibly have liberated the Vietnamese from French rule after the war. That Communists successfully met this challenge speaks to their impressive strategic skills and political commitment. However, that challenge itself was an inadvertent gift from the French.

In Malaya and the Philippines, by contrast, colonial policies eventually undermined rather than enhanced the appeal of revolutionaries. The Communist-led movements in these countries were effectively contained by reforms "from above" and gradual transitions to formal independence. Elections in these countries provided a more effective and less dangerous means for influencing state policies – including the winning of independence itself – than armed insurrection. Moreover, the increasingly discriminate use of force against the insurgents limited the number of people who, fearing military abuses, joined the guerrillas for purposes of self-defense. Neocolonial elites – that is, pro-Western, moderate political leaders, primarily from propertied classes – were the main beneficiaries of these processes.

In Malaya, as we have seen, the British counterinsurgency succeeded primarily because the Communist-led MRLA was unable to expand its base beyond the Chinese working-class and squatter communities. What

---

[10] The Viet Minh's main rivals in southern Vietnam (with the exception of the Trotskyists) were not political parties, but syncretic religious movements whose populist economic programs attracted large peasant followings. These groups, however, did not exercise much influence beyond a few regional enclaves and were uninterested in seizing state power (see Popkin 1979; Tai 1983).

125

accounts for this fatal weakness of the Malayan Communist movement? Why was the Communist Party – which certainly *attempted*, from all accounts, to lead a multiethnic struggle against the British – unable to mobilize the ethnic Malay population?

The British ruled Malaya in a comparatively liberal and inclusionary fashion, preserving much of the traditional status and prerogatives of the Malay aristocracy and sultans (see, e.g., Emerson 1937; Hua Wu Yin 1983). The British also actively promoted Malay employment in the civil service – and legally restricted access to such positions, in fact, to the ethnic Malay population (in effect, the educated Malay elite) (Yeo Kim Wah 1980). Even in the ferment of the immediate postwar period, consequently, "Anti-colonial sentiments hardly existed among non-communist Malayan political leaders" (Pluvier 1974: 467).

The British also relied mainly on Chinese and Indian laborers to work their mines and plantations (see, e.g., Caldwell 1977a); they were particularly concerned with preserving the Malay peasantry and isolating it from other "racial" groups. The Malay Reservations Act of 1913 set aside special "Malay" lands for rice production (in part to feed the colony's growing population) and legally prohibited the sale of such lands to non-Malays.

During the war years, moreover, the Japanese maintained this policy of indirect rule and preferential treatment of ethnic Malays. "[D]ue to the Japanese policy of ingratiating themselves primarily with the Malays," in fact, the Malay community "had few reasons to be anti-Japanese" (Pluvier 1974: 299). Consequently, the anti-Japanese resistance in Malaya consisted almost exclusively of ethnic Chinese. Violent postwar clashes between Communists and ethnic Malays suspected of collaborating with the Japanese drove a further wedge between the Communists and the Malay community; according to one scholar, these clashes "proved to be a disaster, dashing any hope [the Communists] may have had of gaining support among all of Malaya's racial groups" (Stubbs 1989: 45).[11] Moreover, the gradual movement toward Malayan independence in the postwar period also undermined the popularity of the guerrillas among both the Malay *and* Chinese populations, since the elections that were central to this process appeared to be an effective alternative to armed struggle.

---

[11] Another scholar notes that "so chauvinistically Chinese was the orientation and style of the MCP/MPAJA that they came to be called by many Malays simply 'the Chinese Party'" (Stenson 1980: 107–8).

Accounting for Movement Outcomes: Variations in Colonial Rule

Had British rule been more or less equally repressive for all ethnic groups (and classes) in Malaya; had the British not sponsored or tolerated moderate political groups such as the UMNO and MCA; and had the British not initiated a transition to Malayan self-government – in short, had the British acted more like the French in Vietnam – then the Communists just might have been more successful in expanding their following beyond lower-class Chinese. But given the actual political context in Malaya, the Communists' decision to take up armed struggle and to abandon the cities for a rural insurgency – while understandable – would inevitably proved disastrous. This decision

> forced [the party] away from its areas of proven and preferred influence within urban Chinese society into rural areas where Chinese comprised small minorities in the midst of hostile Malay peasants. When the Chinese squatters were successfully relocated and isolated in a new village, as they were during the course of 1950–52, the Party's position became even more tenuous. When the government succeeded, almost despite itself, in stimulating the formation of a stable, conservative, multiracial political alliance, committed to electoral politics and the attainment of independence, the Party's fate was virtually sealed. (Stenson 1974: 146)

As we have seen, the Huk insurgents in the Philippines also came to confront a government – a formally independent government in this case – that was not only militarily strong, but also apparently amenable to at least some popular demands. Like the British in Malaya, the United States came to rule the Philippines in a comparatively liberal and inclusionary fashion, sponsoring elections for local offices and opening up opportunities in the civil service and armed forces that were seized by members of the Philippine landed elite and middle classes (Friend 1965, 1988). In fact, as two harsh critics of U.S. rule in the Philippines point out, in a "virtually unprecedented manner the U.S. government established colonial rule in the Philippines with the declared purpose of self-liquidation of that rule, and enlisted the collaboration of the Philippine elite to this end" (Schirmer and Shalom 1987: 35).[12]

As early as 1916, the Jones Act, which established the Philippine senate, promised eventual independence to the archipelago, and the Philippines attained commonwealth status in 1935. The Philippine landed elite, moreover, prospered economically thanks to the free-trade relationship between

---

[12] It must be noted, however, that the American war of conquest in the Philippines (1899–1903) was extremely brutal, with hundreds of thousands of Filipino casualties (Miller 1994).

the two countries, and it became notoriously "Americanized" in its political outlook and cultural tastes (McCoy 1981). The U.S. government, consequently, was more than willing to hand over formal political power to this conservative elite after the war and then to provide it with substantial material aid with which to fight the Huk insurgents.

Had the Philippine government proven incapable of implementing even modest reforms and had the United States been unable to assist it (as the Communist Party so erroneously predicted), then the Huks just might have grown into a much more formidable movement. As it was, however, the insurgency was unable to expand much beyond its peasant base in Central Luzon, and it began to lose popular support even there after 1951. Benedict Kerkvliet, author of the most exhaustive study of the rebellion, concludes that "the major reasons why the Huk rebellion died down" were "[w]eariness among peasants in Central Luzon, the government's effective use of promises and reforms, and the [Huks'] inferiority compared to the government military's renewed strength and tactics" (Kerkvliet 1977: 245).

In sum, the relatively inclusionary structure and liberal policies of the colonial and neocolonial regimes in Malaya and the Philippines, combined with counterinsurgencies that were as much political as military in nature, prevented the Communist insurgencies in those countries, unlike that in Vietnam, from developing into broad, multiclass (or multiethnic) coalitions; these rebellions remained largely confined to a specific ethnic group or social class, became geographically isolated, and were eventually decimated by counterinsurgencies characterized by limited reforms and increasingly discriminate repression. Counterrevolution in these countries, accordingly, was much cheaper and more effective than in Vietnam, and elicited little opposition in the metropolitan societies. When the colonial rulers of these countries departed, they did not create a power vacuum that only armed revolutionaries could fill; they left behind conservative political leaders with significant popular support.

Excursus: Explaining Variations in Colonial Rule

If liberal, inclusionary, and reformist state policies undermine the appeal of revolutionaries, then why would imperialists who are strongly challenged by revolutionaries maintain an exclusionary and authoritarian form of colonial rule? Why, in other words, did the French rule Vietnam so repressively and refuse to devolve political power to moderate nationalists in order to preempt Communist revolution? And why did the British and Americans, by contrast, not only tolerate but actually sponsor such nationalists?

At least part of the solution to this puzzle seems to lie in the economic value of specific colonies to larger imperial projects. As the first industrial power, Britain traditionally preferred free-trade arrangements with indigenous "import-export elites" to protectionist colonial schemes that required the costly deployment of administrators and military forces. As Tony Smith argues,

> Only the inability of native regimes to maintain themselves in the face of mounting domestic and foreign pressures prompted Britain's direct (and generally begrudging) intervention. With the exception of India, the British far preferred the sort of arrangement they had worked out in Latin America to that they felt obliged to undertake in Egypt and East and West Africa. Although they had finally undertaken to experiment with a protectionist empire during the interwar period, this style never suited the free trade imperialists nearly as well as it had the French. (Smith 1981: 100)

As an emerging industrial giant, the United States also had serious misgivings about colonial forms of imperialism. During World War II, especially, "American policy makers became convinced that the postwar prosperity of the United States and of the world would depend to a large extent on open access to foreign markets and sources of raw materials" (McMahon 1981: 58–9). By this time, the United States had the world's most powerful economy and could be expected, accordingly, to dominate open foreign markets.

France, by contrast, as a relatively weaker economic actor on the international stage, was more inclined to seek the preferential access to raw materials that formal colonies afforded (the same was true of the Netherlands). "This very reliance of the French on an economically protected empire," Smith adds, "meant that those interests involved overseas were usually more intensely committed than their British counterparts, who ... were correspondingly less insistent that colonial nationalism be opposed" (Smith 1981: 100). Economically protectionist empires, in other words, bred political intransigence in the face of anticolonial movements – an intransigence evident in Amsterdam as well as in Paris.

Cultural and ideological factors, however, also played a significant role in shaping the disposition of Western powers to countenance (or not) decolonization "from above." Political elites in the United States, which was itself borne of an anticolonial struggle, were always culturally ambivalent about, if not outright indisposed toward, colonialism. The annexation

129

of the Philippines, in fact, unleashed rancorous political debates in the United States, and, as noted previously, the Americans began taking steps toward eventual Philippine independence well before the Second World War.

French national identity, by contrast, had rather different implications for colonial policy. The French, who generally "did not believe indigenous cultures or institutions offered anything of value," believed that their "civilizing mission" (*mission civilisatrice*) in their colonies required "the repression of colonial nationalism" (Shafer 1988: 142, 149). Humiliated by their experience in World War II, moreover, a broad spectrum of the French political class – from the far right to the non-Communist left – viewed the reconquest of Vietnam and France's other prewar colonies as indispensable for the restoration of the country's "national dignity," collective optimism, and international greatness (see, e.g., Smith 1974; Dalloz 1987). General de Gaulle, for example, asked President Roosevelt how France could possibly recover her national "vigour" if "she loses her African and Asian territories – in short, if the settlement of the war definitively imposes upon her the psychology of the vanquished?" (quoted in Smith 1974: 243). Finally, once the French confronted a strong revolutionary movement in Vietnam, many officials felt that anything less than its swift and total suppression would simply encourage anticolonial movements in other French colonies, especially Algeria.[13] And that, of course, might have meant the end of the French empire – and, for many, of French greatness.

Conclusion to Part 2

The state-centered analysis of Southeast Asian national liberation movements that I have presented in this and the previous chapter is schematically summarized in Figure 4.1.

The figure indicates that two political variables, against a general backdrop of colonial rule, widespread socioeconomic problems, and Japanese occupation, determined whether strong Communist-led national

---

[13] Such concerns were not misplaced. In May 1945, French air and ground forces killed perhaps fifteen thousand Algerians – estimates vary between eight thousand and forty-five thousand – after riots erupted in Sétif; the riots began after demonstrations celebrating Allied war victories and calling for equality among Christians and Muslims were fired upon (Wolf 1969: 235–6).

Conclusion to Part 2

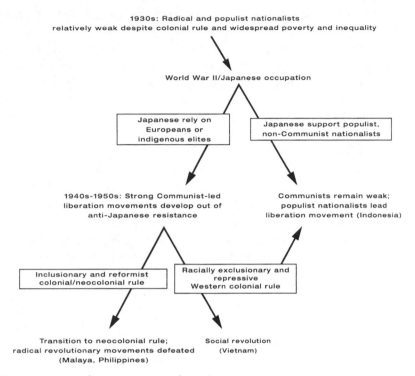

Figure 4.1 Analytic trajectory of revolutionary movements in Southeast Asia, 1930–60.

liberation movements would form and take power in Southeast Asia: the nature of Japanese rule during World War II and the political character of Western colonialism and neocolonialism in each national society. More specifically, the formation and fate of Communist movements depended upon (1) whether the Japanese relied upon Europeans (as in Vietnam) or existing indigenous elites (as in Malaya and the Philippines), on the one hand, or sponsored populist nationalists (as in Indonesia), on the other, and (2) whether the rule of Western powers and/or their local allies, including their reaction to Communist movements, was inclusionary and reformist (Malaya and the Philippines) or exclusionary and repressive (Vietnam). This is not to say that all colonies ruled in a racially exclusionary and repressive fashion have been toppled by revolutionaries; among other factors, the repression may simply be too strong for revolutionaries to overcome (hence the importance in Southeast Asia of the dis-

131

ruptions of the Japanese occupation and World War II), or the geopolitical balance of power may weigh against the revolutionaries (who may lack
the type of needed international support that was available to the Viet
Minh). Still, racially exclusionary and repressive colonialism clearly tends
at once to radicalize and to broaden the potential social base of national
liberation movements – as occurred, for example, in Burma, Algeria,
Portugal's African colonies (Guinea-Bissau, Angola, and Mozambique),
Zimbabwe, and the West Bank and Gaza (see, e.g., Holland 1985; Betts
1991; Low 1991; Goldstone, Gurr, and Moshiri 1991).

What are the implications of this analysis for theories of revolutions?
As noted in Chapter 2, an extraordinarily wide variety of theoretical
perspectives has been applied to revolutionary movements, including
modernization, Marxist, world-systems, geopolitical, Leninist, social-
psychological, demographic, resource-mobilization, network-analytic, and
culturalist theories (see, e.g., Foran 1993; Kimmel 1990; Goldstone 1980).
(In fact, there are now virtually as many theories as there are cases of social
revolutions.) These approaches attribute revolutions to such factors as the
disruptive effects of rapid social change, the incorporation of populations
into the global capitalist economy, the inspiration and material aid of
foreign powers, the formation of new (or threats to old) social classes, the
"organizational weapon" of the vanguard party, widespread relative deprivation, population pressures on valued resources and social positions,
popular access to substantial flows of material resources, threats to populations with dense social ties, and the (re)affirmation of ethnic or national
identities. In fact, all of these factors would undoubtedly appear in any
comprehensive history of modern Southeast Asia, and many of them are
evident, or implicit, in my own brief summaries of the postwar revolutionary movements in the region. Moreover, all of these factors (and still
others) have no doubt figured prominently in several and perhaps many
revolutions, as either proximate or remote causes. One is tempted simply
to add state structures and practices – the analytic pivot of this book – to
this list as just another potential cause of revolutions.

In my view, however, whether any of the factors (or some combination
of them) that are emphasized in extant theories will actually give rise to a
revolutionary movement or to a revolution depends very much upon the
political context in which they are embedded. When these factors, accordingly, are abstracted from such contexts – as "independent variables" – they
cease to explain (or predict) revolutions. My analysis of Southeast Asia
suggests, in fact, that existing theories of revolutions are not only

incomplete, but positively misleading when they ignore the direct and mediating effects of state structures and practices.

There can be no doubt, for example, that the new class and ethnic relations that Western and Japanese imperialism introduced into Southeast Asia were at least potentially conducive to the formation of strong radical movements. But a focus on the transformations of social relations and collective identities in the region that ignores the political context in which these occurred obscures a number of important causal mechanisms. For example, this focus cannot easily explain why such changes engendered radical national liberation movements in some countries but more moderate nationalist movements in others (see Chapter 3). Such a focus also fails to explain one of our principal concerns in this chapter: the quite variable capacity of revolutionary movements to forge broad multiclass and multiethnic alliances, marginalizing movements led by more moderate political leaders in the process. I have argued that this capacity was primarily, albeit unintentionally, determined by variations in colonial rule in Southeast Asia.

More generally, I have argued that the connection between the wide assortment of causal factors that various theories of revolution have specified and actual revolutions is mediated by political contexts characterized by distinctive state structures and practices. In this sense, these structures and practices are *more* than just another potentially important variable. Rather, scholars of revolutions need to pay particular attention to states not only because control of state power is, by definition, central to revolutions (see Tilly 1993: 5), but also because states powerfully determine the precise ways in which a range of other factors may (or may not) contribute to both the mobilization and impact of revolutionary movements. A state-centered approach, in sum, is important not just or even mainly because of the importance of state breakdowns or political opportunities for seizures of power by preexisting movements, but also because the very formation and strength of revolutionary movements vis-à-vis other political challengers are strongly shaped by the ways in which political authorities rule and respond to challengers. The objective possibilities for revolutionary mobilization and transfers of power are constructed, to a very large extent, by the deployment of state power.

PART THREE

Central America

Chronology for Central America

Nicaragua

1893–1909	rule of the Liberal Party dictator José Santos Zelaya
1912–33	era of U.S. military occupation
1927–33	Augusto César Sandino leads guerrilla war against U.S. Marine occupation
1934	Sandino murdered by U.S.-created National Guard
1936–56	dictatorship of Anastasio Somoza García, head of the National Guard
1956	Somoza García assassinated; his elder son, Luis Somoza Debayle, assumes the presidency, and his younger son, Anastasio Somoza Debayle, becomes chief of the National Guard
1961	Sandinista National Liberation Front (FSLN) founded in Honduras
1963	first armed action by FSLN (March); FSLN guerrillas retreat after sustaining heavy losses (June–October)
1967	over two hundred killed by National Guard at opposition rally; Anastasio Somoza Debayle fraudulently "elected" president, beginning twelve years of dictatorial rule (1967–79); his brother Luis dies of heart attack; FSLN guerrilla *foco* at Pancasán retreats after sustaining heavy losses (May–August)
1970	FSLN begins period of "accumulating forces in silence"
1972	earthquake kills eighteen thousand people and destroys central Managua
1974–7	Somoza declares state of siege; two to three thousand killed; FSLN splits into three "tendencies"
1977	Jimmy Carter sworn in as U.S. president; Somoza lifts state of siege (September); FSLN attacks National Guard barracks in San Carlos and several other cities (October)
1978	assassination of *La Prensa* editor and long-time Somoza foe Pedro Joaquín Chamorro sparks protests and business strike (January); insurrection in Monimbó (February); Sandinistas seize the National Palace and obtain release of political prisoners (August); FSLN launches "general offensive" (September 9); U.S.-sponsored mediation between Somoza and moderate opposition begins (October); Costa Rica breaks diplomatic relations with Somoza (November)

1979	formation of the National Patriotic Front (FPN) (January); three FSLN tendencies announce unity accord (March); Mexico breaks relations with Somoza (May); FSLN announces "final offensive" against Somoza (May 30); Organization of American States calls for Somoza's removal (June 23); Somoza resigns (July 17) and Sandinistas enter Managua (July 19), beginning decade of Sandinista rule
1981	Reagan Administration suspends economic aid; U.S.-backed counter-revolutionaries (contras) begin war against Sandinistas
1984	Sandinistas easily win elections (boycotted by some opposition parties at U.S. urging)
1987	new constitution signed after extensive public deliberations; peace plan of Costa Rican president Oscar Arias signed in Guatemala by five Central American presidents, despite U.S. opposition
1988	United States ends military aid to contras; Sandinistas and contras sign cease-fire agreement
1990	coalition led by Violetta Chamorro defeats Sandinistas at polls; contras agree to disarm under U.N. supervision

El Salvador

1871	"Liberal Revolution" ends era of Conservative dominance
1931–44	military coup installs dictatorship of General Maximiliano Hernández Martínez
1932	abortive rebellion by Communist Party led by Farabundo Martí; twenty to thirty thousand peasants massacred (*la matanza*)
1948–79	succession of military governments
1969	"soccer war" with Honduras
1970–8	formation and growth of guerrilla groups and allied "popular organizations"
1972	military steals election from reformist coalition led by Christian Democrat José Napoleón Duarte
1977	Oscar Romero becomes archbishop of El Salvador; Father Rutilio Grande assassinated by death squad, the first of seven priests killed over the following two years; General Carlos Romero assumes presidency through fraudulent elections; violence escalates sharply
1979	martial law imposed (May); military-civilian junta replaces Romero in a bloodless coup (October)
1980	civilians resign from junta; Christian Democrats and the military form new junta; security forces attack a huge demonstration in San Salvador (January); junta announces land reform program and imposes state of siege; violence escalates further; Archbishop Romero assassinated (March); formation of Democratic Revolutionary Front (FDR) (April) and the Farabundo Martí National Liberation Front (FMLN) (November); all-out civil war begins

Guatemala

1981	FMLN launches abortive "final offensive" (January); Reagan Administration vastly increases military and economic aid; army massacre of up to one thousand people at El Mozote (December)
1982	right-wing coalition wins majority in Constituent Assembly elections (March) and suspends important land reform provisions (May)
1983	total number of political killings reaches forty-five thousand
1984	Duarte elected president; abortive peace talks (October–November)
1985	Christian Democrats win legislative and municipal elections; four U.S. marines killed by guerrillas in a San Salvador restaurant; guerrillas kidnap Duarte's daughter, who is later released in exchange for rebel prisoners
1986	labor protests in response to austerity measures; formation of the National Unity of Salvadoran Workers (UNTS); severe earthquake in San Salvador
1987	talks between government and FMLN in San Salvador; human rights leader Herbert Anaya is murdered in death-squad fashion; Guillermo Ungo and Rubén Zamora return from exile and form the Democratic Convergence (CD)
1988	death-squad killings on the rise; ARENA handily wins municipal and legislative elections
1989	ARENA candidate Alfredo Cristiani elected president; talks between the government and FMLN in Mexico and Costa Rica; FMLN calls off talks following the bombing of the offices of FENASTRAS, the country's largest trade union federation; major FMLN offensive in San Salvador and other cities; Jesuit priests murdered at the Central American University (November)
1991	following resumption of peace talks, Salvadoran government and FMLN conclude a peace agreement at the United Nations, New York City (December 31), ending the twelve-year civil war
1992	final peace accords signed in Mexico City (January 16)

Guatemala

1931–44	dictatorship of General Jorge Ubico
1945–50	reformist government of Juan José Arévalo
1950–4	presidency of Jacobo Arbenz; agrarian reform enacted (1952)
1954	General Carlos Castíllo Armas, backed by the United States, overthrows Arbenz, ending a decade of democratic rule
1962	student and labor demonstrations; beginning of guerrilla insurgency (to 1996)
1966–8	guerrilla groups in eastern part of country decimated by U.S.-backed counterinsurgency; some eight thousand unarmed civilians killed by security forces by 1970; right-wing death squads kill thirty thousand more through 1973
1968	U.S. Ambassador John Gordon Mein kidnapped and killed by insurgents
1971	General Carlos Araña Osorio becomes president; repression intensifies
1972–9	resurgence of guerrilla groups in western highlands

139

1974	right-wing General Kjell Laugerud García fraudulently "elected" president
1976	severe earthquake; formation of the National Committee of Trade Union Unity (CNUS); popular mobilization increases
1977	United States ends military assistance to Guatemala after the Guatemalan government already rejected aid conditioned upon improvements in human rights
1978	General Romeo Lucas García assumes presidency following fraudulent elections; formation of the Committee of Peasant Unity (CUC); repression of labor and peasant movements increases; massacre at Panzós; Carter administration bans arms sales to Guatemala
1980	massacre at Spanish embassy; Spain breaks diplomatic relations with Guatemala; guerrilla groups form a loose alliance
1981	army counteroffensive against guerrillas begins; CUC goes underground
1982	guerrilla groups form the Guatemalan National Revolutionary Unity (URNG) (February); junior officers led by General Efraín Ríos Montt oust Lucas García following the fraudulent election of General Aníbal Guevara (March); state of siege is declared and the "scorched earth" campaign against guerrillas intensifies
1983	Reagan administration resumes arms sales to Guatemala; a coup ousts Ríos Montt and installs General Oscar Mejías Víctores, who initiates "model village" program and a return to formal civilian rule
1984	Constituent Assembly writes a new constitution
1985	official U.S. economic and military aid to Guatemala (suspended since 1977) resumes; Guatemalan military reports that it has destroyed 440 villages during the past five years; Democratic Socialist Party (PSD) reestablished; Christian Democrat Vinicio Cerezo elected president
1987	talks between government and URNG in Madrid
1988	exiled leadership of CUC return for a week-long visit; the military cancels its offensive against guerrillas after sustaining heavy casualties; attempted military-rightist coup against Cerezo fails; massacre at El Aguacate
1989	Amoco ends three years of oil exploration in western highlands due to guerrilla harassment; three-month teachers' strike; accords reached in Oslo between URNG and the National Reconciliation Commission (CNR) call for a political settlement to the civil war
1990	Ríos Montt banned from running for presidency; massacre at Santiago Atitlán
1991	Jorge Serrano elected president; peace talks continue in Mexico
1996	URNG and government sign "Accord for a Firm and Lasting Peace" (December 29), some thirty-five years after the guerrilla insurgency began

Honduras

1932–48	dictatorship of General Tiburcio Carías Andino
1954	major strike against U.S. banana companies results in legalization of trade unions

Honduras

1957	Ramon Villeda Morales of the Liberal Party elected president; new labor code and social-security law adopted
1962	first agrarian reform law passed
1963	Villeda overthrown by General Oswaldo López Arellano, who rules until 1971
1969	"soccer war" with El Salvador
1971–2	brief "national unity government" ousted by military
1972–5	period of military reformism; two more agrarian laws enacted
1980	Constituent Assembly elections narrowly won by the Liberal Party
1981	Roberto Suazo Córdova of the Liberal Party elected president
1981–90	increased U.S. military presence in and aid to Honduras; U.S.-backed Nicaraguan contras operate from Honduran bases; human rights abuses escalate
1982	Gustavo Álvárez Martínez appointed military commander in chief
1983	small guerrilla force destroyed in Olancho; most of the guerrillas are executed after capture, including a North American priest, James Carney
1984	Gen. Álvárez overthrown by officer corps and forced to leave country; large demonstrations against U.S. presence
1985	José Azcona Hoyo of the Liberal Party elected president
1986	camps of several dozen guerrillas of the Cinchonero Popular Liberation Movement (MPL) discovered and destroyed
1988	President Azcona demands departure of contras from Honduras and U.N. peacekeeping force to patrol borders
1989	Rafael Leonardo Callejas of the National Party elected president
1991	small guerrilla groups formally renounce armed struggle

5

The Formation of Revolutionary Movements in Central America

> That revolutionary processes broke out only in some countries, even though economic change was a factor across the region, suggests that the disorders of capitalist modernization are not a sufficient explanation for the emergence of radical political challenges. The political conditions and institutions that framed those structural changes and their negative impacts on particular groups and classes must also be considered.
>
> – Carlos Vilas (1995: 79)

> I believe that the people have different motivations for fighting than those acquired by a more sophisticated leadership. Politically, people have more rudimentary motivations: often they simply have no choice, like in the case of the peasantry, such an important component of the struggle in El Salvador, which joined the guerrillas because it couldn't be on the other side, because their families were simply murdered. They know since they were born that the Army is evil and that the guerrillas are against the Army. That's about it.
>
> – Salvador Samayoa, Salvador guerrilla leader
> (quoted in Castañeda 1993: 241–2)

In the preceding chapters, I have tried to demonstrate how a state-centered approach illuminates the uneven development of revolutionary movements in postwar Southeast Asia. But perhaps the power of this approach for that region, at that time, has something to do with the fact that these societies were formal colonies ruled by powerful external states that were then suddenly occupied by yet another foreign power, Japan. Does a state-centered approach also illuminate the formation and fate of revolutionary movements in formally independent peripheral societies? In this and the following chapter, I argue that it does, focusing on Central America in the period following the 1960s.

Scholars have generally argued that the revolutionary upheavals and political violence in Central America during the 1970s and 1980s were the

142

result of the changing, and increasingly polarized, class structures in the isthmus (Brockett 1998; Paige 1987, 1997) and/or of the region's extreme economic dependence upon the United States (LaFeber 1993; Coatsworth 1994). However, these factors, singly or combined, fail to explain why the only revolutionary movement in the region that actually seized state power was the Sandinista National Liberation Front (FSLN) in Nicaragua, a country that, according to a variety of measures, was and remains no more (and in some aspects less) internally inequitable and externally dependent than the others in the region. These factors also fail to explain why no strong revolutionary movement developed during these decades in Honduras, a country that was and remains, according to a variety of measures, as internally inequitable and externally dependent as any in the region (Schulz and Schulz 1994).[1]

In contrast to analyses that focus primarily, or even exclusively, on class relations and transnational economic dependency, I shall argue that the institutional configurations and practices of Central American *states* best explain both the uneven development and the relative success or failure of Central America's revolutionary movements. More specifically, I suggest in this chapter that revolutionary movements became strong only where militarized yet infrastructurally weak states were consistently exclusionary, antireformist, and more or less indiscriminately repressive of their political opponents (moderates and reformists as well as revolutionaries) throughout the 1960s and 1970s. This formula applies to Nicaragua, El Salvador, and Guatemala, but *not* to Honduras, where the military was more tolerant of politically moderate labor and peasant unions and even introduced a significant, if limited, agrarian reform "from above" during the early 1970s (Ruhl 1984; Sieder 1995).

I will also suggest in the following chapter that Nicaragua's FSLN was the only revolutionary movement in the region actually able to seize state power primarily because it confronted a personalistic, "neopatrimonial"

---

[1] No significant revolutionary movement formed in Costa Rica during these years either. However, this is much less of a puzzle than the Honduran case, since Costa Rica has the longest-existing democratic regime in Latin America as well as a substantially more developed economy than the other countries of Central America (e.g., Booth and Walker 1993: 29–32). For these reasons, I have not included Costa Rica in my analysis of revolutionary movements, nor am I tempted to enter the interesting fray concerning the origins of Costa Rican democracy (but see Gudmundson 1986; Yashar 1997; Paige 1997).

143

dictatorship that increasingly alienated large sections of the Nicaraguan bourgeoisie and political moderates, as well as virtually all other sectors of the Nicaraguan population, especially after 1972 (see, e.g., Booth 1985; Wickham-Crowley 1992; Everingham 1996). In the process, this dictatorship also became internationally or geopolitically isolated. By contrast, the revolutionary movements in El Salvador (the Farabundo Martí National Liberation Front, or FMLN) and Guatemala (the Guatemalan National Revolutionary Unity, or URNG) confronted much more cohesive authoritarian states that were dominated by the armed forces *as an institution*, were generally supported by the dominant landowning class, and were recipients (especially in the Salvadoran case) of substantial external assistance.

This analysis obviously "decenters" but is not intended to displace class relations and economic dependence (or, in the Guatemalan case, ethnic conflict) as important causal factors behind the revolutionary conflicts in Central America. Class struggles have undoubtedly been a major cause (and consequence) of the formation of popular revolutionary movements in the region. On the other hand, class struggles did not give birth to a significant revolutionary movement in Honduras, and class conflict in Nicaragua was relatively muted – and even purposively muted by the FSLN – during the multiclass struggle against the Somoza dictatorship in 1978–9 (see, e.g., Arias 1980: 108). Transnational dependency, for its part, has certainly aggravated inequalities of wealth and power in the region and generated demands for "national liberation" from U.S. imperialism. On the other hand, such demands did not give rise to a significant national-liberation movement in Honduras. Even where and when they were undeniably important, moreover, the effects of class relations and economic dependence on the formation and success of revolutionary movements were *mediated* by the institutions and practices of each Central American state. Class relations and external ties, that is, were less important in terms of their *direct* effects on would-be revolutionaries than in terms of how they shaped, constrained, and enabled the deployment of *state power*, which was more immediately significant for the formation and relative success of revolutionary movements.

In responding to political challengers during the 1960s and 1970s, it should be emphasized, Central American states and armies generally relied upon "tried-and-trusted" repertoires of routinized and taken-for-granted practices (see Williams, e.g., 1994) – although, across the region as a whole, these practices would have variable and often unintended conse-

144

quences.[2] In Nicaragua and, to a lesser extent, El Salvador, militarized states persisted in these activities despite accumulating evidence that they were ineffectual and even counterproductive (see, e.g., Stanley 1996). The habitual, unreflective, and deeply ingrained character of these practices accords with a major tenet of the "new institutionalism" in sociological theory – namely, the idea that "taken-for-granted scripts, rules, and classifications are the stuff of which institutions are made" (DiMaggio and Powell 1991: 15).

More generally, my state-centered analysis accords with the new institutionalism in emphasizing the causal importance of institutionalized practices as opposed to broad "social forces" or abstractly defined "variables" such as class or dependency. According to this perspective, political institutions shape the fault lines of collective contention as well as the character and outcome of that contention; political institutions privilege certain actors and disadvantage others by both shaping and constraining the identities, interests, organization, and power of social actors (Thelen and Steinmo 1992). My examination of Central America in this and the following chapter suggests that the structures and practices of state institutions were decisive in determining the uneven distribution and variable outcomes of the revolutionary conflicts in that region.

An Overview of Central America

In July 1979, the Sandinista National Liberation Front successfully overthrew the "dynastic dictatorship" of the Somoza family, which had ruled Nicaragua since 1936, after a relatively brief but bloody popular insurrection that left between forty and fifty thousand people dead (Booth 1985: 183). Strong revolutionary movements also formed (or re-formed) in El Salvador and Guatemala by the late 1970s, but these proved unable to seize state power. Approximately seventy-five thousand people were killed in the decade-long Salvadoran civil war, which was settled through negotiations at the end of 1991; as many as two hundred thousand people were killed in Guatemala during the 1980s and 1990s; peace accords ended that conflict in 1996. In Honduras, however, none of several revolutionary groups

---

[2] The idea that social actors have a limited repertoire of "strategies of action" (Swidler 1986) has generally been employed to explain the activities of social movements and other forms of contentious politics (see especially Tilly 1978, 1986). The idea is also clearly applicable, however, to state actors.

managed to mobilize a significant revolutionary movement during or after the 1970s.

Fortunately, Central America, even more than Southeast Asia, provides especially fertile ground for addressing questions about the causes of revolutionary mobilization and actual transfers of power (see Map 5.1). Indeed, as one observer has suggested, Central America is a veritable "laboratory for theories of revolution" (Krumwiede 1984: 10) because the countries that comprise it (except Costa Rica) share broadly similar social structures, cultures, and histories as well as a common geopolitical location vis-à-vis North America and Western Europe.[3] One cannot in fact find anywhere in the world four contiguous national societies that are more homogeneous. As in Southeast Asia, moreover, we can logically rule out the shared characteristics of these societies as the sufficient causes of the very different political fortunes of the revolutionaries in the region. We can similarly rule out as sufficient causes those factors that, while varying significantly across the region, do not clearly differentiate either Nicaragua and El Salvador (where the most effective and largest revolutionary movements formed, respectively) *or* Honduras (where no significant revolutionary movement formed at all) from the other countries in the region. Once again, the value of this type of regional approach is precisely that it allows one to "control" for a variety of factors that might otherwise be mistaken as causally decisive for either the emergence or political trajectory of revolutionary movements.

Ten regional similarities in Central America are especially important to note:

1. The rapid development, especially in the postwar period, of agroexporting economies dominated by small landowning (and processing) classes or "oligarchies."
2. The transition from traditional haciendas with resident labor forces to more purely capitalist "agribusiness" based on migratory labor forces (landless laborers and "semiproletarians" with very little land).

---

[3] Central America, in fact, was a single political unit – the so-called Kingdom of Guatemala – for more than three centuries of Spanish rule. (This "kingdom," significantly, also included the state of Chiapas in what would become Mexico.) Central America was also briefly a federal union, the United Provinces of Central America, following independence from Spain. Some Central Americans (mainly intellectuals) maintain the dream of a united Central America, arguing that the present "balkanization" of the region is artificial and economically irrational.

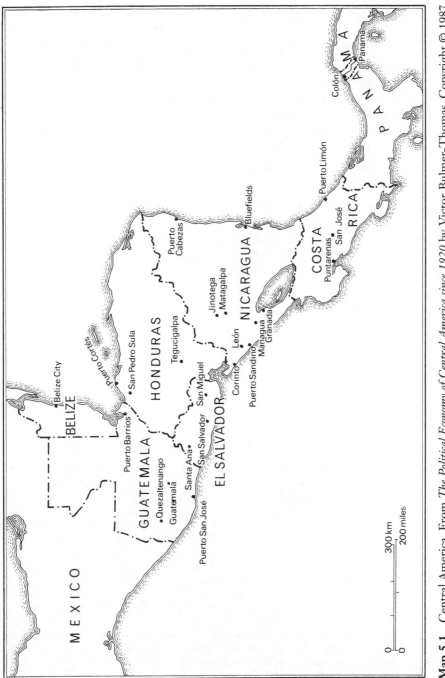

Map 5.1 Central America. From *The Political Economy of Central America since 1920* by Victor Bulmer-Thomas. Copyright © 1987 Cambridge University Press. Reprinted with permission.

3. Rapid population growth.
4. A highly concentrated pattern of land ownership, which has led not only to widespread landlessness and land poverty, but also to massive urban migration, extensive under- and unemployment, and endemic poverty.
5. A tradition of political authoritarianism, typically based on strategic alliances between local oligarchs and the state's armed forces[4] and generally supported by the United States during the Cold War as a bulwark against Communism.
6. Fiscally and infrastructurally weak states that do not effectively penetrate or control all of the national territory that they claim to rule (especially "peripheral" border and/or mountainous regions) – a consequence in part of the exceedingly small tax bases of these societies, which is itself largely a result of the impressive capacity of local oligarchies to veto attempts to tax their wealth (see also Chapter 7, Appendix 2).
7. The predominance of the Roman Catholic religion and the changing institutions and practices associated with it, including, since the late 1960s, the ideas and practices associated with liberation theology.
8. The formation, especially since the 1950s and 1960s, of reform-oriented grass-roots organizations and political parties, including Christian Democratic and social-democratic parties.
9. The formation, also since the 1960s, of predominantly Marxist-Leninist revolutionary organizations that, following the example of the Cuban Revolution, adopted the strategy or "repertoire" of guerrilla struggle for "national liberation" from U.S. imperialism and its local allies (many of these organizations, in fact, split off from older, pro-Soviet Communist parties).[5]

---

[4] Oligarchies have often very severely constrained the options of Central American states and armed forces. As will become clear, however, I reject the view that Central American armies lack any institutional autonomy and are invariably the instrument or "junior partner" of local oligarchies. State autonomy is especially clear, most analysts agree, for the cases of Nicaragua and Honduras, but the institutional autonomy of the armed forces also helps us to explain certain aspects of the Salvadoran civil war (see Stanley 1996) and the Guatemalan conflict (see Anderson and Simon 1987).

[5] The leading cadres of both reformist and revolutionary organizations tend to be of middle-class background; many teachers, students, and professionals tend to be found in top leadership positions, even in those revolutionary groups oriented toward the mobilization of workers and peasants (see Wickham-Crowley 1992: Appendix A.)

10. The concerted attempt by these ideologically radical revolutionary organizations to mobilize mass movements and guerrilla armies within a common "world-historical context." This historical context is characterized by (a) the existence of the Communist regime in Cuba, which not only inspired but also sometimes materially supported revolutionaries in the region; (b) growing Church activism in efforts to alleviate poverty as well as growing Church acceptance of the legitimacy of armed struggle as a "method of last resort"; and (c) intense debates within the United States, in the aftermath of the debacle in Vietnam, over the efficacy and, to a lesser extent, the morality of supporting repressive anti-Communist regimes (i.e., the so-called "Vietnam syndrome").[6]

Before turning to some of the regional variations that are hidden beneath these rather broad similarities, I should note that these similarities have led most observers to conclude, not surprisingly, that the recent revolutionary conflicts in Central America were part of an integrated regional crisis that simply worked itself out at different speeds, and with particular nuances, in each society. These observers speak variously of the crisis of Central American "client states," "neodependency," "liberalism," or "feudalism," by which they all more or less mean landlord-dominated and U.S.-dependent economies and states (see, e.g., Coatsworth 1994; LaFeber 1993; Woodward 1984, 1985: chs. 8–9; Pérez Brignoli 1985; Weeks 1986a; Dore and Weeks 1992). Implicitly or explicitly, many observers also suggested (at least during the early 1980s) that social revolution was a likely or even inescapable outcome of this putatively regional crisis. Indeed, one very learned popular history of the region was entitled *Inevitable Revolutions* (LaFeber 1993).[7] In 1985, James Dunkerley, an astute analyst of the region (whose subsequent writings are more sensitive to national variations [see Dunkerley 1988]), wrote that revolution in Central America

---

[6] These and other regional similarities are discussed in a number of helpful synthetic treatments of Central America: Weeks 1985, Woodward 1985, Pérez Brignoli 1985, Williams 1986, Barry 1987, Bulmer-Thomas 1987, Anderson 1988, Dunkerley 1988, Booth and Walker 1993, Torres Rivas 1993, Weaver 1994, Coatsworth 1994, Vilas 1995, Paige 1997, and Brockett 1998.

[7] The first edition of LaFeber's book was published in 1984, a more optimistic time for revolutionaries than subsequent years.

has been nurtured in the social conditions of states that comprise a region that is politically balkanised but of a relatively homogenous social fabric. If the peculiarities of Nicaragua under the Somoza dynasty proved to be the weakest link in the chain, and the small size, high population density and remarkable omnipotence of the local oligarchy in El Salvador provided an obvious sequitur, there is nothing in the physiognomy of the other countries [in the region] that would confer upon them some kind of immunity. (Dunkerley 1985: 3)

This implies, among other things, that the specific political context within each of the region's balkanized societies may be less causally significant than the region's general characteristics. In this and the following chapter, I suggest that we need to reverse this formulation to understand why El Salvador – let alone Guatemala or Honduras – did *not* become "an obvious sequitur" to Nicaragua.

The Formation of Revolutionary Movements

Most commentators have attributed the emergence of revolutionary movements in Central America to the region's extreme poverty, the vast gulf between rich and poor, extensive landlessness and land poverty in the countryside (and the class struggles that these engendered), the existence of powerful landowning oligarchies, and/or the region's extreme economic dependence on the United States. Surprisingly, however, none of these factors is strongly correlated with the diverse political fortunes of revolutionaries in the region.

Neither absolute impoverishment nor income inequality, for example, is unambiguously associated with the uneven development of revolutionary movements in the region. As Table 5.1 indicates, Honduras was the poorest country in Central America, in per capita terms, through the 1970s, yet, as noted, no revolutionary movement emerged there. And Nicaragua, the lone case where revolutionaries seized power, was actually the *least* impoverished country in the region until the insurrection of 1978–9. In 1980, moreover, there were very high levels of poverty throughout the entire region, and extreme poverty was more prevalent in Honduras than in any other country in the region (see Table 5.2). Income distribution was also very inequitable across the entire region (see Table 5.3). In 1980, the greatest income inequality was found in El Salvador (not Nicaragua), and the least in Guatemala (not Honduras); in fact, income inequality was the same in Nicaragua (where revolutionaries took power) and Honduras (where revolutionaries were of marginal significance) (see Table 5.4).

Table 5.1. *Gross national product per capita in Central America, 1972–82 (constant 1981 dollars).*

Year	Nicaragua	El Salvador	Guatemala	Honduras
1972	1129	808	980	605
1973	1106	825	1032	606
1974	1269	857	1064	599
1975	1260	882	1044	565
1976	1255	881	1098	584
1977	1264	909	1169	614
1978	1110	942	1196	635
1979	818	895	1217	651
1980	910	794	1218	650
1981	946	759	1159	624
1982	878	717	1100	595

Source: U.S. Arms Control and Disarmament Agency 1984: 25, 28–9, 39 (from World Bank data).

Table 5.2. *Percentage of population living in poverty in Central America, 1980.*

Nation	Total	Extreme poverty
Nicaragua	61.5	34.7
El Salvador	68.1	50.6
Guatemala	71.1	39.6
Honduras	68.2	56.7

Source: Economic Commission for Latin America and the Caribbean (CEPAL) 1982: 20–1.

Table 5.3. *Distribution of income in Central America, 1970 and 1980 (percentage of total by stratum).*

Nation	Year	Poorest 20%	Next 30%	Next 30%	Richest 20%
Nicaragua	1970	no data	15.0	25.0	60.0
	1980	3.0	13.0	26.0	58.0
El Salvador	1970	3.7	14.9	30.6	50.8
	1980	2.0	10.0	22.0	66.0
Guatemala	1970	4.9	12.5	23.8	58.8
	1980	5.3	14.5	26.1	54.1
Honduras	1970	3.0	7.7	21.6	67.7
	1980	4.3	12.7	23.7	59.3

Source: CEPAL 1982: 15.

Table 5.4. *Gini coefficient for income distribution in Central America, 1980.*

Nation	Coefficient
Nicaragua	.51
El Salvador	.60
Guatemala	.46
Honduras	.51

Source: CEPAL 1982: 18. .00 = complete equality; 1.00 = greatest possible inequality.

Table 5.5. *Average annual population growth in Central America (percentage).*

Nation	1965–80	1980–89
Nicaragua	3.1	3.4
El Salvador	2.8	1.4
Guatemala	2.8	2.9
Honduras	3.2	3.5

Source: World Bank 1991: 254–5 (Table 26).

Rapid population growth, which may aggravate poverty, social inequalities, and political conflict under certain circumstances (see Goldstone 1991), was also characteristic of the region as a whole during the 1970s and 1980s. Again, population growth was most rapid in comparatively quiescent Honduras *and* in revolutionary Nicaragua (see Table 5.5).

Widespread landlessness and land poverty among Central Americans have typically been portrayed as the "roots" of the revolutionary conflicts in the region (see, e.g., Barry 1987; Barraclough and Scott 1987). As Table 5.6 shows, however, there is no direct connection between the extent of these problems and the fortune of revolutionaries. Landlessness and land poverty were most severe in El Salvador and Guatemala, where revolutionaries did become powerful actors, but they were least severe in Nicaragua, where revolutionaries actually took power.

The figures in Table 5.6 reflect a well-known division within the isthmus: El Salvador and Guatemala have very wealthy, tightly knit, and hence politically powerful landowning oligarchies, while Nicaragua and Honduras have rather less wealthy, divided, and hence less politically

Table 5.6. *Distribution of rural families in Central America by size of landholding, 1970 (percentage).*

Size (hectares)	Nicaragua	El Salvador	Guatemala	Honduras
Landless	33.8	26.1	26.6	31.4
Under .7	1.5	24.4	15.0	10.3
0.7–4	24.2	36.2	42.3	24.1
4–7	7.9	6.2	6.9	11.9
7–35	18.1	4.9	7.4	18.1
35–350	13.5	2.0	1.4	3.9
Over 350	1.0	0.2	0.4	0.3
Landless or insufficient land	59.5	86.7	83.9	65.8

Source: Weeks 1985: 112.

powerful oligarchies (Paige 1987, 1997; Williams 1994). (The reasons for this dichotomy are complex, but are explained mainly by the nature and extent of coffee production, population density, and, in the case of Nicaragua, the effects of the U.S. Marine occupation early in the century [see Paige 1997: 79–80].) Like landlessness and land poverty, however, this dichotomy does not neatly correlate with the fortunes of revolutionaries in the region. Again, revolutionary movements did become strong in those countries with powerful oligarchies (El Salvador and Guatemala), but revolutionaries actually took power in a country with a relatively weak and divided oligarchy (Nicaragua).

Yet another interpretation of the revolutionary conflicts in Central America posits that revolutionaries were responding to, and attempting to end, the region's extreme dependence on the United States. For example, Roger Burbach has suggested that, "Even more so than in Vietnam, Central Americans are rebelling against decades of U.S. domination over all aspects of their society (military, economic, political, and cultural)" (1984: 17). However, the various data on external dependency that are presented in Tables 5.7 through 5.10, like the other data presented thus far, do not strongly correlate with the diverse political fortunes of revolutionaries in the region. As Table 5.7 shows, the importance of exports for the national economies in the region was greatest in Nicaragua on the eve of the revolution in that country; on the other hand, Honduras was somewhat more externally dependent, according to this measure, than both El Salvador and Guatemala.

Table 5.7. *Export earnings in Central America as a percentage of gross domestic product (constant prices).*

Year	Nicaragua	El Salvador	Guatemala	Honduras
1960	24.0	20.4	14.6	20.3
1970	30.1	21.3	19.3	29.6
1975	33.7	24.4	21.2	26.4

Source: Weeks 1985: 52.

Table 5.8. *Net direct foreign investment in Central America, 1960–78 (millions of dollars).*

Years	Nicaragua	El Salvador	Guatemala	Honduras
1960–4	27.1	31.4	54.7	–6.1
1965–9	63.3	42.5	110.4	46.6
1970–4	65.3	42.6	132.8	24.1
1975–8	40.9	112.2	340.6	35.3
Total	196.6	228.7	638.5	99.9

Source: Weeks 1985: 93–4.

Between 1960 and 1978, moreover, direct foreign investment was much greater in Guatemala – and slightly greater in El Salvador – than in Nicaragua (see Table 5.8). Moreover, as Table 5.9 shows, "imperialist exploitation," as measured by profit transfers minus foreign investments, was greatest during this period in Honduras, which experienced the greatest decapitalization or net transfer of wealth. Finally, the data in Table 5.10 indicate that more aid from the United States and U.S.-dominated "multilateral" banking institutions flowed to Guatemala and Honduras than to El Salvador and Nicaragua in the decades leading up to the revolutionary conflicts in the region. Again, there is no clear connection here between economic dependence and the fortunes of revolutionary movements.

If poverty, inequality, the "land question," powerful oligarchs, and external dependence do not adequately explain the uneven development of popular revolutionary movements in Central America, what does? In my view, revolutionary movements became powerful political forces in Nicaragua, El Salvador, and Guatemala because attempts during the 1960s and 1970s to redress a variety of social and political grievances through elections and peaceful organizing were greeted by the authoritarian regimes in those countries with blatant fraud and violent repression. As a

Table 5.9. *Net direct foreign investment in Central America minus net profit transfers, 1960–78 (millions of dollars).*

Years	Nicaragua	El Salvador	Guatemala	Honduras
1960–4	10.8	6.3	−11.1	−16.0
1965–9	−36.3	2.3	−40.6	−42.6
1970–4	−135.0	−21.5	−99.4	−75.1
1975–8	−240.9	−24.7	172.5	−203.8
Total	−401.4	−37.6	21.4	−413.3

Source: Weeks 1985: 93–4.

Table 5.10. *U.S. and multilateral assistance to Central America, 1953–79 (millions of dollars).*

Sources	Nicaragua	El Salvador	Guatemala	Honduras
U.S. economic assistance	345.8	218.4	526.0	305.1
U.S. military assistance	32.6	16.8	41.9	28.4
"Multilateral" banking aid	469.5	479.2	593.0	688.0
Total	847.9	714.4	1060.9	1021.5

Source: Petras and Morley 1983: 225.

result, growing numbers of people joined or collaborated with armed and ideologically radical guerrilla organizations; indeed, even moderate and predominantly middle-class political parties and voluntary associations joined broad alliances that effectively supported armed struggle. The development of popular revolutionary movements in Nicaragua, El Salvador, and Guatemala did not occur, in short, until the authoritarian regimes in those countries had made it absolutely clear that they would neither cede power to their political opponents through electoral means nor accede to the demands of nonviolent reformist movements.[8]

---

[8] Certain Guatemalan guerrillas purposely attempted to provoke abuses by the armed forces during the 1970s and early 1980s in order to recruit supporters, as Stoll (1993, 1999) emphasizes; but it hardly follows from this that the guerrillas in any sense started the violence in Guatemala; that the armed forces were tolerant of *unarmed* challenges "from below"; or that a strategy of armed struggle was therefore irrational or unjustified.

In case of Nicaragua, the Somoza family dominated the political life of that country for nearly a half century mainly by controlling the National Guard.[9] The Guard itself was the principal legacy of the long U.S. military occupation of Nicaragua (virtually continuous from 1912 to 1933), which was originally occasioned by the specter of economic nationalism in Nicaragua, including a fear that an interoceanic canal through the country might end up in the hands of a European power or even Japan.[10]

The dictatorship of Anastasio Somoza García (1936–56), which occasionally enacted populist and prolabor measures in order to secure popular support (see Walter 1993; Gould 1990), came to an abrupt end with the dictator's assassination in 1956. Somoza's sons, however, were able to dominate the state (including, especially, the National Guard) for another twenty years. Anastasio Somoza Debayle, who immediately took control of the Guard following his father's assassination, had himself elected president of Nicaragua in 1967 as the candidate of the so-called Liberal National Party, a quintessentially personalistic patronage party. At least two hundred people were killed by the Guard at an opposition rally prior to Somoza's election, which he won "by the traditional huge majority: this time 70% of the popular vote" (Black 1981: 44). In 1971, with the help of the U.S. ambassador, Somoza struck a deal that guaranteed the Conservative Party some 40 percent of the seats in the legislature and that convened a Constituent Assembly that would rewrite the Constitution to allow Somoza's reelection in 1974. (The Conservative Party was the long-time "loyal opposition" to the dictatorship.) Executive power was formally ceded shortly thereafter to a three-man junta, which included the Conservative leader Fernando Agüero. "The dictator, needless to say, kept control of the National Guard and continued to exercise real power, representing Nicaragua as before as head of state in international forums" (Black 1981: 58). "After the Agüero-Somoza pact of 1971," adds John Booth, "revolutionary student groups began to attract more youths from upper-class backgrounds, both Liberal and Conservative" (Booth 1985: 111). Somoza was easily reelected president in 1974, although the election

---

[9] Helpful accounts of the Nicaraguan Revolution may be found in Black 1981; Booth 1985; Dunkerley 1988: ch. 6; Pezzullo and Pezzullo 1993; and Everingham 1996. Weber 1981 and Vilas 1986 present more interpretive analyses.

[10] Millett 1977, the standard history of the Guard, includes a helpful discussion of the politics surrounding the U.S. occupation. See also Selser 1984, Walker 1985a, and Bermann 1986.

was boycotted by various elite opponents of Somoza, including the publisher Pedro Joaquín Chamorro and the coalition that he led, the Democratic Union of Liberation (UDEL). "For their pains, 27 leaders of the boycott were arrested and deprived of their political rights until March the following year" (Black 1981: 61).

Electoral fraud was also common in El Salvador, where military rule, like the Somoza dictatorship, dates back to the 1930s.[11] The Salvadoran armed forces ruled that country in an "institutional" manner from 1948 to 1979, running their own candidates for office and even creating their own political-patronage party, the so-called National Conciliation Party (PCN) (see Stanley 1996: ch. 3; Williams and Walter 1997: ch. 4). After 1948, no single general, family, or clique controlled the Salvadoran armed forces in the manner in which the Somozas controlled the Nicaraguan National Guard. Instead, *tandas* – tightly knit graduating classes from the military academy – would generally dominate the government (and the spoils that went with it) until they were displaced by another *tanda*. The armed forces also ruled in a close strategic alliance with the powerful Salvadoran oligarchy, providing (and occasionally exploiting) what Stanley (1996) has called a "protection racket" for elite interests.

By the early 1970s, however, institutionalized military rule in El Salvador was coming under increasing electoral threat. In 1972 the military was challenged by the National Opposition Union (UNO), an alliance of Christian Democrats, Social Democrats, and Communists. As it became apparent that UNO's presidential candidate, José Napoleón Duarte, was about to be elected, the army prohibited the announcement of further election returns and declared that the military candidate was the victor. A group of young army officers, with Duarte's support, then tried to stage a coup d'etat, but they were quickly routed. Duarte himself was kidnapped by the armed forces, tortured, and forced into exile.

The mayoral and legislative elections of 1974 "were marked by even more blatant manipulation than had been evident two years earlier" (Montgomery 1995: 67). And the 1977 presidential election was also characterized by massive fraud and violence against the opposition; a post-election rally of some fifty thousand people, which was called to denounce the fraud, was fired upon by the police, resulting in at least forty-eight deaths (Montgomery 1995: 72).

---

[11] Helpful overviews of recent Salvadoran history may be found in Baloyra 1982, Dunkerley 1985, North 1985, McClintock 1985a, Montgomery 1995, and Stanley 1996.

In Guatemala, finally, electoral fraud and violence had been the order of the day since the 1954 CIA-sponsored coup d'etat that placed the armed forces in power in that country, ending a decade of democratic rule.[12] As in El Salvador, the military ruled Guatemala in an "institutional" fashion, although nothing quite so formal as El Salvador's *tanda* system seems to have taken root.[13] As in El Salvador, moreover, military rule came under challenge in the early 1970s. In 1974, Christian Democrats and Social Democrats joined forces to form the National Opposition Front (FNO), nominating for president General Efraín Ríos Montt, who was believed to be one of the very few honest officers in the armed forces. Again, as in El Salvador, this coalition seemed headed for victory when the military began to delay voting results and ultimately declared its own candidate the victor. After speculation that Ríos Montt might lead a coup to overturn these results, he quietly accepted a diplomatic post in Spain instead.[14]

In 1978, the military's candidate, General Romeo Lucas García, easily won the presidency in an election in which only fifteen percent of eligible voters went to the polls. Nonetheless, violence against opposition political parties increased dramatically following General Lucas's election. The leader of the Social Democratic Party (PSD), Alberto Fuentes Mohr, and the head of the social-democratic United Revolutionary Front (FUR), Manuel Colom Argueta, were murdered in 1979. Vinicio Cerezo, secretary-general of the Christian Democratic Party (DCG), himself the target of several assassination attempts, announced that seventy-six party members were killed between September 1980 and May 1981 alone (Handy 1984: 179). (These killings occurred in the context of an escalating "dirty war" against the armed opposition and its supporters, real and imagined [see Chapter 6].) When the military candidate won yet again in the 1982 presidential election, "in another patent example of electoral fraud, all opposition parties once again joined in condemnation of the Lucas government" (Handy 1984: 182).

Electoral fraud and violence, however, were but one facet of the repressive and exclusionary regimes in Nicaragua, El Salvador, and Guatemala.

---

[12] Good accounts of recent Guatemalan history can be found in Black 1984, Handy 1984, Frank and Wheaton 1984, McClintock 1985b, Painter 1987, Jonas 1991, Trudeau 1993, and Perera 1993.

[13] On the Guatemalan armed forces, see Richards 1985, Black 1985, Nairn and Simon 1986, Anderson and Simon 1987, Schirmer 1989, 1996, and Martínez and Loeb 1994.

[14] During the early 1980s, Ríos Montt would lead a military government that waged a brutal counterinsurgency in the Western highlands.

In fact, virtually any type of peaceful political organizing and protest – particularly labor and peasant organizing, strikes, and land occupations – was liable to be attacked violently by the armed forces of these countries (or by allied "death squads") regardless of whether it was undertaken by revolutionaries or by reformists, including groups supported by the Catholic Church. Indeed, incumbent regimes made little distinction between reformists and revolutionaries, or between guerrillas and people merely suspected of collaborating with them. In addition to putative guerrillas and guerrilla sympathizers, rural and urban unions, student groups, Christian "base communities," priests and catechists, and moderate political parties and opposition figures were all singled out for attack by the National Guard in Nicaragua and by the armed forces, paramilitary organizations, and death squads in El Salvador and Guatemala. (One Salvadoran death squad circulated a handbill that advised, "Be a Patriot – Kill a Priest!") At times, in fact, virtually anyone of student age seems to have been regarded by state authorities as a political enemy.

In Nicaragua, notes John Booth, "Repression rose and fell according to the level of opposition activity – with major peaks during the late 1950s, the late 1960s, and from 1974 to the fall of the regime" (Booth 1985: 93). "In 1973 and 1974," notes another observer, "when cotton workers, hospital workers, and banana workers struck, and when slum dweller organizations, market traders, and other groups staged protest actions, the Somoza government tried to crush these organizations by disrupting protest actions and arresting the leaders" (Williams 1986: 167). An attempt to form a union of rural workers in the department of Chinandega resulted in the deaths of three hundred people at the hands of the National Guard (Paige 1985: 107). Somoza declared a state of siege in December 1974, after a group of Sandinistas held a number of the regime's luminaries hostage at a private Christmas party, winning the release of a number of political prisoners as well as the broadcast and publication of two lengthy communiques to the Nicaraguan people. During the state of siege, which was in effect until 1977,

The Guard sought to disrupt the FSLN, to capture and kill as many guerrillas as possible, and to take reprisals against any campesinos [peasants or rural people] who, willingly or not, supported the insurgents. The army often appropriated the resources of peasants without compensation. Whole regions underwent "agrarian reform" – population relocation to break up foci of guerrilla support. Suspected guerrilla collaborators suffered horrifying tortures. The Guard often murdered not only FSLN collaborators, but their families as well.

Estimates of the total number of peasants killed by the Guard begin at three thousand. (Booth 1985: 94–5)

Booth adds that when "in the late 1970s the government began to suspect the FSLN of recruiting mainly teenage males, the Guard seized many – often barely more than children – from Managua's streets and executed them on the shore of [Lake Managua]" (Booth 1985: 95).

In El Salvador, a paramilitary force called the Nationalist Democratic Organization (ORDEN, or *order* in Spanish) was used to attack union and political activists working among peasants and rural workers during the 1970s. (ORDEN was established in the mid-1960s with U.S. assistance [see, e.g., McClintock 1985a].) Father Rutilio Grande, a well-known priest who had worked to establish "base communities" around the town of Aguilares, was murdered by soldiers in March 1977. The Christian Federation of Salvadoran Peasants (FECCAS) and the Union of Rural Workers (UTC) organized a series of peaceful land invasions the following month, demanding that landowners rent unused land at affordable prices:

Two thousand troops came with helicopters and armoured troop carriers and took over the entire region, surrounding Aguilares in the early hours of 19 May. A peasant sleeping in the church tried to ring the church bell to alert the town but was shot and killed. . . . Soldiers moved through the town, ransacking houses, and later announced that one soldier and six civilians had been killed in an armed encounter. Eyewitnesses corrected the numbers: at least 50 townspeople had been shot dead and hundreds taken away by the army. (Pearce 1986: 168.)

Another activist priest, Alfonso Navarro, was killed shortly after the events in Aguilares. In all, ten priests and one seminarian were assassinated between March 1977 and June 1981, and at least sixty priests were expelled from the country or forced into exile.

In May 1979, a recently formed political front or "popular organization," as it was known, occupied the metropolitan cathedral in San Salvador, demanding the release of imprisoned members of the group. "[President Carlos Humberto] Romero's reply was unambiguous: troops fired on the demonstrators outside the cathedral, and some 25 people died in the mad scramble to reach the precarious safety of the church" (Dunkerley 1985: 127). Nearly eight hundred people would be killed in 1979. And on January 22, 1980, when the "popular organizations" organized the largest demonstration in Salvadoran history, with more than two hundred thousand people gathered in San Salvador from all over the country, security forces fired on the crowd, leaving forty-nine dead and hundreds wounded (Montgomery 1995: 108–9).

State violence in Guatemala, although less frequently reported in the United States than that in Nicaragua or El Salvador, was the most deadly in the region. In the predominantly indigenous department of El Quiché alone, 168 cooperative or village leaders – mainly ethnic Ixils – were killed between 1976 and 1978 (Handy 1984: 244). Over one hundred men, women, and children were massacred in the town of Panzós in May 1978, after gathering to protest evictions from nearby lands (Aguilera Peralta 1979). Amnesty International documented some 615 "disappearances" between mid-1978 and November 1980, and the same organization documented the cases of nine Catholic priests who had either "disappeared" or been killed by security forces between April 1980 and July 1981 alone (AI 1987: 3, 24). In one remarkable incident in 1979, seven alleged guerrillas were executed by soldiers in the central plaza of Chajul, El Quiché, following a show trial; one of the bodies was dragged before the church and set afire, and all were dumped in a common grave (Perera 1993: 106).

In January 1980, a group of peasants from El Quiché – including members of the Committee of Peasant Unity (CUC) – participated in an occupation of the Spanish embassy in Guatemala City, demanding that military abuses be investigated:

Despite the demands by the Spanish ambassador that the peasants inside the building not be attacked, the police stormed the building and 39 people were killed including a former vice-president and a foreign minister who were both in the building to talk with the peasants. [Most of those killed died in a fire of uncertain origin.] Only the ambassador and one peasant survived. The peasant was later kidnapped from the hospital where he was recuperating from his injuries. After the attack the Spanish government broke off all diplomatic relations with Guatemala and withdrew its ambassador. (Handy 1984: 245)[15]

Several months later, twenty-five leaders of the National Confederation of Labor (CNT) were abducted from a meeting at their headquarters in

---

[15] Stoll (1999: 76) calculates the number killed as 36. One of those killed was the father of Rigoberta Menchú, the future Nobel Peace Prize winner (see Menchú 1984: ch. 25). Her as-told-to "autobiography" is an excellent case study of the radicalizing effects of state violence; although Menchú herself never actually joined the guerrillas, she helped bring them international legitimacy.

Guatemala City and were never seen again (AI 1987: 118–9; Black 1984: 90–1).[16]

Clearly, Jeane Kirkpatrick's famous suggestion that "traditional," non-Communist autocrats such as those in Central America "do not disturb the habitual rhythms of work and leisure, habitual places of residence, habitual patterns of family and personal relations" (1986: 33) is not a particularly apt characterization. Indeed, given the sort of violence that even moderates and reformists encountered in Nicaragua, El Salvador, and Guatemala during the 1970s, it is hardly surprising that many people came to view armed struggle and the overthrow of extant states as the only viable political strategy in those countries. The radical "political-military organizations," as they were called, that led the popular revolutionary movements in Central America were themselves formed for the most part by dissidents from electorally oriented parties (including Christian Democratic as well as Communist parties), who were repeatedly frustrated, and their lives endangered in many cases, by continual electoral fraud and political repression. Communist parties and political fronts, it should be noted, were not the main "mobilizing structures" of revolutionary movements in the region (as they were in postwar Southeast Asia), although the Salvadoran Communist Party (PCS) and a faction from the divided Guatemalan Communist Party (PGT) did belatedly adopt a strategy of armed struggle after the worst repression had begun in those countries.

Political-military organizations, which at first included no more than a handful of members, ultimately profited from this indiscriminate repression. They did so not only because they seemed more realistic than electoral parties or reformist groups, but also because they could provide protective cover for at least some of those who feared state violence. Indeed, active collaboration with revolutionaries, which might once have invited persecution, came to be seen by many as the only alternative (other than flight) to violent death. "The arbitrariness of the exercise of political-military power by the dictatorship," as Carlos Vilas has written of Nicaragua, "the indiscriminate – and finally, genocidal – character of the repression . . . converted active rebellion and participation in the revolutionary struggle into a defensive question – life or death" (1986: 112–3). This dynamic is also evident in Guatemala and El Salvador. For example, the aforementioned executions in Chajul, Guatemala, notes Victor Perera,

[16] Helpful accounts of state violence against the Guatemalan urban labor movement may be found in Frundt 1987, Goldston 1989, and Levenson-Estrada 1994.

had the opposite effect of what they [state authorities] intended. Hundreds of Ixils continued to join the Guerrilla Army of the Poor; and thousands provided the EGP with food, shelter, and information about the army's movements. By the following year [1980], the army itself estimated that roughly half the population of the [Ixil] triangle [in northern El Quiché] had become active or potential collaborators with the insurgents. (Perera 1993: 106–7; see also Davis 1988: 23)

And in El Salvador, notes Elisabeth Wood,

repression led many people hitherto active only in peasant or student organizations to support the previously inconsequential Salvadoran guerrilla forces. In interviews several FMLN members stated that they joined the guerrillas out of outrage at the actions of the security forces against family members or neighbors. . . . Others joined because they felt they had no choice, some because they had been identified as activists in opposition organizations and were therefore likely targets of the government forces and others because they were reputed to be even if they were not. (Wood 2000a: 47)

Thus, the exclusionary and violently repressive character of the Nicaraguan, Salvadoran, and Guatemalan states unintentionally recruited new members and supporters for the revolutionary movements, particularly in those relatively isolated regions – north-central Nicaragua, northern El Salvador, and the western highlands of Guatemala – that these infrastructurally weak states did not effectively control. As in Southeast Asia, then, states themselves unwittingly helped construct revolutionary movements in Central America.

Radical political-military organizations were themselves born, and eventually coalesced, in this context of political exclusion and violence. Nicaragua's Sandinista National Liberation Front was founded by three political activists in 1961, although it never grew larger than a few hundred people until the eve of the insurrection of 1978–9. The Front was also divided during the 1970s among three political "tendencies" that split over strategic questions. The Front's prime mover, Carlos Fonseca Amador, was a former member of Nicaragua's Communist Party (PSN), which did not itself join the armed struggle against Somoza until the eleventh hour. After a series of setbacks during the 1960s, the Sandinistas managed to establish a sizable network (or "chain," as they called it) of collaborators among the peasants of north-central Nicaragua (see, e.g., Horton 1998: ch. 3). Many of these peasants had been adversely affected by a movement of land enclosures by wealthy cattle ranchers in the area (Williams 1986: 129f). The Sandinistas later recruited rural workers on the Pacific coast, and in March 1978 they formed the Association of Rural Workers (ATC), which "was able to convert itself into a powerful force of the FSLN, not only in building the armed struggle but in organizing political action by workers and peasants in rural areas" (cited in Paige 1985: 108–9).

During the insurrection of 1978–9,

Training camps in Costa Rica, Honduras, and Nicaragua swelled into substantial operations. The overall number of FSLN troops thus ballooned from between five hundred and one thousand in early 1978 to nearly three thousand by late 1978 to around five thousand by July 1979. To incorporate the many irregular volunteers, the FSLN also ran short combat-training sessions for citizens when Sandinista columns occupied a neighborhood. These trained volunteers were the core of the popular militia. (Booth 1985: 149–50)

The Sandinistas were able to recruit these volunteers from a variety of urban groups, especially students and petty tradespeople. According to Carlos Vilas's study of those killed in the insurrection, it was these groups, and not full-time wage earners or peasants, that formed the principal social base of the insurrection (Vilas 1986: 119).

El Salvador's Farabundo Martí National Liberation Front (FMLN), an umbrella group of five political-military organizations that was formed in October 1980, had "two main sources: radicalized religious activists, and the Salvadoran Communist Party" (Leiken 1984: 115). The largest guerrilla group in the FMLN, the Popular Forces of Liberation (FPL), was formed in 1970 by dissidents from the Communist Party, led by Salvador Cayetano Carpio. (The event that precipitated this split was the Communist Party's support for the brief "soccer war" with Honduras in 1969.) The second most important guerrilla group, the Popular Revolutionary Army (ERP), was founded in 1972 by activists from both the Communist and Christian Democratic youth movements. A third group, the Armed Forces of National Resistance (FARN), broke from the ERP in 1975 following the latter group's execution of a well-known intellectual-turned-guerrilla named Roque Dalton, who was charged with being a "Soviet-Cuban and CIA double agent" by the ERP's military staff. (Many of those within the ERP faction that formed the FARN were Protestants, and at least two were Baptist ministers [Montgomery 1995: 104].) The Communist Party and the small Revolutionary Party of Central American Workers (PRTC) also subsequently formed guerrilla groups that joined the FMLN.

Although the social base of the FMLN was quite diverse (Wood 2000b: ch. 6), its backbone seems to have consisted of "semiproletarians" who

164

worked tiny plots of land in the less densely populated northern part of the country (which also happened to be a region, as noted previously, that was not well controlled by the central state).[17] Although they owned or rented land, these poor peasants migrated to cotton, coffee, or sugar estates for part of the year to supplement their meager incomes. Landless laborers and landowning middle peasants, however, also joined or collaborated with the guerrillas in impressive numbers (Cabarrús 1983: 365–7; Pearce 1986: 150–1). And the guerrillas also included, especially at the leadership level, a significant number of urban political and trade union activists, intellectuals, students, and professionals. At its peak numerical strength, in the early 1980s, the FMLN is estimated to have had about eight to twelve thousand guerrillas (Barry 1990: 60; see also Dunkerley 1985: 221; Halloran 1987).

The Guatemalan National Revolutionary Unity (URNG), which was formed in January 1982, began, like the FMLN, as an umbrella organization, in this case of four political-military groups. All of these groups descended (directly or indirectly) from the guerrilla organizations of an earlier and less successful "wave" of revolutionary mobilization in Guatemala during the 1960s (see Wickham-Crowley 1992: pt. 2). The largest component of the URNG, at least until the early 1980s, the Guerrilla Army of the Poor (EGP), was formed in 1972 by radical Christians and survivors of the Edgar Ibarra Guerrilla Front, "one of the strongest guerrilla forces in the continent," which was decimated in the late 1960s (Black 1984: 68, 106). Another important group, the Revolutionary Organization of People in Arms (ORPA), which was not launched publicly until 1979, split from the Rebel Armed Forces (FAR), another group founded in the 1960s, which was close to the Communist Party (PGT). The FAR itself also joined the URNG, having been rejuvenated in the mid-1970s by disaffected Christian Democrats. Finally, a faction from the Communist Party, the so-called Guatemalan Labor Party Núcleo de Dirección, also belatedly organized a guerrilla force after breaking with the Party's central committee in 1978 over the question of armed struggle (Jonas 1991: 138; Black 1984: chs. 4–5; Handy 1984: ch. 11).

Unlike their predecessors of the 1960s, which mainly operated in the eastern part of the country, the Guatemalan guerrilla groups of the 1970s

---

[17] The guerrillas were also strong in parts of Usulután, which was abandoned by most landlords and the armed forces in the early 1980s (Wood 2000b: ch. 3).

(especially the EGP and ORPA) tended to focus their political work on Guatemala's indigenous population in the western highlands.[18] As in El Salvador, the guerrillas seem to have drawn much of their support from the migratory semiproletariat as well as from landless laborers and some middle peasants (Paige 1983: 728; Davis 1988: 14–20; Jonas 1991: 133–4). Unlike the Sandinistas and the FMLN, however, the URNG does not seem to have developed much urban support (see, e.g., Payeras 1987). The causal mechanisms that drove ordinary people into an alliance with armed revolutionaries, however, were very similar to those in Nicaragua and El Salvador:

> Military repression of reformist efforts and community organization led . . . to widespread defensive mobilization: to protect themselves from the landowners and the military, the Indian communities began to organize for the purposes of self-defense. Victimized by the military and lacking alternatives for economic self-improvement, the Indians became increasingly willing to turn to armed opposition, swelling the ranks of the guerrilla movement. By and large, their resistance was a result of state repression, not its cause. (Trudeau and Schoultz 1986: 37–8)

By 1980 the guerrillas numbered between six thousand and eight thousand, with up to half a million active supporters (Jonas 1991: 138).

The combination of electoral fraud and indiscriminate repression by infrastructurally weak states not only swelled the ranks of guerrilla organizations and encouraged those organizations to coalesce, but also prompted many moderate and reformist political groups, including several predominantly middle-class organizations, to enter into more or less open strategic alliances with the guerrillas. Of course, the revolutionaries' own openness to such alliances – which generally involved ideological and programmatic compromises – was also necessary for their formation.[19] These groups were generally helpful in providing material aid, political legitimacy, and foreign support (official and unofficial) for the armed opposition in Nicaragua, El Salvador, and (to a lesser extent) Guatemala. Perhaps just as importantly, their very refusal to participate in "politics as usual" reinforced the perception that armed struggle was the only realistic mechanism for political and social change.

---

[18] Some critics, however, maintain that these groups did not break from a class-reductionist view of the "Indian" or "national question." See, e.g., Smith 1987.

[19] The ideological and strategic dogmatism of the Shining Path guerrilla movement in Peru, which I consider in Chapter 7, ruled out such an alliance, to that movement's undoubted detriment. Here is an important factor that cannot be wholly explained by state structures and practices (see Chapter 2).

In 1977 the Sandinista Front encouraged the formation of the "Group of Twelve," which consisted of prominent anti-Somoza businesspeople, academics, and intellectuals; these individuals were allegedly designated for cabinet posts in a revolutionary government. Exposed and forced to flee Nicaragua, "the Twelve began to lobby against international aid and to organize the anti-Somoza coalitions within Nicaragua" (Booth 1985: 102). The Sandinistas also catalyzed the formation of the so-called United People's Movement (MPU) in the early summer of 1978; this group eventually brought together some twenty-two labor and political organizations, including the main teachers' union, Nicaragua's leading labor and student federations, the country's principal women's organization, and two small left-wing parties. In February 1979, moreover, following the breakdown of negotiations aimed at securing Somoza's resignation (see Chapter 6), two primarily middle-class parties – the Independent Liberal Party (PLI) and the People's Social Christian Party (PPSC), the country's main Christian Democratic organization at the time – joined with the MPU, together with several other groups, to form the so-called National Patriotic Front (FPN). "Given its broader political base," Booth has noted,

the FPN's formal program contained somewhat less far-reaching proposals than that of the MPU.... [H]owever, the FSLN justified the watered-down FPN program as necessary to unite disparate forces seeking a common anti-Somoza objective. (Booth 1985: 155)

The Sandinistas eventually headed a broad "multi-class populist coalition" that included workers and peasants, students and youth, middle-class folk, and part of Nicaragua's elite (Foran, Klouzal, and Rivera 1997: 46–7).

In El Salvador, each of the guerrilla groups was affiliated with a "popular organization" that brought together a large number of labor and political groupings. "Government repression solidified the links between the popular organizations and the guerrilla groups," notes Leiken. "The former came to constitute recruiting ground for the latter" (Leiken 1984: 117). The Popular Forces of Liberation, for example, was closely tied to the Popular Revolutionary Bloc (BPR), the largest of the popular organizations with some sixty thousand members; the BPR included two large unions of peasants and rural workers (FECCAS and UTC), the country's main teachers' union, a shantytown-dwellers' association, and student groups. The Popular Revolutionary Army and the Armed Forces of National Resistance were closely connected to the Popular Leagues of February 28 (LP-28) and the United Popular Action Front (FAPU), respectively; and the Communist Party and the PRTC were aligned with the National Democratic Union (UDN) and the Movement of Popular Liberation (MLP), respectively. In April 1980, these five popular organizations (the BLP, LP-28, FAPU, UDN, and MLP) would join with the social-democratic National Revolutionary Movement (MNR), led by Guillermo Ungo, the Popular Social Christian Movement (MPSC), led by Rubén Zamora, and the Independent Movement of Professionals and Technicians of El Salvador (MIPTES) to form the Democratic Revolutionary Front (FDR). Later that year, the FDR and the FMLN announced their formal alliance. "Throughout the spring and summer," Tommie Sue Montgomery points out,

delegations from the FDR toured Europe and Latin America in a fairly successful effort to gain international support. Four European countries declared their support for the FDR, and the Socialist International, at its June 1980 meeting in Oslo, voted to support it. In Latin America, the strongest early support came from Mexican President José López Portillo, who permitted the FDR to establish political offices in that country. (Montgomery 1995: 111)

In Guatemala, finally, the guerrilla groups were closely tied for some time to two political fronts, the so-called Democratic Front Against Repression (FDRC) and the Popular Front of January 31 (FP-31). The FDRC nominally united over 170 organizations, including the National Committee of Labor Unity (CNUS), the Social Democratic Party (PSD), and the United Democratic Front (FUR). The FP-31 brought together, among other groups, the important Committee of Peasant Unity (CUC), which had ties to the Guerrilla Army of the Poor, and a radical Christian organization (Black 1984: 107–9). The FDRC and the FP-31 merged in February 1982, forming the Guatemalan Committee of Patriotic Unity (CGUP).

In sum, radical organizations were able to mobilize powerful revolutionary movements in Nicaragua, El Salvador, and Guatemala not simply because of rapid social change, widespread social grievances, class struggles, economic crisis, or imperialist domination per se; rather, these groups were effective mobilizers because the brutal and indiscriminate violence with which exclusionary and infrastructurally weak states greeted attempts to bring about change through electoral and other nonviolent means backfired, unintentionally convincing substantial numbers of groups and individuals that armed struggle aimed at overthrowing the state was legitimate and even necessary. To be sure, not all of the grievances that lay behind the resultant revolutionary movements pertained directly to the actions of those states – although abuses by government officials, soldiers, and allied death squads certainly affected thousands of people, many of whom joined or supported the guerrillas as a direct result of such abuses (see, e.g., Danner 1993 on El Salvador; Stoll 1993 on Guatemala; Brockett 1995). Many who joined or supported the revolutionaries had other "local" or particularistic demands – a piece of land, for example, or better wages and working conditions. But these concerns became the "causes" of revolutionary movements only because specific state structures and practices prevented them from being redressed, or even honestly addressed, in a nonviolent, meliorative fashion. As a result of state repression, in fact, by the late 1970s effective reformist organizations were essentially unavailable in these societies to many ordinary folk with an interest in even modest socioeconomic reforms. The plausibility of this analysis is reinforced by the unique success of the Sandinista Front in actually overthrowing the Nicaraguan state – the most autonomous or socially "disembedded" state in the region – despite the fact that land and other socioeconomic issues were generally *less* pressing there, in comparative terms, than elsewhere in Central America. The plausibility of this analysis is also reinforced by the neglected case of Honduras, where no significant revolutionary movement emerged at all, despite tremendous poverty, inequality, and insecurity.

The Function of the Little-Known Case in Theory Formation, or Why Was There No Revolutionary Movement in Honduras?

Just as Honduran elites were flexible enough to provide escape valves for popular discontent, they were never so violent as to inspire large-scale leftist resistance. In recent years, political scientists have become increasingly aware of the critical role played by repression in the creation of revolutionary movements. Of all the factors that account for Honduras's comparative tranquility, this was surely the most important. Whatever else might be said about that country's military, it did not display the massive, often indiscriminate savagery witnessed in El Salvador, Guatemala, and Nicaragua.
      – Donald E. Schulz and Deborah Sundloff Schulz (1994: 319)

At a time when powerful revolutionary movements were forming in Nicaragua, El Salvador, and Guatemala, neighboring Honduras was remarkably quiet.[20] "In a region where the fires of revolution burn white hot," notes Steven Volk, "Honduras has been a model of stability, a bizarre anomaly" (Volk 1983: 225). The absence of a significant revolutionary movement in Honduras does indeed pose a puzzle. As noted earlier, Honduras has historically been the poorest Central American country; like its neighbors, moreover, it experienced a grave economic crisis during the 1970s and 1980s; landlessness and land poverty, while not as severe as in El Salvador or Guatemala, rivaled that of prerevolutionary Nicaragua; and the country is as externally dependent as any other in the region. Honduras, in fact, is the classic "banana republic," a country with a long and unhappy history of dependence on banana exports and of domination by U.S. corporations. (Before bananas, in fact, U.S. corporations bled Honduras of its silver.) Here would seem to lie fertile ground for a radical "national liberation" movement.

The Honduran left, however, and the revolutionary left in particular, were marginal political actors during the 1970s and 1980s. One small guerrilla column, for example, was destroyed after entering the country from Nicaragua in July 1983. Surrounded by the Honduran military, the survivors of this incursion quickly surrendered and were promptly executed; among those murdered was a North American priest, James Carney (Schulz and Schulz 1994: 81). In the mid-1980s, it was estimated that the four main guerrilla organizations in Honduras had a *combined* membership of about six hundred individuals (Halloran 1987), although the number of armed guerrillas would have been smaller. "None of these groups had ever shown any signs of having mass support, much less the ability to coordinate their activities" (Schulz and Schulz 1994: 216).

How then did Honduras manage to avoid the violent civil conflict that befell its neighbors? To paraphrase Werner Sombart (1976 [1906]), why was there no revolutionary movement in Honduras?

Political context is the crucial differentiating factor. The key difference between Honduras and its neighbors, is what might be called the "semi-openness" of the political regimes in Honduras after the 1960s. During this period, Honduras has alternated between civilian and comparatively moderate military rule; most importantly, perhaps, there was a brief period of "military reformism" in the early 1970s, during which time an impor-

---

[20] Good accounts of recent Honduran history may be found in Posas and del Cid 1983, Morris 1984a, Lapper and Painter 1985, Acker 1988, Schulz and Schulz 1994, and Euraque 1996.

tant if flawed land reform was enacted (see, e.g., Sieder 1995; Ruhl 1984). (By contrast, military officers who supported land reform in El Salvador at this time were ousted by military hardliners.) As a result of this political semiopenness, reformist political currents as well as ideologically moderate labor and peasant unions have been unusually free, at least by Central American standards, to operate and organize within Honduras, even during periods of direct military rule. In fact, "in the 1960s, Honduras gave birth to the most militant and, before long, the best-organized peasant movement in Central America" (Volk 1983: 215).

James Morris has noted how the alternation between reformist and conservative rule in Honduras has produced a "cycle of frustration" (Morris 1984a: ch. 9). Paradoxically, however, this cycle has not produced, but may actually account for the absence of, a strong revolutionary movement in Honduras. Intermittent reform and the impermanence and relative mildness of military rule led most leftist and progressive movements in Honduras to eschew a strategy of armed struggle. Even more importantly, this political context has discouraged ordinary people from joining or collaborating with those small guerrilla groups that have attempted to operate in the country.

The semiopenness of Honduran politics essentially dates from the important general strike of 1954 against the powerful U.S. banana companies – "the most extensive industrial and political action in Honduran history" (Lapper and Painter 1984: 35). Although the strike resulted in very small wage increases and prompted the banana companies to lay off thousands of workers, the strikers did win their principal demand: the legal recognition of trade unions (MacCameron 1983). Shortly thereafter, the reformist Ramón Villeda Morales of the Liberal Party was elected president:

Villeda set up a public-works program to provide the nation with some basic infrastructure (as of 1950 the capital city had no paved roads) and to employ some of the thousands of dismissed banana workers. He also ordered a number of land-colonization plans, distributing lands in regions of low population density to peasant families. . . . More important, in September 1962 Villeda pushed through the country's first agrarian-reform law. (Volk 1983: 210)

In 1963, Villeda was overthrown by the armed forces, led by Colonel Oswaldo López Arellano, much to the delight of big landowners and right-wing forces. López, however, "turned out to be a political chameleon"; in 1967, with land occupations by peasant groups on the rise, "López revitalised the agrarian reform, as part of his search for a new political base" (Lapper and Painter 1985: 54, 59). The Honduran government began to harass and evict Salvadoran emigrants who had squatted on public lands, thereby facilitating land transfers without the need of seizing the property of large landowners.

The Honduran government's actions, coupled with the flow of Salvadorans back into their native land, precipitated the "soccer war" of 1969. The results of this short war were quite paradoxical. The return of thousands of land-hungry peasants to El Salvador contributed to the growing crisis in that country, which would soon escalate into a full-blown revolutionary situation. In Honduras, however, the war ultimately served to dampen political conflict. For El Salvador's invasion of Honduras proved to be an embarrassing disaster for the Honduran military. Only the intervention of the Organization of American States (OAS) saved the army from complete defeat. (Salvadoran troops had advanced deeply into Honduran territory before the OAS threatened both countries with an economic boycott [Lapper and Painter 1985: 61].) This disaster for the Honduran armed forces, however, would prove a blessing in disguise for subsequent political stability in Honduras, for what it was worth. The major result of the "soccer war," notes Volk, "was noting short of monumental" for the country, as military defeat

paved the way for reform in Honduras. The Honduran officer corps became increasingly influenced by younger officers who drew their inspiration from military reformers in Peru and Panama. Many of the older, corruption-tainted officers were purged. (Volk 1983: 216–7)

Following a short-lived civilian government, military reformists seized power in 1972, led once again by (now) General López, and enacted yet another agrarian reform law – a reform more thoroughgoing than that enacted a decade earlier by Villeda, the very man whom López had ousted. Peasants were now granted the right to occupy certain public lands, and landowners were obliged either to rent or cultivate their own untilled land. Provision was also made for the return of lands to peasant communities that had been illegally, or quasilegally, expropriated by landlords. In addition, the size of farms liable to expropriation was raised to five hundred hectares (Lapper and Painter 1985: 63–4).

Mark Ruhl estimates that only about 22 percent of landless and land-poor families in Honduras in the mid-1970s directly benefited from the new agrarian reform. But this reform was "very important symbolically,"

Ruhl suggests, because "the program demonstrated the continued flexibility and reform potential of the Honduran government and fostered an 'incrementalist' policy orientation among the peasant organizations":

> The fact that campesinos could win disputes over land titles . . . and force "stolen" land to be returned by landlords was very significant. Such outcomes would have been almost unimaginable in Guatemala, El Salvador, or Nicaragua. The association of the military with land reform during the late 1960s and 1970s also created a much more progressive image for Honduran soldiers than for their counterparts in neighboring countries and demonstrated clearly that the armed forces were not under the control of the Honduran rural oligarchy. (Ruhl 1984: 55)

Thus, the reformist political orientation of at least some Honduran officers during this period had important ideological effects, in turn, on important forces in Honduran society.

Military reformists were, however, pushed out of power by more conservative officers in the late 1970s, but Honduras returned to formal civilian rule, once again, after 1980. As elsewhere in the region, the return to civilian rule coincided with a steep rise in human rights abuses against labor and peasant activists by the armed forces, although these abuses fell far short of the magnitude of those in Nicaragua, El Salvador, and Guatemala. These abuses have been attributed to conservative sectors of the army associated with General Gustavo Álvarez Martínez, who became chief of the armed forces in 1982. During the early 1980s, a U.S.-trained counterintelligence unit known as Battalion 3–16, which Álvarez founded and led, "disappeared" at least 184 "subversives" (CEJIL 1994; Schulz and Schulz 1994: 84–7). In March 1984, however, younger officers deposed Álvarez and forced him into exile, and rights abuses fell sharply. "The fall of Álvarez Martínez," notes Hector Pérez Brignoli, "is an event of great significance: It implies a setback, although perhaps only temporary, of the most repressive military sectors" (Pérez Brignoli 1985: 143).

If the semiopenness of the Honduran polity accounts for the weakness of the revolutionary left in that country, what then accounts for this semiopen political context? Why have the Honduran armed forces, in particular, been less consistently brutal and less politically conservative than their counterparts in Nicaragua, El Salvador, and Guatemala? Two factors deserve special emphasis. Most importantly, Honduras has never had a powerful landowning oligarchy of the Salvadoran or Guatemalan variety. During the nineteenth century, as Ruhl notes,

Coffee did not assume a major role in the Honduran economy and the ejidos [common lands] remained intact. Coffee failed to reorient Honduran agriculture for several reasons including the lack of a high proportion of the rich, volcanic soils conducive to coffee production and the preoccupation of Honduran governments both with intra-elite political conflicts and with encouraging foreign silver mining and other ventures. . . . Because of these various factors, no strong cohesive oligarchy developed in Honduras to dominate the government and to absorb the ejidal lands. (1984: 36; see also Williams 1994: ch. 3)

(Thus does volcanic activity – or the lack thereof – shape the fate of millions!)

Foremost among the foreign "ventures" encouraged by the Honduran government were the huge U.S.-owned banana plantations along the country's north coast, which were operated virtually as states within a state. As Morris notes, however, the "concessions made by the government to foreign investors, though perhaps compromising latitude of action and control, did result in ever-increasing revenues for Honduran administrations" (Morris 1984b: 197). As a result, and because no other lucrative economic opportunities presented themselves, elite political factions vied for control over the state and for the wealth and patronage that went with it. These struggles, moreover, resulted in a very different type of relationship between that elite and Honduras's lower classes – a relationship generally more paternalistic and less coercive than was to be found in Guatemala or El Salvador.

"With little local oligarchy to protect," moreover, "Honduras did not develop a professional military tied to concentrated economic interests, and the military did not view its function as making more or less permanent war on its own people" (Shepherd 1986b: 127). The military's relative autonomy from conservative landowners is most evident from its sponsorship of land reform during the late 1960s and early 1970s. Ironically, it was the more conservative of the two dominant parties in Honduras, the National Party (itself ousted from power by the military in 1972), that became the more insistent voice during the 1970s for a return to civilian rule.

The absence of a powerful oligarchy is, in fact, the single factor that best accounts for the lack of revolutionary mobilization in Honduras. Two related points, however, must immediately be noted. First, this factor has dampened revolutionary mobilization in Honduras in an *indirect* fashion – that is, through the relative autonomy that it has allowed the Honduran state and armed forces. The weak Honduran oligarchy has certainly not

174

inhibited peasant collective action, nor is it sufficient to explain why such collective action has not been channeled in a more radical direction. This is underscored by a second important point: that the absence of a powerful oligarchy obviously did very *little* to dampen revolutionary mobilization in neighboring Nicaragua. The weakness of the oligarchy in that country also helped to make possible the autonomy of the Somoza regime, but in this case state autonomy assumed the form of a highly repressive "above-class" dictatorship whose actions served to facilitate revolutionary mobilization.

A second factor that helps to account for the semiopenness of the Honduran polity – and one closely related to the weakness of the local oligarchy – has been the relatively plentiful supply of public land. This is the result of Honduras's comparatively sparse population and the absence of an oligarchic drive to buy or seize such land for coffee cultivation. (The departure of thousands of Salvadorans before and during the "soccer war" is also important in this respect.) As noted, state control of public lands has made it possible to enact a significant land reform without expropriating, and thereby alienating, large landowners.

Of course, these two factors alone do not by themselves guarantee a relatively open polity. Nicaragua, after all, has also been characterized by a comparatively weak (and divided) oligarchy and by plentiful public lands, yet these factors did not prevent the consolidation of the Somoza dictatorship. Perhaps the key factor that accounts for the very different political trajectory of these two countries, despite similar socioeconomic profiles, has been the nature of their relationship to the United States. For while Honduras has been a historic playground for U.S. corporations, it was not militarily occupied for two decades, like Nicaragua, by the United States. (The compliance of the Honduran political elite and the absence of any possible route through Honduras for an interoceanic canal are undoubtedly crucial factors here.) So while the United States has played a significant role in the evolution of the Honduran armed forces (Ropp 1974), it never bequeathed to Honduras an institution quite so reactionary and repressive as the Nicaraguan National Guard.

At a time when revolutionary conflicts had engulfed its neighbors, Jorge Arturo Reina usefully summarized "the principal reasons why there is no violence for now" in Honduras:

1. The social reforms enacted by the government of Villeda Morales. 2. The exodus of Salvadorans due to the 1969 war. 3. The reforms enacted in the first stage [i.e.,

175

1972–75] of the military government led by General López Arellano. 4. The hope that the electoral road can bring about changes peacefully. 5. The relative tolerance of military rule compared to the reactionary military regimes elsewhere in the region. (Reina 1981: 46)

In sum, the cycle of civilian and comparatively mild military rule in Honduras, however frustrating it has been for those Hondurans who would prefer more stable democratic rule as well as more thoroughgoing socioeconomic reforms, seems to have prevented the emergence of a popular revolutionary movement in that country. The extensive poverty and vast inequalities in Honduras are, to be sure, grievous, tragic, and morally reprehensible; alas, grievances, tragedy, and moral outrage alone do not revolutions make. In this sense, Honduras is a "little-known case" (Kenworthy 1973) of great significance for theories of revolution.

Conclusion

The evidence reviewed in this chapter clearly suggests that the character and practices of Central American states – and not rapid modernization, class structure, poverty, or external dependence per se – determined whether or not armed and ideologically radical revolutionaries could mobilize a substantial revolutionary movement and guerrilla army. Extensive revolutionary mobilization occurred where political exclusion and state repression were the norm during the 1960s and 1970s – that is, in Nicaragua, El Salvador, and Guatemala. By contrast, revolutionaries in Honduras found it impossible to win mass support due to the comparatively more open political regimes in that country during the same period. Accordingly, the revolutionary conflicts that occurred in Central America during the 1970s and 1980s should not be seen as evidence of a generalized regional crisis of "liberal" or "oligarchic capitalism" (see Weeks 1986a; Woodward 1984), but rather of a crisis of *autocratic* capitalism – or capitalist authoritarianism – at the level of specific national societies. As in Southeast Asia, moreover, state violence typically channeled an array of social groups behind the banner of revolutionary organizations, making it extremely difficult to view the resulting movements as representative of any single class.

This analysis, while obviously a state-centered one, turns on its head the familiar claim that collective action requires expanding political opportunities. Far from being a response to political openings, the revolutionary mobilization that occurred in Central America during the 1970s and 1980s was generally a response to political exclusion and violent repression – the *contraction* of political opportunities and the *closing down* of "political space." State structures and practices unintentionally helped to construct revolutionary movements not by lessening repression or providing access to political authorities (to the contrary), but by closing off or destroying for a great many people alternative means of interest representation or even the possibility of living with a modicum of personal security.

This conclusion, it might be noted, accords with that reached by many scholars of working-class politics – including Bendix (1977: ch. 3) and Lipset (1983) – who have argued that political repression, not inequality or exploitation per se, encourages ordinary workers to support revolutionary parties and organizations. In fact, the evidence from both Southeast Asia and Central America strongly suggests that exclusionary states that indiscriminately repress their opponents have unintentionally encouraged revolutionary mobilization, especially in those regions of the national society where state power does not fully penetrate. At least five distinct causal mechanisms or processes are evident in this respect.

First, mundane economic and workplace grievances tend to be politicized and "nationalized" under despotic regimes; not just particular landlords or capitalists, but the state itself comes to be viewed as complicit in, and an obstacle to redressing, such injustices. In this type of political context, other things being equal, movements that promise an altogether new political order – that is, specifically revolutionary movements – come to be viewed favorably by large numbers of people.

Second, despotic regimes provide a common enemy and a highly visible focus of opposition for groups and classes that may have very *different* grievances. The existence of such a common enemy makes it easier for revolutionaries – at least revolutionaries who are astute enough to speak for the nation or national society as a whole – to forge a broad, multiclass coalition. This has been the strategy, in fact, of the most successful revolutionary movements that we have examined – the Vietnamese, Indonesian, Nicaraguan, and, to a lesser extent, Salvadoran.

Third, exclusionary and repressive states render political moderates, reformists, and legalistic opposition groups and leaders relatively impotent and inconsequential. It may become more dangerous, in fact, to associate with such above-ground groups than with armed revolutionaries, whose activities are less open to state surveillance and who can, after all, defend themselves when attacked. In repressive political contexts, political moderates thus tend to lose popular support (if they had any to begin with) or to become radicalized themselves (in their means of struggle if not their ultimate ends) or at least to form strategic alliances with revolutionaries, especially if and when the latter become sufficiently powerful to challenge seriously the extant state. As we have seen, this process of radicalization as well as coalition building between radicals and moderates was especially evident in Nicaragua and, to a lesser extent, El Salvador.

Fourth, popular legitimacy is extremely problematic for those contemporary authoritarian regimes that can no longer appeal to tradition or to religious authorities for their right to rule. Furthermore, rhetorical claims that such regimes stand in defense of freedom, democracy, and the popular will against assorted state enemies (especially Communism) – claims that are intended for foreign as much as for domestic consumption – typically become self-defeating; they often serve, in fact, simply to legitimize Communists, or those whom the state has branded Communists, in the eyes of the general population. Fraudulent elections are especially effective in delegitimizing state authority, and they often stigmatize as well those "loyal" regime opponents who participate in them. Revolutionaries, once again, are the principal if unintended beneficiaries of these dynamics.

Finally, political repression places a premium on precisely the sorts of goods and services that revolutionaries are most willing and able to supply to potential followers, including (first and foremost) means of self-defense (clandestine organizations and networks, guns, safehouses, and perhaps even "liberated" territory) as well as those collective or public goods that state authorities often promise but seldom deliver (including law and order, health services, education, common lands, etc.).

In all of these ways, autocratic capitalism or what has been termed "reactionary despotism" (Baloyra-Herp 1983) inadvertently facilitated and even encouraged, by the end of the 1970s, the formation of mass-based revolutionary movements in Nicaragua, El Salvador, and Guatemala. However, it would be premature to end our analysis of these movements at this point. We still need to explain why only the Nicaraguan revolutionary movement, of the three that became significant political forces in the region, was able to seize state power. Logically, the fact that the Sandinista Front confronted a repressive authoritarian state cannot explain this outcome, since the Sandinistas' counterparts in El Salvador and Guatemala (unlike revolutionaries in Honduras) also confronted violently

Conclusion

reactionary regimes. In the following chapter, I argue that structural differences between the *types* of authoritarian states in Nicaragua, El Salvador, and Guatemala – and the variable response of these states to their opponents – largely explain the relative success or failure of revolutionaries in actually seizing state power.

6

Not-So-Inevitable Revolutions: The Political Trajectory of Revolutionary Movements in Central America

> *The Somocista circle consisted of a vast conglomerate of various enterprises. The mechanisms of the enrichment process resemble – though only formally – those procedures that the grand vizier placed at the disposition of his close circle of favorites in order to assure their prosperity. Because those procedures were accompanied by a high level of physical violence and arbitrariness – while always being perceived as personal concessions from the caliph – they produced a structure of loyalties with striking similarities to the patrimonial game of feudal domination.*
>
> – Edelberto Torres Rivas (1989: 128)

> *El Salvador was different. . . . [T]he regime did not provide the population with a single figure like Somoza, whom everyone loves to hate. The problem in El Salvador was an economic and political system, a far more amorphous enemy.*
>
> – Tommie Sue Montgomery (1995: 115)

The impressive growth, especially in the late 1970s, of popular revolutionary movements in Nicaragua, El Salvador, and Guatemala was predicated upon the violent closure of the infrastructurally weak authoritarian regimes in those countries. Yet these regimes did not prove equally vulnerable to the movements that they unwittingly helped to construct. Only the movement in Nicaragua, which harnessed a vast popular insurrection that it only loosely controlled, actually seized state power, toppling the Somoza dictatorship and the National Guard in July 1979. The Sandinista revolution, moreover, occurred quite rapidly – less than two years after the Sandinistas reemerged publicly following a period of "accumulating forces in silence." Thus, Mario Lungo Uclés refers to the Nicaraguan insurrection as a "revolutionary war of 'rapid definition'" (Lungo 1996 [1990]: 79–80). The Sandinistas were subsequently ousted from power in 1990, but this occurred not through a counterrevolution that reestablished the status quo ante, but through an electoral framework that the Sandinistas themselves had established (Foran and Goodwin 1993).

In El Salvador and Guatemala, by contrast, revolutionary movements failed to conquer state power – although state power also failed to conquer them – after many years of struggle. The conflict in El Salvador stretched into a decade-long, stalemated civil war, punctuated by FMLN offensives in January 1981 and again in November 1989. Neither offensive sparked the sort of broad popular insurrection that occurred in Nicaragua, and neither toppled the government or armed forces. However, the 1989 offensive – which has been called "El Salvador's Tet" (Karl 1992) – did catalyze an emergent "peace process" in that country, and a negotiated settlement to the conflict was reached by 1992 (only a few months, not entirely coincidentally, following the unraveling of the Soviet Union). In Guatemala, a brutal counterinsurgency campaign during the early 1980s proved much more effective than its Salvadoran counterpart in decimating the guerrillas of the URNG and cutting them off from their mass base, which the guerrillas proved largely incapable of defending; here too, however, government forces failed to eliminate the guerrillas, and a "low-intensity conflict" persisted until 1996, when the government and the URNG signed peace accords.

These patterns underscore the fact – as do the postwar insurgencies in Malaya, the Philippines, Greece, Kenya, Peru, and elsewhere – that the factors that "construct" strong revolutionary movements are evidently not exactly the same as those that determine whether such movements will actually seize state power. Clearly, a revolutionary organization may mobilize and sustain an impressive base of popular support, yet lack the capacity to overthrow the state; there is perhaps no better example of this, in fact, than the FMLN. To put it differently, even if a state is unable to prevent the growth of a powerful revolutionary movement, it may be able to hold that movement at arm's length and thereby to survive. This chapter explains why the Salvadoran and Guatemalan states survived, while the Somoza dictatorship in Nicaragua did not; the following chapter says more about why the Salvadoran and Guatemalan states nonetheless failed to defeat the revolutionary movements that they had unwittingly brought into being. The causal processes that led to peace accords (and democratization) in El Salvador and Guatemala lie beyond the scope of this chapter (but see Wood 2000a), although I do briefly discuss the Salvadoran accords in Chapter 7. Suffice it to say that the major factor inducing the governments of these countries to accept negotiated settlements was their inability to defeat the revolutionary movements, which was itself a result in large measure of their own inept and perverse policies.

Why did the state collapse in Nicaragua (and collapse quite rapidly) when confronted by a significant revolutionary challenge, but not in El Salvador or Guatemala? I will argue that the key to this puzzle lies in the manner in which the very differently structured authoritarian regimes in the region responded to the revolutionary situations that they had unwittingly induced. In Nicaragua, the "neopatrimonial" (or "sultanistic") character of the Somoza dictatorship, coupled with Anastasio Somoza Debayle's own unpredictable and self-destructive behavior – which, under the circumstances, was necessarily *state*-destructive behavior – was the key factor behind the rapid Sandinista triumph. The Somoza dictatorship not only alienated most Nicaraguans, including the middle classes and certain elites, but proved incapable of preempting revolution through reforms or, ultimately, of defending itself by force of arms. The Somoza regime not only created its own grave diggers, to paraphrase Marx, but also provided them with shovels and a coffin.

By contrast, the revolutionary movements in El Salvador and Guatemala were unable to seize power because they confronted authoritarian regimes characterized by more corporate or institutional (although hardly fully rationalized) forms of military domination that economic elites largely tolerated and even embraced (at least until the late 1980s) (Paige 1997). In both these cases, moreover, the armed forces agreed to allow (primarily to obtain international aid and legit-imacy) limited political openings that unevenly incorporated into the polity moderate or centrist political forces of the sort that had actively opposed the dictatorship in Nicaragua. Geopolitics also worked to the comparative disadvantage of the revolutionaries in El Salvador and Guatemala, who were unable to secure the broad international support of the type that the Sandinistas obtained in 1979; the military-backed regimes in El Salvador and even Guatemala, by the same token, never faced the same geopolitical isolation as did the Somoza dictatorship during that fateful year. Eventually, the revolutionaries, unable to seize power from these well-armed regimes, were themselves incorporated into the Salvadoran and Guatemalan polities as unarmed political parties. Thus, while the Salvadoran and Guatemalan regimes may have produced their own grave diggers, they did manage to avoid their own funerals. The supposedly "inevitable revolutions" (LaFeber 1993) in these countries never occurred.

Personalistic Versus Institutional Dictatorships

Before developing these arguments in greater detail, let me clarify the central distinction upon which my analysis will pivot: that between personalistic, neopatrimonial dictatorships, on the one hand, and more institutional or corporate forms of authoritarianism, on the other (i.e., forms of authoritarianism in which the regime is dominated not by a single ruler or clique, but by the armed forces as an institution, a dominant political party, or some other collective entity such as an extended kinship network). Like other analysts (e.g., Dix 1984; Midlarsky and Roberts 1985; Goldstone 1986; Wickham-Crowley 1992), I believe that neopatrimonial dictatorships are comparatively more vulnerable to overthrow by revolutionaries than are institutional forms of authoritarianism. Neopatrimonial or sultanistic dictatorships may be differentiated from more institutional or corporate forms of authoritarianism along a number of structural dimensions, the importance of which will become evident in my analysis of the uneven political fortunes of popular revolutionary movements in Central America.

The concept of a neopatrimonial or sultanistic dictatorship, which derives from the political sociology of Max Weber, has been elaborated by several scholars (see Linz 1975; Eisenstadt 1978; Goldstone 1986; Snyder 1992; Bratton and van de Walle 1994; Chehabi and Linz 1998). Neopatrimonial dictatorship refers here to a type of personalistic domination based upon the coercion and threats of the dictator's army or praetorian guard, on the one hand, and upon the distribution of patronage and offices to "clients" in exchange for their political loyalty, on the other. Weber himself referred to "sultanism" as the "extreme case" of patrimonialism, one characterized by "an administration and a military force which are purely personal instruments of the master" (Weber 1978, vol. 1: 231). Sultanistic rule, accordingly, entails "no constitutional, charismatic-revolutionary or traditional legitimacy. . . . *Fear and personal loyalties* are the mainstays of a personalistic government untrammelled by traditional or modern constitutional limitations" (Sandbrook 1985: 89; emphasis added).

Neopatrimonial dictatorship is predicated upon (and reproduces) depoliticized and demobilized masses as well as weak economic elites that are dependent upon the central state; in fact, elites are generally coopted and disorganized by the dictatorship through its distributive practices. As a result, elites tend also to lack broad political influence or hegemony under neopatrimonial regimes (see, e.g., McDaniel 1991: ch. 4). As S. N. Eisenstadt notes, "The weakness of the leading elites in neopatrimonial societies [is] often manifest in their inability either to guide, mobilize, and control in a sustained way the groups that [are] mobilized in situations of upheaval and change or to be able to forge alliances with other elites" (Eisenstadt 1978: 289). Dominant classes tend to be much better organized and more influential, by contrast, under institutional dictatorships, which they often strongly and explicitly influence; organized elites, in fact, tend to prefer the impersonal routines of institutional dictatorships over the more arbitrary and unpredictable practices that are characteristic of neopatrimonial regimes.

Several other structural differences between personalistic and institutional dictatorships deserve special emphasis. First, neopatrimonial dictators, in order to exercise personal control over "their" army and administration, typically create competing offices with ill-defined responsibilities as well as overlapping chains of command. By contrast, corporate forms of authoritarianism tend to be more classically bureaucratic, with state institutions characterized by a single hierarchy of offices with more strictly delimited official responsibilities. The "bureaucratic authoritarianism" (O'Donnell 1973) that arose in Latin America's southern cone during the 1960s and 1970s was an especially rationalized form of what I am calling institutional or corporate dictatorship.

In neopatrimonial dictatorships, furthermore, official appointments and promotions as well as the awarding of state contracts (and other business and professional opportunities channeled through the state) are typically based upon personal loyalty to or affiliation with the dictator (including, typically, kinship). This is a potential basis, it should be emphasized, for intense conflict between the dictatorship and those economic elites who *lack* political or social connections to the regime. Under corporate forms of authoritarianism, by contrast, appointments, promotions, and contracts are generally awarded according to expertise, training, or merit, or at least upon perceived loyalty to the *institution* of the army, the ruling party, or the state as a whole. Again, economic elites tend to prefer these more impersonal, hence predictable, criteria to the often arbitrary decisions of dictators. (Weber repeatedly emphasized how the unpredictability and formal irrationality of sultanistic rule rendered capitalist economic action difficult if not impossible.)

184

In addition, because neopatrimonial dictators groom officials and officers for their personal loyalty, it is relatively difficult for an effective political opposition, in the form of autonomous cliques or factions, to emerge *within* the state apparatus itself. Dictators often rotate or shuttle officials quite rapidly through a series of official positions precisely in order to prevent the crystallization of such cliques. There tends to be more "political space" for the development of such oppositional factions within the comparatively more rational and "settled" forms of corporate authoritarianism.

The administrative and military officials of neopatrimonial dictatorships also tend to be more isolated from the broader political and intellectual currents of "civil society" (as well as from agents of foreign states) than are more bureaucratically organized officials and officers. Indeed, neopatrimonial dictators often purposively segregate officials and officers, socially and even spatially, and purge those who move within social and political circles that are deemed insufficiently loyal or trustworthy. By contrast, more bureaucratically organized officials and officers have somewhat more autonomy and capacity to associate (and, sometimes, to form pacts) with actors in civil society and/or agents of foreign powers.

Finally, official positions in neopatrimonial dictatorships – above all, the office of the "executive" itself – are typically employed for private economic gain. As suggested previously, patronage and corruption are important mechanisms used by dictators to recruit and control elites, officials, and officers. By contrast, official posts are more typically remunerated by fixed salary under corporate forms of authoritarianism; corruption can certainly exist in such regimes, but it tends to be more decentralized and uncoordinated compared to that in personalistic regimes, with no single official in so commanding (or "patronizing") a position as a personalistic dictator.

By all accounts, the regime of Anastasio Somoza Debayle (1967–79) in Nicaragua – which was but the last act of an even longer "family dynasty" – was much closer to the ideal type of neopatrimonial dictatorship than were the elite-backed military regimes in El Salvador (1948–79) and Guatemala (1954–85), which more closely approximated institutional forms of authoritarianism, despite certain patrimonial characteristics. (Other dictators who approximate the neopatrimonial or sultanistic type include Porfirio Díaz of Mexico, Rafael Trujillo of the Dominican Republic, François Duvalier of Haiti, Shah Reza Pahlavi of Iran, Ferdinand Marcos of the Philippines, Mobutu Sese Seko of Zaire, Saddam

Hussein of Iraq, and, to a lesser extent, Chiang Kai-shek of China and Fulgencio Batista of Cuba [Chehabi and Linz 1998].) The following sections of this chapter suggest that this difference in the organization of state power – and in the political practices it facilitated or prevented, including responses to political challengers – was the central factor that accounts for the overthrow of the Somoza regime, on the one hand, and for the inability of the revolutionary movements in El Salvador and Guatemala to seize state power, on the other.

The Nicaraguan Revolution: Channeling the Deluge

> We couldn't say "no" to the insurrection. The mass movement was ahead of the vanguard's capacity to lead it. We couldn't oppose that mass movement, that current. We had to put ourselves at the front of that current [al frente de ese río] in order to more or less direct and channel it.
>
> – Humberto Ortega (1984 [1979]: 33)

The triumph of the popular insurrection of 1978–9 against the Somoza dictatorship was the result of several mutually reinforcing factors: the growing strength and popularity of the FSLN (discussed in Chapter 5); growing elite and moderate opposition to Somoza; increasing international support for the Sandinistas and the concomitant geopolitical isolation of Somoza; the *absence* of a political opening "from above"; and the inability of Somoza's National Guard to contain, let alone halt, the rising tide of armed insurrection.[1] All of these factors are anchored, to one degree or another, in the neopatrimonial character of the Somoza dictatorship.

Despite the turbulence of 1978, the outcome of the struggle against Somoza remained very much in doubt at the start of the new year. The National Guard contained scattered uprisings in September 1978, retaking Sandinista-controlled cities and towns one by one. The events of that month resulted in some five thousand deaths, ten thousand injured, and about eighty-five thousand displaced. Somoza even felt confident enough to release 350 political prisoners. The dictator also bent before U.S. pressure and agreed to negotiate with the moderate opposition – represented by a group called the Broad Opposition Front (FAO) – in talks mediated

---

[1] There are now many helpful accounts of the Nicaraguan Revolution, including Black 1981, Weber 1981, Nolan 1984, Booth 1985, Lozano 1985, Nuñez Téllez 1986 (1980), Pastor 1987, Ruchwarger 1987, Gilbert 1988, Pezzullo and Pezzullo 1993, Chavarría 1994 (1982), and Everingham 1996.

by the Organization of American States (OAS).[2] The Broad Opposition Front, which had been formed in March 1978, included the Democratic Union of Liberation (UDEL), formed by Pedro Joaquín Chamorro; the Nicaraguan Democratic Movement (MDN), a group of businessmen and professionals led by the industrialist Alfonso Robelo Callejas; and the businesspeople and intellectuals known as the "Group of Twelve" (see Chapter 5). Chamorro's assassination in January 1978 led directly to the formation of the FAO.

Nicaraguan businessmen had long complained of Somoza's "disloyal competition" (*competencia desleal*), that is, the use of state power and connections to control business and professional opportunities in the country. Under Somoza, notes Edelberto Torres Rivas, "a structure of loyalties was created which brings to mind the patrimonial character of feudal domination. The administration of public matters . . . became a government of private affairs" (Torres Rivas 1983a: 137). One commentator has even suggested that Nicaragua did not have a capitalist so much as a "Somoza mode of production" (Selser 1984: 273).

Bourgeois opposition to the dictatorship became especially pronounced after the devastating earthquake of December 1972, which destroyed most of downtown Managua and killed nearly twenty thousand people.[3] Somoza not only embezzled huge sums of relief assistance, but he also "cornered the reconstruction of Managua":

His company ESPESA took charge of demolition work; Inmuebles SA of real estate speculation; a host of other companies, generally with a monopoly, took on contracts for concrete, building materials, metal structures, roofing, asbestos, and plastic. (Black 1981: 59–60)

The assassination of Chamorro further deepened the chasm between Somoza and those elites who were not directly tied into the dictator's network of corruption.

Somoza proved intransigent in the OAS-mediated talks with the FAO, and he resolutely refused to step down or to transfer power to an interim

---

[2] The OAS team consisted of representatives from Guatemala, the Dominican Republic, and the United States.

[3] Jaime Wheelock, who became the Sandinista Minister of Agricultural Development and Agrarian Reform, has written an excellent study of the divisions between Somoza and the "non-Somocista bourgeoisie." See Wheelock Roman 1980 (1975): ch. 6. See also Paige 1989, 1997, Spalding 1994, and Everingham 1996.

government until his presidential term officially expired in 1981. The Carter administration was the principal force behind these OAS-mediated discussions. By the end of 1978, U.S. policy had as its goal the quixotic task of removing Somoza while preserving the National Guard, and it was hoped that some type of agreement between Somoza and the conservative opposition would make this possible. Thus, the Carter administration's policy toward Somoza has been aptly described as "sacrificing the dictator to save the state" (Petras and Morley 1990: ch. 4). Unfortunately, the nature of neopatrimonial rule makes it extraordinarily difficult to sacrifice certain dictators without destroying "their" armies and states in the process.

Somoza's intransigence, for its part, can be understood as a calculated attempt to undercut the moderates as an effective political force and to present the Carter administration with an unambiguous choice between supporting his rule or seeing "the Communists" take power. Somoza's actions certainly had the intended polarizing effect, but the United States failed to react as he anticipated:

Somoza's obstinacy frustrated the U.S. effort. Moreover, U.S. support of the conservative sector exacerbated the situation and more liberal factions withdrew one by one from the mediation process, charging that the [OAS] Commission only wanted to establish *Somocismo sin Somoza* (Somozaism without Somoza). At this stage, Somoza's suggestion to hold a plebiscite was immediately encouraged by the U.S. This option, however, fell through because of conflicting conditions demanded by both sides. (Chavarría 1994 [1982]: 163)

On January 9, 1979, Luis Medrano Flores, the leader of a conservative trade union federation and a member of the FAO, was gunned down in Managua. The FAO broke off negotiations with Somoza once and for all on January 19. "The dictator misread the situation," suggests Ricardo Chavarría, "and tried to resolve a societal crisis by adopting exclusively military means" (Chavarría 1994 [1982]: 165).

The breakdown of negotiations between Somoza and the moderate opposition contributed to the growing perception, both in Nicaragua and abroad, that the armed struggle led by Sandinistas was the only viable way out of the Somoza dictatorship. In fact, as Somoza became increasingly intransigent and repressive, elites entered into a strategic alliance with the Sandinistas (and vice versa). After the FSLN announced a "final offensive" against Somoza in late May, the FAO supported a general strike that virtually shut down the country. The FAO and the Superior Council of Private Enterprise (COSEP) later endorsed the five-member Governing Junta of National Reconstruction formed by the Sandinistas, which included the businessman Alfonso Robelo of the MDN as well as Violeta Barrios de Chamorro, the widow of Pedro Joaquín Chamorro. The Sandinistas later accepted a moderate "Program of the Government of National Reconstruction" that was drawn up by Robelo and Alfredo César, who had managed a sugar company before joining the insurrection. In toppling the Somoza dictatorship, then, the Sandinistas did not overthrow an "executive committee" of the bourgeoisie; on the contrary, that "committee" largely supported the revolution – at least until the smoke cleared (see Foran and Goodwin 1993).

The growing elite as well as popular opposition to Somoza certainly encouraged regional and international support for the FSLN and the isolation of Somoza. Especially important in this regard was the ability of the FSLN to operate from base camps in Costa Rica and, to a lesser extent, Honduras; the sanctuaries and transshipment points in these countries made it much easier for the Sandinistas to prosecute the war against Somoza (see Seligson and Carroll 1982). As the Front grew, its agents in these countries acquired additional arms with few difficulties. "This was especially true of Costa Rica after 1978, when the government of President Rodrigo Carazo not only permitted but encouraged arms shipment to the FSLN" (Booth 1985: 152).

Weapons sent from a number of Latin American governments went first to Panama and were then shipped to the Sandinistas by air or ground through Costa Rica. Although the Costa Rican government assured the United States that it was not trafficking in arms, it was subsequently revealed that

in May–July 1979 twenty-one flights by Costa Rican civilian transport planes brought a total of 320 tons of arms from a Havana military base to the FSLN via the airfield at Costa Rica's northern town of Liberia. The cost to the FSLN of this assistance was Costa Rica's retention of half the arms. Virtually every known model of light combat arm manufactured in the United States and Western Europe found its way into the FSLN armory. Light civilian planes flown from Costa Rica even dropped a few bombs on National Guard positions late in the war. (Booth 1985: 153; see also Castañeda 1993: 59–60)

All the while, the Somoza regime became increasingly isolated internationally. U.S. military aid, which had been cut off by President Carter, was never restored. Costa Rica broke diplomatic relations with Somoza as early as November 1978, following a border incident that left four Costa Rican

Civil Guardsmen dead. Mexico broke relations in May 1979, and Panama and Brazil followed suit in June.

Somoza himself flew to Guatemala City on June 13 in an unsuccessful bid to obtain support from the leaders of the Central American Defense Council (CONDECA). Most significantly, on June 21 the OAS rejected a proposal by U.S. Secretary of State Cyrus Vance to send an inter-American "peace-keeping" force to Nicaragua; in a seventeen-to-two vote, the OAS then demanded Somoza's immediate and unconditional resignation. (Somoza would later blame his downfall on this OAS resolution [see Booth 1985: 181].) Over the objections of Vance, President Carter's National Security Adviser Zbigniew Brzezinski proceeded to propose a unilateral U.S. intervention in Nicaragua, but Carter ruled this out. Ultimately, the Carter administration, despite the mixed signals it had sent to Nicaragua, was unwilling either to preserve Somoza's rule or to prevent a Sandinista victory through some type of military intervention.[4] Thus, the actions of the U.S. state (and the Costa Rican and Cuban states, among others) also figured prominently in the fall of the Somoza dictatorship, although these actions were largely conditioned if not directly provoked by those of the Somoza regime.

Short of an external military intervention, perhaps the only fashion in which Somoza might have been deposed and the growing insurrection reversed would have been a coup d'etat by the National Guard, perhaps in conjunction with elite sectors. But no faction within the Guard, which had been closely controlled by the Somoza family for more than forty years, was able to topple the dictator and initiate some sort of political opening "from above." As James Dunkerley notes,

In marked contrast to the pattern in [El Salvador and Guatemala], the Nicaraguan National Guard (GN) did not operate with institutional autonomy, being commanded throughout its history by members of the Somoza family . . . and dedicated as much to furthering their economic and political interests as to fulfilling less narrowly partisan tasks of state control. . . . Subjected by Somoza to tight internal control through dispensation of favours, frequent rotation of postings, and the occasional expulsion of ambitious officers, it was large enough to seem ubiquitous in a small country and yet too small to develop an institutional ethic beyond loyalty to its commander. (Dunkerley 1988: 232)

---

[4] On U.S. policies toward Somoza and the Sandinistas, see especially Pastor 1987, Lake 1989, Pezzullo and Pezzullo 1993, and LeoGrande 1998: ch. 2.

As opposition to Somoza swelled, however, there were certainly rumors that the Guard might attempt to remove him; the Sandinista takeover of the National Palace in August 1978, noted in Chapter 5, was undertaken, according to Humberto Ortega, precisely in order "to foil the imperialist plot which consisted of staging a coup . . . to put a civilianmilitary regime in power and thus put a damper on the revolutionary struggle" (Ortega 1982 [1980]: 69). Eighty-five members of the Guard were subsequently arrested for plotting against Somoza (Booth 1985: 165). On September 9, 1978, furthermore,

General José Ivan Alegrett and several others, who had conveyed to reporters their anger over Somoza's surrender of the National Palace, died in a plane crash. There was widespread speculation that Somoza had them killed to discourage further plots. (Pastor 1987: 72)

Following these events – that is, during the dictatorship's final months – the officer corp (or what remained of it) did prove remarkably loyal to Somoza.

The National Guard, however, which Somoza kept relatively small to maintain tighter control, was unable to contain the spreading insurrection, even though Somoza expanded its troop levels from seven thousand to as many as fourteen thousand by the end of 1978. The insurrection, which, as Ortega has noted, always seemed to move "faster than the vanguard" (Ortega 1982 [1980]: 67), became much better organized and armed by the Sandinistas during 1979. The organizational capacities of the Front were enhanced by external assistance; and the three political "tendencies" that had developed within the Front during the 1970s (see Chapter 5) had merged by March 1979. The Front's ability to wage a coordinated national struggle was also facilitated by its acquisition of wireless communication and by the broadcasts of Radio Sandino in Costa Rica.

Thus, while the FSLN never had more than five thousand armed guerrillas, its "numerical disadvantage was greatly offset by its massive popular support in organization, logistics, and combat. In almost every battle in a populated center, the Front found its members multiplied severalfold by volunteers" (Booth 1985: 176). "We always took the masses into account," according to Ortega,

but more in terms of their supporting the guerrillas, so that the guerrillas as such could defeat the National Guard. This isn't what actually happened. What happened was that it was the guerrillas who provided support for the masses so that they could defeat the enemy by means of insurrection. (Ortega 1982 [1980]: 58)

191

The FSLN's strategy was to spread the National Guard thin by organizing or supporting insurrections in a number of cities and towns throughout the country; to this end, it organized several "fronts" in various parts of the country (see Map 6.1). The primarily urban character of the revolution, at least during this final phase, is reflected in the social background of the rebel combatants killed during the insurrection, most of whom were students and tradespeople (artisans, food vendors, and the like) (see Table 6.1). By early July, the Guard's "profligate use of ammunition, loss of garrison arsenals, and a cutoff of imports had severely cut into their supplies" (Pezzullo and Pezzullo 1993: 168). The Guard became unable to relieve or resupply besieged posts around the country (Chavarría 1994 [1982]: 164). On July 6, the towns of Jinotepe, San Marcos, and Masatepe fell, giving the Front control of the strategic Carazo region and thereby cutting off Guard troops stationed in the southern part of the country from Managua. The important city of León was liberated by the Sandinistas on July 9.

By mid-July, the Sandinistas controlled all the major roads to Managua. Somoza was getting out. On July 16, the dictator announced the retirement of more than one hundred generals and colonels with more than thirty years' service in the National Guard. During the early morning hours of July 17, 1979, Somoza submitted his resignation and fled the country with his family, the general staff of the National Guard (including his son and presumptive political heir, Colonel Anastasio Somoza Portocarrero), and the loyal leadership of his Liberal National Party (which, as the joke goes, was neither liberal, nor nationalist, nor a party). Decapitated, the National Guard began to disintegrate rapidly. On July 18, the Guard's small air force defected to Honduras. Guardsmen stranded in the south fled to El Salvador via the port at San Juan del Sur; many officers headed for Honduras, with or without their troops.[5] There would not be – and, given the nature of the dictatorship, perhaps *could* not be – "Somoza-ism without Somoza" in Nicaragua. On the night of July 19–20, the FSLN moved virtually uncontested into Managua. Some fifty thousand Nicaraguans lay dead, but "the last marine" had finally departed.

Clearly, no single causal factor or process can account for the triumph of the Nicaraguan Revolution, the complexity of which is immensely

---

[5] Dickey (1987: 19–68) provides a useful and vivid account of the disintegration of the Guard, many of whose officers would later reemerge in Honduras as leaders of the counterrevolutionary forces or contras who did battle with the Sandinistas through the 1980s.

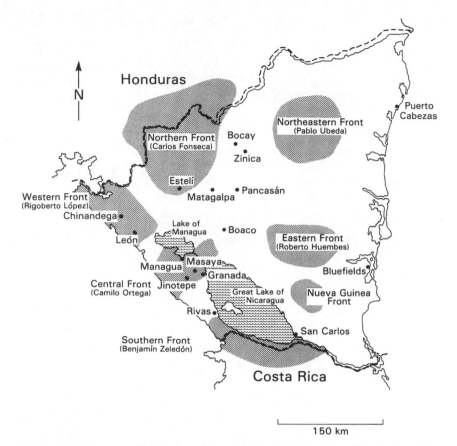

Map 6.1   The guerrilla fronts of the FSLN, 1977–9. From *The End and the Beginning: The Nicaraguan Revolution*, second edition, by John A. Booth. Copyright © 1985 Westview Press. Reprinted with permission.

simplified in the preceding account. Nor was the revolution in any sense inevitable; at various points in time through early 1979, any number of events – including Somoza's resignation and/or a U.S. invasion – might have reversed the growing popular insurrection or, at least, prevented the wholesale collapse of the state and National Guard. At the vortex of virtually all the processes that culminated in the revolution, however, stood the neopatrimonial Somoza dictatorship. Like the authoritarian regimes in El Salvador and Guatemala, this dictatorship radicalized and focused popular resistance on the central government and on the grossest forms of state-sanctioned poverty and inequality.

193

Table 6.1. *Occupation of combatants killed in the Sandinista revolution (percentage).*

Occupation	Percentage
Students	29.0
Tradespeople (artisans, food vendors, mechanics, carpenters, shoemakers, plumbers, etc.)	22.0
Workers and journeymen	16.0
Office employees	16.0
Professionals, technicians, teachers, and professors	7.0
Small merchants and traders	5.0
Peasants, farmers, and others	5.0
Total (n = 542)	100.0

Source: Vilas 1986: 108. Note: Vilas's figures are derived from a random sample of dossiers compiled by the Nicaraguan Institute for Social Security and Welfare (INSSBI) (see Vilas 1986: 278n10).

But more than this, the actions of the Somoza dictatorship also drove elites and moderates into the revolutionary camp; elite opposition to the regime, furthermore, helped to isolate it internationally; and the structure of the dictatorship made it all but impossible for a military coup d'etat, with or without civilian participation, to depose Somoza and undertake initiatives that might have stemmed the tide of revolution. The Sandinistas, for their part, astutely exploited the regime's vulnerabilities, and their capacity to do so was by no means a foregone conclusion. Indeed, as Phil Ryan (2000: 194) has suggested, to some degree the Sandinistas themselves self-consciously "helped forestall a premature regime-change, an elite rapprochement with the regime, as well as direct U.S. intervention" – any one of which might well have aborted the revolution. Ultimately, the National Guard – the backbone of Somoza's rule – proved too small, and became too weak, to save Somoza and his cronies. And with Somoza's flight from the country, this glorified corps of bodyguards became incapable even of defending itself.

Unlike the pattern of certain other revolutions, the Sandinistas did not seize power in Nicaragua because of the political opportunities afforded by a prior breakdown of the state's administrative or military apparatus. Indeed, there was not even a momentary breakdown of political authority – a "window of opportunity" – as in Vietnam in 1945. It would be truer to say that the Sandinistas themselves broke down the state, albeit a state that was infrastructurally weak to begin with and that proved incapable of reform.

Stalemate in El Salvador; Impasse in Guatemala

The major factors that facilitated the actual triumph, as opposed to the popularity or mobilizing capacity, of revolutionaries in Nicaragua were simply not present in El Salvador or Guatemala: The armed forces in these countries were able, through extraordinary repression, to prevent or contain urban insurrections and eventually to arrest the growth of revolutionary movements, although they could not eliminate them. In addition, the armed forces in both countries tolerated and even sponsored flawed but increasingly competitive elections, accepted the opening of limited "political space" for unarmed social movements, and/or implemented modest socioeconomic reforms – all of which denied the revolutionaries potential domestic and international allies. Although these elections, political openings, and reforms did not necessarily please economic elites (or all hard-line military officers), those elites remained at least "semi-loyal" toward the new forms of "electoral authoritarianism" (Montgomery 1995: ch. 7) or "hybrid regimes" (Karl 1995) that emerged in both countries during the 1980s; elites most certainly did not join forces with revolutionaries, as occurred on a large scale in Nicaragua. Partly because of the "semiopening" of these regimes, furthermore, they were much less isolated internationally, and the revolutionaries much more isolated, than was the case in Nicaragua. As a result of these various factors, all of which are closely linked to the institutional character of military domination in these societies, revolutionaries were not able to seize power; instead, they found themselves locked into a stalemated civil war (in El Salvador) and a protracted low-intensity conflict (in Guatemala), with neither side capable of defeating the other. (I examine the reasons for the prolonged character of these conflicts in Chapter 7.)

Important military coups occurred in both El Salvador and Guatemala that overthrew fraudulently "elected" military leaders who were widely viewed as unusually corrupt and incapable of dealing with the strong guerrilla movements that had developed by the late 1970s. In October 1979, shortly after the Sandinista triumph in Nicaragua, and in a context of deepening political polarization, reformist elements within the Salvadoran military, working with civilians of the moderate left, overthrew the unpopular

195

military regime headed by General Carlos Humberto Romero and established a military-civilian junta.[6] The most progressive officers and civilians in this junta, including the social-democrat Guillermo Ungo and Central American University rector Román Mayorga Quiroz, eventually resigned because of their inability to restrain the increasing violence unleashed by the military against popular movements and suspected rebels. However, the junta was reorganized in early 1980 with the participation of the Christian Democratic Party (PDC), including, eventually, José Napoleón Duarte, the 1972 presidential candidate who had been living in exile in Venezuela (see Chapter 5). Under this junta, which ruled until 1982, the armed forces and allied death squads unleashed an incredibly violent and quite indiscriminate war against the guerrilla groups and the popular organizations affiliated with them; simultaneously, however, official violence against the Christian Democratic faction associated with Duarte eased, and preparations were begun for the election of a civilian government, beginning with an elected constituent assembly that would draft a new constitution.[7]

In Guatemala, similarly, General Efraín Ríos Montt – the Christian Democratic candidate for the presidency in 1974, who had subsequently become an evangelical Protestant – took power through a military coup in March 1982; the coup was undertaken to prevent the winner of the fraudulent presidential "election" of that month, General Angel Aníbal Guevara, from assuming office.[8] (The election was manipulated by then-President General Lucas to ensure the victory of Guevara, who served as his defense minister.) This coup also led, as in El Salvador, to an increasingly savage counterinsurgency campaign against the guerrillas and their presumed supporters in the western highlands; at the same time, plans were laid for a transition to an elected civilian government. Ríos Montt himself was overthrown by his defense minister, General Oscar Humberto Mejía Víctores, in August 1983, largely because of the

---

[6] Keogh 1985 provides the best account of the October 1979 coup and its aftermath. See also LeoGrande and Robbins 1980, Baloyra-Herp 1982, and Gordon 1989. I have heard that a popular chant in leftist demonstrations in El Salvador during the late 1970s was "Romero, Somoza son la misma cosa" ("Romero and Somoza are the same thing"). As life itself would prove, nothing could be further from the truth.

[7] Christian Democratic participation in the junta created a crisis among the party's activists; the progressive wing of the party split off in March 1980 and formed the Popular Social Christian Movement (MPSC).

[8] Helpful accounts of the March 1982 coup and its aftermath are found in Black 1984, McClintock 1985b, Handy 1986, and Jonas 1991.

196

growing estrangement between Ríos Montt and the army's high command (among other things, Ríos Montt's moralistic evangelicalism antagonized many officers). However, the Mejía Víctores government continued the "authoritarian transition to democracy" (Torres Rivas 1989a) initiated by Ríos Montt.

It should be emphasized that the very capacity of the armed forces in El Salvador and Guatemala to depose unpopular generals such as Romero and Guevara and to initiate limited political openings reflects their relative institutional autonomy and organizational rationality, which stand in sharp contrast to the Nicaraguan National Guard. The latter organization, as we have seen, was almost totally beholden to a single individual and proved unable (and largely unwilling) to depose that leader even when its own institutional interests would have been served thereby.

The most striking immediate result of both the 1979 coup in El Salvador and the 1982 coup in Guatemala – notwithstanding the preparations for elections and transitions to formal civilian rule – was the rapid escalation of violence by the armed forces. In El Salvador, political murders increased to more than one thousand per month in 1980, claiming (among others) Archbishop Oscar Romero of San Salvador, an increasingly vocal opponent of the U.S.-backed junta; six principal leaders of the Democratic Revolutionary Front (FDR), an umbrella group of the moderate left allied with the FMLN; and four U.S. churchwomen.[9] In the countryside, the Salvadoran army came to rely on indiscriminate "sweeps" through guerrilla-controlled zones, aerial bombardment (believed to be the most extensive in the history of the Western hemisphere), and the cutting off of food and supply lines in order to "drain the sea" of guerrilla supporters. Among numerous massacres, the most notorious atrocity of the war was no doubt the systematic killing, in December 1981, of approximately eight hundred unarmed men, women, and children in and around the village of El Mozote, in the department of Morazán, by the U.S.-trained troops of the Atlacatl Battalion; the victims were shot, hanged, bayonneted, or burned alive, in many cases after being tortured and/or raped (Danner 1993; United Nations 1995: 347–51; Binford 1996). As was typical in such cases, many surviving villagers subsequently joined or supported the guerrillas.

---

[9] Valuable analyses of the Salvadoran counterinsurgency and civil war may be found in Dunkerley 1985, McClintock 1985a, Pearce 1986, Fish and Sganga 1988, Lungo Uclés 1990, Montgomery 1995, and Stanley 1996.

It is not the purpose of this chapter to recount the long, tortuous history of the revolutionary conflict in El Salvador (or Guatemala) during the 1980s and into the 1990s.[10] Suffice it to say that more than a decade after it began, approximately seventy-five thousand Salvadorans had been killed in the civil war, the overwhelming majority of them victims of the armed forces and associated death squads. (The armed forces were expanded from some ten thousand troops in 1979 to a peak of about fifty-six thousand troops during the 1987–91 period [Montgomery 1995: 149; Dunkerley 1994: 146].) In fact, the Truth Commission for El Salvador established by the United Nations as part of the peace accords of 1992 found that 95 percent of the more than twenty-two thousand human rights abuses that it investigated were committed by the armed forces, government-sponsored paramilitary organizations, and death squads (United Nations 1995: 311). It has also been estimated that more than a quarter of the Salvadoran population was displaced by the war (Karl 1985: 306), and perhaps 10 to 15 percent of all Salvadorans were living in the United States by the late 1980s.

State-sponsored violence in Guatemala was even worse. Estimates of the number of victims of the counterinsurgency in that country run as high as one hundred fifty thousand for the 1982–5 period alone (Booth and Walker 1993: 110).[11] (Ricardo Falla [1994] has written an entire book on army massacres of indigenous people just in the northern zone of El Quiché, most of which took place in 1982.) A massive report released in 1998 by the Human Rights Office of the Catholic Church estimated that two hundred thousand people (90 percent of them unarmed civilians) were killed or "disappeared" in Guatemala between the early 1960s and the signing of the peace accords in December 1996; the Church attributed 90 percent of all human rights abuses perpetrated during the conflict to the armed forces, their paramilitary allies, and death squards; guerrilla groups were held responsible for less than 5 percent of all abuses (REMHI 1999: 290).[12] In 1984, the Juvenile Division of the Guatemalan Supreme Court asked mayors to compile lists of children who had lost parents since 1980

---

[10] For details, see the sources cited in footnotes 9 and 11.

[11] Helpful accounts of the Guatemalan counterinsurgency and civil war may be found in McClintock 1985b, Barry 1986, Anderson and Simon 1987, Carmack 1988, Jonas 1991, Perera 1993, Falla 1994, and Schirmer 1998.

[12] The key figure behind this report, Bishop Juan Gerardi, was murdered shortly after its release. Current or former officers of the armed forces were immediately suspected of the murder.

as a result of political violence: "In September 1984 the Guatemalan press reported that some 100,000 children (and perhaps as many as 200,000) had lost at least one parent and that some 20 percent of them were orphans" (AI 1987: 7). During the period from 1981 to 1983, Amnesty International repeatedly received reports of the mass murder of Catholic catechists: "Eye-witness accounts describe incidents in which up to 50 catechists were murdered during army attacks on their villages. Some were garrotted, others were hanged from trees, chopped to pieces with machetes or locked into churches in groups and burned to death" (AI 1987: 24–5).

The Guatemalan army itself admits to having completely destroyed 440 villages under the Ríos Montt and Mejía Víctores governments (Painter 1986: 825). Around this time, as many as two hundred thousand Guatemalans fled to refugee camps in Mexico, and internal refugees came to number about one million (Jonas 1991: 149), including the several thousand people who comprised the so-called Communities of People in Resistance (CPRs), which lived clandestinely in inaccessible mountains and jungles. Some fifty thousand indigenous people, moreover, were relocated into military-controlled "model villages," similar to the "new villages" in Malaya and "strategic hamlets" of South Vietnam (Barry 1986: 31). Beginning in 1982, the military also forced the rural population in strategic areas to participate in so-called Civil Defense Patrols (PACs). By 1986, over one million men and boys, mostly indigenous, were serving without compensation in these patrols (Farnsworth 1987: 528). The armed forces themselves were expanded from fewer than fifteen thousand troops in 1977 to some sixty thousand by 1991 (Dunkerley 1994: 146).

In neither El Salvador nor Guatemala, however, was repression the only response by the state – as it was in Nicaragua – to escalating revolutionary challenges. Following the military coups previously discussed, the armed forces in both countries oversaw transitions to semicompetitive electoral regimes in which centrist and (eventually) moderate social-democratic political parties would participate (but not, of course, the left). In El Salvador, the armed forces tolerated this transition as the price to be paid for massive U.S. aid (discussed later in this section). In Guatemala, the transition to electoralism was part of a calculated effort by the armed forces and its elite allies to reduce Guatemala's international isolation and thereby to secure greater flows of foreign aid, loans, and investments.

Accordingly, a rapid and unprecedented series of elections were held in El Salvador and Guatemala during the 1980s. In El Salvador, elections for a constituent assembly were held in 1982; a presidential election (two rounds) in 1984; legislative assembly elections in 1985 and 1988; and a presidential election in 1989. In Guatemala, constituent assembly elections were held in 1984; a presidential election (two rounds) in 1985; and presidential and legislative elections in 1990. Christian Democratic parties were the initial beneficiaries of these elections, raising popular hopes for peace and social reform. Duarte and fellow Christian Democrat Vinicio Cerezo were the winners of the 1984 and 1985 presidential elections in El Salvador and Guatemala, respectively. In both countries, however, right-wing politicians were subsequently elected to office after Christian Democrats failed to end the civil conflicts, curb human rights abuses by the armed forces, or address popular economic concerns. It would be these rightists, ironically, who would reach negotiated settlements with revolutionaries after concluding that they could not be defeated.

As many commentators have suggested,[13] the winners of the electoral contests of the 1980s would not or could not substantially erode the power of the armed forces or of economic elites. Nor, as noted, did they bring about peace or successfully address popular economic grievances. The most important result of these elections, however, may very well have been to prevent still *further* political polarization. The very fact that the armed forces had allowed civilians to assume office created the perception, or at least the hope, that peace and social justice might yet come about through peaceful means. In this regard, it should be noted that Duarte won the support, at least for a time, of a coalition of labor and peasant groups known as the Popular Democratic Unity (UPD) for his 1984 presidential bid, signing a "social pact" in which he agreed to implement economic reforms, including an accelerated land reform, and to negotiate with the guerrillas.

Duarte was also able to open up limited political space for nonviolent protest, even if much of that space was filled by groups that were disgruntled with his own administration. Duarte used his international backing, furthermore, as leverage to curb some of the worst abuses of the armed forces:

Duarte's success in Washington brought home the message that to receive substantial increases in U.S. aid El Salvador had to maintain a government acceptable to the U.S. Congress. The Salvadoran Armed Forces responded

[13] See especially Karl 1985, García 1989, Acevedo 1991, and Baloyra-Herp 1995 on the Salvadoran elections, and Painter 1986, 1987, Jonas 1991, 1995, and Trudeau 1993 on the Guatemalan elections.

200

positively to this message by restructuring the military command. Four leading rightist officers – including Treasury Police head Nicolas Carranza – known to be . . . linked to death squad activity, were transferred to posts outside El Salvador. In addition, the military agreed to dismantle the intelligence unit of the Treasury Police, the reputed center of death squad activity. (Karl 1985: 318)

Death-squad violence dropped substantially in El Salvador after the early 1980s (especially following Vice President George Bush's visit of late 1983), and a plethora of popular organizations would soon fill the emerging political space (e.g., Lungo Uclés 1996 [1990]; Stahler-Sholk 1994).

In Guatemala, similarly, President Cerezo disbanded the notorious Department of Technical Investigations (DIT), the intelligence branch of the National Police (although most of its members were reassigned and only one, apparently, was ever charged with any crime) (AI 1987: 12–3). Cerezo also replaced or transferred the entire membership of the army's Council of Commanders, which oversees the various regions of the country, and retired a number of generals (Farnsworth 1987: 532). And while Cerezo did not seek a significant agrarian-reform law, his government purchased a small number of farms held by state banks and distributed them to some of Guatemala's estimated four hundred and nineteen thousand landless rural laborers (Farnsworth 1987: 528).

Parties of the moderate left were also able to take advantage of the limited openings in El Salvador and Guatemala. Beginning in 1985, the center-left Social Democratic Party (PSD) contested elections in Guatemala, albeit with extremely limited results. A leftist coalition called the New Guatemala Democratic Front (FDNG) entered the electoral fray shortly before the peace accords were signed. In El Salvador, Guillermo Ungo and Rubén Zamora, leaders of the Democratic Revolutionary Front (FDR), returned to El Salvador in late 1987 after seven years of exile; their Democratic Convergence (CD) party contested the 1989 election, with Ungo as presidential candidate, winning 3.8 percent of the vote. Had even such limited political space not existed, the guerrillas of the URNG would undoubtedly have found additional sympathizers.

Because these political openings represented only a potential threat to Salvadoran and Guatemalan elites, however, it is not surprising they remained "semiloyal" to the new electoral regimes, supportive of elections and civilian rule precisely to the extent that they offered an alternative to the guerrillas that did not threaten their own economic interests. Unlike their Nicaraguan counterparts, certainly, Salvadoran and Guatemalan elites did not close ranks with revolutionaries. In fact, elites skillfully exploited the political openings to build their own formidable political parties and used their considerable influence to control and manipulate – and actually to become – elected officials.

Indeed, while the elections of the 1980s demonstrated that civilians with reformist credentials could actually assume office, the real power of Christian Democratic governments was extremely circumscribed. To begin with, the armed forces let it be known that civilians should not look too deeply into their handling of "security" matters, including human rights abuses by officers and their charges. Military impunity, in short, would continue virtually unchallenged until peace accords were signed (see, e.g., Stanley 1996: chs. 5–6; Williams and Walter 1997: ch. 6; Handy 1986; Simon 1988). The local oligarchies, furthermore, whether through their friends in the military, private-sector associations, or right-wing parties such as the Nationalist Republican Alliance (ARENA) in El Salvador, effectively vetoed reformist legislation, such as it was.

An important centerpiece of the political opening in El Salvador, for example, was supposed to have been the land reform enacted by the military-civilian junta in March 1980. This reform, however, while vigorously opposed by the oligarchy, did not fundamentally change the lot of most rural Salvadorans. Its central provision – which would have affected most of El Salvador's coffee estates – was suspended by the Constituent Assembly in May 1982, and its other provisions were obstructed by the oligarchy or "benignly neglected" by the government. The reform did not even attempt to address the needs of the large wage-earning workforce in the Salvadoran countryside.[14]

Prior to the 1985 presidential election in Guatemala, Cerezo promised that he would not even attempt to enact an agrarian reform or to nationalize any property if elected (Painter 1986: 834) – a promise that he thoroughly fulfilled. Before turning over power to Cerezo, moreover, General Mejía Víctores proclaimed an amnesty for "all people implicated in political crimes" between March 1982 and January 1986. Cerezo, for his part, announced that "we are not going to be able to investigate the past. We would have to put the entire army in jail" (AI 1987: 5–6). And despite preelection promises, Cerezo did not make participation in the Civil Defense Patrols (PACs) voluntary (Farnsworth 1987: 528).

---

[14] Critical analyses of the Salvadoran land reform may be found in Bonner 1984: 191–203, Deere 1984, Barry 1987: ch. 6, and Pelupessy 1991, 1997.

Duarte and Cerezo were rather more accomplished at obtaining international aid and legitimacy. In fact, the tremendous expansion of the armed forces in El Salvador and Guatemala and the counterinsurgency wars that these forces fought would not have been possible without external assistance – mainly but not exclusively from the United States – to the newly elected governments in these countries. A number of knowledgeable observers, in fact, doubt that the Salvadoran armed forces could have prevented a guerrilla victory without massive infusions of U.S. aid. By contrast, as we have seen, such external progovernment support did not materialize in the case of Nicaragua. Indeed, while the Carter Administration was unwilling to intervene unilaterally in Nicaragua in order to prevent a Sandinista victory, both the Carter and Reagan Administrations made the prevention of yet another revolutionary victory in Central America a major foreign policy objective. Consequently, U.S. military assistance to El Salvador grew to massive sums, from $100 million in 1981 to over $400 million in 1984 (Montgomery 1995: 298). In all, U.S. economic and military aid to El Salvador amounted to more than $3.6 billion during the 1980s, or about $1 million per day (Dunkerley 1994: 145).

Because of the ban on U.S. military aid to Guatemala enacted in 1977, the Guatemalan military was forced to turn, at least until 1984, to other countries for military assistance, principally Israel, Taiwan, and South Africa. In 1983, Israel helped Guatemala set up two defense factories for manufacturing munitions, Galil rifles, and armored vehicles (Barry 1986: 86; Jamail and Gutierrez 1987: 35). According to one report, the Israelis outfitted the entire Guatemalan army, "from helmets to standard-issue automatic rifles" (Jamail and Gutierrez 1987: 36). Despite the aid ban, moreover, more than $30 million of trucks, jeeps, and helicopters were sold by private U.S. companies to Guatemala between 1977 and 1984 (Painter 1986: 824). U.S. economic aid to Guatemala, moreover, jumped from $11 million in 1980 to $146 million in 1989 (Dunkerley 1994: 145). In 1982, furthermore, "the [Reagan] Administration formally erased Guatemala from the list of human rights offenders. The policy immediately affected six World Bank and IDB [Inter-American Development Bank] loans, worth a total of $170 million" (Black 1984: 160).

If the elected governments in El Salvador and Guatemala did not experience the same degree of international isolation as the Somoza dictatorship in Nicaragua, revolutionaries in these countries, by contrast, became very isolated indeed. No contiguous country, to begin with, provided sanctuary for Salvadoran or Guatemalan rebels, such as Costa Rica provided for Somoza's opponents. Honduras, under heavy pressure from the United States, proved especially hostile to the Salvadoran rebels, cooperating on a number of occasions with the Salvadoran military in joint operations against guerrillas and their supporters along the Salvador-Honduras border. There is no credible evidence, furthermore, of significant arms shipments to Guatemalan or Salvadoran rebels from Cuba or Nicaragua after 1981 (see North 1985: 115–6; Smith 1987: 90–2), although the Salvadoran rebels did obtain Soviet-made antiaircraft missiles after 1989 (Uhlig 1990). Salvadoran rebel leaders complained, in fact, that they did not lack combatants so much as arms (Montgomery 1995: 116–7).

Although the counterinsurgencies ultimately failed to eliminate the guerrillas, years of state-sponsored violence took their toll on the revolutionary movements, particularly in Guatemala. From the start, the guerrillas found it difficult to mobilize large numbers of noncombatants, especially for the sort of urban insurrections that occurred in Nicaragua. The Salvadoran guerrillas' "final offensive" of January 1981 is illustrative in this regard. This offensive – which the rebels hoped would present the incoming Reagan Administration with a revolutionary fait accompli – did result in a number of strategic military gains, with guerrilla forces reaching as far as Ilopango, fourteen miles from the capital, and briefly controlling the suburbs of the capital, San Salvador. However, the population of the capital, battered by months of state-sanctioned violence, was not well organized, there was little coordination among FMLN commanders, and the armed forces were able to militarize public transportation and factories (Montgomery 1995: 113). A week after it had begun, the offensive was called off.[15]

Despite the failure of the 1981 "final offensive," the guerrilla groups in El Salvador remained strong over the next decade. The guerrillas effectively ruled "zones of control" in relatively isolated parts of northern El Salvador, especially in the less densely populated departments of Chalatenango and Morazán, where the state was infrastructurally weak

---

[15] Joaquin Villalobos, one of the guerrillas' top military strategists, later regretted that the guerrillas had not struck earlier, before the violence worsened. "What happened," he suggests, "is that we lost the propitious moment" (quoted in Harnecker 1984: 175).

(see Map 6.2).[16] In these zones, locally elected bodies known as Local Popular Power (PPL) governed independently of the "official" state (see Pearce 1986; Shaull 1990; Ventura n.d.). After 1984, however, the zones of control were rolled back considerably, and the guerrillas were forced to break up into small, mobile units; the guerrillas and their supporters were often forced to relocate at considerable distances on short notice.

The sheer number of armed guerrillas in El Salvador declined significantly during the 1980s. According to estimates by the U.S. military, the number of guerrillas fell from a peak of as many as eleven thousand in 1982 to from four thousand to eight thousand in the late 1980s (Halloran 1987; LeMoyne 1987; McClintock 1998: 73–4). Another analyst describes a decline from about twelve thousand to seven thousand guerrillas during the same period (Barry 1990: 60).

As noted previously, however, the FMLN did mount an impressive offensive in November 1989 that was crucial in hastening the peace accords of 1992. According to Lungo Uclés (1996 [1990]: 177), the "fundamental purpose" of the offensive "was not to defeat the official armed forces once and for all":

Rather, the uprising sought to provoke a qualitative change in the correlation of forces that would help to restart the stalemated negotiation process for a political solution to the war. Subsequent events, culminating in the signing of the Peace Accords in January 1992, testify to the attainment of this central objective. Nevertheless, some sectors of the FMLN undoubtedly believed that the government army could be decisively defeated through a possible popular insurrection in the capital. . . . although the popular insurrection that some had erroneously envisioned did not take place. (Lungo Uclés 1996 [1990]: 177–8)

The FMLN did receive considerable popular support in certain working-class districts of San Salvador, holding off government forces for nearly a week, but this led the armed forces to bomb these areas indiscriminately (Preston 1990; Montgomery 1995: 217–20). The FMLN then retreated, as "neither the insurrectionists nor the people who supported them were prepared to resist a bombardment of this intensity to sustain the fighting for a prolonged period" (Lungo Uclés 1996 [1990]: 178).

By all accounts, the guerrillas in Guatemala found themselves in much worse straits than those in El Salvador. The brutal counterinsurgency in

[16] One of the constituent groups of the FMLN, the Popular Revolutionary Army (ERP), was also able to maintain a considerable presence in parts of Usulután, an important agroexporting department (Wood 2000b: ch. 3).

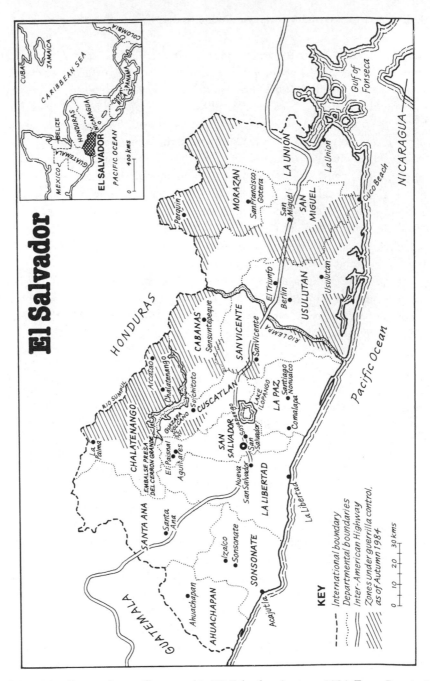

Map 6.2   Zones of guerrilla control in El Salvador, Autumn 1984. From *Promised Land* by Jenny Pearce. Copyright © 1986 Latin America Bureau. Reprinted with permission.

Guatemala during the early 1980s seems to have been particularly effective in cutting off the guerrillas from their mass base of collaborators. According to one sympathetic observer,

Massacres and village burnings struck fear into Indian communities, causing them to think twice about supporting the guerrillas. The wave of violence that swept through the highlands increased Indian hatred of the army but also resulted in widespread disillusionment with the rebel opposition. While the guerrillas demonstrated their ability to strike out at army targets, they did not prove capable of protecting their popular base of support. (Barry 1986: 36; see also Stoll 1993)

The URNG guerrillas, furthermore, had considerably less urban and working-class support than their Salvadoran counterparts, and they were never able to mount the type of urban offensives that the FMLN executed in 1981 and 1989 (see, e.g., Payeras 1987).

The number of armed insurgents in Guatemala declined from a peak of six thousand to eight thousand in 1980–1 (Jonas 1991: 138) to two thousand to three thousand by the late 1980s and early 1990s (Halloran 1987; Taylor and Marshall 1996). Even at the height of their influence, "the armed insurgents themselves were mainly located in the more isolated areas north and south of the densely populated [western] highlands" (Smith 1990: 10). The two most important guerrilla groups, the Revolutionary Organization of People in Arms (ORPA) and the Guerrilla Army of Poor (EGP), operated in the areas west of Lake Atitlán and in the northern highlands, respectively (see Map 6.3).

In sum, the combination of massive state terrorism, the holding of semicompetitive elections, the opening of limited political space, and the declining international isolation of "electoral authoritarian" regimes effectively prevented revolutionary movements from seizing power in El Salvador and Guatemala. However, precisely because the armed forces continued to repress more or less indiscriminately, and with impunity, and because elections were only semicompetitive, the political openings limited, and significant socioeconomic reforms blocked, revolutionaries were able to maintain significant popular support, especially in El Salvador, through the 1980s and into the 1990s. The guerrillas may not have won, but neither did they lose, a reality that I explore more closely in the following chapter.

No single factor, clearly, can account for the failure of revolutionary movements to seize state power in El Salvador and Guatemala – just as no single factor or process can account for the Nicaraguan

Map 6.3 Zones of insurgency in Guatemala, 1981. From *Rebels of Highland Guatemala* by Robert M. Carmack. Copyright © 1995 University of Oklahoma Press. Reprinted with permission.

Revolution. Nor were these failures any more inevitable than was the success of the Sandinistas. In El Salvador, especially, an FMLN victory was hardly unimaginable in the early 1980s. The guerrillas might very well have overthrown a military-dominated government that refused to incorporate Christian Democrats or to open up even limited political space for popular groups, or that failed to receive massive external aid. Nonetheless, the key factors that account for the relative solidity of state power in El Salvador and Guatemala in the face of revolutionary challenges – the capacity of the armed forces to remove ineffectual rulers, to oversee political openings, and thereby to obtain international aid for counterinsurgent wars – can all be traced to the longstanding characteristics of *institutional* military domination of those societies.

Conclusion to Part 3

During the 1970s, as Robert Williams has noted, economic conditions prompted similar patterns of political action throughout the Central American isthmus: "Peasants moved onto idle lands, wage earners demanded cost-of-living adjustments, and large landowners called on the services of the local police and the national security forces. What differed from country to country," he adds, "was the way national governments responded to the pressures from the different camps" (Williams 1986: 166). I have suggested here that it was the longstanding "closure" and indiscriminate repression of authoritarian regimes in Nicaragua, El Salvador, and Guatemala that – against this general backdrop of gross inequality and gathering resistance – unintentionally helped to induce or "construct" popular revolutionary movements. Revolutionary organizations or vanguards were themselves typically formed by dissidents from electorally oriented political parties or reformist social movements, who became frustrated by repeated electoral fraud and political repression. Fraud and violence also created a general political context that allowed these organizations to attract support from, and form alliances with, a broad range of social and political groupings, including peasants, workers, students, and middle strata.

In Honduras, however, a very different "cycle of political frustration" – one based on the alternation of mildly reformist and conservative rule – inhibited the development of a popular armed revolutionary movement, despite profound internal inequities and external dependence. Indeed, the case of Honduras seems to suggest that "political opportunities" for quite modest reforms may sometimes preempt the development of revolutionary insurgencies in otherwise conducive contexts. This is so both because leftist organizations will likely attempt to "fill" even limited political space with less costly, nonviolent forms of contestation – and eschew armed struggle – and because large numbers of ordinary people are unlikely to risk their lives in an armed struggle for state power when opportunities for peacefully attaining incremental reforms are seen to exist.

This is not to imply, however, that popular armed insurgencies, once they are under way, will necessarily dissipate if and when a dictatorial regime introduces reforms or incorporates new social groups into the polity. As the Salvadoran and Guatemalan cases demonstrate, this depends on a number of more specific factors, including the ability of the government to enact reforms that directly benefit real or potential rebel supporters and especially to ensure that revolutionaries and their follow-ers can safely and effectively participate in the electoral arena and civic life more generally (see Chapter 7). Not surprisingly, revolutionaries often decide that it is simply too dangerous for them to lay down their arms, even when the regimes that they confront begin to "open up" to some, perhaps considerable, degree.

This study has also emphasized, however, that the conditions that foster strong revolutionary movements by no means guarantee that such movements will actually seize state power. While revolutionaries became powerful actors in Nicaragua, El Salvador, and Guatemala, they overthrew only the old regime in Nicaragua. This was largely due, I have argued, to the structural differences between the Somoza dictatorship, on the one hand, and the Salvadoran and Guatemalan military regimes, on the other, and to the ways these regimes responded to revolutionary movements. Because of the neopatrimonial character of the Somoza regime, Somoza's personal intransigence, and the consequent difficulty of creating a politi-cal opening in Nicaragua, the Sandinistas were able to build a much broader coalition of both domestic allies (including the anti-Somoza bourgeoisie) and international supporters than were their Salvadoran and Guatemalan counterparts. As Carlos Vilas has noted,

The rise of the Sandinista struggle, international pressure, and the breakup of the ruling bloc isolated the Somoza regime from society as a whole. Sandinista strategy reinforced this effect by concentrating its attack on Somoza and the Guardia Nacional, thereby cushioning the struggle's class repercussions in pursuit of a call for national democratic consensus among a broad spectrum of actors. This was in contrast with the events of the same years in El Salvador and Guatemala, where . . . the political confrontation took on a clearly classist, or at least social, cast. Nicaragua reached a confrontation point pitting the state against society. (Vilas 1995: 97–8)

Salvadoran and Guatemalan revolutionaries confronted more institu-tional military regimes with much greater elite support than the Somoza dictatorship; in the face of revolutionary challenges, furthermore, these military regimes incorporated sectors of the moderate opposition, which themselves demonstrated significant popular support. Partly as a result of these limited openings, furthermore, the Guatemalan and especially the Salvadoran regime were bolstered by external aid, military training, and direct logistical assistance, mainly, although not exclusively, from the United States. Thus, Salvadoran and Guatemalan revolutionaries could find far fewer friends, and confronted a much stronger enemy, than did

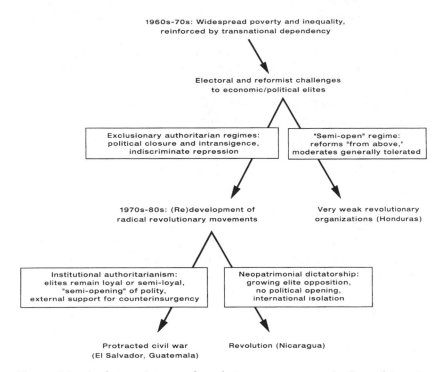

Figure 6.1 Analytic trajectory of revolutionary movements in Central America, 1960–90.

the Sandinistas. There is a clear parallel here with postwar Southeast Asia: Those revolutionary movements that were able to build broad multiclass coalitions (in Vietnam and Indonesia) seized state power, whereas those that could not (in Malaya and the Philippines) did not.

The state-centered analysis of Central American revolutionary movements that I have presented in this and the previous chapter is schematically summarized in Figure 6.1. The figure indicates that two political variables, against a general backdrop of widespread poverty, inequality, dependency, and incipient popular challenges to elites (often supported by the Catholic Church), determined whether radical revolutionary movements would form and take power in Central America. More specifically, the formation and fate of revolutionary movements depended upon (1) whether challengers confronted exclusionary and repressive authoritarian regimes (as in Nicaragua, El Salvador, and Guatemala) or a "semi-open" regime (as in Honduras), and (2) whether the repressive authoritarian

211

regimes were institutional in character and eventually responded to revolutionaries with a "semiopening" of the polity (El Salvador and Guatemala) or were neopatrimonial or sultanistic in character and responded to revolutionaries in a strictly and persistently repressive fashion (Nicaragua). This is not to say that all neopatrimonial or sultanistic dictatorships have been or will be toppled by popular revolutionary movements, radical or otherwise; some, for example, have proven too powerful for revolutionaries to overthrow, perhaps by retaining the loyalty of elites and/or foreign sponsors, and still others have been toppled by coups d'etat (see Snyder 1992, 1998; Everingham 1996; Herb 1999). Still, especially when they are infrastructurally weak, neopatrimonial dictatorships are not only particularly vulnerable to revolutionary overthrow, but also (like exclusionary and repressive forms of colonialism) tend to incubate and broaden the potential social base of the very movements that oppose them. Dictatorships that approximate the neopatrimonial type and which have been overthrown by revolutionaries, whether radical or populist, include the Díaz regime in Mexico, the Batista dictatorship in Cuba (see Chapter 2), the dictatorship of Shah Reza Pahlavi in Iran, the Marcos dictatorship in the Philippines, the dictatorship of Nicolae Ceauşescu in Romania (see Chapter 8), and the regime of Mobutu Sese Seko in Zaire.

The implications of this analysis for a more general understanding of successful revolutionary movements seem clear. Events in Central America support Robert Dix's (1984) argument that revolutionaries will often need to assemble a broad "negative" coalition – a coalition, that is, which opposes the status quo but may not agree on much else – of diverse social classes *and* external allies in order to seize state power. As Dix and others have noted, the assemblage of such a coalition is precisely what distinguishes the Nicaraguan (and Cuban) case from those of El Salvador and Guatemala, not to mention Honduras. My analysis also bears out Dix's assertion that the ability of revolutionaries to construct such a coalition depends less on socioeconomic than on political factors, specifically, "the catalyzing effect afforded by a narrowly-based dictatorship" (Dix 1984: 438) that remains repressive and intransigent in the face of political opposition. To Dix's formulation I would add only the requirement that the dictatorship be infrastructurally weak, for a powerful dictatorship with a reliable army could, in principle, repeatedly and effectively repress any emergent opposition.

This analysis also broadly concurs with that of Timothy Wickham-Crowley (1992), who also emphasizes the special vulnerabilities of corrupt, personalist dictatorships (which he terms "mafiacracies") when confronted by revolutionary movements. More than this, however, I hope to have shown that these dictatorships also unwittingly help to construct the very movements that bury them (see also Goodwin 1994b). To be sure, these movements also grow out of poverty, specific class relations, particular cultural frameworks, the organizational work of ideological revolutionaries, and a host of other potentially important factors; but as the case of Honduras suggests, outside of particular political contexts – contexts characterized above all by political exclusion and/or indiscriminate repression by infrastructurally weak (or weakened) states – none of these factors necessarily gives rise to strong revolutionary movements.

PART FOUR

Further Comparisons and Theoretical Elaborations

7

Between Success and Failure:
Persistent Insurgencies

It was that massacre, the most horrible, that really caused the glass of water to overflow. . . . People flowed out of the zone, either toward Honduras or south . . . or into the guerrillas. A lot of people joined us as combatants then.
      – "Licho," a Salvadoran guerrilla, on the El Mozote massacre
      of December 1981 (quoted in Danner 1993: 101)

The previous chapter characterized the Salvadoran and Guatemalan revolutionary movements as failures, which is true by definition if a revolution, or a "successful" revolution, requires the overthrow of the existing state. But there is another side to the proverbial coin: As we have seen, the Salvadoran and Guatemalan states were themselves unable to defeat militarily the revolutionary movements that challenged them. This raises a question that has received relatively little attention in the literature on revolutionary movements (and social movements more generally): Why have certain movements (but not others) been able to persist for many years or even decades, maintaining a significant base of popular support, even when subjected to extraordinary levels of state violence? To address this question, I compare in this chapter cases of "persistent insurgency" in El Salvador, Guatemala, and Peru (with a glance at Colombia) with major defeated rebellions in Malaya and the Philippines (discussed in Part 2) as well as Venezuela. I will argue that popularly supported guerrilla insurgencies have persisted when and where the armed forces of infrastructurally weak states have employed indiscriminate violence against social sectors suspected of sympathizing with the insurgents. Moreover, insurgencies have persisted in such cases despite the introduction of competitive elections, regardless of whether these rebellions themselves received significant foreign assistance, and regardless of whether state authorities received massive aid from foreign powers. The negotiated settlement of the Salvadoran civil war, furthermore, which I briefly examine, suggests that the termination of persistent insurgencies need not require substantial socioeconomic reforms so much as a reorganization of the state's armed forces.

Recent events in Latin America have raised anew the old question of "why revolutions succeed and fail" (Dix 1984). But do the notions of "success" and "failure" adequately characterize the fate of revolutionary movements in the region? In fact, none of the five major popularly supported armed rebellions that developed (or reemerged) in Latin America during the 1970s and 1980s – in Nicaragua, El Salvador, Guatemala, Colombia, and Peru – unambiguously succeeded *or* failed. To be sure, the Sandinista Front for National Liberation (FSLN) successfully toppled the Somoza dictatorship in Nicaragua in 1979, for reasons that I discussed in the previous chapter. The Sandinista Front thus "made" the only revolution in Latin America since the Cuban. However, largely as a result of intense elite and U.S. opposition, the Sandinistas proved rather less successful at radically reordering Nicaraguan society, and they were eventually voted out of power in 1990 (see, e.g., Foran and Goodwin 1993).

In this chapter, I focus upon the fate of the Salvadoran, Guatemalan, and Peruvian (Shining Path) insurgencies, which, unlike the Nicaraguan, proved incapable of seizing state power. None of these insurgencies, however, "failed" in terms of mobilizing large guerrilla armies and significant popular support over many years. As noted in Chapter 6, the Farabundo Martí National Liberation Front (FMLN) became locked in a military stalemate with the Salvadoran state for more than a decade (1980–92), an achievement that was the key factor leading to the negotiations that ended that civil war. One need not accept inflated claims about a "negotiated revolution" in El Salvador to recognize that the FMLN, although now disarmed, was never militarily defeated and remains a very powerful political actor as a legal political party (see, e.g., Karl 1992). The Guatemalan National Revolutionary Unity (URNG), for its part, while never as strong as the FMLN, survived a particularly savage counterinsurgency in the early 1980s, launched new offensives in the late 1980s, and, in December 1996, signed accords with the Guatemalan government, which also recognized the

URNG as a legal political organization.[1] Unlike the Salvadoran and Guatemalan insurgencies, the insurgency that was led by the Maoist Communist Party of Peru, better known as Sendero Luminoso (Shining Path), *was* effectively defeated during the early 1990s. But this conflict lasted more than a decade and resulted in some thirty-five thousand deaths and $25 billion in damage; several thousand Shining Path guerrillas remained active as late as 1995 (Sims 1996b).[2] How was this possible?

The Need for a Third Category

The prolonged character of the guerrilla insurgencies in El Salvador, Guatemala, and Peru clearly indicates that we need an additional category – besides "success" and "failure" – to characterize accurately their political fortunes. Yet the literature on mass-based rebellions and revolutions seems implicitly to recognize only two possible outcomes: either the rebels seize power, or they are more or less quickly crushed.[3] However, students of revolutionary movements need, at the very least, to make distinctions among (1) those insurgencies or rebellions that *successfully* seize state power; (2) those that are quickly and decisively *defeated* or, at least, driven to the margins of political significance; and (3) those that *persist* for many years or even decades without seizing power, but which maintain significant popular support. This last category includes those undefeated rebellions (like the Salvadoran and Guatemalan) that are terminated only through negotiated settlements. "Successful" insurgencies (in the minimal sense of [1] in the preceding list) include those in Vietnam, Cuba, and Nicaragua; "defeated" revolutionary movements include that led by the Malayan Communist Party (MCP) in British Malaya, the Communist-led Huk rebellion in the Philippines, the Communist-led rebellion in postwar Greece, the Mau Mau uprising in Kenya, and the

[1] The Guatemalan government held an initial round of "conversations" with the URNG as early as October 1987 in order to comply with the Central America Peace Accords of August 1987 (the Esquipulas II Accords), although the army refused even to consider a cease-fire at that time (Jonas 1991: 164–5).

[2] A smaller insurgent group, the Movimiento Revolucionario Túpac Amaru (MRTA), has also been active in Peru. Although the MRTA's dramatic seizure of the Japanese diplomatic residence in Lima made headlines in 1997, it was estimated to have only some three hundred to six hundred members (Sims 1997).

[3] Some scholars, however, have emphasized the persistence of social movements through periods of "abeyance." See Taylor 1989; Whittier 1995.

insurgency in Venezuela during the 1960s led by the Armed Forces of National Liberation (FALN).

This chapter focuses on the neglected third category, that of protracted or persistent insurgency. I do so through a comparative study that employs the method of qualitative comparative analysis (QCA) (Ragin 1987). More specifically, I compare a number of persistent insurgencies with defeated (albeit mass-based) guerrilla movements. To increase the analytic sharpness of my comparisons, I have delimited the universe of cases from which I have drawn my sample of insurgencies (both defeated and persistent) by excluding separatist insurgencies and by requiring that the rebels fielded at least one thousand armed guerrillas at their peak (thereby excluding small rural and/or urban guerrilla movements with relatively little popular support, such as were once found in Latin America's southern cone). I further define "persistent insurgencies" as revolutionary movements that mobilize an average of at least one thousand armed guerrillas for at least a decade.

I should emphasize that I am not directly concerned here, as I was in Chapters 3 and 5, with explaining why some radical groups, but not others, have been able to mobilize extensive popular support in the first place; the particular question that I seek to answer in this chapter is why revolutionary movements that have *already* mobilized large, popularly supported guerrilla armies have sometimes been more or less easily defeated by counterinsurgencies, while others have persevered for many years or even decades.

Which guerrilla movements fall into the category of "persistent insurgency"? Two extraordinary examples may be found in Burma and Colombia.[4] Several ethnic separatist groups have been at war with the Burmese state almost continuously since that country attained independence from Britain in 1948, as were Communists for several decades (see, e.g., Smith 1991); the Colombian insurgency, for its part, has links to the "peasant republics" established in that country during *la Violencia* ("the Violence") of the 1950s, and today's largest Colombian guerrilla group, the Revolutionary Armed Forces of Colombia (FARC), was formally established more than three decades ago (1964) (see, e.g., Arango 1984). These cases clearly demonstrate that armed rebellions

---

[4] Another important case would be East Timor, the former Portuguese colony, where a guerrilla insurgency survived more than two decades of a brutal military occupation by Indonesia (1975–99).

– and, hence, revolutionary situations – can become an integral aspect of a country's "routine politics" under certain circumstances: a virtual "way of life" for rebels and their supporters and "politics as usual" for government officials.[5]

The revolutionary movements in El Salvador, Guatemala, and Peru, on which I focus in this chapter,[6] also count as persistent insurgencies as previously defined: None seized state power and yet none was quickly or easily defeated; all three maintained substantial guerrilla armies and significant popular support for at least a decade. The FMLN, from its founding in 1980 through the 1992 peace accords, maintained a substantial guerrilla army as well as a mass base of collaborators and sympathizers; as we saw in Chapter 5, the so-called political-military organizations that comprised the FMLN developed sizable bases of support in the 1970s (e.g., Montgomery 1995: ch. 4). The insurgency in Guatemala dates back to the early 1960s. Several rebel groups formed or regrouped in that country during the 1970s after a brutal, U.S.-sponsored counterinsurgency in the late 1960s decimated the earlier movement. And, as noted in the previous chapter, the URNG (which was formed from these groups) survived yet another wave of intense repression in the early 1980s (Black 1984; Gruson 1990; Jonas 1991). Finally, Sendero Luminoso began its armed struggle in 1980 in the highland department of Ayacucho and subsequently developed a significant presence in several other regions of the country, including the Upper Huallaga Valley, a coca-producing region, and the shantytowns of Lima, the capital (Degregori 1990; Poole and Renique 1992; Palmer 1994a; Stern 1998).

One of the remarkable aspects of these insurgencies was their capacity to persist in the face of the incredible violence inflicted upon them and their real and putative supporters by government forces. The twelve-year civil war in El Salvador resulted in the deaths of some seventy-five thousand individuals, the vast majority at the hands of the government's armed forces and associated "death squads." As many as one million Salvadorans fled their country, and as many as five hundred thousand others were internally displaced (see, e.g., Barry 1990: 128–9). During the 1981–3 period

---

[5] Charles Tilly (who writes mainly about Western Europe) has implied that (1) insurrections and (2) coups, among other phenomena, fall outside of what he variously terms "politics as usual" and "routine politics" (Tilly 1978: 196 [Figure 7-1], 198 [Figure 7-3]). The first claim would surprise a Colombian or Guatemalan, the second a Bolivian.

[6] I examine these particular cases because they are the ones that I know best and, not coincidentally, because there exists a fairly substantial scholarly literature on each.

alone, I noted earlier, the Guatemalan government's "scorched earth" counterinsurgency resulted in the destruction of more than 440 villages and the deaths, according to some estimates, of between one hundred thousand and one hundred fifty thousand individuals. This counterinsurgency created as many as one million internal refugees, and as many as two hundred thousand Guatemalans fled to southern Mexico. The armed forces in Peru, finally, were implicated in numerous massacres of peasants, indiscriminately bombed rural areas, and summarily executed many of the nearly three hundred Shining Path prisoners killed in prison uprisings in 1986. The United Nations reports that the Peruvian government had the worst human rights record of any country in the world from 1987 to 1991 in terms of "disappearances" (Palmer 1994b: 271), and the war also produced as many as two hundred thousand internal refugees (Kirk 1991). As we shall see, earlier insurgencies in the Philippines, Malaya, and Venezuela were defeated outright more quickly and with much less bloodshed.

The persistence for more than a decade of the Shining Path insurgency in Peru is particularly puzzling, given that movement's unusual ideological dogmatism and well-documented use of terrorism against its perceived civilian opponents, including the leaders of other leftist parties and community organizations as well as ordinary Peruvians suspected of anti-Sendero activities or even sentiments (see, e.g., Poole and Renique 1991, 1992; Starn 1992). The human rights organization Americas Watch concluded that the "murder of the defenseless, often in grotesque fashion, is Sendero policy" (Americas Watch [hereafter, AW] 1992: 64).[7] The inability of the Peruvian government to contain Sendero after its emergence in 1980, at least until the early 1990s, emerges as a particularly puzzling problem that I hope to unravel.

---

[7] This is not to say that guerrillas in El Salvador and Guatemala never violated human rights. Salvadoran guerrillas, for example, occasionally engaged in summary executions, kidnapping for ransom, forced "recruitment," and the indiscriminate use of land mines, among other practices (see AW 1991: ch. 4). And the Guatemalan guerrillas, among other abuses (see Stoll 1993, 1999), have been implicated in at least one major massacre of villagers (in Chacalté, El Quiché) whom they apparently suspected of betraying them to the armed forces (see, e.g., Taylor 1997). However, these violations do not even begin to approach the scale of human rights abuses committed by Sendero or by the incumbent regimes in any of the three countries that I discuss in this chapter. As Jennifer Harbury has aptly written, "Suggestions that the guerrilla forces [in Guatemala] were somehow as abusive as the military are ridiculous. . . . Comparing the two is like saying the French Resistance was as bad as the Third Reich" (Harbury 1997: A14).

Persistence Versus Failure

Why compare persistent insurgencies with the defeated rebellions in the Philippines, Malaya, and Venezuela? The Venezuelan insurgency was selected because it was the largest Latin American guerrilla movement of the 1960s, inspired by the Cuban Revolution, that was decisively defeated; the Salvadoran and Guatemalan regimes, moreover, explicitly (if unsuccessfully) attempted to emulate the Venezuelan counterinsurgency "model" (Karl 1985: 309; Jonas 1991: 154). (Salvadoran President José Napoleón Duarte remarked in 1983 that, "We are following the Venezuelan example and I am Rómulo Betancourt," the Venezuelan president who presided over the early phase of that country's famously effective counterinsurgency [quoted in Karl 1985: 309].) As we have seen in Part 2 of this book, the Huk rebellion and the Malayan Communist insurgency were also major revolutionary movements, fielding impressive guerrilla armies – and both have been fairly well studied by scholars.

The following analysis will examine several hypotheses about counterinsurgency that concern the nature of the insurgency itself, geopolitical factors, and the actions of the states that revolutionaries have sought to overthrow. Before turning to these hypotheses, however, let me address one "commonsense" explanation for the differences that I have highlighted: Persistent insurgencies have persisted, presumably, because they are especially large and popular; defeated insurgencies were defeated because they were much smaller and, accordingly, more vulnerable to counterinsurgency. Unfortunately, this hypothesis is difficult to test since estimates of the number of people who support revolutionary movements in one form or another vary dramatically depending upon their source. Fortunately, there is rather more agreement among scholars about the (generally much smaller) number of armed guerrillas that insurgent movements have been able to mobilize, although here too estimates vary considerably and should be regarded as only very approximate.

Table 7.1 shows estimates of the size of insurgent armed forces in the six cases that I am examining as well as a measure of the number of guerrillas relative to each country's total population. As can be seen, the relationship between the "density" of the insurgent forces and the persistence of the insurgency is not nearly as strong as common sense might suggest. By this measure, two of the defeated insurgencies (the Philippine and Malayan) were clearly larger than the Shining Path rebellion in Peru and were roughly as large as the Guatemalan insurgency. Only the

223

Table 7.1. *Size of guerrilla armed forces.*

Nation	(a) Number of guerrillas	(b) Total population	(c) Guerrillas per capita*
Persistent			
Guatemala	6–8,000 (1962–96)	6.6 million (1980–1)	90.9–121.2 (1978)
El Salvador	8,000 (1980–92)	4.7 million (early 1980s)	170.2 (1989)
Peru	10,000 (1980–95)	21.9 million (1991)	45.7 (1992)
Defeated			
Philippines	11–15,000 (1946–54)	19.2 million (1949–51)	57.3–78.1 (1948)
Malaya	6,000+ (1948–55)	6.3 million (1954)	95.2+ (1957)
Venezuela	1–2,000 (1962–9)	7.5 million (1962–3)	13.3–26.6 (1961)

Note: * (c) = (a)/(b) × 100,000.

Sources: Guatemala: (a) Jonas 1991: 138; (b) World Bank 1980: 110. El Salvador: (a) McClintock 1998: 73–4; (b) Gettleman et al. 1986: 3. Peru: (a) McClintock 1998: 73–5; (b) AW 1992: xxv. Philippines: (a) Kerkvliet 1977: 210; (b) Rigg 1991: 70. Malaya: (a) Short 1975: 350; (b) Jomo 1988: 324. Venezuela: (a) Wickham-Crowley 1992: 54; (b) Blank 1973: 37.

Salvadoran insurgency was substantially larger than all three defeated rebellions. The explanation for persistent insurgencies, accordingly, would seem to involve more than size or popularity alone. The hypothesis that especially large and popularly supported insurgencies are the ones that tend to persist also begs the question as to *why* they were able to remain large and popular for so long.

One possible explanation is that insurgencies that are "racial" or ethnic in nature *as well as* rooted in class or socioeconomic grievances are likely to be particularly intractable, whereas rebellions that are merely class-based will be more easily defeated or coopted. The decades-long conflicts in Burma, South Africa, and Israel/Palestine come to mind here. In fact, this hypothesis seems to be confirmed by two of the persistent insurgencies in our sample, Guatemala and Peru, where rebels drew disproportionate support from indigenous peoples, who comprise about half the population and a majority of the rural poor in these countries. (It should be emphasized, however, that Shining Path, unlike at least two guerrilla groups within the URNG (Black 1984: ch. 4), based its strategy exclusively upon a class analysis of Peruvian society and used "*none* of the usual repertoire of 'Incan symbols'" that are prominent in Peruvian political discourse [Poole and Renique 1991: 145; emphasis in original].)

This hypothesis, however, does not accurately differentiate persistent from defeated rebellions. One of the persistent insurgencies in our sample, the Salvadoran, was not, for the most part, a "racialized" struggle (according to most estimates, less than 10 percent of the Salvadoran population consists of indigenous people), whereas one of the defeated rebellions, in Malaya, was clearly such, pitting predominantly Chinese guerrillas against the British colonial regime and a conservative ethnic Malay elite (e.g., Stenson 1974; Short 1975). The racialization of an insurgency, therefore, is neither necessary nor sufficient for it to persist.

Another plausible explanation for the persistence of large-scale insurgencies is that revolutionary movements have only been defeated where incumbent regimes have received substantial foreign assistance, particularly military aid. Where such assistance is absent, by contrast, revolutionaries have presumably been able to wage protracted struggles against regimes that simply lack the means to eliminate or demoralize them and their supporters.

In fact, this geopolitical hypothesis is generally confirmed by our sample of *defeated* insurgencies. The colonial government in Malaya, for example, while financing its counterinsurgency mainly through duties on locally produced tin and rubber (whose prices skyrocketed during the Korean War), was also able to draw upon the services of approximately thirty thousand colonial soldiers – who comprised *all* the combat troops used against the rebels – from Britain and the Commonwealth (including Australians, Fijians, East Africans, and Gurkhas); the Malayan government also received arms and helicopters from the United States (Caldwell 1977b: 233, 246).[8] The United States also lent substantial economic and military aid (as well as counterinsurgency experts and trainers) to the Philippines during the Huk rebellion of the early 1950s; indeed, the counterinsurgency in that country was virtually run by the CIA and the Joint U.S. Military

---

[8] Perhaps the major U.S. "contribution" to the Malayan counterinsurgency, however, was its abandonment of its longstanding anticolonial stance toward British Malaya in recognition of Britain's financial dependence on that colony as Britain attempted to rebuild its economy after the war (see Rotter 1987: ch. 3).

Advisory Group (JUSMAG) (Shalom 1977, 1986: ch. 3). According to one
scholar, U.S. aid to the Philippines, which totaled $500 million from 1951
to 1956, "probably saved the government from total economic collapse"
(Kerkvliet 1977: 243).[9]

This hypothesis also seems to explain the persistence of the Shining
Path rebellion, since the Peruvian government did *not* receive substantial
external assistance during the 1980s (McClintock 1992: 234–5; Mauceri
1991: 104).

Notwithstanding these supportive examples, this geopolitical hypothesis also fails to distinguish accurately persistent insurgencies from defeated
rebellions. To begin with, it should be noted that not *all* successful counterinsurgencies have been dependent upon substantial foreign support.
U.S. military aid to the Venezuelan government during the 1960s, for
example, averaged no more than 5 percent of that country's total military
expenditures; in addition, Venezuela received virtually no weapons grants
from the United States, and relatively few of its military personnel received
U.S. counterinsurgency training (Wickham-Crowley 1992: ch. 5). With
its extensive oil revenues, however, Venezuela proved fully capable of
financing its own successful counterinsurgency.

The persistence of insurgency in Guatemala also raises questions about
this hypothesis. Although the Guatemalan government did not receive
official U.S. military assistance from 1977 to 1984 due to human rights
concerns, it continued to purchase arms and other military goods from the
United States during this period. Moreover, because of *previous* U.S. aid
and training during the 1960s and 1970s, which was quite substantial
indeed (see, e.g., Wickham-Crowley 1992: ch. 5), as well as arms and
assistance from Taiwan, Argentina (until the Falklands/Malvinas War),
and especially Israel, the Guatemalan army was able to wage a brutal
counterinsurgency in the 1980s (Jonas 1991: 204–7). Ironically, armed
insurgents in Guatemala began to regroup and to initiate new offensives
in the late 1980s – precisely, that is, when official U.S. military aid began
to flow once again to the regime.

The inability of substantial foreign aid always to defeat an armed rebellion is, however, demonstrated particularly clearly – leaving aside the case
of Vietnam for present purposes – by the case of El Salvador. As we have
seen, the insurgency led by the FMLN persisted throughout the 1980s
despite U.S. aid to the Salvadoran regime that totaled more than $1

[9] For an alternative but, to me, unpersuasive perspective, see Shafer 1988: ch. 8.

million *per day*. Between 1980 and 1990, El Salvador received from the United States about $3 billion in economic aid – exceeding the Salvadoran government's own contribution to its budget – and approximately $1 billion in military aid, not to mention counterinsurgency expertise, training, and intelligence data; U.S. Marines are even reported to have led a number of attacks against the guerrillas (Karl 1992: 150; Barry 1990: 143, 149, 178). In sum, the Salvadoran case demonstrates quite clearly that even massive foreign aid does not always make it possible for an incumbent regime to defeat an armed insurgency.

Another plausible hypothesis emphasizes the importance of foreign assistance to the *insurgent* forces: In this view, revolutionary movements that receive significant external aid will be able to persist, while those that do not, will not. This hypothesis seems to be generally confirmed, again, by our sample of *defeated* insurgencies. There is no evidence, for example, that the Huk rebels in the Philippines or the Malayan Communists received external aid during the course of their failed insurgencies (see, e.g., Lieberman 1966: 27, Pomeroy 1963b: 248–9 on the Philippines; Stubbs 1989: 254 on Malaya).[10]

The question of foreign assistance to the FMLN in El Salvador is more controversial. A case can be made that the FMLN received substantial foreign aid, but it is doubtful that this explains the longevity of the insurgency. The FMLN certainly received arms from Nicaragua and Cuba, most notably on the eve of its January 1981 offensive and then again after its November 1989 offensive, when it came into possession of some much-publicized Soviet-made antiaircraft missiles (Uhlig 1989). However, the 1981 rebel offensive suffered in part due to *insufficient* armaments, and, as noted in the previous chapter, guerrilla leaders complained openly about a lack of weapons in the early 1980s (Petras 1986 [1981]: 332; Montgomery 1995: 116). Moreover, the FMLN was forced to rely upon *homemade* antiaircraft weapons for most of the war – weapons that were apparently useless during the 1989 rebel offensive in San Salvador, when the Salvadoran air force did "not hesitate to strafe, rocket, [and] even bomb crowded urban communities" (Preston 1990: 6). During guerrilla attacks on urban military barracks, "amateurish weapons and the inexperience of the combatants caused more casualties among civilian bystanders than within the barracks" (Miles and Ostertag 1991: 229, 235). In sum, even if

[10] Edgar O'Ballance claims that the Malayan rebels did receive some very limited assistance from China (O'Ballance 1966: 138), but provides no documentation.

the assistance that the FMLN received from abroad was in some sense significant, that aid clearly did not transform it into a particularly well-armed movement. "If such outside aid were ended," recognized one observer (in 1989) who *did* judge such assistance to be important, "the guerrillas . . . would remain a potent challenge. The rebels are well organized and have enough popular support to continue fighting for years" (LeMoyne 1989: 120).

There is, moreover, an even better reason to believe that this particular hypothesis does not accurately differentiate persistent from defeated insurgencies. Some *defeated* rebellions have received significant if not massive external aid. The guerrilla movement in Venezuela, for example, received considerable assistance from Cuba and, to a lesser extent, China, before it succumbed. Indeed, from 1964 to 1967 "the Cubans . . . candidly acknowledged their role in training and otherwise assisting the Venezuelan insurgents" (Wickham-Crowley 1992: 88–9). And there is clear evidence that some insurgencies have not required significant external assistance in order to *persist*: Both the URNG in Guatemala as well as Peru's Sendero Luminoso received virtually no such aid (see Jonas 1991: 139 on Guatemala; Gonzales 1992, *inter alia*, on Peru).

When one steps back from the evidence, it is not surprising that these geopolitical hypotheses do not seem to explain very much. The idea that regimes will always need external assistance to fight effectively is not only problematic in its own right, but usually rests upon an even more dubious assumption: the notion that a purely coercive or military response to rebellion will in fact always be effective. "Coercion may seem a necessary course of action to the incumbents," as Claude Welch has noted,

yet their use of force may further inflame popular resentment. . . . Nothing may better drive persons into opposition than the realization that life and livelihood may be at stake. Escalation of violence by the government forcing an all-or-nothing choice can confirm rather than break the will to resist. (Welch 1980: 279, 331)

Accordingly, many students of counterinsurgency (including Welch) have argued that rebellions can be defeated only if their "root causes" are eliminated. Increasingly, in fact, even military officers have recognized that an effective counterinsurgency requires some sort of reforms in addition to coercion (see, e.g., Barry et al. 1987; Manwaring 1991). This raises the question of what exactly the "root causes" of insurgencies *are* that need to be eradicated. In other words, what exactly must incumbent regimes reform in order to defeat armed rebellions? This brings us to a second set of hypotheses about counterinsurgency – hypotheses that refer to the actions of the incumbent regimes that revolutionaries are attempting to overthrow.

Land Reform and Elections

Students of popular insurgencies often suggest that they can be permanently resolved only through social reforms that alleviate the poverty and inequality that presumably are the "root cause" of such rebellions. James Painter, for example, one of the more astute observers of the Guatemalan insurgency, suggested in 1986, with apparent prescience, that "It is hardly controversial to predict that without social reforms the URNG and the popular movement will inevitably recover their strength and once again offer a serious challenge to the status quo" (Painter 1987: 111). Jenny Pearce, the author of an important book on El Salvador, concluded that only "a far-reaching agrarian reform . . . carried out within a broad process of radical social transformation can possibly pave the way for lasting peace" in that country (Pearce 1986: 303). Jeffery Paige similarly describes "the root cause of the civil war" in El Salvador as "coffee" – that is, the concentration of the country's best land in the coffee estates owned by that country's small oligarchy (Paige 1996: 136). Indeed, one plausible hypothesis is that incumbent regimes need to implement a significant land reform in order to defeat revolutionary movements, since, in this view, peasant grievances associated with poverty, tenancy, and landlessness are, in fact, the "root causes" of large-scale insurgencies, at least in agrarian Third World societies (see, e.g., Paige 1975; Barry 1987). (In fact, all of the persistent and defeated rebellions examined in this chapter had substantial, if not exclusive, peasant support.) Insurgencies will persist, if not actually seize power, on the other hand, where no land reform – or a patently inadequate land reform – is enacted.

This land-reform hypothesis does seems to be supported by the cases of persistent insurgency in Guatemala, El Salvador, and (to some extent) Peru. The case of Guatemala, where land distribution is the most unequal in all of Latin America, is straightforward: Prior to the peace accords of 1996, the government did not adopt *any* land redistribution law, even on paper – the only Central American country not to have done so – or even express a commitment to some future land reform (Jonas 1991: 178). (An earlier agrarian reform, it should be noted, was reversed following the U.S.-backed coup in 1954.) The Salvadoran regime, for its part, did enact a much-heralded agrarian reform in 1980 (see Chapter 6), but its actual results are plainly inadequate when measured against the extent of rural poverty and inequality in that country. (I discuss the agrarian aspects of the negotiated settlement of the Salvadoran conflict later in this chapter.) The most important aspect of the 1980 reform, which would have expropriated the bulk of the oligarchy's coffee plantations, was repeatedly postponed and was considerably weakened by a law written into the Salvadoran constitution in 1983. The other elements of the reform, moreover, only benefited about one-third of the already very limited target group of small tenants and permanent agricultural workers. As a result, concludes one analysis of the reform,

The vast majority of small farmers, tenants, semi-proletarians and seasonal workers were untouched by the agrarian reform. The landless – presently more than one quarter of all rural families – were completely left out of the reform. (Pelupessy 1991: 48)

Between 1980 and 1983, only 12 percent of rural households in El Salvador benefited in any way from the agrarian reform (Paige 1996: 136).

The land-reform hypothesis is also supported to some extent by the case of Peru, although the Sendero rebellion "is novel in taking place *after* a major agrarian reform," a reform that by most criteria was "the second most sweeping in Latin America after that of Cuba" (McClintock 1984: 49; emphasis in original). The peasants of the department of Ayacucho, however, where the Sendero rebellion first developed, received fewer benefits from this reform than those of any other agrarian zone; indeed, "the reform barely benefited them materially" (McClintock 1984: 66, 80; see also Palmer 1986: 136–7). Once the insurgency began, in any case, the Peruvian government pursued an almost exclusively military approach toward it: A development program for Peru's southern highlands, which provided peasants with interest-free loans from the state Agrarian Bank as well as technical assistance, was begun in 1985, but this program "collapsed when the economic crisis of 1988 left the Agrarian Bank without funds" (Mauceri 1991: 94–5); in addition, as of the early 1990s there were no long-term crop substitution or economic development projects implemented in the Upper Huallaga valley, where the coca-eradication efforts of a U.S. Drug Enforcement Agency project alienated peasants, who were not offered an alternative to coca production, and thereby helped to consolidate Sendero's influence in the region (AW 1992: 127). (However, while no significant land reform was implemented in Peru, the Shining Path insurgency *was* finally defeated in the early 1990s, as I discuss later in this chapter.)

The land-reform hypothesis is better supported by the successful counterinsurgency in Venezuela, where between 1958 and 1968 the Acción Democrática (AD) regime established more than eight hundred agricultural settlements with a "full panoply of coordinated [government] services" that "directly affected the lives of as many as 100,000 peasant families, bringing them slowly into the main channels of the national economy" (Powell 1971: 110). "Enough peasants received land and other benefits to forestall widespread support for guerrillas" of the FALN (Hellinger 1991: 107). All told, between 1959 and 1975 more than a quarter of rural households in Venezuela benefited from the reform; by this measure, the Venezuelan reform was the third most extensive nonsocialist agrarian reform in Latin America, after the Bolivian and Mexican reforms associated with the revolutions that took place in those countries (Paige 1996: 136). Although by the end of the 1960s the agrarian reform program "slowed down to a calculated, orderly, and time-consuming process," bringing charges that "the AD leadership [had] 'sold out' the interests of its clienteles" (Powell 1971: 114), by then the guerrilla insurgency had all but disintegrated.

Notwithstanding these supportive (or partially supportive) cases, the successful counterinsurgencies in the Philippines and Malaya suggest that a significant land reform may *not* in fact be necessary to defeat a rebellion. In the Philippines, the government of Ramon Magsaysay undertook a number of initiatives, at least on paper and with much public fanfare, that were allegedly aimed at improving the plight of the peasantry. But many of these efforts "came after 1953 – after the rebellion had begun to recede" (Kerkvliet 1977: 240). Moreover, Magsaysay's most ambitious projects "covered relatively few people and were always short of money" (Lieberman 1966: 29). Perhaps the most publicized agrarian reform program, the Economic Development Corps (EDCOR), resettled only about 950 families on new homesteads, and less than 250 of these families had been involved in the Huk movement (Kerkvliet 1977: 239; see also Shalom 1986: 79–80). (When an overzealous U.S. land reform adviser proposed a modest land redistribution program, he was denounced by the speaker of the Philippine House of Representatives as a Communist and was later recalled from Manila [Shalom 1986: 84–5].) In sum, there was no significant land reform in the Philippines during the 1950s (or subsequently, for that matter).

In Malaya, the principal counterinsurgency tool of the British colonial regime was the resettlement of about six hundred thousand Chinese rural squatters – one of the main sources of popular support for the Communist insurgents – into heavily guarded "New Villages" (see, e.g., Renick 1965; Tilman 1966).[11] Those who were resettled had access to relatively little land, although many former squatters who were "deprived of their land by forced resettlement were able to find work on rubber smallholdings and Asian-owned estates and tin mines," which were prospering due to the Korean War (Stubbs 1989: 173). The New Villages, in other words, amounted to a sort of land reform *in reverse*, depriving people of access to land, converting many of them into wage earners, and rendering "the economic stability of the New Villages dependent upon the international prices of rubber and tin" (Stubbs 1989: 174). In sum, the cases of the Philippines and Malaya clearly suggest that a significant land reform may not be necessary, let alone sufficient, to defeat a serious rural insurgency.

Another plausible hypothesis is that rebellions will persist in opposition to a military or some other type of authoritarian regime, but are doomed to failure when incumbent regimes have introduced competitive elections. The assumption here is that elections allow people to express their grievances at a much lower cost and with far fewer risks than armed rebellion.

This "electoral" hypothesis is generally confirmed by the successful counterinsurgencies in the Philippines, Malaya, and Venezuela. In each of these cases, elections played an important role in undermining popular support for guerrilla movements. In the Philippines, the elections held after 1950 were marked by substantially less fraud and violence than those of the immediate postwar period (see Chapter 4). Both the local elections of 1951 and the presidential election of 1953 were relatively peaceful, and Huk leader Luis Taruc later noted that peasants came to see "elections as alternatives to rebellion" (Kerkvliet 1977: 238). The introduction of elections in British Malaya beginning in 1951, which would culminate in full independence in 1957, also undercut the Communist insurgency in that country (see, e.g., Stockwell 1987; Lee 1981). More specifically, the success of the alliance between the United Malays National Organization (UMNO) and the Malayan Chinese Association (MCA) in the 1955 federal election "helped to put the MCP back on the defensive and set the stage for the winding down of the Emergency," the government's euphemism for the rebellion (Stubbs 1989: 220). Finally, large numbers of workers and

[11] The "strategic hamlets" of South Vietnam were modeled on this program.

232

peasants voted for Presidents Rómulo Betancourt (1959–64) and Raúl Leoni (1964–9) of the Acción Democrática party in competitive elections in Venezuela. "[O]pposition to the AD governments was highly vehement and vocal," Wickham-Crowley has noted,

> but the bulk of government and opposition activity was *within* the legal system and the electoral process. Obviously, the very "openness" of the Venezuelan electoral system . . . provided a political space for the moderate opponents of the regime, weakening any attractions that the radical left might have held for them. (Wickham-Crowley 1992: 196; emphasis in original)

The elections of December 1963, in particular, proved to be "a major political defeat for the guerrillas" (Gott 1970: 210). For despite the FALN's boycott campaign, about 90 percent of the registered electorate voted, a development that led many individuals and organizations, including the Communist Party of Venezuela (PCV), to rethink their support for the FALN (Gott 1970: pt. 2, chs. 5–6; see also Ellner 1988: ch. 3).

The validity of this "electoral" hypothesis, however, is much more ambiguous in the cases of El Salvador and Guatemala, if only because the general political context in which elections were held in these countries during the 1980s makes it extremely difficult to speak of genuinely democratic elections (see Herman and Brodhead 1984: ch. 4; Karl 1986; and Acevedo 1991 on El Salvador; Trudeau 1989 and Jonas 1991: chs. 10–11 on Guatemala). What *is* clear, however, is that the attempt by both the Salvadoran and Guatemalan regimes to use elections for counterinsurgency purposes had limited results in each case, despite the initial election of "centrist" Christian Democratic presidents who had themselves been persecuted by the armed forces in these countries. The insurgencies in El Salvador and Guatemala persisted, moreover, even after small social-democratic parties contested elections, producing an ideological spectrum of competing parties that was certainly as broad as that in the Philippines or Malaya during the 1950s or in Venezuela in the 1960s.

The case of Peru is even more telling on this issue. Prior to President Alberto Fujimori's so-called *autogolpe* (or "self-coup") in April 1992, elections in that country were simply not effective at undermining the Shining Path insurgency, even though a remarkably wide spectrum of political parties competed, including Marxist parties (see, e.g., Woy-Hazleton and Hazleton 1994). Indeed, as many analysts have noted, the great irony is that Shining Path began its armed struggle at the very moment when Peru

233

was attempting to democratize after a period of military rule (see, e.g., McClintock 1994, 1998; Degregori 1999). What is perhaps even more surprising is that the rebels were able to expand their influence during a period when several competitive elections were held. The insurgency was effectively defeated, moreover, after 1992, a period characterized by increasingly unfair and undemocratic elections (although, as I detail below, Shining Path had provoked widespread popular resistance well before then). The historical record clearly indicates, then, that while elections may *sometimes* prove helpful or even necessary for defeating insurgencies, this is not always the case.

A Theory of Persistent Insurgency, or the Perversity of Indiscriminate Violence by Weak States

What exactly explains this last, curious finding? Why would large numbers of people support or even fight on behalf of an illegal and persecuted organization if it is possible to articulate political grievances peacefully through elections? My hypothesis is that competitive elections – which, as many have suggested, should not be equated with democracy – do not in fact always guarantee that groups *can* make political demands, however peacefully, without suffering violent repression. Elections, therefore, will not induce guerrillas to give up their fight, or their supporters to abandon them, when to do so will not significantly reduce, and may very well increase, the likelihood of violent injury or death. A popular insurgency cannot be defeated, it follows, until rebels can lay down their guns – and they and their supporters can engage in peaceful political activities – without fear of being violently attacked.

This suggests that the crucial factor that explains the persistence or defeat of insurgencies may lie in the variable capacity of political authorities to tolerate, or at least not to repress indiscriminately, organized dissent and protest. We may hypothesize, that is, that mass-based insurgencies will not be easily defeated unless the armed forces of such regimes broadly tolerate peaceful political protest or at least do not indiscriminately repress presumed regime opponents. This, in turn, may require a significant reorganization of the structure and personnel of the armed forces and the effective disbandment of death squads and abusive paramilitary groups. By contrast, the continuous, indiscriminate repression of social sectors presumed to be sympathetic to the rebels will serve – however unintentionally – to prolong and perhaps even strengthen a mass-based insurgency, *even if* incumbents have introduced competitive elections and/or receive substantial foreign assistance.

Indiscriminate state violence is especially likely to backfire, generating ever greater levels of armed resistance, when states do not fully penetrate and control the territories they claim to rule. When repressive states are infrastructurally weak, that is, revolutionaries can more easily mobilize popular support in such territories. In fact, all the states confronted by the insurgents in our sample were more or less infrastructurally weak: Guerrillas were able to retreat to areas that were (at best) only tenuously or irregularly controlled by government forces. These areas included the northern departments of El Salvador, along the Honduran border; the western highlands of Guatemala, especially near the Mexican border; the southern highlands, the Upper Huallaga Valley, and the shantytowns of Lima in Peru; the Sierra Madre of Luzon in the Philippines; the interior jungles of Malaya (peninsular Malaysia); and the Andean departments of Venezuela. (See also Appendix 2 to this chapter.)

The hypothesis that indiscriminate violence by weak states unintentionally fuels insurgencies is supported by the successful counterinsurgencies in the Philippines, Malaya, and Venezuela. Peaceful political dissent generally came to be tolerated and abuses by the armed forces were largely, if far from entirely, curbed during the course of the insurgencies in these countries – despite reservations about such policies among many officers. In the Philippines, as noted previously, political violence associated with elections abated after 1950, and the military became much less abusive under the leadership of Ramon Magsaysay, first when he was secretary of defense (1950–3) and then during his presidency (1954–7). While defense minister, "Magsaysay was given unprecedented authority . . . to make field promotions and to order courts-martial, and he used both extensively to punish random abuses against the civilian population and to reward combat prowess" (McClintock 1992: 113). According to Benedict Kerkvliet,

Former rebels and nonrebels alike claimed that Magsaysay "cleaned up the PC [Philippine Constabulary] and Philippine army" so that soldiers no longer stole from peasants, "got rid of the civilian guards" [notoriously abusive forces that were paid in part by landlords], "promised amnesty to Huks and kept his word about it," and "understood that we weren't criminals and that we wanted only what was rightfully ours." (Kerkvliet 1977: 208)

Jesus Lava, secretary general of the Communist Party at the height of the rebellion, noted that when "Magsaysay started making reforms in the

Philippine army . . . it had an impact not only on the movement's mass support but on the armed [Huk] soldiers as well. Many left because repression was ending" (quoted in Kerkvliet 1977: 238). Moreover, while no significant land reform was enacted and "living conditions . . . improved little – if at all – after the revolt," the government generally tolerated the activities of the Federation of Free Farmers (FFF) and the Free Farmers Union (MASAKA), both of which "grew directly out of the Huk movement" (Kerkvliet 1977: 268).

In Malaya, similarly, the government and armed forces became much less abusive after Sir Gerald Templer – who emphasized the importance of "winning the hearts and minds" of Malayans – was appointed high commissioner in early 1952. Templer abolished a regulation that permitted mass detentions and deportations. Furthermore, Operation Service, an effort to reform the colonial police, "exceeded initial expectations. Because of better training, and the new equipment sent from Britain . . . the police gained confidence in their own abilities, were less ill-disposed towards the general public, and less inclined to treat all Chinese [the principal ethnic base of the rebellion] as suspects" (Stubbs 1989: 157, 166; see also O'Ballance 1966: 129).[12] Better training and equipment also reduced the use of "coercion and intimidation tactics" and improved the morale of combat troops, changes that were "particularly welcome," according to Richard Stubbs, to "the ordinary people in the rural areas" (Stubbs 1989: 159). Most of the New Villages of resettled Chinese, furthermore, which might have become hotbeds of political discontent, were governed by elected local councils by the end of 1955. These councils were, at least in some cases, "an effective liaison between the villages and state and federal officials, as well as a means by which grievances could be aired" (Stubbs 1989: 215). A series of well-publicized amnesties for guerrillas were also proclaimed (despite opposition from sectors of the armed forces), and surrendered insurgents were not only well treated, but were offered substantial rewards for intelligence information (see O'Ballance 1966: 150, 156, 159, 174).[13] In the months following the August 31, 1957,

---

[12] Collective curfews and fines, however, continued to be imposed occasionally on villages, although "some of the more extreme measures were discarded by Templer presumably because they were judged ineffective or counter-productive" (Stubbs 1989: 166).

[13] One member of the MCP Politburo defected in exchange for a bribe of nearly half a million dollars. Tunku Abdul Rahman, a leading Malay politician and the first prime minister of independent Malaya, allegedly remarked that "He is now richer than any of us" (O'Ballance 1966: 160).

independence day celebrations, "a series of mass surrenders brought about an almost complete collapse of the communist guerrilla army" (Stubbs 1989: 240), which had already been severely weakened.

There is comparatively little published information about the character of the counterinsurgency in Venezuela during the 1960s, but the same general pattern of growing tolerance for peaceful political activities seems evident, despite the virulent anti-Communism of the elite troops within the army and political police (Wickham-Crowley 1992: 200). Most importantly, the AD governments of the 1960s not only tolerated but actively encouraged the organization of peasants, who became the regime's strongest supporters. After the massive turnout for the 1963 elections, moreover, the Communist Party (PCV) gradually withdrew its support for the FALN – to the great chagrin of Fidel Castro, who supported the insurgency – and began preparations to contest the elections of 1968, which it eventually did, with President Leoni's consent, through a front organization called United to Advance (Hellinger 1991: 112). The PCV was formally relegalized by President Rafael Caldera in early 1969. "Caldera's pacification policy, which allowed for the admission of guerrilla fighters as full citizens if they gave up armed struggle, proceeded despite occasional military opposition" (Aguero 1990: 264). Many former guerrillas, in fact, subsequently served in the Venezuelan congress (Ellner 1988).[14]

We find an entirely different response to insurgency in El Salvador, Guatemala, and (initially) Peru, even after the introduction of elections. In these countries, competitive elections occurred alongside what can only be described as the grossest abuses of human rights by the armed forces, including frequent indiscriminate attacks on merely presumed regime opponents. Here, I can do little more than summarize some of the more egregious examples of the systematic violation of human rights in these countries. This summary, moreover, refers only to human rights abuses *after* the introduction of elections in each country, although it should be kept in mind that tens of thousands of people were murdered by the armed forces in El Salvador and Guatemala before the advent of these elections (i.e., during the late 1970s and early 1980s).

On the eve of the negotiated settlement in El Salvador, Americas Watch concluded that "the human rights situation has not fundamentally

---

[14] Guerrilla leader Douglas Bravo, who was expelled from the PCV, did not accept a government amnesty until 1979, but the FALN had already been pushed to the margins of political significance by 1969, if not earlier (see Loveman and Davies 1985: 258).

changed" in that country since 1980, when the civil war began (AW 1991: 138). Political killings "remain routine and continue to go unpunished," and left-of-center politicians were unable "to participate in elections freely without fear of reprisals" (AW 1991: 138–9). Several leaders of the Democratic Revolutionary Front (FDR), the social-democratic grouping allied to the FMLN, were "disappeared" in October 1982 along with several affiliated union activists; the highest ranking FDR spokesperson who remained in the country was murdered the following year (AW 1991: 11). The Salvadoran air force, furthermore, deliberately used its "aerial power to drive civilians out of areas in which the guerrillas were active and seemed to enjoy substantial peasant support" (AW 1991: 53). Massacres of unarmed civilians suspected of pro-FMLN sympathies continued throughout the decade: More than one hundred people were killed by the U.S.-trained Atlacatl Battalion in Copapayo, San Nicolas department, and nearby towns in November 1983; at least fifty people were killed in August 1984 at the Gualsinga River in Chalatenango, fleeing government troops; ten peasants were massacred by the Jiboa Battalion in San Francisco, San Vicente, in September 1988; a bomb that detonated at the headquarters of the leftist National Federation of Salvadoran Workers (FENASTRAS) killed ten unionists in October 1989; and during the guerrilla offensive in San Salvador of the following month, uniformed soldiers of the Atlacatl Battalion grotesquely murdered six Jesuit priests, their housekeeper, and her daughter (AW 1991: 15, 35, 50–2, 60). In addition, "the Salvadoran security forces continue to torture prisoners, using beating, simulated drowning, rape, electric shock, stabbing, whipping, and near asphyxiation, as well as other cruel and degrading treatment" (AW 1991: 83). Despite this record, however, not a single military officer was even brought to trial, let alone convicted of a crime, during the 1980s. "The very forces charged with protecting citizens not only remain the most deadly threat to their security but continue to act with complete impunity" (AW 1991: 86).[15] In sum, the numerous elections that were held in El Salvador during the 1980s "did not establish the rule of law, the supremacy of civilian authority over the authority of the armed forces, or the guarantee of fundamental human rights for the Salvadoran people" (AW 1991: 136). A

---

[15] After the Americas Watch report was published, two officers (among others) were tried and found guilty of murder in the Jesuit case, although many believe that a cover-up abetted by the Salvadoran Defense Minister and the U.S. embassy protected the actual instigators of the murders (see, e.g., *Envio* 1991).

238

Pentagon-commissioned study concluded that the Salvadoran armed forces had a human rights record that "no truly democratic and just society could tolerate" (quoted in Karl 1992: 150).

Massive human rights abuses also continued in Guatemala after the introduction of elections in that country in 1984. Four days before the inauguration of President Vinicio Cerezo in 1986 – the first civilian president in Guatemala since the late 1960s – the military regime of General Mejía Víctores passed an amnesty decree that exempted all members of the security forces from prosecution for political or related common crimes. As we have seen, Cerezo did not seek to overturn the decree, noting that "we are not going to be able to investigate the past" because "we would have to put the entire army in jail" (quoted in Simon 1988: 6).

Guatemala's indigenous population, along with trade union, community, and human rights activists, was the principal target of army abuses. Peasants were pressured to join "voluntary" Civil Defense Patrols; those who refused were threatened with death and accused of being subversives (Goldston 1989: xii). The human rights situation in Guatemala deteriorated significantly after a coup attempt in May 1988 by ultrarightist officers – the first of three attempts to depose Cerezo during 1988 and 1989. Disappearances and occasional massacres continued through the late 1980s and 1990s: Twenty-two peasants were killed in the village of El Aguacate in November 1988; fifteen people were massacred in Santiago Atitlán in December 1990; and twelve returned refugees were killed in the settlement at Xamán in late 1995. During the first two years of the Cerezo government, six unionists were killed, eight disappeared, and dozens were threatened; eleven teachers were assassinated (Goldston 1989: 53). The Council on Hemispheric Affairs named Guatemala as the Latin American country with the most human rights violations in 1988 (Barry 1989: 27), yet not a single military officer was prosecuted, let alone convicted, of abusing civilians. In 1988, Americas Watch concluded that "the apparatus of state terror [in Guatemala] remains intact and undiminished in strength" (AW 1988: 104).

Until about 1992, the Peruvian armed forces also committed extensive and largely indiscriminate human rights abuses in a "dirty war" against Shining Path. Soon after the insurgency began, "more than half of Peru's twenty million citizens [were placed] under a sustained state of emergency, effectively governed by the military and lacking basic protections against arbitrary arrest, disappearance, and extrajudicial execution by the armed

239

and police forces or the paramilitary groups they tolerated" (AW 1992: xxi). According to Lewis Taylor,

Anti-state and pro-guerrilla sentiments were also encouraged by the blundering and bloody actions of the Sinchis, special police units supposedly trained for counter-insurgency campaigns, who were sent to Ayacucho in late 1980 and 1981. Instead of winning the "hearts and minds" of the population, brutal Sinchi "sweep and search" operations acted . . . as "recruiting drives" for [Shining Path]. The outcome was that by December 1982 the insurgent organisation had managed to consolidate itself to a degree that surprised most analysts and probably the party leadership as well. (Taylor 1998: 42)

"After an interval of less spectacular abuses" during the mid-1980s, according to a 1992 Americas Watch report, "the army has again engaged in killing large numbers of civilians together, often combining murder with inhumane treatment and humiliation" (AW 1992: 142). Approximately thirty people were killed by the army in Cayara, Cangallo province, in May 1988, and twelve individuals were murdered and eight disappeared in Chumbivilcas, Cusco, in April 1990. Paramilitary agents murdered sixteen people, including children, in a Lima neighborhood in November 1991, and nine students and a professor from the national university of La Cantuta disappeared in July 1992. As noted earlier, there were more disappearances in Peru between 1987 and 1991 – the vast majority carried out by the armed forces – than in any other country in the world. Americas Watch noted, "It is, by now, beyond serious dispute that disappearance is one of the instruments the Peruvian military has chosen in its war on the insurgency" (AW 1992: 20). Torture, furthermore, was "systematically used on both political and nonpolitical detainees in Peru," and "conditions in the prisons of Lima and Callao are among the worst anywhere" in the world (AW 1992: 7, 11).

Given this indiscriminate state violence, it is hardly surprising that guerrillas and their supporters in El Salvador, Guatemala, and Peru would not choose unilaterally to lay down their arms and to pursue their political demands through legal channels, including elections; to do so would have simply increased their exposure to state violence. In fact, based on the preceding examination of successful counterinsurgencies, it could have been safely hypothesized that political authorities in these and similar societies would not permanently erode popular support for large-scale insurgencies until peaceful political dissent or at least the basic civil rights of noncombatants, including presumed rebel supporters, were widely tolerated.

This hypothesis is further supported by the case of Colombia, where, as noted previously, a guerrilla insurgency has persisted since the 1960s and became quite powerful by the late 1990s. Colombia's traditionally dominant Liberal and Conservative political parties have contested elections throughout most of this period, yet the armed forces and (increasingly) allied paramilitary groups of a chronically weak state (Boudon 1996) have also persistently committed gross abuses against presumed rebel sympathizers.[16] The main guerrilla army, the Revolutionary Armed Forces of Colombia (FARC), which broke from the Colombian Communist Party in 1964, had approximately fifteen thousand soldiers by the year 2000. After the mid-1990s, moreover, FARC earned as much as $400 to $600 million annually by taxing coca growers and traffickers in southern Colombia; during this same period, soldiers and paramilitary forces – with growing U.S. assistance – killed thousands of peasants suspected of supporting the guerrillas and displaced hundreds of thousands (see, e.g., Rohter 2000). As elsewhere, however, state-sponsored violence backfired: "Rather than fading away, FARC consolidated its base of support and became the effective government over large tracts of Colombian territory" (Cala 2000: 59). Following a series of FARC military victories in 1998, the state ceded to the guerrillas a demilitarized zone about the size of Switzerland as an inducement to negotiate. However, as Rafael Pardo points out,

Most members of armed groups fear that once they sign a peace accord and give up their weapons, they will likely be killed or thrown in jail. These concerns are entirely legitimate, given that during an earlier attempt at peace talks with FARC in the late 1980s, an entire FARC-backed political party was annihilated. More than 3,500 members of that group, the Unión Patriótica, either were murdered or disappeared – a crime that not only increased rebel suspicions but lowered the prospects for the eventual creation of a democratic leftist political party. (Pardo 2000: 72)

Any viable negotiated settlement to the Colombian conflict will presumably have to address the rational fears of the rebels and their supporters, as suggested by the Salvadoran peace settlement that I discuss later in this chapter.[17]

---

[16] On human rights abuses in Colombia, see, e.g., Human Rights Watch 1996, 2000, Giraldo 1996, Arnson and Kirk 1993, and WOLA 1989. On the Colombian guerrillas, see Cala 2000, Chernick 1999 (including appendix), Pizarro 1992, Wickham-Crowley 1992, and Arango 1984.

[17] Like their Guatemalan and Salvadoran counterparts, the guerrillas in Colombia hardly have an unblemished human rights record. They have been accused of forced recruitment,

241

The perversity of indiscriminate state violence – and of indiscriminate *counterstate* violence – is also demonstrated by the eventual *defeat* of the Shining Path insurgency in Peru during the early 1990s. Indeed, analysts generally attribute this defeat to three key factors: (1) decreasing abuses by the Peruvian armed forces after about 1991; (2) Shining Path's own heavy-handed violence and ideological dogmatism; and, as a result of these factors, (3) increasing peasant resistance to Shining Path during the late 1980s and early 1990s, particularly in the form of armed *rondas campesinas* (peasant rounds or patrols). According to Orin Starn,

Already by 1985 . . . and especially with the evident ability of the rebels to survive the storm of [state] violence, many officers recognized the need to combine intimidation and persuasion in a so-called "integral" strategy, including "socioeconomic development" and "civic action" to build support among the peasantry. Selective killing began to predominate over wholesale slaughter, as civilian deaths at the hands of the military declined by more than two-thirds after 1983–1984. (Starn 1998: 237–8; see also Taylor 1998: 50; McClintock 1999: 242)

In 1991 the army began to distribute more than ten thousand shotguns to *rondas*, and a 1992 law recognized the right of ronderos to bear arms, "signaling the confidence of [President] Fujimori and his generals in the strength of their unlikely alliance with the peasantry in the war against the Shining Path" (Starn 1998: 232).

The main factor behind the expansion of the *rondas* was growing peasant disenchantment with Shining Path guerrillas, especially after 1989, when Shining Path concluded that it had reached a "strategic equilibrium" with the government and began to increase its demands for food and recruits and to execute suspected *soplones* or stool pigeons (Degregori 1999: 252; Starn 1998: 236). Shining Path also assassinated members of rival social movements and political parties, killing more than fifty union leaders in early 1989 alone and forty-four leaders of grassroots organizations between 1991 and 1992 (McClintock 1998: 294). According to Taylor,

Anti-guerrilla sentiment was also fuelled by the arbitrary removal of established community leaders and their replacement with younger [Shining Path] cadres, who were held in lower regard and invariably acted in an authoritarian fashion. Substantial hostility was also generated by the extreme violence [of the guerrillas]:

the recruitment of children, kidnapping civilians, and summary executions (including the execution of three North American indigenous activists in February 1999). However, these abuses pale in comparison to those perpetrated by paramilitary groups (see, e.g., Krauss 2000).

242

while villagers might agree that exploitative and delinquent individuals deserved to be punished, in most cases they balked at the *senderistas'* practice of sanction through assassination. Rebel involvement in mass killings that rivalled the brutality of the military was also rejected by most *campesinos* and lost the [Shining Path] much support. As one disillusioned captured member aptly noted, "How are they going to win by massacring peasants? You only attract hatred." (Taylor 1998: 49)

Indeed, indiscriminate violence can backfire when perpetrated by revolutionaries as well as reactionaries. As Cynthia McClintock notes,

The shift toward repudiation of Sendero among many peasant communities in Peru contrasts with the continuation of support for revolutionary movements in Guatemala and El Salvador, and this difference is the most important factor explaining the relative success of *rondas* in Peru [as opposed to] their relative failure in the Central American countries. (McClintock 1999: 235)

The results of the preceding analysis are summarized in Table 7.2, a Boolean truth table in which "1" indicates the presence of a variable and "0" its absence (Ragin 1987). (A brief technical analysis of Table 7.2 is presented in Appendix 1 to this chapter.) In addition to Colombia, I have also included in Table 7.2 the persistent insurgency in the Philippines (where a new armed conflict began in the late 1960s) as well as the defeated rebellion in Greece following World War II. I will not present a thorough analysis of these latter cases, but, based on my understanding of them, I believe that they support my argument about the perversity of indiscriminate state violence by weak states.[18]

Popular insurgencies, one may note, including two that received significant external aid (i.e., Greece and Venezuela), were defeated by regimes that introduced competitive elections and came to tolerate dissent or at least not indiscriminately attack presumed rebel supporters – and they were defeated whether or not incumbent regimes implemented a significant land reform or received substantial foreign assistance (although the latter was undoubtedly crucial in three of the four cases). By contrast, large-scale insurgencies persisted where and so long as incumbent regimes committed extensive and indiscriminate human rights abuses – and they persisted despite the holding of competitive elections and whether or not either side to the conflict received significant foreign assistance. Thus, while no single factor is *sufficient* to account for the persistence of mass-based revolutionary movements, indiscriminate state violence would

---

[18] See, e.g., Jones 1989 on the Philippines and Close 1995, Iatrides 1993, and Wittner 1982 on Greece.

Table 7.2. *Boolean truth table: Persistent versus defeated revolutionary movements.*

Variable:	Movement		Geopolitics		Incumbent regime	
Country	(A) "Racial" or ethnic as well as class-based	(B) Significant foreign aid to rebels	(C) Substantial foreign aid to incumbent regime	(D) Major land reform implemented	(E) Competitive elections introduced	(F) Indiscriminate, extensive human rights abuses
Persistent						
Colombia (1962–)	0	0	0[1]	0	1	1
Guatemala (1962–96)	1	0	1	0	1 (after 1984)	1
Philippines (1969–)	0	0	1	0	1 (after 1986)	1
El Salvador (1980–92)	0	1	1	0	1 (after 1982)	1
Peru (1980–95)	1	0	0	0[2]	1[3]	1[4]
Defeated						
Philippines (1946–54)	0	0	1	0	1	0 (after 1950)
Greece (1946–9)	0	1	1	0	1 (after 1950)	0
Malaya (1948–55)	1	0	1	0	1 (after 1951)	0 (after 1952)
Venezuela (1962–9)	0	1	0	1	1	0

Notes: [1] U.S. aid became substantial after 1998.
[2] A major, albeit very uneven, land reform was implemented *prior* to the insurgency.
[3] Elections became increasingly less fair and competitive after 1992.
[4] Abuses became more discriminate after 1991.

appear to be a *necessary* condition for such persistence.[19] As we have seen repeatedly, such violence, especially when perpetrated by weak states, unintentionally bolsters revolutionary movements.

The Peace Accords in El Salvador

> *We want the government to face the fact that reforms are valueless if they are carried out at the cost of so much blood. In the name of God, in the name of this suffering people whose cries rise to heaven more loudly each day, I implore you, I beg you, I order you in the name of God: stop the repression.*
>
> – Archbishop Oscar Romero, March 23, 1980 (quoted in AW 1991: xxii)[20]

Implicit in the hypothesis that insurgencies persist because of indiscriminate violence by weak states is the view that the "root cause" of *armed* rebellions that seek the overthrow of the state – as distinct from other forms of political conflict – is not poverty, exploitation, or inequality per se. Rather, armed revolutionary movements result from *the violent suppression of the peaceful political activities of aggrieved people who have the capacity to rebel*. As John A. Hall has argued, collective violence is not a direct, unmediated response to poverty and economic difficulties; rather, "revolutionaries are the result of authoritarian state behavior" (Hall 1987: 120; Gude 1975).[21]

This interpretation of persistent insurgencies is supported by the nature of the peace accords that ended the twelve-year-long civil war in El Salvador and the decades-long insurgency in Guatemala. In this section, I will focus on the January 1992 accords that successfully brought the armed conflict in El Salvador to an end. Although the FMLN was undoubtedly

---

[19] Unfortunately, my sample of insurgencies does not include a case where a major land reform was implemented at the same time that human rights were indiscriminately violated (although El Salvador most closely approximates this situation). I cannot, therefore, *logically* rule out the possibility that this improbable combination of factors would defeat a large-scale insurgency. The *theoretical* logic of this chapter, however, would lead me to predict that an insurgency would persist in such a case.

[20] The following day, Archbishop Romero was assassinated while performing mass.

[21] McClintock argues (based primarily on interviews with thirty-three Senderistas from one region) that "socioeconomic misery [was] the key impetus to their decision to join the revolutionary movement" (McClintock 1998: 273). Significantly, however, many of her respondents blamed the government, President Fujimori, "the political system," "elected demagogues," "too much bureaucracy," or "genocidal soldiers" for this misery (see, e.g., McClintock 1998: 274–81). Poverty per se also fails to explain why someone would join a specifically revolutionary movement as opposed to some other type of political movement (which many did in Peru).

influenced by the collapse of the Soviet bloc and the electoral defeat of the Sandinistas in Nicaragua, it clearly did not decide to disarm because it lacked the means (or popular support) to continue its armed struggle. And the armed conflict certainly did not come to an end because the popular grievances that grew out of poverty, landlessness, and other economic problems had been redressed (Diskin 1996; Paige 1996; Seligson 1996). In fact, the "far-reaching agrarian reform" and "radical social transformation" that Jenny Pearce and others saw as the only possible path to peace in El Salvador have not occurred (Pearce 1986: 303). As George Vickers notes, the accords did not end "the economic and political dominance of the coffee-growing elite" and in no way "guarantee[d] a new social and economic order for El Salvador" (Vickers 1992: 5–6). (The same can be said of the negotiated settlement in Guatemala [see Jonas 1997, 2000].)

To be sure, the accords obliged the government, albeit in very general and somewhat vague terms, to attempt to purchase land from absentee owners that was occupied by guerrillas or their supporters, or to attempt to relocate these squatters on land in the same general area. However, the total number of beneficiaries of land transfers will not exceed 47,500, which includes fifteen thousand former soldiers from El Salvador's regular armed forces (United Nations Security Council 1992: 12). Moreover, government promises to purchase land for FMLN guerrillas and supporters,

nebulous as they are, apply only to the conflictive zones. The government makes no commitment to land reform outside these zones beyond pledging to carry out existing law. Neither do the accords directly address problems of urban misery and employment needs outside the conflictive zones. (Vickers 1992: 6)

Furthermore, as Jeffery Paige notes,

Even if the peace accords are carried out fully, the Salvadoran reform . . . will still leave a huge number of Salvadorans without access to adequate land. . . . [A]grarian problems persist and are likely to be exacerbated in the short run by neoliberal economic policies and rising land prices. (Paige 1996: 136, 138)

The FMLN opted to disarm neither because social justice had finally been achieved in El Salvador nor because the putative socioeconomic "root causes" of the rebellion had been removed; the guerrillas laid down their arms, rather, because they realized they could not win the war *and*, just as importantly, because the government agreed to reorganize fundamentally

246

its armed forces under United Nations supervision. In fact, the FMLN quite reasonably viewed reform of the Salvadoran military as the basic precondition for its own transformation into an unarmed political party. The government's concessions on military reform – "the most difficult item on the agenda" of the negotiations, according to U.N. mediator Alvaro de Soto (quoted in Karl 1992: 155) – included a substantial reduction in the size of the armed forces; the disbanding of the notoriously abusive National Guard, Treasury Police, and U.S.-trained Immediate Reaction Infantry Battalions; the establishment of a "Truth Commission," composed of three foreign jurists, that investigated eight well-known cases of human rights abuse (including the 1980 assassination of Archbishop Oscar Romero, the bombing of FENASTRAS, and the massacre of the Jesuits); and the formation of a new national police force, under civilian control, to which former FMLN guerrillas could apply (see Vickers 1992: 6; Karl 1992: 157–8). The accords also resulted in a purge of approximately one hundred military officers whom an independent commission determined were implicated in human rights abuses, including Defense Minister René Emilio Ponce.

These measures have not brought about social justice in El Salvador, but they should at last make it possible for the FMLN and its supporters – and indeed all Salvadorans – to engage in peaceful political activities without fear of government repression. As the preceding analysis has suggested, nothing less can permanently end the sort of popular insurgency that developed in El Salvador.

Conclusion

The analysis developed in this chapter suggests that the persistence or defeat of large-scale revolutionary movements hinges crucially upon the variable capacity of armed forces to respect the rights of noncombatants and broadly tolerate peaceful political dissent while democratic regimes are consolidated. The case of Peru, where elections became increasingly undemocratic after Fujimori's *autogolpe* of 1992, also suggests that a persistent insurgency may itself be defeated if the armed forces do not indiscriminately repress those suspected of supporting the (in this case, increasingly unpopular) insurgency. Military practices, unfortunately, have received surprisingly little analysis in studies of democratization. As Alfred Stepan has noted, "the military has probably been the least studied of the factors involved in . . . newly democratizing polities" (Stepan

247

1988: xi). Three factors, however, which I will only briefly touch upon, seem especially relevant for understanding this issue and should be an important focus, accordingly, for future research on negotiated settlements of civil wars: (1) the pervasiveness of racism among military officers (or, by extension, religious sectarianism or other particularistic mentalities); (2) the extent of corruption within the officer corps; and, perhaps especially, (3) the extent of "military prerogatives" within the polity.

Particularistic mentalities such as racism obviously make it much easier for military officers and/or their charges to abuse people who are seen as "naturally" or culturally inferior; in fact, military abuses of noncombatants in Guatemala and Peru in particular were clearly associated with the endemic racism of military officers, as well as political and economic elites, in those countries (see, e.g., McClintock 1985b; Jonas 1991 and Schirmer 1998 on Guatemala; Poole and Renique 1992 on Peru).[22] Here is an instance in which state-centered analysis becomes more powerful by taking into consideration the cultural frameworks of state elites.

Widespread corruption among officers, furthermore, including profiteering from the special circumstances of counterinsurgency itself, renders such officers particularly resistant to the extension of the sort of civilian oversight or control that might reduce human rights abuses; profiteering from counterinsurgency, in fact, gives officers a perverse interest in the very persistence of the insurgency they are supposed to quell (Stanley 1996).

Finally, and perhaps most importantly, extensive military prerogatives within the polity virtually guarantee the impunity of the armed forces. "Military prerogatives," as Stepan defines them, refer to

those areas where . . . the military as an institution assumes they have an acquired right or privilege, formal or informal, to exercise effective control over [the military's] internal governance, to play a role within the extramilitary areas within the state apparatus, or even to structure relationships between the state and political or civil society. (Stepan 1988: 93)

Where such prerogatives are vast, effective prosecution of military personnel for human rights abuses becomes virtually impossible. And by

---

[22] When asked how he could justify a massacre of peasants in which "maybe five or six of the hundred or so dead will be insurgents," one Peruvian officer responded, "They are only Indians; who cares?" (quoted in Manwaring, Prisk, and Fishel 1991: 95).

Stepan's measures, certainly, the armed forces of El Salvador, Guatemala, and Peru have historically had very extensive military prerogatives, acquired through decades of direct military rule.[23]

In sum, while more research on this issue is clearly necessary, it seems that those armed forces whose officer corps are deeply racist, dependent upon (and therefore protective of) extensive corruption, and/or possessive of extensive prerogatives are unlikely to respect human rights when challenged by popular revolutionary movements. And for that very reason, if not others, the historical record suggests, such movements will persist and negotiated settlements will be difficult to achieve.

Appendix 1: Boolean Analysis

If P = persistent insurgency and D = defeated insurgency, and uppercase letters indicate the presence of the variable ("1" numerically) and lowercase letters its absence ("0" numerically), then Table 7.2 can be represented as follows:

$$P = abcdEF + AbCdEF + abCdEF + aBCdEF + AbcdEF$$

$$D = abCdEf + aBCdEf + AbCdEf + aBcDEf$$

The strings of letters in these equations represent the five persistent and four defeated insurgencies in the order in which they are listed in Table 7.2. Minimization and factoring (see Ragin 1987: 93–5, 100–1) result in the following simplified equations:

$$P = aCdEF + bdEF = dF (ABce + aCE + bE)$$

$$D = aBcDEf + aCdEf + bCdEf = Ef (aBcD + aCd + bCd)$$

These equations indicate that, no single variable or combination of variables produces either persistence or defeat; however, based on the cases examined, we may conclude that both the absence of a major land reform (d) and indiscriminate state violence (F) are necessary for an insurgency to

---

[23] Specifically, 1931–79 in El Salvador; 1931–44, 1954–66 and 1970–85 in Guatemala; and 1948–56, 1962–3, and 1968–80 in Peru. See McClintock 1985a, Millman 1989, Stanley 1996, and Williams and Walter 1997 on El Salvador; Black 1984: ch. 2, McClintock 1985b, Jonas 1991, and Schirmer 1998 on Guatemala; and Cotler 1986, Abugattas 1987: 139, AW 1992, and Obando 1998 on Peru.

persist (see note 19), and both the introduction of competitive elections (E) and the absence of indiscriminate state violence (f) are necessary to defeat a large-scale insurgency (though competitive elections were not a factor in the defeat of Shining Path in Peru).

Furthermore, there are two general patterns of persistent insurgency and three general patterns of defeated insurgency in our sample of cases. The Philippine (post-1969) and Salvadoran patterns of persistence combine to produce aCdEF (i.e., the insurgency persists despite massive external aid to the government). The Colombian, Guatemalan, Philippine, and Peruvian patterns combine to produce bdEF (i.e., the insurgency persists despite the absence of significant external aid to the guerrillas).

The Venezuelan pattern of defeat (aBcDEf) cannot be "minimized" – the Venezuelan government, uniquely among my sample, enacted a major (if flawed) land reform. The Philippine (Huks) and Greek patterns of defeat combine to produce aCdEf (i.e., an increasingly less repressive and externally supported regime defeats a nonracialized insurgency). Finally, the Philippine and Malayan patterns of defeat combine to produce bCdEf (i.e., an increasingly less repressive and externally supported regime defeats an insurgency without external support).

Appendix 2: On Infrastructural Power

There can be no simple numerical measurement of a state's infrastructural power, for two reasons. First, states penetrate and control national territories through a wide variety of means, not all of which are easily quantified, including overt surveillance and policing, covert surveillance (e.g., spying), education and propaganda, mundane administrative practices, and (not least) direct coercion and threats of coercion. Second, infrastructural power is by its very nature uneven in spatial and social terms – a state may be infrastructurally powerful in an elite urban enclave, for example, and yet wield very little power in a shantytown just ten miles away. Or a state may be quite powerful in urban areas generally, yet have very little power in peripheral rural regions or in mountainous areas – even those that may be relatively close to urban centers. For these reasons, any claim that a particular state is infrastructurally "strong" should ideally specify *where*, *for whom*, and *how*.

Nonetheless, certain gross crossnational statistics do convey, in necessarily general terms, the relative infrastructural power of states. The five variables in Table 7.3 provide suggestive glimpses of the comparative

Appendix 2: On Infrastructural Power

Table 7.3. *Measures of state infrastructural power.*

Country	Variable (1)	(2)	(3)	(4)	(5)
Nicaragua	21	3.0	13.0	3	12.8
El Salvador	10	2.1	51.2	8	11.6
Guatemala	10	2.5	25.3	3	8.9
Honduras	11	4.1	8.7	2	13.2
Peru	33	5.2	5.6	2	14.6
Philippines	8	1.6	54.2	4	12.4
Malaysia*	54	6.0	19.2	8	20.3
Venezuela	80	3.9	9.2	1	18.5

United States	722	11.1	70.7	26	17.6
United Kingdom	406	6.6	156.0	97	32.6
France	331	10.8	283.2	41	33.4
West Germany**	313	8.2	194.5	76	25.3
Sweden	425	9.3	36.0	19	32.4

Poland	277	9.6	128.9	20	38.7
East Germany**	422	11.9	194.5	11	na
Hungary	258	14.0	180.3	11	56.5
Czechoslovakia***	412	15.2	68.0	44	na
Romania	200	10.5	205.5	11	na

Notes:

* The figures for variables (3) and (4) are based on the land area of peninsular Malaysia only.

** The figures for variables (3) and (4) are based on the land area of all Germany; the figure for variable (3) is based on the total kilometers of railroads and highways in all Germany in 1995.

*** The figures for variables (3) and (4) are based on the combined land areas of the present Czech Republic and Slovakia.

Variables: (1) Military expenditures per capita (constant 1981 dollars) in 1972; (2) armed forces (including paramilitary forces) per 1,000 population in 1972; (3) kilometers of railroad and highway (paved and unpaved) per square kilometer of land area in 1995 ($\times$100); (4) military aircraft (including helicopters, transports, and reconnaissance aircraft) per square kilometer of land area in 1971 ($\times$10,000); (5) total government current revenue as a percentage of GNP in 1972 (in 1989 for Poland and Hungary).

Sources: (1) and (2): U.S. Arms Control and Disarmament Agency 1984; (3) author's calculations, based on Central Intelligence Agency [CIA] 1995; (4) author's calculations, based on Sellers 1971 and CIA 1995; (5) World Bank 1991: 226–7 (Table 12).

infrastructural power of samples of three general types of states: (1) states of the capitalist periphery (i.e., the site of the revolutionary movements discussed in this chapter as well as in Parts 2 and 3 of this book), (2) states of the capitalist core (i.e., advanced capitalist societies), and (3) states of the erstwhile socialist periphery of Eastern Europe, which I discuss in the following chapter.

The first two variables in Table 7.3 – military spending and armed forces per capita – roughly measure the state's *means of coercion*, both technological and human, relative to the level of economic development and population of the national society ruled by that state. Variables (3) and (4) – railroads and highways per square kilometer, on the one hand, and military aircraft per square kilometer, on the other – roughly measure the density of the *technological infrastructure* that is available to a state for deploying its means of coercion (as well as other means of social control), relative to the geographical size of the national society. (Note that some forms of technological infrastructure – jet fighters, for example – are themselves means of coercion.) Finally, the fifth variable – government revenue as a percentage of gross national product (GNP) – very roughly measures the state's taxing or *"extractive" capacity*, which provides the indispensable material means for the state's administrative and coercive activities, although states may also receive substantial resources from foreign allies. (Most of the data in Table 7.3 is from the years 1971 and 1972, which lie near the midpoint of the historical period – the Cold War era – examined in this book.)

Not surprisingly, the data in Table 7.3 indicate that the states from the capitalist periphery were – at least in the early 1970s – significantly weaker, according to all five measures of infrastructural power, than states from both the capitalist core and from the former socialist periphery. Compared to the latter states, Third World states generally (including those discussed in this chapter and in Part 3) had much less formidable means of coercion (even relative to their smaller economies and typically smaller populations), had access to less developed technological infrastructures, and had less formidable extractive capacities. By contrast, the states of the socialist periphery of Eastern Europe – despite lower levels of economic development – were generally as infrastructurally powerful as those of the capitalist core. To be sure, military spending per capita and especially military aircraft per square kilometer were lower in Eastern Europe than in the core, but it is important to note that the figures for Eastern Europe do not include Soviet or Warsaw Pact troops, aircraft, or other military hardware. Moreover, armed forces per capita as well as state extractive capacities were generally *greater* in Eastern Europe than in the capitalist core. In the following chapter, I suggest how the infrastructural strength of Eastern European states helps to explain some of the unique dynamics of the Eastern European "refolutions" and rebellions of 1989.

Chronology for Eastern Europe

1945 Yalta agreements (February); Soviet army controls much of Eastern Europe

1945–8 imposition of Communist rule

1948 Soviet blockade of Berlin and Allied airlift

1949 formation of the Council for Mutual Economic Assistance (CMEA or Comecon)

1953 Stalin dies; mass strikes in East Germany

1955 Warsaw Pact formed following West Germany's entry into NATO

1956 unrest in Poland; Soviet Union suppresses rebellion in Hungary (more than twenty thousand killed)

1961 Berlin Wall erected

1968 Hungary introduces New Economic Mechanism; "Prague spring" reforms in Czechoslovakia suppressed by Soviet and Warsaw Pact intervention; unrest in Polish universities

1970 riots and strikes in Poland (five hundred to six hundred workers killed)

1976 more unrest in Poland; formation there of Workers' Defense Committee (KOR)

1977 Charter 77 circulated in Czechoslovakia; miners' strike in Romania

1980 demonstration in Prague; Vaclav Havel and others arrested (January); mass strikes in Poland; Polish government recognizes independent trade union Solidarity (August)

1981 martial law declared in Poland (formally lifted in 1983), Solidarity banned (December)

1985 Mikhail Gorbachev assumes Soviet leadership

1987 large demonstration in Brasov, Romania

1988 mass strikes in Poland; large demonstration in Prague on the twentieth anniversary of Warsaw Pact intervention (August)

1989 roundtable meetings between Polish government and Solidarity (February); Hungarian government approves independent parties (February); Hungary opens border with Austria (May); Solidarity candidates win elections in Poland (June); formation in Poland of first non-Communist government in Eastern Europe since 1948 (August); Hungarian Communist Party dissolves itself; demonstrations in East Germany (October); East German

254

government resigns and the Berlin Wall is opened; Civic Forum formed in Czechoslovakia (November); Czech government resigns and Vaclav Havel elected president; demonstrations in Timişoara lead to further protest and streetfighting in Romania; the dictator Ceauşescu and his wife are executed (December)

1990   "shock therapy" economic reforms introduced in Poland (January); prounification parties dominate East German elections (March); Jozsef Antall of the Hungarian Democratic Forum elected prime minister (March); Ion Iliescu of the National Salvation Front elected president in Romania (May); Civic Forum wins 48 percent of the vote in elections in Czechoslovakia (June); two Germanies united after forty-five years (October); Lech Walesa elected president in Poland (December)

8

"Refolution" and Rebellion
in Eastern Europe, 1989

When they saw so many ridiculous, ramshackle institutions, survivals of an earlier age, which no one had attempted to co-ordinate or adjust to modern conditions and which seemed destined to live on despite the fact that they had ceased to have any present value, it was natural enough that thinkers of the day should come to loathe everything that savored of the past and should desire to remold society on entirely new lines. . . .

– Alexis de Tocqueville (1955 [1856]: 140)

De Tocqueville called the French Revolution history's largest property transaction; but the legacy of 1789 is easily matched by the privatization that followed 1989.

– Harold James (1997: 6)

If one set out in the spring of 1980 to analyze recent revolutions – inspired, perhaps, by the dramatic events of the previous year in Iran, Nicaragua, and Afghanistan – one's attention would have been drawn inexorably and indeed *exclusively* to the Third World. At that time, certainly, there did not seem to be anything particularly revolutionary occurring in the "Second World" of the Soviet bloc (and certainly not in the "First World" of advanced capitalist societies). Indeed, opposition movements in Eastern Europe seemed extraordinarily weak or simply nonexistent. The fact that powerful movements within and without the ruling Communist parties had been bloodily suppressed by the Soviet Union in Hungary in 1956 and rather more easily, but no less thoroughly, in Czechoslovakia in 1968 only underscored the apparently insurmountable difficulties in opposing the extant Communist regimes. (The emergence of the Solidarity movement in Poland was still a few months away.)

On the international scene, moreover, Communism seemed as powerful as ever, if not more so. Indeed, during the mid- to late 1970s it was possible to discern what Fred Halliday termed "a new period of Third World revolutions" (Halliday 1986: ch. 4) – most of them supported materially or at least rhetorically by the Soviet Union: The U.S.-backed South Vietnamese regime finally fell in April 1975, and Communist forces seized power in Cambodia and Laos about the same time; after years of revolutionary conflict, furthermore, Portugal finally abandoned to radical nationalists its African colonies of Guinea-Bissau, Mozambique, and Angola; pro-Soviet regimes also emerged following coups in Ethiopia and Afghanistan, which Soviet troops invaded in December 1979; and leftist, Cuban-supported movements seized power in Grenada and Nicaragua in 1979. Only the dramatic revolution against the U.S.-backed dictatorship in Iran in 1978–9 was not more or less openly championed by the Soviet Union, Cuba, or (as in the case of Cambodia) China – although this was hardly a revolution calculated to cheer Western governments and the United States in particular.

And yet, little more than a decade later something truly revolutionary had occurred: The Soviet bloc was no more. In 1989 one of the most startling and almost completely unanticipated revolutions – actually, a series of linked revolutions and "refolutions" (a term explained later in this chapter) – destroyed the Communist regimes of Eastern Europe and all that went with them: the political monopoly of the ruling Communist parties; state organizations (including armies and secret police) thoroughly penetrated by these parties; state control over the means of production; and extensive state economic planning. How could this have happened?

In an ironic twist, there is a strong if largely unnoticed Marxist flavor to both popular and academic understandings of the collapse of Communism and of the events of 1989 in Eastern Europe in particular. Indeed, even resolutely anti-Marxist commentators tend to emphasize (sometimes exclusively) the role of *economic factors* in the demise of Communism. In this view, Communism collapsed because it represented a form of economic organization that, because of state ownership and planning, was thoroughly inefficient, technologically stagnant, and, accordingly, incapable of keeping pace with the capitalist West. In 1989, the political superstructure of Communist societies, having become a fetter on the development of the means of production, was burst asunder.

There is yet another popular interpretation of 1989. Some view the events of that year as reflecting the triumph of a new "civil society" in Eastern Europe. In this view, the old regime – weak though it may have been – was pulled down by a combination of political dissidents and

257

capitalist entrepreneurs, groups that had emerged within the region's political (and intellectual) underground and the "second" or informal economy, respectively – the interstices, as it were, of the old order.

Finally, the events of 1989 have been explained by what Albert Hirschman has aptly described as "a deus ex machina" (Hirschman 1993: 196) – namely, Mikhail Gorbachev. In this view, the fall of Communism in Eastern Europe was an inevitable result of the reformist orientation of the Soviet leader and, more particularly, of his refusal to employ Soviet forces to defend the Soviet Union's satellite regimes in that region (i.e., his rejection of the so-called Brezhnev Doctrine).

All of these explanations certainly capture important aspects of 1989, and I shall invoke them in the analysis that follows. And yet they also beg crucial questions that a state-centered perspective can address more adequately, as I hope to show in this chapter. Neither the economic nor the "Gorbachev" explanation for 1989, for example, explains why there was so little interest, as there once had been, in "fixing" or reforming Communism in Eastern Europe as opposed to overthrowing it. (This, after all, was precisely what Gorbachev was attempting to do in the Soviet Union itself.) "Civil society," moreover, was relatively underdeveloped in 1989 (a legacy of Communist despotism felt to this day), more so in some countries than in others, and its generally antisocialist orientation needs to be explained, not simply assumed. Finally, we need to ask why Communist leaders in the region (outside of Romania) did not *themselves* attempt to defend their privileges, through violence if necessary – which some did, actually, almost until the bitter end. Why was there so little counterrevolutionary violence in Eastern Europe during 1989? Economic stagnation may explain why people were generally unhappy in Eastern Europe, and Gorbachev's leadership may explain why *Soviet* troops were not employed to suppress their protests, but neither of these explanations adequately explains the rapid and relatively bloodless overthrow of Communist rule in 1989.

An alternative perspective on 1989 is to view the events of that year as a reaction by both political dissidents *and* important elements within the regimes themselves to the long-established practices of the satellite states of an overextended imperialist power. Although certainly a year of democratic revolutions in Eastern Europe, 1989 was also, for that very reason, a year of *anti-imperialist* revolutions directed against Soviet domination of the region.

The dissolution of empires, formal and informal, has in fact been one of the distinguishing and most consequential characteristics of the twentieth century, and one for which revolutionaries can take substantial credit.[1] The popular struggles for national sovereignty that have helped to destroy empires have sometimes (although certainly not always) been fused with attempts to change radically the socioeconomic institutions inherited from the imperialists. The result of this fusion has been nationalist revolution – or revolutionary nationalism – another phenomenon largely unique to the present century. Eastern Europe is only the most recent example of how imperial domination not only has generated nationalist opposition, but has also unwittingly radicalized it – albeit in a very peculiar way that this chapter attempts to explain. Thus, the Eastern European revolutions of 1989, as Pavel Campeanu has pointed out, had "a dual nature: social, since their goal was to destroy the socioeconomic structures of Stalinism, and national, since they aspired to re-establish the sovereignty of the countries in question" (Campeanu 1991: 806–7).

This chapter argues that, despite obvious differences in their form and ideology, the combined national and social revolutions in Eastern Europe display a number of similarities with revolutions in the peculiar type of dependent Third World societies that we have examined in earlier chapters.[2] (Perhaps this is not so surprising, since Eastern Europe was after all the "first" Third World – that is, the original periphery of Western Europe. "Most of these countries before World War II were on the periphery or semi-periphery of Europe" [Szelenyi and Szelenyi 1994: 214].) There are some striking similarities, in particular, between the old-regime states and the opposition movements that those states unintentionally helped to constitute or construct in both the Second and Third Worlds. The following analysis assumes, as in previous chapters, that one cannot understand the breadth, ideological character, or the political fortunes of rebellious movements "from below" without reference to the nature of the states "above" them.

The model for this particular mode of state-centered analysis is Alexis de Tocqueville's classic study of the French Revolution (Tocqueville 1955 [1856]) (see Chapter 2). A "Tocquevillian" analysis, as Theda Skocpol notes, emphasizes how the "organizational configurations [of states], along

[1] The literature is quite vast. See, e.g., Barkey and von Hagen 1997; Low 1991; Betts 1991; Holland 1985; Albertini 1982 [1966]; Smith 1981; Fieldhouse 1965; Easton 1960; Emerson 1960.
[2] Much of the following analysis also applies to the "internal" empire of the former Soviet Union, especially the Baltic states and Transcaucasia (see, e.g., Lieven 1994; Suny 1990).

with their overall patterns of activity, affect political culture, encourage some kinds of group formation and collective political actions (but not others), and make possible the raising of certain political issues (but not others)" (Skocpol 1985: 21). I have referred to this mode of analysis as "state constructionism." Certain types of states, I have suggested, are especially likely to engender or construct specifically *revolutionary* forms of political opposition. And a particular subset of *these* states is especially likely to collapse or capitulate when confronted by powerful revolutionary movements.[3]

Were the events in Eastern Europe in 1989 "revolutionary"? "Social revolution" denotes a fundamental and relatively rapid transformation of a national society's state structure, economic institutions, and/or culture; these changes, furthermore, are initiated and/or achieved, at least in part, by popular mobilizations, including armed movements, strikes, and/or demonstrations.[4] While the events of 1989 largely fit this definition, especially in Czechoslovakia and East Germany, the process of revolutionary change in Eastern Europe was certainly unusual compared to most revolutions (see Dix 1991; Bunce 1999: 152–6). To begin with, the undeniably radical transformations that have taken place in Eastern Europe – including the collapse of Communist Party rule, the elimination of longstanding military and economic ties to the former Soviet Union, and the transition to a distinctively Eastern European capitalism (see Stark 1996) – occurred (except in Romania) virtually without armed conflict. In addition, these transformations were at least partly the result of reformist movements or factions within the ruling Communist parties themselves. For this reason, Timothy Garton Ash has described the events in Poland and Hungary as "refolutions" – a hybrid of reform and revolution (1990: 14). These distinctive characteristics of Eastern European revolutions obviously require some explanation. This chapter, accordingly, not only suggests some important similarities between Second and Third World revolutions, but also tries to account for the uniquely peaceful character of revolutionary change in Eastern Europe as well as its actual encouragement "from above" in certain countries.

---

[3] Goldstone (1993) employs a similar "top-down" approach to explain the collapse of the Soviet Union.

[4] This definition is a slightly revised version of Skocpol's influential formulation (1979: 4) (see Chapter 1). For an excellent discussion of the implications of recent events in Eastern Europe for theories of revolution, see Dix 1991. For reviews of the most recent social-science analyses of revolutions, see Foran 1993 and Goodwin 1994b.

My analysis has two parts: The first emphasizes the *similarities* between Second World revolutions, on the one hand (especially the cases of Poland, Hungary, Czechoslovakia, and East Germany), and certain Third World revolutions, on the other (including such cases as Mexico, Vietnam, Cuba, Iran, and Nicaragua); the second half of the analysis focuses on the *differences* between these sets of cases. More specifically, after discussing some of the similarities between both the old regimes and the opposition movements in the Second and Third Worlds – similarities that have been largely overlooked in recent discussions of Eastern Europe – I turn to some of the differences in the forms or processes of these revolutions; here, I focus particularly on the unusually nonviolent nature and "bourgeois" ideological orientation of the revolutions in Eastern Europe.[5] Finally, I also examine the "exceptional" (i.e., violent) events in Romania in December 1989, the upheaval in Eastern Europe that seems most similar to previous revolutions against neopatrimonial or sultanistic dictatorships in the Third World – a characterization that is in fact only partly accurate.

Similarities: The Old Regimes and Revolutionary Mobilization

The structures and practices of the old-regime states of Eastern Europe share a number of similarities with two particular types of Third World regimes that, as we have seen, have proven exceptionally vulnerable to revolutionary overthrow: neopatrimonial, personalist dictatorships, on the one hand (such as once ruled Mexico, Iran, Cuba, and Nicaragua), and racially exclusionary and repressive colonial regimes, on the other hand (such as were once found in Vietnam, Algeria, Angola, and elsewhere). These state structures and practices became the target of an extremely broad nationalist opposition and, by rendering these regimes "unreformable," unintentionally served to radicalize these oppositions as well. In the Second World no less than the Third, in other words, certain types of states helped to construct the very movements that would bury them.[6]

---

[5] This chapter does not take up the much larger task of explaining the collapse (or persistence) of state socialism in those countries where it was established through indigenous revolutions (e.g., the Soviet Union, Yugoslavia, Albania, China, Cuba, and Vietnam). On the Soviet Union and Yugoslavia, see Bunce 1999: chs. 5–6; on Cuba, see Pérez-Stable 1999.

[6] The following analysis of events in Eastern Europe is based generally on Echikson 1990, Garton Ash 1990, Gati 1990, Glenny 1990, Brown 1991, Ramet 1991, Mason 1992, Simons 1993, Stokes 1993, Ekiert 1996, and Bunce 1999, and on the essays in Prins 1990 and Banac

What are these lethal state structures and practices? Both Second and Third World revolutions destroyed states that were simultaneously (1) highly *autonomous* of, or "disembedded" from, weakly organized domestic social classes, interest groups, and associations in "civil society"; (2) economically and/or militarily *dependent* upon, and in many cases installed by, foreign powers; (3) indiscriminately *repressive* of independent opposition movements (including reformist oppositions as well as radical and disloyal movements); and (4) intimately implicated in the ownership or control of important *economic* sectors, if not the economy as a whole; in other words, there was a very close connection between, if not actual fusion of, political authoritarianism and economic decision making – even closer in the Second World, in fact, than in most formal colonies or in neopatrimonial dictatorships with attendant forms of "crony capitalism."

In both Second and Third World contexts, in other words, the combination of extreme (domestic) state autonomy, external dependence, exclusionary authoritarianism, and a politicized economy proved to be an especially explosive mixture. In Eastern Europe, these factors gradually generated widespread disgruntlement with Communist regimes, some of which never had substantial legitimacy in the first place due to their foreign imposition. (This is not to say that Communism did not have significant legitimacy in certain Eastern European countries in the immediate postwar period, especially Czechoslovakia and East Germany, due in part to the role of Communists in the antifascist resistance [see, e.g., Naimark 1992a and Chirot 1991: 9–10].) Opposition to Communism not only became widespread (although it was seldom well organized, given the infrastructural power of Communist regimes), but it was also focused upon the state, increasingly radicalized, and closely linked to demands for national liberation from foreign (i.e., Soviet) domination. The next section examines in more detail the characteristics of these old-regime states. (The fourth characteristic – the fusion of political despotism and economic authority – is discussed in the subsequent analysis of opposition movements.)

Old-Regime States

The domestic "hyper-autonomy," to use Walter Connor's term (1988: 9), of the Soviet-backed states in Eastern European has long been empha-

1992. My understanding of Eastern Europe has also benefited enormously from exchanges with Valerie Bunce.

sized in the social-science literature on Soviet-type societies.[7] In this respect, these states were structurally quite similar to those Third World states that have proven most conducive to the formation of powerful revolutionary movements. As Eric Wolf has argued, the penetration of "North Atlantic capitalism" into non-European societies – like the penetration of Soviet-style Communism into Eastern Europe – weakened or destroyed traditional elites and thereby encouraged "the rise or perpetuation of a dominant central executive, attempting to stand 'above' the contending parties and interest groups":

Díaz ruled over Mexico . . . France exercised autocratic rule in Vietnam and Algiers through her governor general, vastly more authoritarian than the head of government at home; and Cuba was dominated by Batista. (Wolf 1969: 284.)

The prerevolutionary states in Iran and Nicaragua (see Chapter 6) were also highly autonomous and personalistic dictatorships (see, e.g., Farhi 1990: ch. 2; Wickham-Crowley 1992: ch. 11).

The (domestic) autonomy of Eastern European regimes, in fact, like that of prerevolutionary Third World states, was predicated on and reproduced by their historic intolerance of "civil society" – independent associations and ideological currents. Indeed, this latter characteristic of totalitarian regimes was thought by many analysts to preclude the very possibility of radical change in Eastern Europe. However, after the 1960s, many of the Eastern European regimes – Romania being the clearest exception – largely shed their totalitarian pretensions, abandoning the goal of ideological conformity among the population, *even among Party members*, and sometimes tolerating small "islands of autonomy" (Bunce 1999: 32) within civil society so long as these did not seem to threaten the regime (see, e.g., Kolankiewicz 1988). This change is nicely captured in the Hungarian leader Janós Kádár's famous reversal of the formula that "He who is not with us is against us" into "He who is not against us is with us." Indeed, "After the Stalinist period, the state accepted an implicit 'pact of non-aggression' with society, allowing citizens to pursue private and egoistic ends in exchange for withdrawal from public life and politics" (Ekiert 1990: 2; see also Walicki 1991). In other words, there eventually emerged in most of Eastern Europe what scholars have referred to as post-totalitarian regimes (Linz and Stepan 1996: ch. 3, pt. 4).

---

[7] Schöpflin refers to the "hyper-etatism" of Communist regimes (1991: 189); see also Bunce 1985, 1999; Csanadi 1990; and Waller 1993.

The posttotalitarian policy of "salamis for submission," as the Czechs called it, suggests that Second World totalitarianism was gradually evolving, at least in certain respects, into a form of rule that was increasingly similar to Third World authoritarianism.[8] The post-Stalinist "social compact," however, even as it opened up some limited space for the development of a civil society, also placed the thin popular legitimacy of these regimes on a new, nonideological, and, as it developed, even more tenuous basis: If the regime could not provide sufficient salami, it had no right to expect submission.[9] As Valerie Bunce wryly observes,

Regimes that had long castigated capitalism for its short-term horizons and that prided themselves on the long-term vistas enabled by planning, state ownership of the economy, and Communist Party rule were increasingly placed in the position of making decisions in response to a single question: what have you done for me lately? (Bunce 1999: 56–7)

The politicized economies of Eastern Europe, in fact, proved increasingly incapable of "delivering the goods," particularly quality consumer goods, during the 1970s and 1980s (although there were certainly important variations in this regard among individual countries). To be sure, these regimes were relatively adept at heavy industrialization through the "extensive" mobilization of ever-greater resources (including labor) during their first two decades, but "intensive" economic growth based on the efficient utilization of such resources and routine technological innovation was systematically undermined by the politicized (and militarized) nature of state-socialist economies (see, e.g., Stokes 1993: 9–11). Above all, the "soft budget constraints" of state enterprises that are characteristic of such economies – the practical impossibility, that is, of firms going bankrupt, owing to their receipt of state subsidies – provided few incentives for efficient production, quality control, or the development of labor-saving tech-

---

[8] The Polish regime of the 1980s, according to Andrzej Walicki, "became similar to traditional authoritarian regimes" (Walicki 1991: 97; see also Jowitt 1983: 277). The convergence only goes so far: State ownership of the economy, central planning, Leninist parties, and armed forces generally subordinate to civilian authorities, among other factors, clearly differentiated the Eastern European regimes from most authoritarian regimes in the Third World.

[9] On the implicit "social compacts" in Eastern Europe, see Pravda 1981 and Pakulski 1986. J. F. Brown notes that the reputation of Kádár, the Hungarian leader who is perhaps most closely associated with the idea of a consumerist compact, "could not survive the unraveling of the social compact" during the economic downswing of the early 1980s: "Once he failed to deliver, he was vulnerable" (Brown 1991: 104).

nologies.[10] In this economic context, moreover, as Katherine Verdery has noted, "many workers developed an opposition cult of *non*-work, imitating the Party bosses and trying to do as little as possible for their paycheck" (Verdery 1993: 4).

The "success" of economic enterprises in Eastern Europe, as in neopatrimonial dictatorships and racially exclusionary colonies in the Third World, was typically less dependent on economic rationality than on access to state resources and protection from would-be competitors. Such access, in turn, was generally determined by political loyalty to state leaders, party membership, personal connections, outright corruption, and other extra-economic factors (on corruption, see Holmes 1993). In addition, Eastern Europe's dependence on the Soviet Union – not unlike (neo)colonial dependence in the Third World – also discouraged initiatives aimed at more efficient and integrated national economies. Economically protected, at least until the 1970s, from competition with the global capitalist economy and militarily protected from potential geopolitical rivals, the Eastern European regimes were thus insulated from two of the most powerful forces that have encouraged economic rationalization in the modern world.[11]

Economic stagnation, in fact, led a number of Eastern European states to borrow heavily from the West during the 1970s, which simply compounded problems of external dependence (see Borocz 1992; Szelenyi and Szelenyi 1994). As in the Third World, furthermore, these states also came to tolerate the "second," "black," or "gray" economies that developed throughout the region, at least so long as this sphere – like nascent civil societies – acted as a safety valve that complemented rather than threatened the official state-controlled economies (see, e.g., Sampson 1986).

Economic stagnation in the region also led to a number of experiments with economic liberalization and decentralization during the post-Stalin era. The (despotically) politicized nature of state-socialist economies, however, impeded the sort of fundamental political and economic reforms that might have increased enterprise efficiency or, at least, made economic

---

[10] See especially Kornai 1980, as well as Burawoy and Lukacs's important reformulation (1992: ch. 3).

[11] Eastern Europe's relative insulation from global capitalism distinguishes it from the dependent capitalist societies of the Third World. On the other hand, certain formal Western empires were largely autarchic trading blocs that operated in ways not completely dissimilar to those of the Soviet bloc's Council for Mutual Economic Assistance (CMEA, or Comecon).

austerity more palatable. Significant economic and political liberalization, including greater reliance upon markets and/or the inclusion of new groups within the planning process, threatened political elites and well-connected enterprise managers with the loss of access to state-centered economic resources. The nomenklatura's loss of *political* authority, in others words, threatened its *economic* authority and privileges. The result was that state-socialist regimes – again, like neopatrimonial dictatorships and racially exclusionary colonies in the Third World – generally proved incapable of reform "from above" (see Chirot 1991: 4). "Major reform was as necessary as it was politically impossible" (Bunce 1999: 37). (During the late 1980s, however, as I discuss later in this chapter, Communist elites belatedly and hastily began to disentangle economic and political authority.) When serious efforts at reform *were* initiated at the top, furthermore, as in Hungary in 1956 and Czechoslovakia in 1968, the Soviet Union stepped in to "restore order" and "normalize" the situation (Ekiert 1996).

Since the "carrot" of reform was thus unavailable, Eastern Europe's state-socialist regimes – or, if need be, their Soviet patron – almost invariably employed the "stick" against their political opponents. As in many Third World dependencies, however, indiscriminate repression of opposition movements ultimately backfired in Eastern Europe; repression severely impeded overt oppositional activities, to be sure, but at the cost of further undermining the regime's legitimacy and swelling the ranks of those who identified with an increasingly radicalized (i.e., anti-Communist) opposition.[12] As Adam Michnik noted for Poland, "If martial law was a setback for independent society, it was a disaster for the totalitarian state" (quoted in Echikson 1990: 161).

Repression and political exclusion, in fact, predictably weaken the appeal of those opposition groups calling for "mere" reforms or accommodations with the existing regime – such as dissident socialists in Eastern Europe – and strengthen those "radicals" who argue that the entire social and political order is thoroughly bankrupt and must be recast from top to bottom. As Tocqueville argued, highly centralized despotic regimes tend to encourage a utopian desire for "total revolution" among their political

---

[12] By "indiscriminate," I do not wish to suggest that political repression in Eastern Europe was especially or uniformly violent. By Third World standards, certainly, it was not – excepting, of course, the Hungarian counterrevolution, in which more than twenty thousand people were killed. "Indiscriminate" indicates rather that even reformist and potentially loyal oppositions – dissident Marxists and socialists, for example, in the Eastern European context – were generally not tolerated as legitimate political actors.

opponents – a "desire to remold society on entirely new lines" (Tocqueville 1955 [1856]: 140). Calls for the partial reform of such regimes seem wholly inadequate as well as impractical.[13]

Opposition Movements

Successful revolutionary movements in the Second and Third Worlds, as these last observations suggest, also exhibit a number of striking similarities, a fact that is perhaps not so surprising given the aforementioned similarities among the old regimes that they confronted. Just as certain regime types are especially vulnerable to revolutionary overthrow, so certain types of revolutionary movements are especially likely to seize power; more than this, certain regime types (and policies) actually help to produce, however unwittingly, their own grave diggers in the form of revolutionary, as opposed to reformist or loyal, oppositions. In fact, the opposition movements in Eastern Europe in 1989 generally shared *five* characteristics with most successful Third World revolutionary movements: They were (1) multiclass movements that were unified by (2) widespread anger against state authorities as well as by (3) nationalism or patriotism, and they were (4) led by "radical" leaderships with (5) largely imitative and "reactive," albeit quasi-utopian, ideologies. Let us examine some of these characteristics of revolutionary oppositions in more detail.

While the opposition movements that exploded in Eastern Europe in 1989 were not and, given the infrastructural power of their enemies, *could* not be openly or formally organized, let alone armed, they generally drew on broad, multiclass, and, in some cases, multiethnic support and sympathy – including support from both intellectuals and producers.[14] Opposition to Communism was certainly not confined to the poorest or most oppressed segments of these societies; it reached from peasants and workers to intellectuals and professionals and, ultimately, into the nomenklatura itself.

This broad opposition to Communism was characterized and indeed "glued" together by a widespread hostility toward political authorities – a

---

[13] The exception in Eastern Europe to this generalization was East Germany, as is discussed later in this chapter.

[14] The exceptions here are Hungary and East Germany, where the working class was generally (although not entirely) passive and marginal to the events of 1989 (see Brown 1991: 112–3, Fagan 1991, and Burawoy and Lukacs 1992 on Hungary, and Fuller 1999 on East Germany).

267

broadly shared anger that helped to "paper over" the latent conflicts of interest within this opposition (at least until Communist rule was dismantled). Indeed, what made public anger so politically important in Eastern Europe was its pervasive character as well as the fact that it was targeted specifically at the party-state apparatus (see Bunce and Chong 1990; Bunce 1999: ch. 2). Most political systems, by contrast, including many types of authoritarian regimes, are structured in ways that obscure or deflect state responsibility for social and economic conditions – not least by allowing the "invisible hand" of the market to allocate most resources. This type of political deflection, moreover, is not generally regarded as illegitimate given the constitutional insulation of the political (or "public") and economic ("private") spheres that is more or less characteristic of capitalist societies (see Giddens 1987: ch. 5).

However, what Bartlomiej Kamiński has termed "the fusion principle" of state socialism – that is, the fusion of the despotic state and the economy – rendered political authorities responsible for all that happened in Eastern Europe (whether good or ill), since the state centrally planned, "owned," and distributed virtually all economic resources and consumer goods (Kamiński 1991: 8). This fusion encouraged the *politicization* and *nationalization* of initially local struggles over, for example, the prices of goods, the organization of work, pollution, and censorship.[15] In fact, when the public became dissatisfied, it did not (or could not) blame fate, itself, the market, or even local bosses, but generally came to blame Communist Party rule as such.[16] "The very forms of Party rule in the workplace," for example, "tended to focus, politicize, and turn against it the popular discontent that capitalist societies more successfully disperse, depoliticize, and deflect" (Verdery 1993: 5). As Jens Reich, an East German dissident, describes it,

Always the state was to be blamed, even in intimate matters: in people's midlife crises. . . . There was an all-pervading conviction that "They," the State, the Party,

---

[15] The relative isolation of these systems from the larger global capitalist economy also prevented the development of anger targeted at forces outside of the Soviet bloc, such as the International Monetary Fund. So-called "IMF riots" have become rather common, by contrast, in the Third World (see Walton and Ragin 1990).

[16] In the crucial Polish elections of June 1989, for example, the success of Solidarity in each electoral district was directly and strongly related not so much to the prior organizational strength of Solidarity in that district as to the degree of antigovernment sentiment as reflected in the proportion of voters who rejected a "national list" of unopposed Communist candidates (Heyns and Bialecki 1991: 356).

the authorities, were responsible. They had to provide a flat. They had to organize a builder to repair the house or a plumber to unblock the drains. They allocated places at the university to the children who had kept quiet about their true political convictions. (Reich 1990: 78–9)

A similar logic of opposition, as we have seen, has been encouraged in the Third World context by neopatrimonial dictatorships and by racially exclusionary colonial regimes. These regimes are not only characterized by repressive authoritarianism, but also by extensive economic powers and modes of intervention, blatant political and economic favoritism toward privileged clients, and pervasive corruption based on racism and/or "cronyism." Accordingly, these regime types and their typical practices also unintentionally focus a wide array of social and economic grievances upon the state (and thence upon its foreign backers), because the successful resolution of *socioeconomic* conflicts requires a redistribution of *political* power within the state, if not its actual overthrow. A number of recent studies have emphasized the extremely broad social base and nationalist character of revolutionary movements in Vietnam, Algeria, Cuba, Iran, and Nicaragua, where just such a fusion of externally supported despotism and pervasive state-centered economic influence was found (see, e.g., Goldstone 1986; Farhi 1990; Wickham-Crowley 1992).

A wide variety of social and economic grievances, in fact, were "nationalized" in a *double* sense in the particular Second and Third World contexts that I have been discussing: First, grievances that might otherwise have remained localized or diffuse were both aggregated and channeled, as it were, toward the central state; second, such grievances were also redirected or displaced, at least in part, toward the colonial or hegemonic power that stood behind that state. For example, the everyday economic conflicts of Angolan and Vietnamese peasants with landlords tended to escalate into political struggles with the local Portuguese and French colonial states and, ultimately, into nationalist struggles with the Portuguese and French metropolitan states (and their allies). Similarly, the quotidian struggles of Polish shipbuilders invariably escalated into political conflicts with the Polish Communist Party and, ultimately, into a patriotic struggle against that party's Soviet patrons.

Given the peculiar logic of social protest in such contexts, it follows that it is all but impossible to weigh with any precision the extent to which Second and Third World revolutions have been motivated by "socioeconomic," "political," or "nationalist" grievances. The key point here is that

269

certain types of regimes and policies inextricably *meld* all of these analytic types of grievances into one quite potent empirical form – which is precisely one of the principal weaknesses of these regimes.

Finally, most of the leaders of the Eastern European opposition were, at least by 1989 and in the particular context in which they found themselves, decidedly "radical." They were adherents, that is, of an ideology and outlook *fundamentally* at odds with the status quo. This was not always the case. As Tina Rosenberg notes, "In a July 1968 poll – which was probably as reliable as polls could get under communism – only 5 percent of Czechoslovaks said they wanted capitalism; 89 percent wanted to continue on the road to 'socialism with a human face'" (Rosenberg 1995: 18). (By closing that road, the Soviet invasion of the following month also helped to destroy that ideal.) "Workers' self-management," moreover, was the "pivotal component" of the Solidarity movement's political program less than a decade before the fall of Communism (Fields 1991: 106; see also Mason 1989: 54–5; Ost 1989). By the late 1980s, however, Eastern European dissidents largely rejected the idea of a "reformed" Communism and embraced the liberal discourse of human rights, pluralism, free markets, and economic privatization (Judt 1988: 191–5; Scruton 1988a, 1988b). "It was only in 1989 that capitalism as a goal entered the agenda – from a means leading to democracy, the 'building of capitalism' turned into an ethical imperative, into a goal analogous to what 'socialism' was for communists during the late 1940s" (Szelenyi and Szelenyi 1994: 219).

Eastern European radicalism was also, like the ideology of many Third World revolutionaries, strikingly "reactive" and imitative, although not without certain utopian strains. It was, in many ways, a simple inversion of the ideology of "actually existing socialism." For many Eastern Europeans, that is, if Communism (or "the power," as many referred to it) was opposed to markets, private ownership, free elections, a free press, and "decadent" bourgeois culture, then who could doubt that all of these things were unproblematically *good*?

East Germany is the proverbial exception that "proves" the preceding generalization. For until they were pushed aside by a broad wave of popular support for the unification of Germany, leading oppositionists in the GDR consisted in large part of dissident Communists who looked askance at nationalist or patriotic rhetoric. A number of factors explain this East German "exceptionalism" (see Joppke 1995; Torpey 1995), but perhaps the most important were the unusual opportunities for "exit" to West Germany. Even after the construction of the Berlin Wall in 1961,

270

East German authorities allowed between ten thousand and forty thousand refugees, migrants, and ransomed political prisoners to move to West Germany each year (Hirschman 1993: 179). This policy, Albert Hirschman suggests, powerfully shaped the ideological character of the East German opposition:

> The comparison with Poland, Czechoslovakia, and Hungary – where there was no exit alternative to speak of – is . . . instructive. Here dissenters stayed put. . . . Not so in the GDR; here most vocal opponents of the regime had been pushed out to the Federal Republic. . . . What dissident voices were to be heard in the GDR in 1988–89 came largely from a narrow band of reform-minded communists that had remained inside the [Communist] party (SED) and criticized the "really existing socialism" exclusively in the name of some "true" Marxism or socialism. (Hirschman 1993: 185)

However, even East German dissidents, like others in Eastern Europe, did not see themselves as the "midwives" of a radically new historical era. As S. N. Eisenstadt has noted, the events of 1989 did not draw, as in 1789 or 1917, on a new ideological vision "rooted in eschatological expectations of a new type of society" (Eisenstadt 1992: 25). "With all the fuss and noise," Francois Furet remarked at the time, "not a single new idea has come out of Eastern Europe in 1989" (quoted in Dahrendorf 1990: 27). Timothy Garton Ash, who also notes that "The ideas whose time has come are old, familiar, well tested ones," suggests that "the free market is the latest Central European utopia," "a cure for all ills, social and political as well as economic" (Garton Ash 1990: 152, 154; see also Habermas 1990).[17] The Reverend Christian Führer, whose church in Leipzig was a center of dissent, later remarked, "You have to remember that we East Germans had no real picture of what life was like in the west. We had no idea how competitive it would be. The whole system was unknown" (Kinzer 1996).

The reason for this absence of ideological innovation is undoubtedly quite simple: "Bourgeois" liberalism and free-market capitalism were appealing in Eastern Europe principally because – like Marxism-Leninism and the "Soviet model" in the Third World of the recent past – they seemed to represent the most viable alternative social order. Liberal capitalism, that is, came to be viewed as both practically and morally superior to a clearly insupportable status quo – an alternative, moreover, that seemed unquestionably successful in what were regarded, with not a little

---

[17] This is not to say that the *tactic* of a "self-limiting revolution" was not profoundly innovative.

wishful thinking, as similar countries in Western Europe. Like Third World revolutionaries, moreover, the leaders of the Eastern European opposition came to view the relative backwardness of their societies primarily as a result of a larger system of imperial domination; consequently, they believed that such backwardness could only be overcome by switching geopolitical allegiances and "world systems."

Revolutionary change in both the Second and Third Worlds is linked to the politics of hegemonic powers in yet another way. In the Third World, revolutionary change has been possible when colonial or neocolonial powers at last grew weary of the high costs of empire, although this typically did not occur until after long and bloody wars of counterinsurgency aroused opposition among the metropolitan power's *domestic* population (cases include, among others, the French in Vietnam and Algeria, the United States in South Vietnam, and the Portuguese in Africa). In Eastern Europe, similarly, a revolutionary breakthrough at last became possible when the Soviet Union grew weary of the high costs of its empire.[18] Neither Soviet forces in Eastern Europe nor colonial troops in the Third World were *militarily* expelled; the decision to withdraw them came, rather, after the progressive attrition of their governments' political will to deploy them in the face of continuing, yet by no means overwhelming, nationalist resistance (see Mack 1975: 177).

As many analysts have noted, moreover, Gorbachev's reform policies at home and his abandonment of the Brezhnez Doctrine abroad both demoralized conservative, hard-line Communist leaders in Eastern Europe and invigorated their opponents inside as well as outside the ruling parties. Communism in Eastern Europe, in other words, was delegitimated "from above and outside" as well as "from below." The increasingly clear understanding that reformist initiatives would be tolerated and perhaps even welcomed by the Soviet leadership certainly helped to fuel popular opposition movements in Eastern Europe through the course of 1989, producing what one observer has termed a "revolutionary bandwagon," as previously hidden, denied, or "falsified preferences" for regime change could be openly expressed (see Kuran 1991: 36).

Generally, there were two distinct, and temporally sequential, patterns of revolutionary change in 1989 in Eastern Europe's posttotalitarian regimes – one initiated primarily "from above" and the other "from

---

[18] On the transformation of the Soviet Union's Eastern European empire from asset to liability, see Bunce 1985, 1989. On Soviet imperial overextension, see Collins 1995.

below." (I discuss the "exceptional" case of Romania later in this chapter.) Where Communist "soft-liners," or reformers in the Gorbachev mold, predominated, allowing for the development of a comparatively strong civil society, the regime initiated round-table discussions with civic groups – in the wake of serious strikes and protests in 1988 in Poland – which led to negotiated transitions (or "pacted transitions") to democracy and, eventually, capitalism. These "negotiated revolutions" or "refolutions," as Garton Ash calls them, occurred in Poland and Hungary (see Gross 1992 and Staniszkis 1991b on Poland; Hankiss 1900 and Tökés 1996 on Hungary). However, in those posttotalitarian regimes in which Communist "hard-liners" held sway, and civil society was especially weak, regime intransigence in the context of the transitions under way in Poland and Hungary provoked massive (and nonviolent) protests of a more or less spontaneous nature. In these cases (Czechoslovakia and East Germany), the hard-liners eventually capitulated when confronted by popular protest, for reasons that I discuss later in this chapter (see Garton Ash 1990 and Wheaton and Kavan 1992 on Czechoslovakia; Joppke 1995, Hirschman 1993, and Naimark 1992b on the GDR).

In summarizing this brief and necessarily schematic analysis of the similarities between Second and Third World revolutions, it bears reemphasizing that in the Second World no less than the Third, indiscriminately repressive and highly autonomous states that are supported by foreign powers have provided an unambiguous "common enemy" against which a broad, multiclass, and patriotic opposition coalesced, infused with a reactively "radical" and quasi-utopian ideology. Throughout Eastern Europe, Garton Ash has noted,

stress was laid on the self-conscious unity of intelligentsia, workers and peasants. Of course in part this unity was created by the common enemy. . . . [T]hey were all united by consciousness of the one great divide between the communist upper/ruling class, the *nomenklatura*, and all the rest. (Garton Ash 1990: 146)

In Poland, for example, the representatives of the intelligentsia, workers, and peasants within Solidarity "identified themselves as simply 'the society,' *spoleczenstwo*, as one single 'us' against 'them' (*oni*)" (Garton Ash 1991: 50). In Czechoslovakia, similarly, during the crucial general strike of November 27, 1989,

The two main, often opposing, trends in Czechoslovak politics – the intellectual "liberal" and the worker "socialist" – had joined in their disgust with the regime that had ruled for twenty years. Just as important, the demonstrations in Slovakia showed that the Czechs and Slovaks, the two nations of Czechoslovakia, often at odds with one another, had joined in opposition. (Brown 1991: 178)

(Not surprisingly, perhaps, Czechs and Slovaks decided to go their separate ways *after* Communism fell.)

This sense of a broad, familiar "us" pitted against an alien "them" has not only arisen under state socialism in the Second World, but also under personalist dictatorships and racially exclusionary colonialism in the Third World. In fact, externally dependent and domestically repressive regimes that are strongly "fused" with economic authority are the institutional frameworks that have most consistently led to revolution – not capitalism or socialism per se. What collapsed in Eastern Europe was not socialism, but a type of dependent authoritarian socialism – just as what collapsed in the Third World has not been capitalism or even "backward" capitalism, but authoritarian modes of colonial and "crony" capitalism.

Differences: Revolutionary Processes and the Question of Violence

Before examining some crucial differences in the processes of Second and Third World revolutions, one final similarity should be noted. As the previous section implies, the initial success of opposition movements in Eastern Europe, culminating in the collapse of the old regimes, is best understood not as the handiwork of a particular "rising class" but of a multiclass, national, or "societal" movement against a more or less commonly despised, autonomous despotic state with quite constricted social support. Once this type of old regime has been toppled, a variety of latent conflicts within the revolutionary coalition – including class conflicts and national antagonisms – may emerge in a more overt form (as subsequently happened throughout parts of the region).[19] But the initial *overthrow* of the old order in Eastern Europe was not the "project" of a specific social class (see Chirot 1991: 18). In fact, the "successful" completion of Eastern Europe's revolutions along their current trajectories will result in the dominance of a social class, the bourgeoisie, that hardly existed in 1989.

This similarity notwithstanding, there are at least three striking differences between revolutionary processes in Eastern Europe and those of most successful Third World revolutions: (1) the generally spontaneous

---

[19] For an attempt to theorize the outcomes of multiclass revolutions in the Third World, see Foran and Goodwin 1993.

and peaceful nature of the mass mobilizations of 1989; (2) the primarily urban character of these mobilizations; and (3) the absence of counter-revolutionary violence. "A unique feature of eastern Europe's revolutions," notes Robert Dix, "is that supposedly invulnerable 'totalitarian' political and economic systems were changed so drastically in so short a time by varying combinations of largely nonviolent [and urban-based] popular uprisings and rather abrupt capitulation by the governing elites" (Dix 1991: 236).

The relatively spontaneous and nonviolent character of the mass mobilizations in Eastern Europe – from the strikes in Poland in 1988 to the demonstrations in Timişoara, Romania, in December 1989 – has been emphasized by most observers (see, e.g., Garton Ash 1990; Kuran 1991; Eisenstadt 1992). This contrasts starkly with most Third World revolutionary movements, which have typically been organized and led, usually over many years and even decades, by tightly knit vanguard parties that have necessarily relied heavily, although not exclusively, on a strategy of armed struggle, including guerrilla warfare. As Mao Zedong memorably put it,

a revolution is not a dinner party, or writing an essay, or painting a picture, or doing embroidery; it cannot be so refined, so leisurely and gentle, so temperate, kind, courteous, restrained and magnanimous. A revolution is an insurrection, an act of violence by which one class overthrows another. (Mao 1971 [1927]: 30)

The popular rebellions in Eastern Europe were not dinner parties either, of course, but they were, for the most part, remarkably restrained and magnanimous – "civil" as opposed to violent.

What accounts for this difference? As noted earlier, mass protests in Eastern Europe could *only* have been of a relatively spontaneous and peaceful nature, if they were to occur at all, given the tremendous "infrastructural" as well as "despotic" power, in Michael Mann's terms (Mann 1986: 113), of the Communist regimes in the region (Bunce 1999: 23–4; see also Appendix 2 to Chapter 7). Moreover, despite the serious economic difficulties noted previously, the political crises in Eastern Europe in 1989 did *not* entail the actual breakdown of the coercive or administrative power of these states, as in many other revolutionary situations (see Skocpol 1979; Goldstone 1991). Certainly, these states did not suddenly lose their monopoly of the means of violence; it was the ruling parties' political will actually to *employ* counterrevolutionary violence that surprisingly foundered in 1989.

In the Eastern European context, then, there could be no question of establishing "liberated areas" or a situation of "dual power" by force of arms, as revolutionaries have typically done in the Third World. This was not only a pragmatic decision based on limited organizational capacities (although it was certainly that), but also a result of "historical learning" based on previous confrontations with the state. The Hungarian Revolution of 1956, for example, demonstrated that a strategy of armed struggle would be suicidal. "In retrospect," a leading East German dissident has written,

I do not think that the Honecker regime could have been overthrown by an alternative and formal political party. It could only fall to this kind of [spontaneous] popular uprising. A more organised force would have had its head chopped off at once by the Stasi [i.e., the secret police]. (Reich 1990: 74)

Moreover only a very few institutions in Eastern Europe (notably the Catholic Church in Poland and the Lutheran Church in East Germany) could provide the "free space" required for organized opposition activities. Consequently, formal opposition groups like Charter 77, Civic Forum, and Public Against Violence in Czechoslovakia, the New Forum in East Germany, and the Democratic Forum and Free Democrats in Hungary were, in comparative terms, rather small organizations that often brought together people with a variety of ideological and strategic viewpoints (note the preference for "forums").[20] Even the Solidarity movement in Poland, Eastern Europe's best organized opposition, was decimated by the martial law regime of the 1980s, losing roughly four-fifths of its membership.

However widespread, then, opposition to Communism was *not* particularly well organized in much of Eastern Europe. "Civil societies" were certainly in the process of formation, especially in Poland and Hungary, but they were still relatively underdeveloped and vulnerable to repression. For this reason, attempts to explain the events of 1989 primarily in terms of the emergence or triumph of civil societies are one-sided at best (see, e.g., Arato 1993). Of equal if not greater importance for revolutionary change was not simply the eventual capitulation of the nomenklatura, but the transformation of many of its members into outright (albeit opportunistic) *advocates* of fundamental change (as described later in this section).

[20] On the hectic and impromptu activities of Civic Forum, see Garton Ash (1990: 78–130), who notes that its membership ranged "from the neo-Trotskyist Petr Uhl to the deeply conservative Catholic Vaclav Benda" (86). See also Wheaton and Kavan 1992: pt. 2.

Strong civil societies did not overwhelm weak states in 1989; rather, the leaders of still strong states either reached out to emergent civic groups (as in Poland and Hungary) or capitulated to relatively disorganized but suddenly disruptive civil societies (as in Czechoslovakia and East Germany).

It is precisely because independent associations and networks were so weak in Eastern Europe – and because most dissidents were morally opposed to the sort of "vanguardist" politics associated with Communism – that the development of a dense, ideologically diverse, yet tolerant (i.e., "civil") society became the self-conscious goal of much of the opposition (see, e.g., Michnik 1985 [1976]). Most Third World revolutionaries, by contrast (even non-Marxist revolutionaries in Mexico and Algeria) have considered something like an armed vanguard party as essential for mobilizing the masses of people necessary to overthrow the old order and create a new one; they have also tended, not surprisingly, to distrust independent, unaffiliated organizations (and individuals) as much as the states that they have sought to overthrow (a tendency particularly strong, we have seen, in the case of the Shining Path insurgency in Peru).

Mass mobilization, however, does not always require a vanguard party or even strong associational ties (see, e.g., Pfaff 1996; Opp and Gern 1993). The peoples of Eastern Europe, significantly, had been concentrated in urban areas, mass-educated, and of course politicized by four decades of Communist rule. Accordingly, relatively little formal organization was *needed* to bring massive numbers of angry people into the streets or, more typically, into easily accessible central plazas.[21] Indeed, there is more than a little irony in the fact that the large public spaces used or even created by the Communists for ritualized mass rallies would prove useful for their opponents. By contrast, the largely peasant populations of the Third World often require, given their geographical dispersion and/or social atomization, the organization and leadership of (originally) urban-based parties if they are to engage in, or at least successfully sustain, revolutionary movements on a national or even regional scale. This is a theme, for example, of numerous studies of the Chinese, Vietnamese, Cuban, Nicaraguan, and other guerrilla-based revolutions (see, e.g., Moore 1966: ch. 4; Wolf 1969: chs. 3–4; Skocpol 1979: chs. 3, 7; Wickham-Crowley 1992).

---

[21] See Opp and Gern 1993. With the exception of the Iranian Revolution, the revolutions of 1989–91 in the former Soviet bloc have been the only successful revolutions in history of a more or less exclusively urban character.

The primarily rural character of most Third World revolutions (excepting the case of Iran) and the predominantly urban character of Second World revolutions can be understood to some extent in terms of Samuel Huntington's distinction between "Eastern" and "Western" revolutions (Huntington 1968: ch. 5). "Eastern" revolutions are characterized by the rise of popular movements and (typically) guerrilla warfare against weak central states that do not strongly penetrate and control peripheral territories. "Western" revolutions, by contrast, involve mass mobilizations, especially urban conflicts, that arise *after* the collapse of old-regime states due to other causes (e.g., defeat in war). The Communist regimes of Eastern Europe, to be sure, did not collapse before the onset of the mass protests of 1989; however, the eventual unwillingness of Communist leaders to employ violence against demonstrators encouraged ever-larger (because less fearful) masses of people to mobilize near the very centers of state power.[22]

Is Eastern Europe a case, then, in which expanding "political opportunities" resulted in mass protest that overthrew extant regimes (see, e.g., Bunce 1999: ch. 4)? Yes and no. Certainly, the emergence of popular protest in the region following Gorbachev's rejection of the Brezhnev Doctrine seems to suggest as much, and yet there are problems with this thesis – even if we leave aside the case of Romania, where loyalists defended the regime with force. First, as we have seen, revolutionary change came to Poland and especially Hungary primarily "from above." In these cases of "refolution," in other words, there is comparatively little mass protest that needs to be explained. Such political opportunities as existed may have encouraged the efforts of reform Communists within the ruling parties and certain groups in "civil society," but they did not spur a great deal of popular mobilization during 1989.

In the cases of East Germany and Czechoslovakia, moreover, mass protest did not so much *result* from expanding political opportunities as it gradually revealed and indeed helped *create* such opportunities. Gorbachev or no Gorbachev, regime opponents in both countries initially feared, for good reason, that public demonstrations would be violently repressed by

[22] As Dix points out, however, there a number of important differences between the revolutions of 1989 and the "Western" pattern of revolutions in France and Russia. Among other things, "the regimes of eastern Europe were certainly not 'traditional,' nor were they, at least ostensibly, weak, as Huntington would characterize the old regimes in Russia and France" (Dix 1991: 238).

local authorities. After all, Communist hard-liners were in charge in these countries, reform Communists were largely invisible, and the authorities threatened protesters and violently attacked them virtually until the moment when these authorities abruptly capitulated. In East Germany, notes Timothy Garton Ash,

It is important to recall that right up to, and during, the fortieth-anniversary celebrations [of the founding of the GDR] on 7 October, the police used force, indeed gratuitous brutality, to disperse these protests and intimidate any who might have contemplated joining in. Young men were dragged along the cobbled streets by their hair. Women and children were thrown into prison. Innocent bystanders were beaten. (Garton Ash 1990: 67)

Many of those who demonstrated on October 7, in fact, were badly injured and many more were arrested. There were rumors, moreover, that the government was planning a violent "Chinese solution" in response to a demonstration planned for October 9 in Leipzig. As it happened, local Communist officials, in consultation with leaders of the opposition, including the conductor Kurt Masur, decided to allow the demonstration – which drew an estimated seventy thousand people – to take place without police interference (Naimark 1992b: 90–1). According to Jens Reich,

In the event, we escaped without bloodshed. But it was not known at the time that we would. There was a real, objective threat of violence. . . . We escaped a Romanian or a Chinese solution by the skin of our teeth. It could easily have been the other way around, with a re-established leadership sitting on heaps of corpses, and being ostracised entirely by the civilised world. I think that this was a real possibility. (Reich 1990: 86, 88)

It was only after October 9 when the authorities began to tolerate mass demonstrations – which quickly multiplied in numbers and size – and the hard-liners within the regime were gradually displaced.

"The concept of political opportunities," notes John K. Glenn, also "provides a limited account of the velvet revolution in Czechoslovakia" (Glenn 2000: 18). Glenn notes that the formation of the Solidarity-led government in Poland in August 1989 did not stop the Czechoslovak state from repressing a demonstration in Prague on the twenty-first anniversary of the Warsaw Pact invasion. In addition, a demonstration held on October 28, the anniversary of the founding of the Czechoslovak state, was met with force. "At least initially," Glenn suggests, "it was in fact the *continued* state repression in the case of the student demonstration on November 17th which provoked the emergence of Civic Forum and Public Against Violence" (Glenn 2000: 6; author's emphasis). Only *after* widespread outrage was expressed at the repression of this student demonstration did the regime come to tolerate public demonstrations and reform Communists came to the fore, eventually abandoning the party's "leading role."

It obviously mattered that demonstrators in Eastern Europe were not shot down in the streets, that Soviet tanks were not deployed, and that mass protests were eventually tolerated. A final major difference between Second and Third World revolutions, in fact, has to do with the issue of state violence. The unusually peaceful nature of revolutionary change in Eastern Europe (excepting Romania) is due in the first instance to the fact that the incumbent rulers there did ultimately engage in a full-scale retreat from power that allowed radical change to occur unimpededly, even where mass protest forced this retreat. Most rulers in the Third World, on the other hand, have fought ferociously against revolutionary movements, usually after (as well as before) revolutionaries seized power. But in Eastern Europe, as Garton Ash notes, "the ruling elites, and their armed servants, distinguished themselves by their comprehensive unreadiness to stand up in any way for the things in which they had so long claimed to believe" (Garton Ash 1990: 142). What exactly explains this curious and momentous fact? Why did Eastern Europe's Communist rulers capitulate so readily, for the most part, in 1989?

Combinations of the following *four* factors seem to explain, for any particular country, the relatively peaceful nature of the Eastern European revolutions (see Bruszt and Stark 1992; Csanadi 1992).[23]

Of first importance is the "Gorbachev factor." The Soviet leadership's weariness of empire certainly provided a necessary if not sufficient condition for revolutionary change. Gorbachev's abandonment of the Brezhnev Doctrine meant that "external guarantees of political order were effectively removed by the dominant regional power" (Ekiert 1990: 2). In fact, Gorbachev actively *encouraged* Eastern Europe's Communist rulers to reform. ("Life itself punishes those who delay," he pronounced on his visit to the GDR in October.) The result, Garton Ash wittily concludes, was

---

[23] The following discussion draws heavily on conversations and correspondence with Valerie Bunce, as well as on Goodwin and Bunce 1991 and Bunce 1999. For a fairly similar theoretical approach to state violence, see Gurr 1986.

that "Throughout East Central Europe, the people at last derived some benefit from their ruling elites' chronic dependency on the Soviet Union" (Garton Ash 1990: 141).[24] Gorbachev, in short, created the sort of "permissive world context" for revolutionary change that has often been important in the Third World context (see Goldfrank 1979; Foran 1992, 1997b).

Second, some Communists undoubtedly perceived liberalization and open elections not as forces that would sweep them away, but as elements of a purely *strategic* retreat that was necessary – and not for the first time – precisely in order to hold on to their power and privileges in the long run.[25] In Poland, for example, Communists seemed to believe that they could win at least sufficient support in contested elections to form or enter into a coalition government. By thus sharing democratically legitimated power – and, thereby, responsibility for economic austerity – they seem to have calculated that they could begin to repair their reputations, at least relative to that of their opponents. These calculations initially proved overly optimistic, to say the least – an indication of how poor isolated Communist regimes had become at comprehending popular sentiment.[26] On the other hand, this strategy did not prove wholly unsuccessful. A number of (reorganized) Communist parties in the region subsequently managed to maintain or even expand their popular support while their opponents oversaw transitions to capitalism which led, at least in the short term, to declining standards of living for broad social sectors.

Third, it should be emphasized that Eastern Europe's ruling elites, unlike elites in other revolutionary situations, were not physically threatened by their opponents. This opposition was renowned, after all, for its civility and its "self-limiting" and even "antipolitical" aspirations, in part because of the seemingly formidable character of Communist regimes (see, e.g., Konrád 1984; Michnik 1985 [1976]). Moreover, the boundaries between the Communist parties and their opponents were rather perme-

[24] For this same reason, those elites in the region that were *least* dependent on the Soviets – for example, in Romania, Yugoslavia, and Albania – proved more willing to employ coercion against their opponents.

[25] It has also been suggested that by 1989 Communist leaders no longer believed in their own *moral* right to rule. Garton Ash, who refers to this as the "Tocqueville" factor, argues that this was "perhaps the ultimately decisive factor" in the Communists' decision not to suppress violently the revolution "from below" (Garton Ash 1990: 141).

[26] However, where opposition forces were exceptionally weak – for example, in Bulgaria and Albania – this strategy was at least initially successful (see Bruszt and Stark 1992).

able in some cases; the opposition in Poland and Hungary, in particular, included many former party members. And not least, the opposition (unlike most revolutionary movements in the Third World) was unarmed. The institutional integrity of the armed forces and state administration, therefore, was not immediately threatened by the opposition in a way that might have provoked a violent backlash.[27]

A final relevant factor for understanding the full-scale Communist capitulation in 1989 is what some have termed the "embourgeoisement" or "self-privatization" of the Communist elite during the late 1980s. In the posttotalitarian era, and in the Gorbachev years in particular, many educated and opportunistic party members, particularly younger technocrats and professionals, came to view reform, and the transition to a private market economy in particular, not as a threat to their careers but, on the contrary, as a way of improving their income and status. "At the burial of Communism," goes one Polish joke, "many people jumped from the coffin into the funeral procession," and they had clear economic motives for doing so. In Czechoslovakia, for example, more than a hundred joint production ventures with Western companies were already under way by mid-1986 – the permitted foreign share of equity having been raised from 40 to 49 percent (Brown 1991: 157). In Poland, "privatization from above" was begun in 1987, two years before the fall of the Communist government (Staniszkis 1991a: 128). Consequently, the "radicalization" of the opposition in Eastern Europe – a parallel process of embourgeoisement – took on added significance: The opposition's gradual adoption of an unalloyed procapitalist ideology (and concomitant abandonment of such earlier ideals as "socialism with a human face" and workers' self-management) served to undermine whatever opposition that technocrats and professionals within the nomenklatura might otherwise have mounted against "radical" change. The party and society were, for once, moving together.

This factor, moreover, clearly distinguishes Eastern Europe's Communist rulers (or a substantial fraction thereof) from other elites that have confronted revolutionary movements. Revolutions, after all, have by their very nature threatened the entire "way of life" (economic as well as polit-

---

[27] Only a relative handful of Communist officials and functionaries have been arrested thus far throughout the whole of Eastern Europe, and only Nicolae and Elena Ceauşescu, so far as I am aware, have been executed.

ical) – if not the very lives – of ruling and privileged elites; hence the unmitigated violence with which most such elites have greeted revolutionary movements and governments. "Since no deep revolution has won to power," notes Katharine Chorley, "without leaving in its wake a trail of dispossessed and embittered classes, this implies that a revolutionary government on the morrow of its seizure of power will probably be met with a certain degree of violent opposition, whether spasmodic and spontaneous or organized into open rebellion" (Chorley 1943: 185). Yet while the Eastern European revolutions were certainly "deep revolutions" in many ways, they did not wholly dispossess the nomenklatura. It would thus seem that if ruling elites, or powerful segments thereof, can actually expect to *thrive* in a radically new society, then counterrevolutionary violence will not occur.

In the Eastern European context, so long as the nomenklatura's exploitation of state resources and of its own technical knowledge (and social connections) was strictly dependent on the retention of political authority – so long, in other words, as ownership and rulership were fused and collectivized – then violent opposition to democratic change could be expected to follow. But once those resources and skills were privatized and made marketable, a nonviolent transition to capitalism became feasible. Elemér Hankiss notes that when the nomenklatura in Hungary discovered in the late 1980s "the possibility of transferring their power into a new and more efficient socioeconomic system and of becoming part of an emerging new and legitimate ruling class or *grande bourgeoisie*, they lost their interest in keeping the Communist Party as their instrument of power and protection" (Hankiss 1990: 31; see also Verdery 1993: 16). "Making owners of the nomenklatura," as Jadwiga Staniszkis puts it "may have . . . helped to eliminate the nomenklatura as a political mechanism" (Staniszkis 1991a: 139).

In short, if the chronic fusion of economic authority and political power in Eastern Europe served gradually to nationalize and radicalize dissent and opposition, then the eleventh-hour disengagement of economic and political authority during the 1980s, however partial, helped to ensure (along with the Soviet disengagement from the region) that radical change would occur peacefully. This is not to say that post-Communist economies in Eastern Europe are owned and managed *primarily* by ex-Communists; but such economies have provided a relatively "soft landing" for many of the region's former rulers.

Romanian "Exceptionalism": The Collapse of Neopatrimonial Socialism

The case of Romania presents something of a paradox. On the one hand, the process of change there was apparently the most "revolutionary" among the Eastern European cases, characterized as it seemed to be by the brief but bloody confrontation between the population, soon joined by sections of the army, and the Ceauşescu regime. Indeed, in Romania for the first time in history a "Communist" regime was apparently overthrown through force of arms, and the Communist Party itself (unlike those elsewhere in the region) was quickly outlawed. On the other hand, the immediate outcome of the events of December 1989 was the *least* revolutionary among the Eastern European cases, since those events initially produced a government dominated by people with more or less strong ties to the Romanian Communist Party (RCP). Hence, the Romanian "revolution" did *not* lead to an unambiguous break with the past.[28]

The "revolutionary" process in Romania is certainly familiar to students of Third World revolutions. After all, the Ceauşescu regime – which has been described as "dynastic socialism" (Georgescu 1988), "socialist patrimonialism" (Linden 1986), and "socialism in one family" (de Flers 1984) – was not by any means a typical Communist party-state, but more nearly a neopatrimonial, personalist dictatorship of totalitarian intent. As we have seen, such dictatorships have proven especially vulnerable to revolutionary overthrow, at least when they have been infrastructurally weak or weakened.[29] And yet the events in Romania in December 1989 bear relatively little resemblance to the Mexican, Cuban, Iranian, or Nicaraguan revolutions against neopatrimonial dictators. A much closer parallel is the series of events in Haiti in 1986, which resulted in the flight of the dictator Jean-Claude "Baby Doc" Duvalier but *not* in the seizure of power by an organized revolutionary movement.

Like Haiti, in fact, Romania experienced something of a "half-way" or "aborted" revolution (see Fischer 1990; Gilberg 1990). The spontaneous protests of December (like earlier protests in Haiti) were sufficiently

[28] My understanding of the events of 1989 in Romania is based generally, in addition to the sources cited, on Campeanu 1991, Codrescu 1991, Ratesh 1991, and Verdery and Kligman 1992.

[29] On these vulnerabilities, see Dix 1984, Goldstone 1986, and Wickham-Crowley 1992: ch. 11; on Romania's "socialist patrimonialism," see Linden 1986, Georgescu 1988, Tismăneanu 1989, and Fischer 1990.

widespread to cause sectors of the army to defect, and thereby assure the dictator's downfall, but they were *not* strong enough nor sufficiently well organized to thrust their own representatives into positions of power. Instead, state power was reconsolidated by dissident (and not-so-dissident) members of the RCP and the army grouped into the so-called National Salvation Front, an entity that *did* have the solidarity and connections, not to mention the guns, to take power. The result was a "neo-Communist" regime, as its opponents labeled it, just as the Duvalier regime in Haiti was immediately followed by a "neo-Duvalierist" regime.[30]

What accounts for this "exceptional" pattern of change in Romania in 1989? To begin with, the opposition in Romania was remarkably weak, even by Eastern European standards, due to the extraordinary penetration and disorganization of civil society by Ceauşescu's secret police, the Securitate, which essentially acted as his praetorian guard.[31] (Duvalier's infamous Tontons Macoutes played a similar role in Haiti.) The anti-Ceauşescu protests in Timişoara in December, consequently, were of a highly spontaneous nature, and the first protest in Bucharest actually began during a rally called by Ceauşescu himself to denounce the earlier demonstrations in Timişoara. In any event, there was no preexisting opposition network in Romania, like those that emerged out of Solidarity in Poland or Charter 77 in Czechoslovakia, which could place itself at the head of the popular unrest.

The refusal of the regular army to suppress the demonstrations was due in part to its alienation from Ceauşescu as a result of the dictator's coddling of the Securitate and his use of it to spy on and divide the army (a typical ploy of neopatrimonial regimes):

Having starved the armed forces of resources and built up the secret police as the real guardians of the regime, the military was made to dig ditches as cheap labor. It was the grand risk of the Ceauşescu clan that they would not have to call on the

---

[30] The National Salvation Front is *not* "neo-Communist" because it attempted to retain all the old Stalinist institutions. As Verdery and Kligman (1992) emphasize, this is not in fact the case; among other things, the Front began to privatize the economy. However, the regime may accurately be termed "neo-Communist" because of the background (and certain mentalities) of its principal leaders.

[31] The membership of one Romanian opposition group that claims to have been founded before Ceauşescu's fall, the so-called Antitotalitarian Forum, consisted of three families. According to its leader, "If we had taken anybody else in, it would have exposed the group to infiltration by the Securitate" (see Echikson 1990: 51). According to one survey, there were only two independent movements in Romania in June 1989, compared to nine in the GDR, twenty-one in Hungary, and sixty in Poland (Pehe 1989).

army, because if they ever did, the leadership made it almost certain that the troops would not defend them. (Segal and Phipps 1990: 965)

Ceauşescu's highly personalist and nepotistic rule also antagonized members of the RCP and completely marginalized would-be party re-formers and soft-liners. As Vladimir Tismaneanu has noted, the party "remained the only cohesive social stratum" that could possibly "oppose Ceauşescu's plans to turn Romania into a Third World dictatorship. This is the main reason why the General Secretary . . . resorted to permanent rotation of cadres, to that perpetual game of musical chairs which makes everyone insecure and fearful" (Tismaneanu 1989: 374).

Some soft-line RCP members and army officers who became alienated from the regime began plotting to replace Ceauşescu, allegedly with Soviet knowledge. Ultimately, on the back of the spontaneous protests, they suc-ceeded. This entire process is nicely summarized by Richard Snyder:

A wave of spontaneous mass protests, which began in the city of Timişoara on 17 December 1989 and soon swept the country, created an opportunity for army and party soft-liners to throw off the sultanistic ruling clique that had ridden piggy-back on their institutions for two decades. The clash of soft-liners and hard-liners took the form of pitched battles between disloyal and loyal security forces (mainly Securitate members), which lasted until Ceauşescu's capture on 23 December by military rebels and his execution several days later. The absence of well-organized moderate or maximalist opposition groups enabled the National Salvation Front (FSN), a civilian-led coalition with close ties to both the Communist Party and the military, to take control without contest. (Snyder 1998: 78)

The National Salvation Front also easily won the first "free" elections of May 1990, largely because they were held too quickly for other parties to organize effectively and because the Front controlled access to television (Verdery and Kligman 1992: 123). Ironically, then, the most violent and "revolutionary" events of 1989 thrust into power the least revolutionary and most compromised leadership. Nevertheless, the Romanian case demonstrates as well as any in Eastern Europe how state structures and practices shaped the possibilities for (and limitations of) radical change "from below."

Conclusion

After the startling "refolutions" in Poland and Hungary, Eastern Europe experienced a conjuncture of events that is quite familiar to students of Third World revolutions: popular mobilizations "from below," the failure

Conclusion

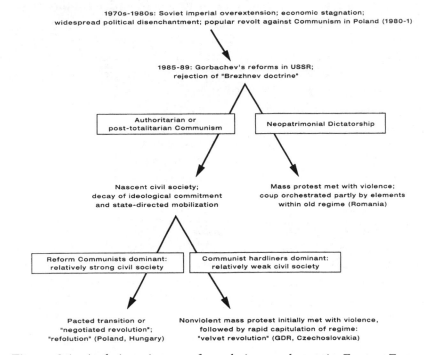

Figure 8.1 Analytic trajectory of revolutionary change in Eastern Europe, 1970–1989.

of states to suppress such protest "from above," and a decision against military intervention "from outside" by the hegemonic imperial power in the region. As in the Third World, this conjuncture resulted in revolution, toppling old regimes and thrusting "radical" dissidents into positions of political power.

Figure 8.1 schematically summarizes the state-centered analysis of revolutionary change in Eastern Europe in 1989 that I have presented in this chapter. The figure indicates that two political variables, against a general backdrop of economic stagnation, widespread political disenchantment, and Gorbachev's reformist rule in Moscow, largely determined how such change would occur in the region: whether the regime was posttotalitarian or neopatrimonial in nature, and, if the former, whether reform Communists or hardliners were dominant. Where the regime was a neopatrimonial dictatorship (i.e., Romania), and civil society virtually nonexistent, change occurred through more or less spontaneous popular

287

demonstrations that led in turn to the defection of sections of the army, a violent response from regime loyalists, and a coup orchestrated partly by elements within the old regime. Change also occurred through popular protest where posttotalitarian regimes were led by hard-liners and civil society was relatively weak (i.e., East Germany and Czechoslovakia), only here the results were "velvet revolutions," as the regimes more or less rapidly capitulated, with minimal violence, following the displacement of hard-liners within the ruling parties. Finally, in those posttotalitarian regimes in which reform Communists were dominant and civil society relatively strong (i.e., Poland and Hungary), roundtable discussions between the regime and opposition groups – after a resurgence of strikes in the case of Poland – led to negotiated or "pacted transitions" from Communism (i.e., "refolutions").

I have argued that the breadth, ideology, and success of the civic groups and popular mobilizations "from below" in these dependent state-socialist societies cannot be understood without reference to the states (and state-elite alliances) that dissidents confronted. I have suggested, more specifically, that the structure and practices of Eastern Europe's Communist regimes – like those of certain regimes in the Third World – unintentionally politicized and nationalized grievances that might otherwise have remained localized and diffuse; these regimes also unwittingly fostered the hegemony of precisely those opposition leaderships that were committed to fundamentally restructuring the state, economic institutions, transnational relations, and even the culture of these societies. In the Second World no less than in the Third, in sum, the formation as well as the success of radical opposition movements has been a consequence not simply of certain class relationships or socioeconomic ills, but also, and more directly, of the violent, arbitrary, and authoritarian practices of states that were internationally dependent, domestically autonomous, and economically intrusive.

9

Conclusion: Generalizations and Prognostication

> *People do not make revolution eagerly any more than they do war. There is this difference, however, that in war compulsion plays the decisive role, in revolution there is no compulsion except that of circumstances. A revolution takes place only when there is no other way out.*
> — Leon Trotsky (1961 [1932], III: 167)

Between the incineration of Hiroshima and the disintegration of the Soviet Union, dozens of revolutionary conflicts shook the world. Most revolutionary movements of the Cold War era, including several quite powerful ones, were defeated. But many successfully seized state power, remaking large parts of the globe and, in the process, the international balance of power. In East Asia, revolutionaries seized power in China, North Korea, Vietnam, Cambodia, and Laos, and challenged imperial and neoimperial rule in several other countries, including Burma, Malaya, and the Philippines. In Africa, French Algeria and Portugal's far-flung colonies violently threw off imperial rule, and popular revolts in Kenya, Zimbabwe, Namibia, and South Africa hastened the demise of imperial and/or white-supremacist rule in those countries. In Latin America, meanwhile, revolutionaries seized power in Bolivia, Cuba, and Nicaragua, nearly triumphed in El Salvador, and powerfully shook Venezuela, Guatemala, Peru, and Colombia. Finally, a series of popular rebellions in 1989 finished off the more recalcitrant Communist regimes of Eastern Europe, which had been demoralized by Gorbachev's reforms in the Soviet Union and his rejection of the Brezhnev Doctrine. All told, the revolutions of the Cold War era helped to destroy European colonialism, toppled some of the century's most notorious and bloody dictators, and humbled the superpowers themselves, contributing in the end to the demise of the weaker one, the Soviet Union. The period from 1945 to 1991 was indeed an age of revolutions, if ever there were one.

289

This book has attempted to solve a series of puzzles raised by a variety of revolutionary movements in Southeast Asia, Central America, and Eastern Europe. I have argued that state-centered approaches provide compelling solutions to these puzzles, although these approaches certainly do not pretend to provide an exhaustive causal explanation of any of the movements that I have examined (see Chapter 2). Nor can I offer by way of a conclusion a simple, unitary theory of revolutions or even of "peripheral" revolutions. I have not discovered a parsimonious formula that indicates the necessary and sufficient causes of each and every revolutionary movement or revolution of the Cold War era (e.g., intense demographic pressures or a certain class structure). Perhaps I have not dug deeply nor seen clearly enough. More likely is the sheer implausibility of a general theory of revolutions or peripheral revolutions. As Charles Tilly has suggested, such a theory would assume "a political world in which whole structures and sequences repeat themselves time after time in essentially the same form. That would be a convenient world for theorists, but it does not exist" (1995b: 1596).

In fact, the revolutionary movements of the Cold War era do not fit easily into a single mold. These movements had rather different social bases or constituencies, that held distinctive cultural beliefs; their leaders adhered to different ideologies (even the Marxists seldom shared the *same* Marxism); they pursued different strategies and employed different tactics; they faced different enemies, including differently organized states and regimes; and, as we have seen, they had quite different political fortunes. There were, in short, multiple paths to the formation of revolutionary movements and to actual revolutions during the Cold War era, including many cul-de-sacs.

This said, there is a logic to my principal findings and claims, which are summarized in Figures 4.1, 6.1, and 8.1. In all the cases I have examined, revolution was a response not only to economic exploitation or inequality, but also to political oppression, usually brutal, by a few specific types of states. Revolutionary movements developed and sometimes thrived in opposition to repressive and exclusionary authoritarian states that were infrastructurally weak or weakened, even if these states held more or less competitive elections; and revolutionary movements were most likely to actually seize state power when the repressive states that they confronted were especially autonomous of (or disembedded from) civil society – including middle classes and even elites in addition to lower classes – and organized along patrimonial or clientelistic as opposed to rational-bureaucratic lines (see Figures 1.3 and 1.4). In fact, the great revolutions of the Cold War era were incubated by, and overthrew, precisely three rather peculiar types of political order: the rigidly exclusionary colonies of relatively weak imperial powers; personalistic, "above-class" dictatorships; and dependent, Soviet-imposed Communist regimes. These particular political orders were not sufficient to cause revolutions, but they were certainly essential.

In Southeast Asia, armed revolutionary movements emerged in much of the region during and after the Second World War due to the Japanese occupation, which severely weakened Western colonial domination, if only momentarily, and thereby provided unprecedented political opportunities for the formation of armed national liberation movements. Whether these movements were led by Communists or nationalists depended on the nature of Japanese rule during the war. Where the Japanese relied upon existing indigenous elites that had collaborated with Western colonial rulers, Communist-led movements developed (as in Vietnam, Malaya, and the Philippines). By contrast, where the Japanese proactively sponsored popular non-Communist nationalists, the latter would emerge as leaders of the postwar struggle for independence (as in Indonesia). Furthermore, whether or not Communist-led movements were actually able to seize state power depended on the character of the (reimposed) Western colonial or neocolonial rule that these movements confronted after the war. Where Western rule was, and had historically been, racially exclusionary and indiscriminately repressive, revolutionaries were able to seize power (as in Vietnam). By contrast, where Western rule was or became more inclusionary and reformist, revolutionary movements failed and a successful transition to neocolonial rule took place (as in Malaya and the Philippines).

In Central America, radical revolutionary movements developed, or reemerged, during the 1970s where reformist and/or electorally oriented movements collided with indiscriminately repressive, yet infrastructurally weak, authoritarian regimes (as in Nicaragua, El Salvador, and Guatemala). Where the regime was at least "semiopen," by contrast, revolutionary organizations were unable to mobilize significant movements (as in Honduras). Where institutional or corporate forms of authoritarianism prevailed, furthermore, the armed forces were able to oversee transitions to formal civilian rule and the opening of limited political space for nonviolent movements, thereby securing greater international aid and legitimacy. In this context, popular revolutionary movements were unable to seize power, although neither were they defeated (as in El Salvador and Guatemala). By contrast, revolutionaries *were* able to seize power where they confronted a neopatrimonial or "sultanistic" dictatorship

291

that attempted to defeat them through purely military means (as in Nicaragua).

In Eastern Europe, finally, Gorbachev's rule in the Soviet Union opened up opportunities for radical change, but did not at all determine how that change would occur, if at all. In those "posttotalitarian" regimes in which Communist reformers held sway, allowing for the emergence of a relatively strong civil society, negotiated transitions ("refolutions") to democratic capitalism occurred (as in Poland and Hungary). By contrast, in those posttotalitarian regimes in which Communist hard-liners were dominant and civil society was correspondingly weak, Communist rule collapsed only after massive, more or less spontaneous, and decidedly nonviolent protests occurred (as in Czechoslovakia and the German Democratic Republic). Finally, where a neopatrimonial or "sultanistic" Communist dictator ruled (i.e., Romania), only a violent split within the regime and armed forces – provoked by the spontaneous rebellion of a very weakly organized society – resulted in the overthrow of the dictator by groups and personalities with close connections to the old regime.

The breakdown of political authority and other types of expanding political opportunities played a role in the development and trajectory of some of the movements I have examined. For example, by disrupting Western colonial rule in Southeast Asia, the Japanese occupation of World War II facilitated (and indeed provoked) the formation of revolutionary movements in that region (although it did not determine their subsequent fate). And it is difficult to imagine that the revolutionary events of 1989 in Eastern Europe would or could have occurred had Soviet force been energetically deployed to stop them. Nonetheless, we have also seen that revolutionary movements were more consistently a response to severely constricted or even contracting political opportunities, including chronic and even increasing state repression. Ordinary people joined or supported revolutionary movements when no other means of political expression were available to them, or when they or their families and friends were the targets of the violent repression that was perpetrated or tolerated by relatively weak states. In this way, I have suggested, certain types of states and regimes unintentionally helped to construct revolutionary movements or, more precisely, the type of political contexts in which revolutionaries were able to thrive. And these movements themselves were sometimes able to create, and not simply exploit, opportunities for seizing state power. They did not have to wait for state crises or breakdowns, that is, but sometimes created these themselves. In the terminology of Chapter 2, the revolutionary movements and revolutions of the Cold War era are greatly illuminated by the state-constructionist (or "Tocquevillean"), state-capacity, state-autonomy, and (sometimes) political-opportunity perspectives.

The preceding summary of my major findings and claims points toward the appropriate criteria for criticizing this study and developing a more powerful theoretical analysis than the one offered here. Such an analysis must clearly present more than a descriptively richer or more detailed account of the events that I have analyzed, for any description of events, thick or thin, must be conceptually and theoretically organized (if only implicitly), and any particular theoretical account may utterly fail on empirical grounds. Similarly, analyses that emphasize the importance for revolutionary movements of causal factors or mechanisms other than those highlighted by this study's state-centered perspective – factors such as class struggle, gender, social networks, resource mobilization, and culture, to name but a few – may be quite illuminating, but they may or may not provide persuasive solutions to the specific puzzles about movement formation and success that are addressed in this book.

Accordingly, more powerful solutions to these puzzles must entail a demonstration that some theoretical approach (or combination of approaches) other than a state-centered perspective both (1) accurately distinguishes or parses the differences in the incidence and trajectory of the revolutionary movements I have examined and (2) does so more convincingly – by connecting more relevant facts to this approach – than a state-centered perspective. Simply adding more factors, let alone facts, to the analysis that I have presented here will not necessarily, and will certainly not automatically, provide better answers to the questions this analysis has addressed. In sum, more empirical details or theoretical complexity may be added to the stories that I have told. But the critical discussions that I hope this book opens up will require something more specific – namely, better theoretical solutions than my own to the particular substantive puzzles that I have addressed herein.

Is the Age of Revolutions Over?

So much for the main findings and claims of this study. What are its implications for the future of revolutions as a repertoire of contention – that is, as a type of political struggle and social change? Based on our understanding of the past, what does the future hold for revolutionaries in the post–Cold War period?

Table 9.1. *Armed movements in Latin America, 1959–2000.*

Country	1959–c. 1985	Late 1990s
Argentina	(MPN) Montoneros	–
	ERP	
Bolivia	ELN	–
Brazil	ALN	–
	VPR	
Chile	MIR	–
	FPMR	
Colombia	FARC ----------------------------	FARC
	ELN ----------------------------	ELN
	EPL	
	M-19	
Costa Rica	–	–
Cuba	M-26-7	–
Dominican Republic	M-14	–
Ecuador	AVC	–
El Salvador	FMLN*	–
Guatemala	URNG*	–
Honduras	FPR	–
	MPL (Cinchoneros)	
	PRTC-H	
Mexico	L-23	EZLN
	PROCUP	EPR
Nicaragua	FSLN (Sandinistas)	–
Panama	–	–
Paraguay	–	–
Peru	ELN	
	MIR	
	Sendero Luminoso --------------	Sendero Luminoso
	MRTA ----------------------------	MRTA
Uruguay	(MLN) Tupamaros	–
Venezuela	FALN	–

Note: * multigroup alliances.

Extrapolating from the events of the past two decades, *armed* revolutionary struggle would seem to be on the wane. This trend is especially evident in Latin America in the wake of the peace settlements in El Salvador and Guatemala. Whereas armed movements could be found in virtually every Latin American country during the 1960s and 1970s, such movements were active in only three countries (Colombia, Mexico, and Peru) by the late 1990s (see Table 9.1). Beginning with the Iranian Revo-

Table 9.2. *Major unarmed antigovernment protests, 1978–2000.*

Country	Years
Iran	1978–9
Poland	1980–1
South Africa	1982–5
Chile	1983–6
Sudan	1985
Haiti	1985
Philippines	1986
South Korea	1987
Burma	1987–8
West Bank and Gaza	1987–93
Tibet	1987–9
China	1989
Eastern Europe	1989
Mali	1990–1
Kenya	1990–?
Madagascar	1991–3
Kosovo	1991–7
Nigeria	1993–?
Indonesia	1998
Serbia	2000

Note: Dates are approximate and refer to the peak year(s) of protest.
Source: Adapted from Zunes 1994.

lution of 1978–9, moreover, a growing number of *nonviolent* or at least unarmed popular insurgencies have arisen against authoritarian states. During the 1980s and 1990s, in fact, more than a dozen major instances of unarmed antigovernment protests occurred (see Table 9.2). Most of these protest movements were repressed by government authorities, sometimes quite violently, but others succeeded in overthrowing authoritarian regimes (as in the Philippines and Eastern Europe) and still others contributed indirectly to democratic transitions (as in South Africa, Chile, and Haiti).

Nonviolent protest, including protest aimed at overthrowing or fundamentally reshaping political regimes, is hardly new. The nationalist movement against British rule in India, protest by black South Africans during the 1950s, and the civil rights movement in the United States all employed nonviolent strategies of protest. Still, there does seem to be a trend toward nonviolent or unarmed antigovernment protest during the final decades of the twentieth century.

What might account for this trend? Analysts have pointed to several factors that may explain the appeal of nonviolent protest (e.g., Zunes). Unless state repression is overwhelming, nonviolent protest often facilitates greater popular mobilization than armed struggle, and it need not be confined to peripheral or thinly populated regions where the state's infrastructural power is weak. There may also be a growing recognition that state violence against unarmed protesters, while often compelling some of them to take up arms, may swell the ranks of nonviolent movements, especially if such violence is only erratically and haphazardly employed. Indeed, the use of force against nonviolent protesters may create dissension and divisions among the state's armed forces, which may in turn facilitate regime change. There has also occurred an international diffusion of the ideological principles and techniques of nonviolent protest, especially in the writings of Mohandas K. Gandhi and Martin Luther King, Jr.

Perhaps the central reason for the increasing prevalence of nonviolent or unarmed protest, however, is the general expansion of most states' infrastructural power since the Second World War (see, e.g., World Bank 1997). New military, transportation, and surveillance technologies have made it extremely difficult for would-be revolutionaries to defeat a regular army by force of arms, unless that army has been weakened in war or by political dissension within its ranks. (The latter type of schisms, however, may themselves be generated by extensive nonviolent protest as well as by armed struggle.) Given the infrastructural power of such contemporary authoritarian states as those in China, Cuba, and Iraq, revolutions are only likely to occur in those countries – if they occur at all – as a result of unarmed protest that divides the military. It bears emphasizing, in fact, that few *armed* revolutionary movements that have seized state power actually defeated regular armies on the battlefield. More often, armed revolutionaries have triumphed when the armies that they have confronted broke apart during wartime (as in Russia), were very deeply divided along political lines (as in Bolivia), or eventually refused to fight in defense of an unpopular regime (as in Cuba). In colonial situations, moreover (including, as we have seen, those in Vietnam and Indonesia), armed revolutionaries have usually triumphed by gradually eroding the political will of the colonial power to maintain its rule, typically by waging guerrilla warfare and carrying out economic sabotage over many years or even decades. In these cases, armed revolutionaries eventually won by not losing. But this sort of "prolonged popular warfare" is enormously costly even when the state is infrastructurally weak, and it is thus usually adopted only as a last resort. Nonviolent protest, if and when it proves effective, is generally preferred by protesters, whether they seek to overthrow the state or not.

Will there be more nonviolent revolutions in coming decades? Indeed, what does the future hold for revolutions, violent or nonviolent, during the twenty-first century? Does either "globalization" (i.e., the increasingly transnational character and integration of capitalism) or the demise of the Soviet bloc herald the end of revolution as a distinctive mode of political conflict and change? Is the age of revolutions now over? I believe that it probably is, although not for the reasons that some have proposed. To be sure, revolutions will continue to occur during the post–Cold War era, and revolutionary movements and popular insurgencies will persist in a number of countries and are likely to burst forth in still others. We have already witnessed (among other events) a popular rebellion in Chiapas, Mexico, the violent demise of the personalistic dictatorship of Mobutu Sese Seko in Zaire (now renamed the Democratic Republic of the Congo), and the resignation of the dictator Suharto in Indonesia following mass protests and riots. And revolutions may yet occur in the remaining occupied territories, military dictatorships, and patrimonial regimes sprinkled across the globe – perhaps in Myanmar (formerly Burma), Iraq, or Tibet. Popular movements may also challenge the Communist regimes that still remain in North Korea, Vietnam, Cuba, and China – although these regimes, which are themselves the products of popular revolutions, retain considerably more nationalist legitimacy than did those in Eastern Europe, which were more or less imposed (outside of Yugoslavia and Albania) by the Soviet Union. Moreover, several of these regimes, including the Chinese and Vietnamese, have initiated market reforms that seem to have inaugurated a gradual, nonrevolutionary transition toward a type of capitalist economy.

Revolutionary movements, moreover, will continue to thrive – or at least survive – in the peripheries that lie beyond the reach of authoritarian states, as in Mexico, Colombia, Myanmar, and Algeria.[1] However, while these movements are able to exert pressure on incumbent regimes to a greater or lesser extent, none of them seems capable of actually seizing state power in the near future. In several of these countries, revolutionaries are feared and disliked by broad social sectors, not just elites. Indeed,

---

[1] See Foran (1997a) for a discussion of the likelihood of revolutions in some of the aforementioned countries.

some of these movements may be important mainly for their "radical-flank effects." At a national level, that is, these movements may be most politically significant to the extent that they open up greater political space for other, more moderate political movements and organizations.[2] It is doubtful, finally, whether those revolutionary movements that *do* seize state power in the years ahead will seriously challenge the remaining superpower or radically alter global politics, as did many revolutions of the Cold War era. The recent "revolutions" in Zaire and Indonesia, if we may call them that, are cases in point.

My principal prognostication, however, is that revolutionary movements are rather less likely to arise and social revolutions less likely to occur during the contemporary period than during the Cold War era – especially, but not exclusively, movements and revolutions that would seriously challenge the capitalist world-system. As both a repertoire of contention and a motivating ideal, revolution seems to have lost much of its popular appeal and influence. Why is this? Why has an age of revolutions – an era marked by several waves of widespread revolutionary conflict – now passed? And might another return?

Two possible keys to our nonrevolutionary times may be globalization and the demise of Soviet Communism. Some have suggested that globalization has destroyed the very rationale for revolutions. According to this perspective, state power – the traditional prize of revolutionaries – has been dramatically eroded by the growing power of multinational corporations and by the increasingly rapid and uncontrollable movements of capital, commodities, and people. These realities, according to Charles Tilly, "undermine the autonomy and circumscription of individual states, make it extremely difficult for any state to carry on a separate fiscal, welfare or military policy, and thus reduce the relative advantage of controlling the apparatus of a national state" (1993: 247). In other words, as globalization increasingly diminishes and hollows out state power, the less rational becomes any political project aimed at capturing state power, including revolution.

Globalization has indeed made revolutions less likely, but not for this dubious reason. Rather than uniformly diminishing states, globalization

---

[2] In certain authoritarian contexts, civil society as a whole often benefits from the presence of a strong "radical flank" of revolutionaries. The guerrilla movements in El Salvador and Guatemala, for example, while unable to seize state power, certainly had important radical-flank effects for the more moderate opposition and thereby contributed both directly and indirectly to the process of democratization in those countries.

has been just as likely to spur attempts to employ and, if necessary, expand state power for purposes of enhancing global competitiveness. Historically, in fact, there has been a strong *positive* correlation between a country's exposure to external economic competition and the size of its public sector (Evans 1997). To a significant extent, some have argued, globalization is itself a *project* of strong states (e.g., Weiss 1997). Popular support for revolutionaries, at any rate, is not usually based on estimations of their likely success in instituting a new fiscal policy or even enhancing a country's long-term global competitiveness. As we have seen, ordinary folk have typically supported revolutionaries because they have spoken up for them when no one else would (or could), defended their traditional rights, provided for their subsistence, and, not least, protected them from state violence. As Jorge Castañeda has argued, popular support for revolutionary movements typically derives less from attractive visions of the future than from a conviction that the status quo is unendurable:

The rationale for revolution, from seventeenth-century England to Romania at the close of the second millennium, has always lain as much in the moral indignation aroused by an unacceptable status quo as in the attraction exercised by an existing blueprint for the future. The most powerful argument in the hands of the left in Latin America – or anywhere else – has never been, and in all likelihood will never be, exclusively the intrinsic merit or viability of the alternative it proposes. Its strong suit is the morally unacceptable character of life as the overwhelming majority of the regions' inhabitants live it. (Castañeda 1993: 254)

There seems little reason to believe that in the future people will accept the depredations of authoritarian states on the grounds that "state power ain't what it used to be."

Another, and perhaps more obvious, explanation for the declining prospects for revolution is the collapse of the Soviet bloc. Many revolutionaries of the Cold War era – especially those who did not live particularly close to the Soviet Union's borders – were certainly emboldened by the existence of a powerful noncapitalist industrial society, one that was itself dependent and "backward" in the not-too-distant past. If modernization in a single generation was possible in the Soviet Union, perhaps it was possible anywhere. The appeal of Soviet Communism was all the greater because the Soviets were the self-proclaimed foes of the capitalist powers (above all the United States) which provided aid and comfort – in the name of anti-Communism – to many a brutal and authoritarian regime. Yet I have argued here that it was, in the first instance, precisely the brutality and authoritarianism of so many states during the Cold War era – including the Soviet-backed regimes in Eastern Europe – that provided the seed bed for widespread revolutionary conflicts. For much of the Cold War era, vast tracts of the globe suffered more or less violent and exclusionary forms of colonial rule, imperial domination, military occupation, or postcolonial despotism. In these political contexts, popular rebellions, usually armed and necessarily violent, were often the only practical or even sensible repertoire of political struggle. Moderates and reformists, by contrast, seemed utopian or even suicidal.

Today, however, this seed bed for revolution is virtually desiccated, thanks in no small measure, ironically, to the revolutions of the Cold War era: Colonialism is all but dead; Soviet domination of Eastern Europe is no more; and U.S. hegemony in the Third World – even in its Central American "backyard" – is increasingly challenged by rival powers (see, e.g., Coatsworth 1994). Most importantly, and partly because of these very developments, a transnational "wave" of democratization has swept across large parts of East Asia, Eastern Europe, Latin America, and (to a lesser extent) Africa over the past decade or two (see Markoff 1996; Huntington 1991). While there were precious few democratic regimes in South America in the late 1970s, for example, transitions to democracy were under way virtually everywhere on that continent just fifteen years later, even though much of the region had suffered a serious economic crisis (Mainwaring 1999). Thanks in large part to revolutionary movements themselves, moreover, democratic transitions have also been under way in Central America (Paige 1997). But with democracy has also come the pacification of these revolutionaries (Dunkerley 1994).

The coming decades are unlikely to exhibit the same scale of revolutionary conflict as the Cold War era precisely because of this striking and widespread *political* transformation. The likelihood of future revolutions, that is, rests largely upon the future of democracy. For while we may debate the underlying causes of democratization, and the causes of the most recent wave of democratization in particular, it seems difficult to deny democracy's predominantly counterrevolutionary consequences. *No popular revolutionary movement, it bears emphasizing, has ever overthrown a consolidated democratic regime.*[3] The great revolutions of the Cold War era toppled violently exclusionary colonial regimes (as in Vietnam and Algeria), brutal personalist dictatorships (as in Cuba, Iran, and Nicaragua),

---

[3] Rightist movements did destroy democratic regimes in Germany, Italy, and Spain, although these regimes were of recent vintage and far from fully institutionalized.

and the Soviet-imposed Communist regimes of Eastern Europe. However, none overthrew a regime that even remotely resembled a democracy. And no longstanding, institutionalized democracy is today even remotely threatened by revolutionaries – not in Western Europe, Japan, North America, Costa Rica, Australia, or New Zealand. As one noted sociologist has written,

There is now no substantial reason to believe that marxist revolutions will come about in the foreseeable future in any major advanced capitalist society. In fact, the revolutionary potential – whatever the phrase may reasonably mean – of wage-workers, labor unions and political parties, is feeble. This is true of the generally prosperous post–World War II period; it was also true of the thirties when we witnessed the most grievous slump so far known by world capitalism. Such facts should not *determine* our view of the future, but they cannot be explained away by references to the corrupt and corrupting "misleaders of labor," to the success of capitalist propaganda, to economic prosperity due to war economy, etc. Assume all this to be true; still the evidence points to the fact that, without serious qualification, wageworkers under mature capitalism do accept the system. Wherever a labor party exists in an advanced capitalist society, it tends either to become weak or, in actual policy and result, to become incorporated within the welfare state apparatus. (Mills 1962: 468–9)

These words were written several decades ago (although they require no revision) not by a conservative, but by the radical sociologist C. Wright Mills.

Why exactly is democracy so inhospitable to revolutionaries? First and foremost, democracy largely pacifies and institutionalizes – but hardly does away with – many forms of social conflict. Lipset (1960: ch. 7) has aptly referred to elections as a "democratic translation of the class struggle." Indeed, democracy "translates" and channels a variety of social conflicts – including, but not limited to, class conflicts – into party competition for votes and the lobbying of representatives by interest groups. This "translation" has sometimes taken violent forms, especially when and where the fairness of electoral contests is widely questioned. But the temptation to rebel against the state (which is rarely seized without trepidation under any circumstances, given its life-or-death consequences) is generally quelled under democratic regimes by the knowledge that new elections are but a few years off – and with them the chance to punish incumbent rulers. Just as importantly, democracies have generally afforded a political context in which popular protest can win concessions from economic and political elites, although this often requires a good deal of disruption, if not violence (see, e.g., Gamson 1975; Piven and Cloward 1977). But armed struggles that are aimed at overthrowing elected governments rarely win much popular support – unless such governments (or the armies that they putatively command) effectively push people into the armed opposition by indiscriminately repressing suspected rebel sympathizers. As Che Guevara wrote:

It must always be kept in mind that there is a necessary minimum without which the establishment and consolidation of the first [guerrilla] center [*foco*] is not practicable. People must see clearly the futility of maintaining the fight for social goals within the framework of civil debate.... Where a government has come into power through some form of popular vote, fraudulent or not, and maintains at least an appearance of constitutional legality, the guerrilla outbreak cannot be promoted, since the possibilities of peaceful struggle have not yet been exhausted. (Guevara 1985 [1960]: 50–1)

(Unwisely, Guevara later abandoned this view, claiming that even democracies could be toppled by revolutionaries.) With very few exceptions, to paraphrase Alan Dawley (1976: 70), the ballot box has been the coffin of revolutionaries.

Does this mean that political radicalism and militancy go unrewarded in democratic societies? Hardly. Democracy, to repeat, by no means eliminates social conflict; in fact, in many ways democracy encourages a veritable flowering of social conflict by providing the "political space" or "political opportunities" with which those organized groups outside ruling circles can make claims on political authorities and economic elites (Tarrow 1994).[4] Not just political parties, then, but a whole range of interest groups, trade unions, professional associations, social movements, and even transnational networks become the main organizational vehicles of political life in democratic polities. These institutions of "civil society," however, are generally just that – civil. Their repertoires of contention include electoral campaigns, lobbying, strikes, boycotts, demonstrations, and civil disobedience – forms of collective action that may be undertaken with great passion and militancy (sometimes for quite radical ends), and that sometimes involve or provoke violence, but which are not aimed at bringing down the state. (Nor are riots – from which democracies are hardly immune – revolutionary in this sense.) So whereas radicals and mil-

---

[4] Unfortunately, the political opportunities concept has been defined and operationalized so as to include virtually every environmental factor that facilitates political protest. The claim that such opportunities are a necessary precondition for protest has thus become something of a tautology. See Goodwin and Jasper 1999.

itants may survive and even thrive under democracy – or at least some democracies – true revolutionaries seldom do.

Democracy, then, dramatically reduces the likelihood of revolutionary change, but *not*, I should emphasize, because it necessarily brings about social justice (although justice *is* sometimes served under democracies). Formal democracy is fully compatible with widespread poverty, inequality, and social ills of all sorts – which is precisely why Marx rightly criticized "political emancipation" and so-called bourgeois democracy in the name of "human emancipation." The prevalence of poverty and other social problems is precisely why extraparliamentary movements for social justice so often arise in democratic contexts. But, again, these movements almost always view the state as an instrument to be pressured and influenced, not as something to be seized or smashed. To be pessimistic, at any rate, about the likelihood of social revolutions during the current period is not at all to be pessimistic about the likelihood of struggles for social justice. (And we should recall that the record of past revolutions in achieving social justice is mixed at best.)

Even imperfect and poorly consolidated democracies tend to diffuse revolutionary pressures. The neglected case of Honduras, which I examined in Chapter 5, illustrates this well. During the 1980s, violent conflicts raged in neighboring countries, but Honduras remained relatively quiescent. No significant revolutionary movement challenged the Honduran state, despite social problems and inequalities that rivaled those of its neighbors. Although several elections took place in Honduras during the 1980s, the democratic regime in that country was (and remains) very deeply flawed. The two dominant political parties were (and remain) virtually indistinguishable. A special battalion in the armed forces, moreover, "disappeared" dozens of suspected radicals. Still, trade unions and peasant organizations were generally tolerated and occasionally won concessions through militant protest. Dissident intellectuals and human rights activists spoke out against the government. And, perhaps most important, the armed forces in Honduras never indiscriminately attacked peasant villages or popular organizations in the manner of their Salvadoran or Guatemalan counterparts. As a result, Hondurans never felt the need to join or support revolutionaries in order to defend themselves or to improve their welfare. So while Honduras's quasidemocracy did few things well, it was remarkably effective at preventing the emergence of a popular revolutionary movement.

The recent wave of democratization, then, while certainly uneven and incomplete, has destroyed the basis for revolutionary conflicts in those

303

societies that it has reached. Yet some scholars insist that the "new world order" has not at all diminished the likelihood of revolutions and, at least in certain respects, may even make them more probable in the years ahead, at least in developing or "Southern" societies (see, e.g., Walt 1996: 349–51; Foran 1997a; Selbin 1997). These scholars point out that many countries remain impoverished, dependent upon and subordinate to the wealthy "North," and vulnerable to external economic downturns. They also suggest that, despite the collapse of Communism, a range of dissident ideologies and "cultures of opposition" remains available to would-be revolutionaries, including radical nationalism and religious fundamentalism.

These points are indisputable. Yet while these factors may generate widespread popular grievances, history tells us that these grievances are not sufficient to cause revolutions or even to generate significant revolutionary movements or popular rebellions. After all, revolutionary movements develop not simply because people are angry, but because the state under which they live provides no other mechanism for social change and violently represses those who peacefully seek incremental reforms. And revolutionary movements, even those with strong popular support, rarely succeed in seizing power unless the authoritarian states that they confront are very weak or suddenly weakened (through war, for example).

John Foran (1997a), who is well aware of this line of reasoning, still maintains that the prospects for revolutions have not decreased appreciably in the post–Cold War era. He bases his view on the claim that "exclusionary, personalist states, while out of vogue in the post-1980 movement towards formally democratic polities in much of the world, are still an option for dependent developers (and this global democratisation process remains fragile)" (Foran 1997a: 814). Foran is certainly right to claim that personalist dictatorships have proven unusually vulnerable to revolutionary overthrow, as the cases of Cuba, Iran, and Nicaragua testify. But the personalist dictatorship *is* an increasingly rare and anachronistic state form that clearly seems headed for extinction. The soil in which such dictatorships sunk their roots – a predominantly rural populace, weak landed and industrial elites, demobilized masses, praetorian armies, and massive external aid to combat Communism – has all but dried up. Revolutions may yet topple dictators like Saddam Hussein in Iraq, but few other personalist dictatorships remain.

Foran and Eric Selbin (1997b) also suggest that the end of the Cold War has opened up more geopolitical space for revolutionary movements. By this, they seem to mean that the United States no longer has an excuse for intervening against democratic revolutionaries. However, with the demise of the countervailing power of the Soviet bloc, geopolitical space has surely *contracted* for those revolutionaries, democratic or otherwise, who threaten the perceived interests of the U.S. government. Witness the growing intervention of the United States in the counterinsurgency in Colombia (see Chapter 7). To be sure, thanks mainly to its unfortunate experience in the revolutionary conflict in Vietnam, the U.S. armed forces (and the general public) are loath to commit large numbers of troops to dangerous overseas conflicts. But there are currently no substantial external, geopolitical constraints on the projection of U.S. power abroad in such forms as military aid, long-range missiles, and air power. This does not bode well for revolutionaries who are seen as enemies by the U.S. government.

A more serious challenge to my pessimism about future revolutions is Foran's warning about the fragility of the recent global spread of democracy. For the future of revolutions is indeed inextricably bound to the future of democracy. A new era of widespread revolutionary conflict will dawn, if my analysis is right, only if this most recent wave of democratization recedes in coming years. We will undoubtedly witness new waves of revolutionary conflict if the nascent democracies in Eastern Europe, East Asia, Latin America, and Africa are replaced by violent, authoritarian regimes. Fortunately, this scenario seems unlikely, if only because economic and political elites, including even army officers, have become increasingly aware of the growing economic costs of the political disorder, corruption, and cronyism that authoritarianism breeds. Here is where globalization may truly matter. The unprecedented speed and mobility of financial resources in the current era hangs like the sword of Damocles over those on both the left *and* right who would disrupt predictable business climates and "investor confidence." In the new world order, the fear of capital flight or boycott may stay the hand of would-be Pinochets as well as that of would-be Lenins. Globalization, in other words, notwithstanding its often disastrous socioeconomic effects, may actually help preserve formally democratic and quasidemocratic regimes and undermine the most brutal and corrupt forms of authoritarianism. As a political project of the most advanced capitalist countries (and their "Southern" allies), especially the United States, globalization seeks to undermine all forms of economic nationalism and autarchy, whether of the left or right, and foster the type of free trade that powerful multinational corporations will inevitably dominate. Globalization thus abhors the autocratic and

305

oligarchic forms of "crony capitalism" that have nurtured so many revolutionary movements during the past century. In short, Lenin was undoubtedly right to argue that formal democracy – whether more or less inclusionary, more or less representative – provides the best "political shell" for capitalism.

History, however, admittedly provides less room for optimism. Past waves of democratization, alas, have in fact been regularly followed by antidemocratic waves. Yet this should give little comfort to revolutionaries, for "the overwhelming majority of [past] transitions from democracy" were not the result of popular revolts, but "took the form of either military coups ... or executive coups in which democratically chosen chief executives effectively ended democracy by concentrating power in themselves" (Huntington 1991: 291). Needless to say, very few people would welcome such coups today, even if, in the long run, they make revolutions more likely. In fact, the left as a whole (including former revolutionaries) – perhaps more than any other segment of the political spectrum in newly democratic countries – has come through hard experience to value bourgeois democracy and the rule of law, warts and all. The contemporary left, with few exceptions, is generally keen on avoiding actions, including armed rebellions, that might provide a pretext for, or unintentionally legitimate, antidemocratic coups. (In Latin America, this means that the left – with some exceptions – has returned to the outlook that prevailed prior to the Cuban Revolution, which leftists initially denounced as "putschist" and "adventurist.") The left itself, in short, today stands, and should stand, as an important obstacle to one of the most basic and necessary preconditions for revolution: political authoritarianism. But history, of course, is full of such paradoxes.

Annotated Bibliography

The following bibliography includes all the sources cited in the text as well as a number of other works that have shaped my understanding of the revolutionary movements examined in this book. The annotations are intended to be a guide for those who wish to pursue certain topics in more detail than I have provided. However, what follows certainly does not pretend to be an exhaustive bibliography for the theoretical issues, regions, countries, or periods in question. (The section on Eastern Europe is particularly sketchy, including few items other than those cited in the text.) Excellent general bibliographies on revolutions and cognate phenomena include Tilly 1995a and Lanzona 1993; there is also an extensive bibliography in Zimmermann 1983.

In organizing this bibliography, I have attempted to place works that could legitimately fall under two or more of the headings outlined below within the more *specific* category. For example, Popkin 1979 is placed under "Vietnam," and Scott 1976 under "General Studies" of Southeast Asia, although both might also have been listed as works of theory.

Entries are organized according to the following outline:

I. Theory, Methodology, and General Studies
II. Southeast Asia
  A. General Studies (Including Asia Generally)
  B. Vietnam
  C. Indonesia
  D. Malaya
  E. The Philippines
III. Central America
  A. General Studies (Including Latin America Generally)

B. Nicaragua
C. El Salvador
D. Guatemala
E. Honduras
IV. Eastern Europe (Including the Soviet Union)

I. Theory, Methodology, and General Studies

Abrams, Philip. 1988 (1977). "Notes on the Difficulty of Studying the State." *Journal of Historical Sociology* 1:58–89. Emphasizes the importance of the ideological notion of the state, or "state idea," in addition to the structures and practices of state institutions.

Ahmad, Eqbal. 1971. "Revolutionary Warfare and Counter-Insurgency." Pp. 137–213 in *National Liberation: Revolution in the Third World*, edited by Norman Miller and Roderick Aya. New York: Free Press. One of the best general statements on the subject. Develops the idea of revolutionary movements as statelike organizations.

Albertini, Rudolph von. 1982 (1966). *Decolonization: The Administration and Future of the Colonies, 1919–1960*. New York: Africana Publishing Company. An extensive comparative study.

Almond, Gabriel, et al. 1954. *The Appeals of Communism*. Princeton, NJ: Princeton University Press. A Cold War classic.

Amenta, Edwin, Bruce G. Carruthers, and Yvonne Zylan. 1992. "A Hero for the Aged? The Townsend Movement, the Political Mediation Model, and U.S. Old-Age Policy, 1934–1950." *American Journal of Sociology* 98:308–39. The authors' political mediation model emphasizes the importance of what I am calling "political context."

Anderson, Benedict. 1991. *Imagined Communities: Reflections on the Origin and Spread of Nationalism*. Revised edition. London and New York: Verso. One of the most important recent studies of nationalism; the author is a Southeast Asia specialist.

Anderson, Perry. 1974. *Lineages of the Absolutist State*. London: Verso. A wide-ranging Marxist analysis of absolutist states in Western and Eastern Europe.

Archer, Margaret. 1988. *Culture and Agency: The Place of Culture in Social Theory*. Cambridge, UK: Cambridge University Press. Difficult but important.

Aya, Rod. 1990. *Rethinking Revolutions and Collective Violence: Studies on Concept, Theory, and Method*. Amsterdam: Het Spinhuis. Develops some important insights, although Aya engages in a nasty polemic against Walton (1984) and calls for a narrowly instrumentalist understanding of social action.

Barkey, Karen and Mark von Hagen, eds. 1997. *After Empire: Multiethnic Societies and Nation-Building: The Soviet Union and Russian, Ottoman, and Habsburg Empires*. Boulder, CO: Westview Press. How four empires ended, and the consequences thereof.

I. Theory, Methodology, and General Studies

Bearman, Peter. 1993. *Relations into Rhetoric: Local Elite Structure in Norfolk, England, 1540–1640.* New Brunswick, NJ: Rutgers University Press. On the elective affinities between networks and ideologies.

Bendix, Reinhard. 1977 (1964). *Nation-Building and Citizenship.* Berkeley and Los Angeles: University of California Press. A minor classic. How citizenship builds nations and typically deradicalizes workers.

Betts, Raymond F. 1991. *France and Decolonisation, 1900–1960.* New York: St. Martin's Press. A very useful short overview.

Birnbaum, Pierre. 1988. *States and Collective Action: The European Experience.* Cambridge, UK: Cambridge University Press. State-centered to a fault.

Boswell, Terry and William J. Dixon. 1993. "Marx's Theory of Rebellion: A Cross-National Analysis of Class Exploitation, Economic Development, and Violent Rebellion." *American Sociological Review* 58:681–702. This defense of Marx's theory argues that the positive effect of economic development on rebellion (see Muller and Seligson 1987) is due to the former's impact on proletarianization, class exploitation, and market crises.

Bratton, Michael and Nicolas van de Walle. 1994. "Neopatrimonial Regimes and Political Transitions in Africa." *World Politics* 46:453–89. An exemplary state-centered study, focusing on the problems of democratization in neopatrimonial regimes. See also Snyder 1992.

Brooker, Paul. 1997. *Defiant Dictatorships: Communist and Middle-Eastern Dictatorships in a Democratic Age.* New York: New York University Press. Argues that defiance against external foes – often with a new or renewed emphasis on nationalism – has been the principal stabilizing force behind eight persistent dictatorships.

Burawoy, Michael. 1989. "Two Methods in Search of Science: Skocpol Versus Trotsky." *Theory and Society* 18:759–805. A hostile critique of Skocpol (1979), emphasizing the pitfalls of John Stuart Mill's canons of induction.

Callinicos, Alex. 1982. "Trotsky's Theory of Permanent Revolution and Its Relevance to the Third World Today." *International Socialism* 2:98–112. A critique of Löwy (1981) that emphasizes some of the limitations of Trotsky's theory.

Calhoun, Craig. 1982. *The Question of Class Struggle: Social Foundations of Popular Radicalism during the Industrial Revolution.* Chicago: University of Chicago Press. Develops the notion of "reactionary radicalism."

Cammack, Paul. 1989. "Review Article: Bringing the State Back In?" *British Journal of Sociology* 19:261–90. Develops a number of important criticisms of state-centered sociology, although the author overlooks or obscures some of the more important insights of this perspective.

Central Intelligence Agency [CIA]. 1995. *The World Factbook 1995.* Washington, DC: CIA, Office of Public and Agency Information. A helpful source of national-level data.

Chaliand, Gérard. 1989. *Revolution in the Third World: Currents and Conflicts in Asia, Africa, and Latin America.* Revised edition. New York: Penguin Books. A rather disorganized set of ruminations, often insightful, on development, armed struggle, and socialism.

309

Chehabi, H. E. and Juan J. Linz, eds. 1998. *Sultanistic Regimes*. Baltimore, MD: Johns Hopkins University Press. A fascinating volume on a type of regime that has proven unusually susceptible to revolutionary overthrow.

Chorley, Katharine. 1943. *Armies and the Art of Revolution*. London: Faber and Faber. A neglected classic; argues that revolutions are usually impossible when the armies they confront are unified.

Close, David H. 1995. *The Origins of the Greek Civil War*. London: Longman. A very helpful and well-written overview of a defeated revolutionary movement by a leading expert.

Cohan, A. S. 1975. *Theories of Revolution: An Introduction*. London: Nelson. A handy primer, although now somewhat dated.

Cohen, Jean L. and Andrew Arato. 1992. *Civil Society and Political Theory*. Cambridge, MA: MIT Press. The most thoughtful and comprehensive statement on "civil society."

Colburn, Forrest D. 1994. *The Vogue of Revolution in Poor Countries*. Princeton, NJ: Princeton University Press. A short overview; the author may exaggerate the role of ideas (particularly Marxism-Leninism) in Third World revolutions, as opposed to political and social structures.

Collins, Randall. 1993. "Maturation of the State-Centered Theory of Revolution and Ideology." *Sociological Theory* 11:117–28. A sympathetic review, emphasizing geopolitics.

1995. "Prediction in Macrosociology: The Case of the Soviet Collapse." *American Journal of Sociology* 100:1552–93. Collins predicted it, if not quite the precise timing.

Darby, Phillip. 1987. *Three Faces of Imperialism: British and American Approaches to Asia and Africa, 1870–1970*. New Haven and London: Yale University Press. Examines the strategic, economic, and moral dimensions of imperialism.

Dawley, Alan. 1976. *Class and Community: The Industrial Revolution in Lynn*. Cambridge, MA: Harvard University Press. A marvelous study of (among other things) the deradicalizing effects of democracy.

DiMaggio, Paul J. and Walter W. Powell. 1991. "Introduction." Pp. 1–38 in *The New Institutionalism in Organizational Analysis*, edited by Walter W. Powell and Paul J. DiMaggio. Chicago: University of Chicago Press. On the cognitive and mythic foundations of institutions.

Dunn, John. 1972. *Modern Revolutions: An Introduction to the Analysis of a Political Phenomenon*. Cambridge, UK: Cambridge University Press. Includes eight case studies, including an interesting chapter on Vietnam.

Easton, Stewart C. 1960. *The Twilight of European Colonialism: A Political Analysis*. New York: Holt, Rinehart, and Winston. Includes a discussion of the contrasting colonial policies of Britain, France, Belgium, and Portugal.

Eckstein, Harry. 1975. "Case Study and Theory in Political Science." Pp. 79–137 in *Handbook of Political Science, Volume 7: Strategies of Inquiry*, edited by Fred I. Greenstein and Nelson W. Polsby. Reading, MA: Addison-Wesley. A defense of the case-study method, but one with many interesting implications for comparative analysis.

I. Theory, Methodology, and General Studies

Eisenstadt, S. N. 1978. *Revolution and the Transformation of Societies: A Comparative Study of Civilizations*. New York: Free Press. Includes some interesting reflections on revolutions in neopatrimonial societies.

Eisinger, Peter K. 1973. "The Conditions of Protest in American Cities." *American Political Science Review* 67:11–28. An early statement about the importance of political opportunity structures.

Elias, Norbert. 1978 (1970). *What Is Sociology?* New York: Columbia University Press. A brilliant little volume, in every way. Includes important reflections on how *intra*society relations are embedded within a larger "figuration" of *inter*society relations.

Emerson, Rupert. 1960. *From Empire to Nation: The Rise to Self-Assertion of Asian and African Peoples*. Boston: Beacon Press. The author views non-Western nationalism as primarily a product of imperialism; varieties of the former, moreover, are largely the result of variations of the latter.

Emirbayer, Mustafa and Jeff Goodwin. 1996. "Symbols, Positions, Objects: Towards a New Theory of Revolutions and Collective Action." *History and Theory* 35:358–74. A synthetic approach in broad strokes.

Evans, Peter. 1995. *Embedded Autonomy: States and Industrial Transformation*. Princeton, NJ: Princeton University Press. Examines how particular state structures and practices inhibit or foster economic development.

———. 1997. "The Eclipse of the State? Reflections on Stateness in an Era of Globalization." *World Politics* 50:62–87. Important considerations from a skeptic.

Fairbairn, Geoffrey. 1974. *Revolutionary Guerrilla Warfare: The Countryside Version*. Harmondsworth, UK: Penguin Books. Looks at China, Southeast Asia, and Cuba. Dated, but still helpful.

Farhi, Farideh. 1990. *States and Urban-Based Revolutions: Iran and Nicaragua*. Urbana, IL and Chicago: University of Illinois Press. A short, provocative comparative study that attempts to rework Skocpol's (1979) ideas.

Fieldhouse, D. K. 1965. *The Colonial Empires: A Comparative Survey from the Eighteenth Century*. New York: Delacorte Press. A standard overview.

Fishman, Robert M. 1990. "Rethinking State and Regime: Southern Europe's Transition to Democracy." *World Politics* 43:422–40. Develops the distinction between state and regime and shows how it matters for democratization.

Foran, John. 1992. "A Theory of Third World Social Revolutions: Iran, Nicaragua, and El Salvador Compared." *Critical Sociology* 19:3–27. A multicausal, "additive" theory of revolutions.

———. 1993. "Theories of Revolution Revisited: Toward a Fourth Generation." *Sociological Theory* 11:1–20. Analyzes recent attempts to introduce culture and agency into more "structural" theories of revolution. See also Selbin 1997.

———. 1997a. "The Future of Revolutions at the *Fin-de-Siècle*." *Third World Quarterly* 18:791–820. Despite recent failures, claims the author, revolutions are here to stay.

———. 1997b. "The Comparative-Historical Sociology of Third World Social Revolutions: Why a Few Succeed, Why Most Fail." Pp. 227–67 in *Theorizing Revolutions*, edited by John Foran. London: Routledge. A sweeping attempt to explain Third World revolutions in terms of five causal factors.

Foran, John and Jeff Goodwin. 1993. "Revolutionary Outcomes in Iran and Nicaragua: Coalition Fragmentation, War, and the Limits of Social Transformation." *Theory and Society* 22:209–47. Why revolutions turn out as they do.

Foucault, Michel. 1990. *The History of Sexuality, Vol. 1: An Introduction.* New York: Vintage. Includes some interesting yet problematic ruminations on power.

Friedland, Roger and Robert R. Alford. 1991. "Bringing Society Back In: Symbols, Practices, and Institutional Contradictions." Pp. 232–63 in *The New Institutionalism in Organizational Analysis,* edited by Walter W. Powell and Paul J. DiMaggio. Chicago: University of Chicago Press. Includes some hit-and-miss strikes at the statist tradition.

Furedi, Frank. 1989. "Britain's Colonial Emergencies and the Invisible Nationalists." *Journal of Historical Sociology* 2:240–64. Analyzes the British response to radical nationalism in Kenya, Malaya, and British Guiana (Guyana); emphasizes British manipulation of communalism and the transfer of power to collaborationists.

  1993. "Creating a Breathing Space: The Political Management of Colonial Emergencies." *Journal of Imperial and Commonwealth History* 21:89–106. Suggests that the British government declared "emergencies" in its colonies in order to create a "breathing space" in which to deal with radical nationalists.

Gamson, William A. 1975. *The Strategy of Social Protest.* Homewood, IL: Dorsey. Violence works in democracies more often than one might think.

Giddens, Anthony. 1987. *The Nation-State and Violence.* Berkeley, CA, and Los Angeles: University of California Press. Part of the author's critique of Marxism.

Giugni, Marco, Doug McAdam, and Charles Tilly, eds. 1999. *How Social Movements Matter.* Minneapolis, MN: University of Minnesota Press. Essays on the consequences of movements, intended and unintended.

Goffman, Erving. 1974. *Frame Analysis: An Essay on the Organization of Experience.* New York: Harper and Row. An influential if seldom read book.

Goldfield, Michael. 1989. "Worker Insurgency, Radical Organization, and New Deal Labor Legislation." *American Political Science Review* 83:1257–82. The class struggle wins concessions.

Goldstone, Jack A. 1980. "Theories of Revolution: The Third Generation." *World Politics* 32:425–53. A helpful review essay; see also Foran's (1993) update.

  1986. "Revolutions and Superpowers." Pp. 38–48 in *Superpowers and Revolution,* edited by Jonathan R. Adelman. New York: Praeger. An excellent discussion of the weaknesses of neopatrimonial states, although see Snyder (1992) for a more differentiated view.

  1991. *Revolution and Rebellion in the Early Modern World.* Berkeley, CA, and Los Angeles: University of California Press. A sweeping study that develops a "demographic/structural" explanation of state breakdowns.

Goldstone, Jack A., Ted Robert Gurr, and Farrokh Moshiri, eds. 1991. *Revolutions of the Late Twentieth Century.* Boulder, CO: Westview Press. Includes a number of excellent case studies.

I. Theory, Methodology, and General Studies

Goodwin, Jeff. 1994a. "Old Regimes and Revolutions in the Second and Third Worlds: A Comparative Perspective." *Social Science History* 18:575–604. An earlier version of chapter 8 in this volume.

　　1994b. "Toward a New Sociology of Revolutions." *Theory and Society* 23:731–66. Reflections on the state of the art.

Goodwin, Jeff and James M. Jasper. 1999. "Caught in a Winding, Snarling Vine: The Structural Bias of Political Process Theory." *Sociological Forum* 14:27–54. Discusses some of the conceptual problems with the political process approach to "contentious politics" and especially with the privileged concept of "political opportunities."

Goodwin, Jeff and Theda Skocpol. 1989. "Explaining Revolutions in the Contemporary Third World." *Politics and Society* 17:489–507. A broad overview from a (mainly) state-centered perspective.

Gould, Roger V. 1995. *Insurgent Identities: Class, Community, and Protest in Paris from 1848 to the Commune.* Chicago: University of Chicago Press. How identities emerge from social ties. And vice versa?

Gurr, Ted Robert. 1970. *Why Men Rebel.* Princeton, NJ: Princeton University Press. Works outward from anger, grievances, and deprivation.

　　1986. "Persisting Patterns of Repression and Rebellion: Foundations for a General Theory of Political Coercion." Pp. 149–68 in *Persistent Patterns and Emergent Structures in a Waning Century*, edited by M. Karns. New York: Praeger. Why rebellions persist.

Gusfield, Joseph R. 1967. "Tradition and Modernity: Misplaced Polarities in the Study of Social Change." *American Journal of Sociology* 72:351–62. An early critique of modernization theory.

Hagopian, Mark N. 1974. *The Phenomenon of Revolution.* New York: Dodd, Mead. Nicely synthesizes an earlier generation of work; now quite dated.

Hall, John A. 1987. *Liberalism: Politics, Ideology and the Market.* Chapel Hill, NC: University of North Carolina Press. Contains some analytic gems.

Halliday, Fred. 1986. *The Making of the Second Cold War.* Second edition. London: Verso. Includes an informative chapter on revolutionary upheavals of the 1970s.

　　1991. "Revolution in the Third World: 1945 and After." Pp. 129–52 in *Revolution and Counter-Revolution*, edited by E. E. Rice. Oxford, UK: Basil Blackwell. An interesting descriptive survey, but one that fails to explain how radicals came to lead certain national liberation movements but not others, and why some of these movements were rather more successful than others.

Herb, Michael. 1999. *All in the Family: Absolutism, Revolution, and Democracy in the Middle Eastern Monarchies.* Albany, NY: State University of New York Press. An interesting discussion of "dynastic monarchism" as a form of stable, corporate rule.

Herman, Edward S. and Frank Brodhead. 1984. *Demonstration Elections: U.S.-Staged Elections in the Dominican Republic, Vietnam and El Salvador.* Boston: South End Press. Staged elections as camouflage for counterinsurgency.

Hobsbawm, E. J. 1962. *The Age of Revolution, 1789–1848*. New York: New American Library. A well-known Marxist looks (mainly) at Europe.

Holland, R. F. 1985. *European Decolonization, 1918–1981: An Introductory Survey*. New York: St. Martin's Press. One of the best such surveys.

Huntington, Samuel P. 1968. *Political Order in Changing Societies*. New Haven, CT, and London: Yale University Press. Argues that revolutions happen when political institutions do not accommodate the popular mobilization entailed by modernization. A tad overgeneralized, but on the right track.

———. 1991. *The Third Wave: Democratization in the Late Twentieth Century*. Norman, OK, and London: University of Oklahoma Press. Democracy, like social movements and revolutions, comes in cycles.

Iatrides, John O. 1993. "The Doomed Revolution: Communist Insurgency in Postwar Greece." In *Stopping the Killing: How Civil Wars End*, edited by Roy Licklider. New York and London: New York University Press. Insights on a failed revolution.

Jasper, James M. 1990. *Nuclear Politics: Energy and the State in the United States, Sweden, and France*. Princeton, NJ: Princeton University Press. Weds cultural and state-centered analysis.

———. 1997. *The Art of Moral Protest: Culture, Biography, and Creativity in Social Movements*. Chicago: University of Chicago Press. The best recent treatment of social movements.

Johnson, Chalmers. 1982. *Revolutionary Change*. Second edition. Stanford, CA: Stanford University Press. The classic statement on revolutions from a structural-functionalist perspective.

Katz, Mark N. 1997. *Revolutions and Revolutionary Waves*. New York: St. Martin's Press. Applies the concept of "revolutionary wave" to Marxist-Leninist, Arab nationalist, and Islamic fundamentalist revolutions.

Katznelson, Ira and Aristide R. Zolberg, eds. 1986. *Working-Class Formation: Nineteenth-Century Patterns in Western Europe and the United States*. Princeton, NJ: Princeton University Press. Attempts to bury teleological forms of Marxism, among other bugaboos.

Keddie, Nikki R. 1992. "Can Revolutions Be Predicted; Can Their Causes Be Understood?" *Contention: Debates in Society, Culture, and Science* 1 (2):159–82. Answers: no; yes.

Kennedy, Paul. 1987. *The Rise and Fall of the Great Powers: Economic Change and Military Conflict from 1500 to 2000*. New York: Random House. An influential study of the dangers of imperial overextension.

Kiernan, Victor. 1995 (1969). *The Lords of Human Kind: European Attitudes to Other Cultures in the Imperial Age*. London: Serif. An expansive survey.

Kimmel, Michael S. 1990. *Revolution: A Sociological Interpretation*. Philadelphia: Temple University Press. The best recent book-length overview of theories of revolution.

Kirkpatrick, Jeane. 1986 (1979). "Dictatorships and Double Standards." Pp. 14–35 in *El Salvador: Central America in the New Cold War*, edited by Marvin E. Gettleman, Patrick Lacefield, Louis Menashe, and David Mermelstein. Revised edition. New York: Grove Press. (Originally published in *Commen-*

tary [Nov. 1979] 68:34–45.) Why the U.S. should support friendly dictators. Foolish and wrong.

Kitschelt, Herbert. 1986. "Political Opportunity Structures and Political Protest: Anti-Nuclear Movements in Four Democracies." *British Journal of Political Science* 16:57–85. A seminal discussion of the importance of political opportunity structures.

Kolko, Gabriel. 1988. *Confronting the Third World: United States Foreign Policy, 1945–1980.* New York: Pantheon. A sweeping radical analysis; much better on Southeast Asia than Central America.

———. 1990 (1968). *The Politics of War: The World and United States Foreign Policy, 1943–1945.* New York: Pantheon. A detailed, revisionist examination of the final years of World War II.

Kramnick, Isaac. 1972. "Reflections on Revolution: Definition and Explanation in Recent Scholarship." *History and Theory* 11:26–63. Some interesting reflections indeed, although they are now rather dated.

Kriger, Norma J. 1992. *Zimbabwe's Guerrilla War: Peasant Voices.* Cambridge, UK: Cambridge University Press. A provocative study of the role of peasants in Zimbabwe's guerrilla insurgency. The author's account, however, is rather contradictory, emphasizing both guerrilla coercion of peasants and peasant manipulation of guerrillas.

Lanzona, Maria Vina A. 1993. "A Bibliography on Third World Revolutions." Working Paper No. 157, Center for Studies of Social Change, New School for Social Research. Includes sections on theory and comparative studies, Africa, Latin America, the Middle East, and Southeast Asia.

Lenin, V. I. 1943 (1917). *State and Revolution.* New York: International Publishers. Lenin's view of the state is highly questionable, but his understanding of its centrality to revolutions most certainly is not.

———. 1974 (1917). "One of the Fundamental Questions of the Revolution." Pp. 370–7 in V. I. Lenin, *Collected Works*, Vol. 25. Fourth English edition. Moscow: Progress Publishers. The question concerns state power.

———. 1997 (1917). *Will the Bolsheviks Maintain Power?* Gloucestershire, UK: Sutton Pubishing. Answer: yes. More interesting reflections on revolution and the state.

Levi, Margaret. 1988. *On Rule and Revenue.* Berkeley, CA, and Los Angeles: University of California Press. A rational-choice approach.

Lieberman, Robert C. 1995. "Social Construction (Continued)." *American Political Science Review* 89:437–41. Develops the concept of the "political construction" of group identities, akin to my notion of state constructionism.

Lieberson, Stanley. 1991. "Small N's and Big Conclusions: An Examination of the Reasoning in Comparative Studies Based on a Small Number of Cases." *Social Forces* 70:307–20. Emphasizes the pitfalls of John Stuart Mill's methods of agreement and difference.

Linz, Juan J. 1975. "Totalitarian and Authoritarian Regimes." Pp. 175–411 in *Handbook of Political Science, Volume 3: Macropolitical Theory*, edited by Fred I. Greenstein and Nelson W. Polsby. Reading, MA: Addison-Wesley. A seminal, book-length discussion of the characteristics of various regime types; includes some interesting reflections on "sultanistic" regimes.

Linz, Juan J. and Alfred Stepan. 1996. *Problems of Democratic Transition and Consolidation: Southern Europe, South America, and Post-Communist Europe.* Baltimore: Johns Hopkins University Press. A magisterial comparative analysis of democratization that emphasizes the opportunities and constraints created by distinctive regime types.

Lipset, Seymour Martin. 1960. *Political Man: The Social Bases of Politics.* Garden City, NY: Doubleday. A classic of political sociology.

    1970. *Revolution and Counterrevolution: Change and Persistence in Social Structures.* Revised edition. Garden City, NY: Anchor. Emphasizes the role of values in accounting for differences in national states and societies.

    1983. "Radicalism or Reformism: The Sources of Working-Class Politics." *American Political Science Review* 77:1–18. Repression radicalizes.

Lipsky, William E. 1976. "Comparative Approaches to the Study of Revolution: A Historiographic Essay." *Review of Politics* 38:494–509. Still helpful, though dated.

Low, D. A. 1991. *Eclipse of Empire.* Cambridge, UK: Cambridge University Press. Focuses on British colonialism and its aftermath in South Asia and Africa, although there is also some discussion of Southeast Asia, including non-British colonies.

Löwy, Michael. 1981. *The Politics of Combined and Uneven Development: The Theory of Permanent Revolution.* London: Verso. A rather schematic application of Trotsky's theory to recent revolutions; for an interesting critique, see Callinicos (1982).

McAdam, Doug. 1982. *Political Process and the Development of Black Insurgency, 1930–1970.* Chicago: University of Chicago Press. An influential deployment of the political-process theory of social movements. See Goodwin and Jasper (1999) for a critique.

    1986. "Recruitment to High-Risk Activism: The Case of Freedom Summer." *American Journal of Sociology* 92:64–90. Beliefs are not enough; networks matter.

McAdam, Doug, Sidney Tarrow, and Charles Tilly. 1997. "Toward an Integrated Perspective on Social Movements and Revolutions." Pp. 142–73 in *Comparative Politics: Rationality, Culture, and Structure*, edited by Mark Irving Lichbach and Alan S. Zuckerman. Cambridge, UK: Cambridge University Press. The authors convincingly argue that social movements and revolutions belong on the same causal continuum, although their "integrated perspective" – which privileges "political opportunities" – is debatable (see Goodwin and Jasper 1999).

McCarthy, John D. 1997. "The Globalization of Social Movement Theory." Pp. 243–59 in *Transnational Social Movements and Global Politics: Solidarity Beyond the State*, edited by Jackie Smith, Charles Chatfield, and Ron Pagnucco. Syracuse, NY: Syracuse University Press. Moving beyond the assumption of monadic national states and societies.

I. Theory, Methodology, and General Studies

McCarthy, John D. and Mayer N. Zald. 1977. "Resource Mobilization and Social Movements: A Partial Theory." *American Journal of Sociology* 82:1212–41. An influential statement of the resource-mobilization perspective on social movements.

McClintock, Michael. 1992. *Instruments of Statecraft: U.S. Guerrilla Warfare, Counterinsurgency, and Counterterrorism, 1940–1990*. New York: Pantheon. Extremely well researched; perhaps the best book on the subject. Includes discussions of counterinsurgency in the Philippines, Vietnam, and Central America.

McDaniel, Tim. 1991. *Autocracy, Modernization, and Revolution in Russia and Iran*. Princeton, NJ: Princeton University Press. Emphasizes the perils of "autocratic modernization"; a conceptually rich and well-researched study.

Mack, Andrew. 1975. "Why Big Nations Lose Small Wars: The Politics of Asymmetric Conflict." *World Politics* 27:175–200. Argues that revolutionaries don't have to defeat foreign or colonial troops in order to win, but need merely persist.

Mahoney, James. 1999. "Nominal, Ordinal, and Narrative Appraisal in Macrocausal Analysis." *American Journal of Sociology* 104:1154–96. Nicely analyzes the strengths and weaknesses of three strategies of causal inference.

Mann, Michael. 1984. "The Autonomous Power of the State: Its Origins, Mechanisms and Results." *Archives Européennes de Sociologie* 25:185–213. Develops the concept of the state's "infrastructural power," among other important ideas.

　1988. *State, War and Capitalism*. Oxford, UK: Basil Blackwell. A collection of important essays, including the preceding article.

　1993. *The Sources of Social Power, Vol. 2: The Rise of Classes and Nation-States, 1760–1914*. Cambridge, UK: Cambridge University Press. A sweeping analytic history.

　1995. "Sources of Variation in Working-Class Movements in Twentieth-Century Europe." *New Left Review* 212:14–54. One hugely important source is the nature of the state.

Mao Zedong. 1971 (1927). "Report on an Investigation of the Peasant Movement in Hunan." Pp. 23–39 in *Selected Readings from the Works of Mao Tse-Tung*. Peking: Foreign Languages Press. Includes some interesting reflections on the nature of revolutions.

March, James G. and Johan P. Olsen. 1984. "The New Institutionalism: Organizational Factors in Political Life." *American Political Science Review* 78:734–49. Provocative and justly influential; how organizations matter for politics.

　1989. *Rediscovering Institutions: The Organizational Basis of Politics*. New York: Free Press. A fuller elaboration of ideas in the preceding article.

Markoff, John. 1996. *Waves of Democracy: Social Movements and Political Change*. Thousand Oaks, CA: Pine Forge Press. Nicely expands on some of the themes in Huntington 1991.

Marx, Anthony W. 1992. *Lessons of Struggle: South African Internal Opposition, 1960–1990*. New York and Oxford, UK: Oxford University Press. Examines

317

the shifting ideology and strategy of the opponents of apartheid; includes interesting observations on the give and take between authoritarian states and their opponents.

1996. "Race-Making and the Nation-State." *World Politics* 48:180–208. An exemplary state-centered analysis of racial politics in South Africa, Brazil, and the United States.

Mason, T. David and Dale A. Krane. 1989. "The Political Economy of Death Squads: Toward a Theory of the Impact of State-Sanctioned Terror." *International Studies Quarterly* 33:175–98. Terror doesn't always work.

Migdal, Joel S. 1974. *Peasants, Politics, and Revolution: Pressures Toward Political and Social Change in the Third World*. Princeton, NJ: Princeton University Press. Emphasizes the important role that political organizations may play in peasant-based revolutions.

1988. *Strong Societies and Weak States: State-Society Relations and State Capabilities in the Third World*. Princeton, NJ: Princeton University Press. Important reflections on Third World states, although the title falsely conveys a zero-sum relationship.

Migdal, Joel S., Atul Kohli, and Vivienne Shue. 1994. "Introduction: Developing a State-in-Society Perspective." Pp. 1–4 in *State Power and Social Forces: Domination and Transformation in the Third World*, edited by Joel S. Migdal, Atul Kohli, and Vivienne Shue. Cambridge, UK: Cambridge University Press. Some states are embedded "in" societies more than others.

Mills, C. Wright. 1962. *The Marxists*. New York: Dell. Provocative reflections on the Marxist tradition; includes extensive excerpts from the classics.

Mitchell, Timothy. 1991. "The Limits of the State: Beyond Statist Approaches and Their Critics." *American Political Science Review* 85:77–96. Poststructuralist reflections on the state-society "boundary problem."

Moghadam, Valentine M. 1997. "Gender and Revolutions." Pp. 137–67 in *Theorizing Revolutions*, edited by John Foran. London: Routledge. Provocative reflections, although the author doubts that gender has played an important role in causing revolutions.

Moore, Barrington, Jr. 1966. *Social Origins of Dictatorship and Democracy: Lord and Peasant in the Making of the Modern World*. Boston: Beacon Press. A magisterial and enormously influential work of historical sociology; virtually all subsequent major comparative studies of revolutions are deeply indebted to it.

1978. *Injustice: The Social Bases of Obedience and Revolt*. White Plains, NY: M.E. Sharpe. Includes an extensive discussion of the failed revolution in Germany following World War I.

Mouzelis, Nicos. 1986. *The Politics of the Semi-Periphery*. London: Macmillan. An interesting effort to compare Greece with Latin America's Southern Cone.

Muller, Edward N. 1985. "Income Inequality, Regime Repressiveness, and Political Violence." *American Sociological Review* 50:47–61. Argues that political violence is positively correlated with income inequality and has a curvilinear (i.e., inverted "U") relation to regime repressiveness.

Muller, Edward N. and Mitchell A. Seligson. 1987. "Inequality and Insurgency." *American Political Science Review* 81:425–51. Argues that (in a context of a repressive regime and economic development) income inequality has a greater effect on insurgency than land maldistribution.

Newton, Vern W. 1983. "Great Expectations: The Real Cause of Revolution." *Washington Monthly* (October), pp. 33–8. Well, not *really*.

Olson, Mancur. 1965. *The Logic of Collective Action*. Cambridge, MA: Harvard University Press. Explores the "problems" (e.g., "free riding") that ensue if one begins from some simple (and simple-minded) assumptions about human behavior.

Paige, Jeffery M. 1975. *Agrarian Revolution: Social Movements and Export Agriculture in the Underdeveloped World*. New York: Free Press. An influential class-analytic explanation of various types of rural protest movements, including nationalist and socialist variants. For an important critique, see Somers and Goldfrank (1979).

1983. "Social Theory and Peasant Revolution in Vietnam and Guatemala." *Theory and Society* 12:699–737. Extends Paige's theory into Central America. (Paige 1975 includes an extensive – and, in my view, problematic – discussion of Vietnam.)

1999. "Conjuncture, Comparison, and Conditional Theory in Macrosocial Inquiry." *American Journal of Sociology* 105:781–800. Persuasively advocates "historically conditional generalization" as opposed to universalizing theories.

Petras, James. 1978a. "Toward a Theory of Twentieth Century Socialist Revolutions." Pp. 271–314 in *Critical Perspectives on Imperialism and Social Class in the Third World*. New York: Monthly Review Press. The author links socialist revolutions, rather mechanically in my view, to the imperialist expansion of capitalism.

1978b. "Socialist Revolutions and their Class Components." *New Left Review* 111:37–64. A Marxist analysis.

Piven, Frances Fox and Richard A. Cloward. 1977. *Poor People's Movements: Why They Succeed, How They Fail*. New York: Vintage. A touchstone in the literature; much maligned for its denigration of mass-membership organizations.

Porter, Andrew. 1994. *European Imperialism, 1860–1914*. London: Macmillan. A helpful short introduction to the historiographic debates on the subject; includes an extensive bibliography.

Portes, Alejandro. 1976. "On the Sociology of National Development: Theories and Issues." *American Journal of Sociology* 82:55–85. A very helpful overview, though now somewhat dated.

Putnam, Robert D. 1993. *Making Democracy Work: Civic Traditions in Modern Italy*. Princeton, NJ: Princeton University Press. Civil society makes democracy work.

Ragin, Charles C. 1987. *The Comparative Method: Moving Beyond Qualitative and Quantitative Strategies*. Berkeley, CA, and Los Angeles: University of California Press. The most influential recent statement on the subject; Ragin shows how Boolean algebra can be used to sort out the "multiple conjunctural causation" of various social phenomena, including revolutions. See, e.g., Wickham-Crowley 1992.

Rex, John. 1982. "Racism and the Structure of Colonial Societies." Pp. 199–218 in *Racism and Colonialism*, edited by Robert Ross. The Hague: Martinus Nijhoff. Emphasizes the variable importance of racism for imperial domination.

Robinson, Ronald. 1972. "Non-European Foundations of European Imperialism: Sketch for a Theory of Collaboration." Pp. 117–42 in *Studies in the Theory of Imperialism*, edited by Roger Owen and Bob Sutcliffe. London: Longman. The most influential essay on the topic.

Rostow, W. W. 1967 (1961). "Guerrilla Warfare in Underdeveloped Areas." Pp. 108–16 in *The Viet-Nam Reader*, edited by Marcus G. Raskin and Bernard B. Fall. Revised edition. New York: Random House. Communists as "scavengers of the modernization process" (p. 110).

Rule, James B. 1988. *Theories of Civil Violence*. Berkeley, CA, and Los Angeles: University of California Press. An even-handed overview of some influential theoretical perspectives, not including the statist tradition.

Sandbrook, Richard. 1985. *The Politics of Africa's Economic Stagnation*. Cambridge, UK: Cambridge University Press. Includes interesting reflections on neopatrimonial or sultanistic dictatorships.

Scott, James. 1990. *Domination and the Arts of Resistance: Hidden Transcripts*. New Haven, CT: Yale University Press. Resistance when public protest isn't possible.

Seidman, Gay W. 1994. *Manufacturing Militance: Workers' Movements in Brazil and South Africa, 1970–1985*. Berkeley, CA, and Los Angeles: University of California Press. This detailed analysis argues that militant working-class movements developed in the crucible of "savage capitalism," i.e., dependent authoritarian industrialization.

Selbin, Eric. 1997a. "Revolution in the Real World: Bringing Agency Back In." Pp. 123–36 in *Theorizing Revolutions*, edited by John Foran. London: Routledge. People make their own history.

Sellers, Robert C., ed. 1971. *Armed Forces of the World: A Reference Handbook*. Third edition. New York: Praeger. Some powerful and interesting crossnational statistics.

Selznick, Phillip. 1979 (1952). *The Organizational Weapon: A Study of Bolshevik Strategy and Tactics*. New York: Arno Press. How Communists organize themselves and (sometimes) classes.

Sewell, William H., Jr. 1985. "Ideologies and Social Revolutions: Reflections on the French Case." *Journal of Modern History* 57:57–85. A culturalist critique of Skocpol's interpretation of the French Revolution; see Skocpol's important rejoinder (1985).

Shafer, D. Michael. 1988. *Deadly Paradigms: The Failure of U.S. Counterinsurgency Policy*. Princeton, NJ: Princeton University Press. A provocative critique of counterinsurgency doctrine; however, the case study of the Philippines (the author also discusses Greece and Vietnam) vastly understates the U.S. role in the defeat of the Huk rebellion.

Sharabi, Hisham B. 1966. *Nationalism and Revolution in the Arab World*. Princeton, NJ: Van Nostrand. Suggests that different types of European domination strongly shaped the nature of independence movements and postcolonial regimes.

Skocpol, Theda. 1979. *States and Social Revolutions: A Comparative Analysis of France, Russia, and China*. Cambridge, UK: Cambridge University Press. Still far and away the most influential contribution to the sociology of revolutions since its publication – and rightly so. Skocpol's many critics include Sewell (1985), Taylor (1988), Burawoy (1989), and Cammack (1989).

1982. "What Makes Peasants Revolutionary?" *Comparative Politics* 14:351–75. An important review of the work of Migdal, Paige, Scott, and Wolf.

1984. "Emerging Agendas and Recurrent Strategies in Historical Sociology." Pp. 356–91 in *Vision and Method in Historical Sociology*, edited by Theda Skocpol. Cambridge, UK: Cambridge University Press. Interesting reflections on comparative analysis. See also Skocpol and Somers 1980.

1985. "Cultural Idioms and Political Ideologies in the Revolutionary Reconstruction of State Power: A Rejoinder to Sewell." *Journal of Modern History* 57:86–96. In response to Sewell (1985), Skocpol bends in a more cultural direction, yet remains state-centered.

1992. *Protecting Soldiers and Mothers: The Political Origins of Social Policy in the United States*. Cambridge, MA: Harvard University Press. A detailed case for a "polity-centered" approach to social policy, as against "socially determinist" perspectives.

Skocpol, Theda and Kenneth Finegold. 1990. "Explaining New Deal Labor Policy." *American Political Science Review* 84:1297–304. Claims that Goldfield (1989) gets it all wrong.

Skocpol, Theda and Margaret Somers. 1980. "The Uses of Comparative History in Macrosocial Inquiry." *Comparative Studies in Society and History* 22:174–97. Evaluates three types of comparative analysis: the "contrast-oriented," "parallel," and "macro-analytic" approaches.

Smelser, Neil J. 1962. *Theory of Collective Behavior*. New York: Free Press. An often-cited, and much-maligned, study that views movements and revolutions as responses to social strains.

Smith, Anthony D. S. 1979. *Nationalism in the Twentieth Century*. New York: New York University Press. Includes a very interesting chapter on "Communist nationalisms."

Smith, Tony. 1981. *The Pattern of Imperialism: The United States, Great Britain, and the Late-Industrializing World Since 1815*. Cambridge, UK: Cambridge University Press. Includes an important comparative analysis of colonial nationalism.

Snow, David A. and Robert D. Benford. 1992. "Master Frames and Cycles of Protest." Pp. 133–55 in *Frontiers of Social Movement Theory*, edited by Aldon D. Morris and Carol McClurg Mueller. New Haven, CT: Yale University Press. An important statement by two leading theorists of "framing processes."

Snyder, Richard. 1992. "Explaining Transitions from Neopatrimonial Dictatorships." *Comparative Politics* 24:379–99. This and the following essay contain some very important reflections on cases of nonrevolutionary transitions from neopatrimonial or "sultanistic" dictatorships; they add some important nuances to a number of recent studies that claim that such dictatorships are particularly vulnerable to revolutionary movements.

1998. "Paths out of Sultanistic Regimes: Combining Structural and Voluntarist Perspectives." Pp. 49–81 in *Sultanistic Regimes*, edited by H. E. Chehabi and Juan J. Linz. Baltimore: Johns Hopkins University Press.

Sombart, Werner. 1976 (1906). *Why Is There No Socialism in the United States?* White Plains, NY: International Arts and Science Press. One answer: roast beef and apple pie. Counterfactual history at its best.

Somers, Margaret R. and Walter L. Goldfrank. 1979. "The Limits of Agronomic Determinism: A Critique of Paige's *Agrarian Revolution*." *Comparative Studies in Society and History* 21:443–58. An important critique of Paige (1975), focusing on the conflation of movement and revolution and the anomalous Angolan case.

Swidler, Ann. 1986. "Culture in Action: Symbols and Strategies." *American Sociological Review* 51:273–86. The author conceptualizes culture not as "values," but as a repertoire or "tool kit" of habits, skills, styles, and beliefs from which "strategies of action" are constructed.

Tarrow, Sidney. 1994. *Power in Movement: Social Movements, Collective Action and Politics*. Cambridge, UK: Cambridge University Press. The most influential recent work on the subject, emphasizing the importance of "political opportunities" for social movements. Cf. Goodwin and Jasper 1999.

Taylor, John G. 1979. *From Modernization to Modes of Production*. London: Macmillan. A useful primer on approaches to economic development.

Taylor, Michael. 1988. "Rationality and Revolutionary Collective Action." Pp. 63–97 in *Rationality and Revolution*, edited by Michael Taylor. Cambridge: Cambridge University Press. A rational-choice critique of Skocpol's (1979) account of peasant rebelliousness, albeit one that (like Skocpol herself) emphasizes the importance of peasant "community" (as opposed to selective material incentives) for collective action.

Taylor, Verta. 1989. "Social Movement Continuity: The Women's Movement in Abeyance." *American Sociological Review* 54:761–75. Develops the notion of "abeyance structures" to explain social-movement continuity.

Thelen, Kathleen and Sven Steinmo. 1992. "Historical Institutionalism in Comparative Politics." Pp. 1–32 in *Structuring Politics: Historical Institutionalism in Comparative Analysis*, edited by Sven Steinmo, Kathleen Thelen, and Frank Longstreth. Cambridge, UK: Cambridge University Press. A helpful overview of the institutionalist perspective.

Tilly, Charles. 1973. "Does Modernization Breed Revolution?" *Comparative Politics* 14:351–75. Not always and never directly.

1975. "Revolutions and Collective Violence." Pp. 483–555 in *Handbook of Political Science, Volume 3: Macropolitical Theory*, edited by Fred I. Greenstein and Nelson W. Polsby. Reading, MA: Addison-Wesley. A earlier, condensed version of Tilly 1978.

1978. *From Mobilization to Revolution*. Reading, MA: Addison-Wesley. The most complete theoretical statement of Tilly's influential political-contention perspective, including his conceptual models of revolutionary situations and outcomes.

1984. *Big Structures, Large Processes, Huge Comparisons.* New York: Russell Sage Foundation. Reflections on various types of comparative analysis.

1986. *The Contentious French: Four Centuries of Popular Struggle.* Cambridge, MA: Harvard University Press. Charts changes in popular repertoires of contention.

1992. *Coercion, Capital, and European States, AD 990–1992.* Revised edition. Cambridge, MA: Blackwell. A characteristically sweeping account of the European states system.

1993. *European Revolutions, 1492–1992.* Oxford, UK: Blackwell. Another sweeping analytic history, emphasizing how revolutions have changed as states have changed.

1995a. "Selected Readings on Political Change." Working Paper No. 192, Center for Studies of Social Change, New School for Social Research. This lengthy (115 page) annotated bibliography includes sections on collective action, political conflict, and revolution and rebellion.

1995b. "To Explain Political Processes." *American Journal of Sociology* 100:1594–610. A trenchant critique of general, invariant theories that feature self-contained and self-motivated units of analysis.

Tocqueville, Alexis de. 1955 (1856). *The Old Regime and the French Revolution.* Garden City, NY: Doubleday. A fascinating yet insufficiently appreciated state-centered account of revolution.

1981. *Democracy in America.* New York: Modern Library. Explodes with insights.

Trimberger, Ellen Kay. 1978. *Revolution from Above: Military Bureaucrats and Development in Japan, Turkey, Egypt, and Peru.* New Brunswick, NJ: Transaction Books. The most important work on revolutions from above.

Triska, Jan F., ed. 1986. *Dominant Powers and Subordinate States: The United States in Latin America and the Soviet Union in Eastern Europe.* Durham, NC: Duke University Press. Interesting papers comparing two empires.

Trotsky, Leon. 1961 (1932). *The History of the Russian Revolution.* New York: Monad Press. One of the most interesting, and perhaps the most successful, applications of Marxist theory to a case of revolution.

U.S. Arms Control and Disarmament Agency. 1984. *World Military Expenditures and Arms Transfers, 1972–1982.* Washington, DC: U.S. Arms Control and Disarmament Agency. Important crossnational statistics.

Valenzuela, J. Samuel and Arturo Valenzuela. 1978. "Modernization and Dependency: Alternative Perspectives in the Study of Latin American Underdevelopment." *Comparative Politics* 10:535–57. A devastating critique of modernization theory.

Wallerstein, Immanuel. 1979. *The Capitalist World-Economy.* Cambridge, UK: Cambridge University Press. A collection of Wallerstein's seminal essays on the capitalist "world system."

Walt, Stephen M. 1996. *Revolution and War.* Ithaca, NY: Cornell University Press. Interesting reflections on the tendency of revolutions to induce international conflict.

Walton, John. 1984. *Reluctant Rebels: Comparative Studies of Revolutions and Under-development*. New York: Columbia University Press. A provocative study of the Huk rebellion in the Philippines, *la Violencia* in Colombia, and the so-called Mau Mau revolt in Kenya.

Walton, John and Charles Ragin. 1990. "Global and National Sources of Political Protest: Third World Responses to the Debt Crisis." *American Sociological Review* 55:876–90. An important account of "IMF riots."

Weiss, Linda. 1997. "Globalization and the Myth of the Powerless State." *New Left Review* 225:3–27. See also Evans 1997.

Welch, Claude E., Jr. 1980. *Anatomy of Rebellion*. Albany, NY: State University of New York. A carefully crafted, astute, and yet surprisingly neglected comparative study of several near-revolutions in Asia and Africa.

White, Gordon, Robin Murray, and Christine White, eds. 1983. *Revolutionary Socialist Development in the Third World*. Lexington, KY: University of Kentucky Press. Explores socialism as an alternative path to development in the Third World.

Whittier, Nancy. 1995. *Feminist Generations: The Persistence of the Radical Women's Movement*. Philadelphia: Temple University Press. An interesting case study of how social movements persist.

Wittner, Lawrence S. 1982. *American Intervention in Greece, 1943–1949*. New York: Columbia University Press. A critical study of the U.S. role in the Greek counterinsurgency.

Wolf, Eric R. 1969. *Peasant Wars of the Twentieth Century*. New York: Harper. Includes six excellent case studies; emphasizes the role of "middle" and "free" (or "peripheral") peasants in revolutions.

Wood, Elisabeth Jean. 2000a. *Forging Democracy from Below: Insurgent Transitions in South Africa and El Salvador*. Cambridge, UK: Cambridge University Press. A brilliant comparative analysis of insurgency and democratization.

World Bank. 1980. *World Development Report, 1980*. New York: Oxford University Press. This and the following two volumes are loaded with important statistical data.

1991. *World Development Report 1991: The Challenge of Development*. New York: Oxford University Press.

1997. *World Development Report 1997: The State in a Changing World*. New York: Oxford University Press. Reports of the death of the state may be premature.

Wuthnow, Robert. 1985. "State Structures and Ideological Outcomes." *American Sociological Review* 50:799–821. How the former shapes the latter; fascinating.

Young, Crawford. 1994. *The African Colonial State in Comparative Perspective*. New Haven, CT: Yale University Press. Includes some interesting reflections on the peculiar nature of the colonial state.

Zimmermann, Ekkart. 1983. *Political Violence, Crises, and Revolutions: Theories and Research*. Cambridge, MA: Schenkman. A very useful review of the literatures on political violence, military coups, and revolutions, plus a little of the author's own model building; includes a very extensive bibliography.

Zunes, Stephen. 1994. "Unarmed Insurrections Against Authoritarian Governments in the Third World: A New Kind of Revolution." *Third World Quarterly* 15:403–26. An overview of what the author views as an important historical trend since the late 1970s; most of the insurrections examined are relatively moderate prodemocracy movements.

II. Southeast Asia

A. General Studies (Including Asia Generally)

Bagley, John. 1974. "Burmese Communist Schisms." Pp. 151–68 in *Peasant Rebellion and Communist Revolution in Asia*, edited by John Wilson Lewis. Stanford, CA: Stanford University Press. An important study of the Burmese Communist movement.

Bastin, John and Harry J. Benda. 1968. *A History of Modern Southeast Asia: Colonialism, Nationalism, and Decolonization*. Englewood Cliffs, NJ: Prentice Hall. A solid overview by two area specialists.

Benda, Harry J. 1956. "Communism in Southeast Asia." *The Yale Review* 45:417–29. Provocative reflections by one of the deans of Southeast Asian studies.

    1965. "Political Elites in Colonial Southeast Asia: An Historical Analysis." *Comparative Studies in Society and History* 7:233–51. An important comparative analysis.

    1966. "Reflections on Asian Communism." *The Yale Review* 56:1–16. Develops the ideas in Benda 1956.

    1967. "The Japanese Interregnum in Southeast Asia." Pp. 65–79 in *Imperial Japan and Asia: A Reassessment*, edited by Grant K. Goodman. New York: East Asian Institute, Columbia University. Reprinted, in a slightly revised form, in Bastin and Benda (1968).

Caldwell, Malcolm. 1970. "Subversion or Social Revolution in South-East Asia?" Pp. 74–106 in *Nationalism, Revolution, and Evolution in South-East Asia*, edited by Michael Leifer. Centre for South-East Asian Studies, University of Hull. London: Inter-Documentation Co. Provocative analysis by a radical scholar.

Chen, King C. 1975. "Some Comparisons Between the Chinese and Vietnamese Revolutions." *Asian Profile* 3:227–41. Emphasizes the importance of nationalism and the weakness of non-Communist nationalists.

Christie, Clive J. 1998. *Southeast Asia in the Twentieth Century: A Reader*. London: I.B. Tauris. The title is somewhat misleading, as this helpful book includes both a selection of important writings by others and extensive introductory material by the author-editor. Much of the book focuses on the reaction to colonialism.

Crozier, Brian. 1968. *South-East Asia in Turmoil*. Revised edition. Baltimore: Penguin Books. A short overview of the postwar period.

Dixon, Chris. 1991. *South East Asia in the World-Economy*. Cambridge, UK: Cambridge University Press. A survey of the region's place in the world economy, from the precolonial period to the present.

Dower, John W. 1986. *War Without Mercy: Race and Power in the Pacific War*. New York: Pantheon Books. Includes a fascinating chapter on Japanese policy-makers' self-understanding of the "Greater East Asia Co-Prosperity Sphere."

Elsbree, Willard H. 1953. *Japan's Role in Southeast Asian Nationalist Movements, 1940–1945*. Cambridge, MA: Harvard University Press. An early study of an important subject; focuses largely on Indonesia.

Emerson, Donald K. 1980. "Issues in Southeast Asian History: Room for Interpretation." *Journal of Asian Studies* 40:43–68. Charts the growing emphasis on regional diversity, change, and dependency.

Emerson, Rupert. 1937. *Malaysia: A Study in Direct and Indirect Rule*. New York: Macmillan. A classic study of British Malaya and the Dutch East Indies.

Fay, Peter Ward. 1993. *The Forgotten Army: India's Armed Struggle for Independence, 1942–1945*. Ann Arbor, MI: University of Michigan Press. The most comprehensive account of the Japanese-sponsored Indian National Army.

Friend, Theodore. 1988. *The Blue-Eyed Enemy: Japan Against the West in Java and Luzon, 1942–1945*. Princeton, NJ: Princeton University Press. An excellent comparative analysis of Indonesia and the Philippines from late colonialism to independence; includes critical commentary on Anderson's (1972) influential interpretation of the Indonesian revolution.

Furnivall, J. S. 1948. *Colonial Policy and Practice: A Comparative Study of Burma and Netherlands India*. New York: New York University Press. A seminal comparative analysis of colonialism.

Ghosh, Amitav. 1997. "India's Untold War of Independence." *The New Yorker* (June 23–30), pp. 104–21. An interesting account of the Indian National Army. See also Fay 1993.

Goodall, B. B. 1966. *Revolutionary Warfare in South East Asia*. Johannesburg: University of the Witwatersrand. Includes a short analytic section on the causes of the success and failure of revolutionary movements.

Goodwin, Jeff. 1989. "Colonialism and Revolution in Southeast Asia." Pp. 59–78 in *Revolution in the World-System*, edited by Terry Boswell. New York: Greenwood Press. An earlier, telescoped version of the argument that I develop in Part 2 of this book.

Hanna, Willard A. 1964. *Eight Nation Makers: Southeast Asia's Charismatic Statesmen*. New York: St. Martin's Press. Includes short biographical studies of Sukarno and Tunku Abdul Rahman, among others. To call Hanna's prose purplish would be an understatement.

Ienaga, Saburō. 1978 (1968). *The Pacific War, 1931–1945: A Critical Perspective on Japan's Role in World War II*. New York: Pantheon. A passionately antimilitarist analysis.

Isaacs, Harold R. 1967 (1947). *No Peace for Asia*. Cambridge, MA: MIT Press. Fascinating eyewitness accounts and reflections by a respected Asianist.

Jackson, Karl D. 1985. "Post-Colonial Rebellion and Counter-Insurgency in Southeast Asia." Pp. 3–52 in *Governments and Rebellions in Southeast Asia*, edited by Chandran Jeshurun. Singapore: Institute of Southeast Asian Studies. A rather mechanical and ahistorical examination of how economic growth, economic reforms, religion, ethnicity, etc., influence rebellion.

II. Southeast Asia

Kahin, George McT. 1977. "The United States and the Anticolonial Revolutions in Southeast Asia, 1945–1950." Pp. 338–61 in *The Origins of the Cold War in Asia*, edited by Yonosuke Nagai and Akira Iriye. Tokyo: University of Tokyo Press; New York: Columbia University Press. A superb analysis of U.S. policy toward Indonesia and Vietnam, emphasizing the effects of Eurocentrism and anti-Communism.

Lebra, Joyce C. 1977. *Japanese-Trained Armies in Southeast Asia: Independence and Volunteer Forces in World War II*. New York: Columbia University Press. Emphasizes the impact of Japanese doctrines on nationalist military leaders; includes an informative chapter on the Peta in Indonesia.

McCoy, Alfred W., ed. 1980. *Southeast Asia Under Japanese Occupation*. New Haven, CT: Yale University Southeast Asia Studies. Essays on the local effects of the Japanese "interregnum."

McLane, Charles B. 1966. *Soviet Strategies in Southeast Asia*. Princeton, NJ: Princeton University Press. An exceptional study; includes useful chronologies and biographical information.

McVey, Ruth T. 1958. *The Calcutta Conference and the Southeast Asian Uprising*. Ithaca, NY: Southeast Asia Program, Department of Far Eastern Studies, Cornell University. A leading export on Indonesia questions whether the February 1948 conference issued a directive for revolution in the region.

———. 1964. "The Southeast Asian Insurrectionary Movements." Pp. 145–84 in *Communism and Revolution: The Strategic Uses of Political Violence*, edited by Cyril E. Black and Thomas P. Thornton. Princeton, NJ: Princeton University Press. A short but solid comparative treatment of the postwar revolts in Malaya, the Philippines, Indonesia, and Burma; emphasizes the poor timing of the revolts.

Osborne, Milton. 1970. *Region of Revolt: Focus on Southeast Asia*. Harmondsworth, UK: Penguin Books. A good short study of the postwar insurgencies.

———. 1983. *Southeast Asia: An Introductory History*. Sydney: George Allen and Unwin. The best short introduction to the region.

Pluvier, Jan. 1974. *South-East Asia from Colonialism to Independence*. Kuala Lumpur: Oxford University Press. An ambitious and largely successful comparative study; extraordinarily informative, although somewhat undertheorized.

Purcell, Victor. 1965. *The Chinese in Southeast Asia*. Oxford, UK: Oxford University Press. The best overview of the subject, by a British scholar–civil servant intimately familiar with Malayan affairs.

Rigg, Jonathan. 1991. *Southeast Asia: A Region in Transition*. London: Unwin Hyman. One of the better regional histories.

Rotter, Andrew J. 1987. *The Path to Vietnam: Origins of the American Commitment to Southeast Asia*. Ithaca, NY, and London: Cornell University Press. The economic recovery of Japan and Europe is the key, not wild-eyed Cold War ideology.

Scott, James C. 1972. "The Erosion of Patron-Client Bonds and Social Change in Rural Southeast Asia." *Journal of Asian Studies* 32:5–37. The erosion is necessary for and indeed fosters change.

1976. *The Moral Economy of the Peasant: Rebellion and Subsistence in Southeast Asia*. New Haven, CT: Yale University Press. This influential study includes an interesting discussion of the rebellion of 1930–1 in Vietnam, although the role of the Communist Party is slighted.

Smith, Martin. 1991. *Burma: Insurgency and the Politics of Ethnicity*. London: Zed Books. A massive study of the country's Communist and ethnic rebellions; the best book on the subject.

Smith, R. B. 1988. "China and Southeast Asia: The Revolutionary Perspective, 1951." *Journal of Southeast Asian Studies* 19:97–110. Examines developments in Vietnam, Malaya, and, to a lesser extent, the Philippines, in the wake of the Chinese Revolution.

Steinberg, David Joel, ed. 1987. *In Search of Southeast Asia: A Modern History*. Revised edition. Honolulu: University of Hawaii Press. Along with Pluvier's (1974) more focused work, this counts as the best general study of Southeast Asia.

Tarling, Nicholas. 1998. *Nations and States in Southeast Asia*. Cambridge: Cambridge University Press. A wide-ranging interpretive essay.

Thompson, Sir Robert. 1966. *Defeating Communist Insurgency: The Lessons of Malaya and Vietnam*. New York: Praeger. Reflections of a British expert on counterinsurgency. See Taylor 1998 (on Peru) for a more recent application of the author's ideas.

Thorne, Christopher. 1986. *The Far Eastern War: States and Societies 1941–45*. London: Unwin. The best overview of the complex international relations in East Asia during the war.

van der Kroef, Justus M. 1980. *Communism in South-East Asia*. Berkeley, CA, and Los Angeles: University of California Press. A useful comparative analysis.

Williams, Lea E. 1976. *Southeast Asia: A History*. New York: Oxford University Press. A short but solid historical overview.

Yoshihiko, Tanigawa. 1977. "The Cominform and Southeast Asia." Pp. 362–77 in *The Origins of the Cold War in Asia*, edited by Yonosuke Nagai and Akira Iriye. Tokyo: University of Tokyo Press; New York: Columbia University Press. Another look at the Calcutta Conference of February 1948 (see McVey [1958]).

Zagoria, Donald S. 1974. "Asian Tenancy Systems and Communist Mobilization of the Peasantry." Pp. 29–60 in *Peasant Rebellion and Communist Revolution in Asia*, edited by John Wilson Lewis. Stanford, CA: Stanford University Press. Argues that "family-size tenancy in conditions of heavy pressure on the land ... is particularly conducive to rural instability" (p. 29).

B. Vietnam

Buttinger, Joseph. 1967. *Vietnam: A Dragon Embattled*. 2 volumes. New York: Praeger. Still an important source; a treasure-trove of information.

1977. *Vietnam: The Unforgettable Tragedy*. New York: Horizon Press. Interesting reflections by a long-time observer of Vietnam, an anti-Stalinist social democrat who shamefully backed Diem.

Chen, King C. 1969. *Vietnam and China, 1938–54*. Princeton, NJ: Princeton University Press. The best book-length treatment of this important relationship.

Chesneaux, Jean. 1955. "Stages in the Development of the Vietnam National Movement 1862–1940." *Past and Present* 7:63–75. A good, short synopsis by a respected French scholar.

——— 1969. "The Historical Background of Vietnamese Communism." *Government and Opposition* 4:118–35. Emphasizes the internationalism of the party and its independence from Moscow.

Chovanes, Andrew B. 1986. "On Vietnamese and Other Peasants." *Journal of Southeast Asian Studies* 17:203–35. A critical examination of the work of Scott (1976) and Popkin (1979).

Clodfelter, Michael. 1995. *Vietnam in Military Statistics: A History of the Indochina Wars, 1772–1991*. Jefferson, NC: McFarland & Company. A helpful compendium of statistical information.

Dalloz, Jacques. 1987. *The War in Indo-China, 1945–1954*. Translated by Josephine Bacon. Dublin: Gill and Macmillan; Savage, MD: Barnes and Noble. One of the few good books on the First Indochina War; draws extensively, and exclusively, on French sources.

Duiker, William J. 1976. *The Rise of Nationalism in Vietnam, 1900–1941*. Ithaca, NY: Cornell University Press. An excellent political history by one of the leading scholars on Vietnam; examines the rise of Communism to a position of dominance within the nationalist movement.

——— 1981. *The Communist Road to Power in Vietnam*. Boulder, CO: Westview Press. One of the very best general studies of the subject.

——— 1983. *Vietnam: Nation in Revolution*. Boulder, CO: Westview Press. An excellent short introduction.

——— 1989. "Vietnamese Communism and the Strategy of the United Front." Pp. 173–201 and 335–9 (endnotes) in *Coalition Strategies of Marxist Parties*, edited by Trond Gilberg. Durham, NC: Duke University Press. An excellent overview of the Communists' changing approach to class alliances.

Dunn, Peter M. 1985. *The First Vietnam War*. New York: St. Martin's Press. One of the most extensive accounts of the subject.

Elliott, Mai. 1974. "Translator's Introduction." Pp. 1–30 in *Reminiscences on the Army for National Salvation*, Memoir of General Chu Van Tan. Data Paper No. 97, Southeast Asia Program. Ithaca, NY: Department of Asian Studies, Cornell University. Includes a discussion of the role of ethnic minorities in the Viet Minh.

Fall, Bernard B. 1958. "Post Mortems on Dien-Bien-Phu." *Far Eastern Survey* 27:155–8. A review of General Henri Navarre's *Agonie de l'Indochine* (Paris: Librairie Plon, 1956) and Joseph Laniel's *Le Drame Indochinois* (Paris: Librairie Plon, 1957). Fall sharply disputes Laniel's belief that the French war could have been continued after Dien Bien Phu.

——— 1967a. *Two Vietnams: A Political and Military Analysis*. New York: Praeger. Still informative.

1967b. *Street Without Joy*. Fourth edition. New York: Schocken Books. A political and military history, interspersed with Fall's personal adventures and reflections; focuses primarily on the First Indochina War.

ed. 1967c. *Ho Chi Minh on Revolution: Selected Writings, 1920–1966*. New York: Praeger. The best compilation of Ho's writings.

Fitzgerald, Frances. 1972. *Fire in the Lake: The Vietnamese and the Americans in Vietnam*. New York: Vintage Books. This popular, Pulitzer Prize–winning book, which is not highly regarded by all scholars of Vietnam, is strongly influenced by the work of Paul Mus (see Mus 1949 and McAlister and Mus 1970). For a trenchant critique, see Nguyen Khac Vien (1973).

Frederick, William H. 1973. "Alexandre Varenne and Politics in Indochina, 1925–1926." Pp. 96–159 in *Aspects of Vietnamese History*, edited by Walter F. Vella. Honolulu: Asian Studies at Hawaii, No. 8, University Press of Hawaii. Another episode of abortive reform.

Gardner, Lloyd C. 1988. *Approaching Vietnam: From World War II Through Dienbienphu*. New York: Norton. Well researched; traces the growing involvement of the United States.

Gates, John M. 1990. "People's War in Vietnam." *Journal of Military History* 54:325–44. Argues that the Communists never waged a "conventional war," even in the years running up to 1975; "from beginning to end it was a people's or revolutionary war in which both irregular and conventional forces played important roles" (p. 343).

Giap, Vo Nguyen. 1975. *Unforgettable Days*. Hanoi: Foreign Languages Publishing House. A detailed memoir of the immediate postwar period by the famous military strategist.

Goldner, Loren. 1997. "The Anti-Colonial Movement in Vietnam." *New Politics* (Summer), Vol. 6 (new series), No. 3, pp. 135–41. A short but interesting discussion of the Trotskyist movement; criticizes Marr's (1995) otherwise comprehensive study for slighting this movement and the Viet Minh's elimination of it.

Hammer, Ellen J. 1955. *The Struggle for Indochina, 1940–1955*. Stanford, CA: Stanford University Press. One of the better political histories of the First Indochina War.

Harrison, James Pinckney. 1982. *The Endless War: Vietnam's Struggle for Independence*. New York: McGraw-Hill. A very good general history and interpretive synthesis.

Herring, George C. 1986. *America's Longest War: The United States and Vietnam, 1950–1975*. New York: Alfred A. Knopf. One of the best histories of U.S. intervention in Vietnam; includes a chapter on the First Indochina War.

Herring, George C. and Richard H. Immerman. 1984. "Eisenhower, Dulles, and Dienbienphu: 'The Day We Didn't Go to War' Revisited." *Journal of American History* 71:343–63. Examines why the U.S. decided not to support the French with air strikes at Dien Bien Phu; emphasizes Franco-American disagreements more than Congressional opposition.

Hodgkin, Thomas. 1981. *Vietnam: The Revolutionary Path*. London: Macmillan. A sweeping work of historical synthesis, from ancient times to the August Revolution of 1945; about a third of the book focuses on the two decades between 1925 and 1945.

Hunt, David. 1982. "Village Culture and the Vietnamese Revolution." *Past and Present* 94:131–57. An important and fascinating study of the complex role of popular culture in the revolution.

Huynh Kim Khanh. 1971. "The Vietnamese August Revolution Reinterpreted." *Journal of Asian Studies* 30:761–82. The best short study of its subject.

1982. *Vietnamese Communism, 1925–1945*. Ithaca, NY: Cornell University Press. The best analysis of the Party during this period.

Johnson, George and Fred Feldman. 1974. "Vietnam, Stalinism, and the Postwar Socialist Revolutions." *International Socialist Review* 35:26–61. A Trotskyist critique of Rousset (1974).

Kahin, George McTurnan. 1987. *Intervention: How America Became Involved in Vietnam*. Garden City, NY: Anchor Books. The best book on the subject; exhaustively researched.

Kahin, George McTurnan and John W. Lewis. 1967. *The United States in Vietnam*. N.p.: Delta. A good, critical overview of the period from the Second World War to 1966, by two noted East Asianists.

Karnow, Stanley. 1983. *Vietnam: A History*. New York: Viking Press. A popular synthesis, one that is not highly regarded by many country specialists (or opponents of the U.S. war). Still, Karnow pulls together a great deal of useful material, including a helpful biographical index.

Kiernan, Ben. 1992. "The Vietnam War: Alternative Endings." *American Historical Review* 97:1118–37. An interesting review essay by a leading Cambodia specialist; argues that the U.S. war simply could not have been won.

Kolko, Gabriel. 1985. *Anatomy of a War: Vietnam, the United States, and Historical Experience*. New York: Pantheon. An important general history and provocative radical analysis; one of the very best volumes on Vietnam.

Lacouture, Jean. 1967. *Ho Chi Minh*. Translated by Peter Wiles. Harmondsworth, UK: Penguin Books. Still the best biography.

Lancaster, Donald. 1974 (1961). *The Emancipation of French Indochina*. New York: Octagon Books. Badly dated.

Lockhart, Greg. 1989. *Nation in Arms: The Origins of the People's Revolutionary Army of Vietnam*. Sydney: Allen and Unwin. The title of this very important book is somewhat misleading; this is one of the best general accounts of the 1940–54 period.

Luong, Hy V., with the collaboration of Nguyen Dac Bang. 1992. *Revolution in the Village: Tradition and Transformation in North Vietnam, 1925–1988*. Honolulu: University of Hawaii Press. A fascinating village-level study of Son Duong (near Hanoi); the bulk of the book covers the pre-1954 period and includes an interesting analysis of the 1930 Yen Bay revolt by the Vietnamese Nationalist Party (VNQDD).

McAlister, John T., Jr. 1967. "Mountain Minorities and the Viet Minh: A Key to the Indochina War." Pp. 771–844 in *Southeast Asian Tribes, Minorities, and Nations, Volume II*, edited by Peter Kunstadter. Princeton, NJ: Princeton University Press. The best analysis of the subject; a corrective to accounts of the revolution as a simple assertion of ethnic Vietnamese nationalism.

1969. *Vietnam: The Origins of Revolution*. Garden City, NY: Doubleday. Very well researched; includes a good analysis of the immediate postwar period.

McAlister, John T., Jr. and Paul Mus. 1970. *The Vietnamese and Their Revolution*. New York: Harper and Row. An interpretive account that emphasizes the role of Vietnamese cultural traditions. This book is based on a reworking of some of Mus's previous publications, including his notoriously complex *Viet Nam: sociologie d'une guerre* (Paris: Editions du Seuil, 1952) and Mus (1949).

Marr, David. 1981a. *Vietnamese Tradition on Trial, 1920–1945*. Berkeley, CA, and Los Angeles: University of California Press. A fascinating study of intellectuals and intellectual currents by one of the foremost scholars on Vietnam.

1981b. "Vietnam: Harnessing the Whirlwind." Pp. 163–207 in *Asia – The Winning of Independence*, edited by Robin Jeffrey. London: Macmillan. An excellent short overview of the revolution.

1995. *Vietnam 1945: The Quest for Power*. Berkeley, CA, and Los Angeles: University of California Press. A magisterial account of the August Revolution and antecedent events; but see the critical comments of Goldner 1997.

Modelski, George. 1964. "The Viet Minh Complex." Pp. 185–214 in *Communism and Revolution: The Strategic Uses of Political Violence*, edited by Cyril E. Black and Thomas P. Thornton. Princeton, NJ: Princeton University Press. In a word, unsympathetic.

Morrock, Richard. 1967. "Revolution and Intervention in Vietnam." Pp. 218–49 in *Containment and Revolution*, edited by David Horowitz. Boston: Beacon Press. A short critical analysis.

Murray, Martin J. 1980. *The Development of Capitalism in Colonial Indochina (1870–1940)*. Berkeley, CA, and Los Angeles: University of California Press. A meticulously researched Marxist analysis; a gold mine of information.

1992. "'White Gold' or 'White Blood'?: The Rubber Plantations of Colonial Indochina, 1910–40." *Journal of Peasant Studies* 19:41–67. Brutal exploitation in southern Vietnam.

Mus, Paul. 1949. "The Role of the Village in Vietnamese Politics." *Pacific Affairs* 23:265–72. See McAlister and Mus 1970 for the full story.

Ngo Vinh Long. 1978. "The Indochinese Communist Party and Peasant Rebellion in Central Vietnam, 1930–1931." *Bulletin of Concerned Asian Scholars* 10:15–34. One of the best analyses of this episode.

1990. "Communal Property and Peasant Revolutionary Struggles in Vietnam." *Journal of Peasant Studies* 17:121–40. How the land question fueled revolutionary politics.

1991a (1973). *Before the Revolution: The Vietnamese Peasants Under the French*. New York: Columbia University Press. Perhaps the best book on the subject; includes translations of some fascinating Vietnamese literature of the colonial period.

1991b. "Vietnam." Pp. 9–64 in *Coming to Terms: Indochina, the United States, and the War*, edited by Douglas Allen and Ngo Vinh Long. Boulder, CO: Westview Press. An excellent short overview.

Nguyen The Anh. 1985. "The Vietnamese Monarchy Under French Colonial Rule 1884–1945." *Modern Asian Studies* 19:147–62. How the monarchy became a rather ineffective French anti-Communist tool.

Nguyen Khac Vien. 1973. "Myths and Realities." *Bulletin of Concerned Asian Scholars* 5:56–63. A critique of Fitzgerald (1972) by one of the preeminent Vietnamese scholars.

  1974. *Tradition and Revolution in Vietnam.* Berkeley, CA: Indochina Resource Center. Contains some provocative reflections on the similarities – but also differences – between Confucianism and Communism.

Nguyen Xuan Lai. 1976. "The First Resistance (1945–1954)." *Vietnamese Studies*, No. 44:9–141. Emphasizes the importance of land policies for the Viet Minh's success; an extensive discussion that includes some interesting and important data.

O'Ballance, Edgar. 1964. *The Indo-China War, 1945–1954: A Study in Guerilla Warfare.* London: Faber and Faber. Focuses on the military dimension of the conflict. See his companion study on Malaya (O'Ballance 1966).

O'Neill, Robert J. 1968. *Indo-China Tragedy, 1945–1954.* Melbourne: F.W. Cheshire. A short but useful analysis.

Patti, Archimedes L. A. 1980. *Why Viet Nam? Prelude to America's Albatross.* Berkeley, CA, and Los Angeles: University of California Press. A detailed and fascinating memoir of the immediate postwar period by a leader of the OSS team in the country.

Pike, Douglas. 1978. *History of Vietnamese Communism, 1925–1976.* Stanford, CA: Hoover Institution Press. A useful reference work, despite its simplistic Cold War frame.

Pluvier, Jan. 1973. "The Vietnamese War of Independence (1945–1954) and Historical Objectivity." *Journal of Contemporary Asia* 3:277–91. Attacks the widespread assumption that Vietnamese Communists could not be nationalists.

Popkin, Samuel L. 1979. *The Rational Peasant: The Political Economy of Rural Society in Vietnam.* Berkeley, CA, and Los Angeles: University of California. Contains a wealth of information on Vietnamese peasant society; the author's "rational choice" perspective, however, disappears when he turns to idealistic "political entrepreneurs."

Post, Ken. 1989. *Revolution, Socialism and Nationalism in Viet Nam, Volume One: An Interrupted Revolution.* Belmont, CA: Wadsworth Publishing Company. The first in a projected multivolume study, this provocative interpretive history covers the period up to the late 1950s; like Lockhart (1989), Post emphasizes the importance of Marxist-Leninist ideology – as opposed to nationalism pure and simple – for understanding the revolution.

Race, Jeffrey. 1972. *War Comes to Long An: Revolutionary Conflict in a Vietnamese Province.* Berkeley, CA, and Los Angeles: University of California Press. An important and fascinating study; focuses on the post-1954 era, but contains some material on the pre-Geneva period.

Rousset, Pierre. 1974. "The Vietnamese Revolution and the Role of the Party." *International Socialist Review* 35:4–24. A Trotskyist analysis.

1984. "The Peculiarities of Vietnamese Communism." Pp. 321–44 in *The Stalinist Legacy*, edited by Tariq Ali. Harmondsworth: Penguin Books. This and the previous article argue that the "Vietnamization" of the Communist Party, not its Stalinization, account for the Party's success. For an orthodox Trotskyist critique, see Johnson and Feldman (1974).

Sacks, I. Milton. 1959. "Marxism in Viet Nam." Pp. 102–70 and 315–29 (endnotes) in *Marxism and Southeast Asia*, edited by Frank N. Trager. Stanford, CA: Stanford University Press. Still useful.

Shipway, Martin. 1993. "Creating an Emergency: Metropolitan Constaints on French Colonial Policy and Its Breakdown in Indo-China, 1945–47." *Journal of Imperial and Commonwealth History* 21:1–16. Suggests that French plans to reform the empire after the war foundered on the shoals of domestic politics.

Smith, R. B. 1969. "Bui Quang Chieu and the Constitutionalist Party in French Cochinchina, 1917–1930." *Modern Asian Studies* 3:131–50. Explains why Chieu did not become Vietnam's Manuel Quezon or Tunku Abdul Rahman.

1972. "The Development of Opposition to French Rule in Southern Vietnam 1880–1940." *Past and Present* 54:94–129. A helpful overview, though now rather dated.

1978a. "The Japanese Period in Indochina and the Coup of 9 March 1945." *Journal of Southeast Asian Studies* 9:268–301.

1978b. "The Work of the Provisional Government of Vietnam, August–December 1945." *Modern Asian Studies* 12:571–609. This and the previous article closely examine an important period in the development and consolidation of Communist power.

Short, Anthony. 1989. *The Origins of the Vietnam War*. London and New York: Longman. Perhaps the most comprehensive synthesis on the period from 1920 to 1965, with an exceptional discussion of the crucial years 1952–4.

Smith, Tony. 1974. "The French Colonial Consensus and People's War, 1946–58." *Journal of Contemporary History* 9:217–47. An important article on the France's reluctance to decolonize; emphasizes the collaboration of the French non-Communist left in policies of colonial repression.

Starobin, Joseph. 1968 (1954). *Eyewitness in Indo-China*. New York: Greenwood Press. Interesting contemporary observations by a U.S. Communist leader, who later quit the party, who traveled to Viet-Minh-controlled areas during the French war.

Tai, Hue-Tam Ho. 1983. *Millenarianism and Peasant Politics in Vietnam*. Cambridge, MA: Harvard University Press. The best study of the topic; fascinating.

1984. "The Politics of Compromise: The Constitutionalist Party and the Electoral Reforms of 1922 in French Cochinchina." *Modern Asian Studies* 18:371–91. Emphasizes the Vietnamese bourgeoisie's fear of mass politics.

1992. *Radicalism and the Origins of the Vietnamese Revolution*. Cambridge, MA: Harvard University Press. Examines several modes of non- or pre-Communist "radicalism" during the interwar period.

Tonnesson, Stein. 1991. *The Vietnamese Revolution of 1945: Roosevelt, Ho Chi Minh and de Gaulle in a World at War*. London: Sage Publications. The most comprehensive analysis of the August Revolution, covering its social, political, and international dimensions; exhaustively researched.

Trullinger, James W. 1994 (1980). *Village at War: An Account of Conflict in Vietnam*. Stanford, CA: Stanford University Press. The view from the grassroots (or the rice paddies) in a village in central Vietnam; includes rich material on the French era as well as the on the post-Geneva period.

Truong Nhu Tang, with David Chanoff and Doan Van Toai. 1985. *A Vietcong Memoir*. New York: Vintage Books. Memoirs of the scion of an elite southern family who became an official of the National Liberation Front and later defected to the West.

Vu Ngu Chieu. 1986. "The Other Side of the 1945 Vietnamese Revolution: The Empire of Viet-Nam (March–August 1945)." *Journal of Asian Studies* 45:293–328. Includes an interesting discussion of the ways in which the Japanese-sponsored government of Tran Trong Kim unwittingly played into the hands of the Viet Minh.

White, Christine Pelzer. 1974. "The Vietnamese Revolutionary Alliance: Intellectuals, Workers, and Peasants." Pp. 77–95 and 322–5 (endnotes) in *Peasant Rebellion and Communist Revolution in Asia*, edited by John Wilson Lewis. Stanford, CA: Stanford University Press. An important corrective to portraits of the revolution as a "peasant rebellion" pure and simple.

1983a. "Peasant Mobilization and Anti-Colonial Struggle in Vietnam: The Rent Reduction Campaign of 1953." *Journal of Peasant Studies* 10:187–213. A very important analysis of the dilemmas of class struggle in a war of national liberation.

1983b. "Mass Mobilization and Ideological Transformation in the Vietnamese Land Reform Campaign." *Journal of Contemporary Asia* 13:74–90. Explores the problems Communists confronted in trying to develop class as opposed to national consciousness among peasants.

1986. "Everyday Resistance, Socialist Revolution and Rural Development: The Vietnamese Case." *Journal of Peasant Studies* 13:49–63. A sober critique of the recent turn toward analyses of "everyday forms of peasant resistance" (see Scott [1985] and Kerkvliet [1990]).

Wintle, Justin. 1991. *The Viet Nam Wars*. New York: St. Martin's Press. Includes chapters on the August Revolution and the war against the French.

Woodside, Alexander. 1971. "The Development of Social Organizations in Vietnamese Cities in the Late Colonial Period." *Pacific Affairs* 44:39–64. Focuses on primarily nonpolitical, elite voluntary organizations, although Woodside suggests that traditional ideologies and practices slowed the rise of popular organizations.

1976. *Community and Revolution in Modern Vietnam*. Boston: Houghton Mifflin. An outstanding interpretive history, focusing on the struggle to build new social organizations or what would now be called "civil society."

1989. "History, Structure, and Revolution in Vietnam." *International Political Science Review* 10:143–57. Emphasizes the role of Confucianism, including the tradition of peasant revolts led by provincial intellectuals.

Young, Marilyn B. 1991. *The Vietnam Wars, 1945–1990*. New York: HarperCollins. Scholarly and humane; focuses primarily on the Second Indochina War, but includes some material on the pre-1954 period.

Zhai, Qiang. 1993. "Transplanting the Chinese Model: Chinese Military Advisers and the First Vietnam War, 1950–1954." *Journal of Military History* 57:689–715. Examines the role of Chinese advisers and military aid more generally during the war against the French.

C. Indonesia

Alexander, Jennifer and Paul Alexander. 1991. "Protecting Peasants from Capitalism: The Subordination of Javanese Traders by the Colonial State." *Comparative Studies in Society and History* 33:370–94. Colonialism, not culture, as an explanation for the historic weakness of the Javanese bourgeoisie.

Anderson, Benedict R. O'G. 1966. "Japan: 'The Light of Asia.'" Pp. 13–50 in *Southeast Asia in World War II: Four Essays*, edited by Josef Silverstein. New Haven, CT: Southeast Asia Studies Monograph Series No. 7, Yale University. An excellent study of the Japanese impact on Indonesia, and especially on youth.

   1970–1. "The Cultural Factors in the Indonesian Revolution." *Asia* 20:48–65. Emphasizes the role of the *pemuda*, i.e., activist youth. Anderson argues, not very convincingly, that the Indonesian revolution was "almost purely cultural" (p. 61).

   1972. *Java in a Time of Revolution: Occupation and Resistance, 1944–1946*. Ithaca, NY: Cornell University Press. An indispensable, classic study of the "*pemuda* revolution"; includes an extensive biographical appendix.

   1983. "Old State, New Society: Indonesia's New Order in Comparative Historical Perspective." *Journal of Asian Studies* 42:477–96. A provocative interpretation, from colonialism to Suharto.

Benda, Harry J. 1958. *The Crescent and the Rising Sun: Indonesian Islam Under the Japanese Occupation, 1942–1945*. The Hague: W. van Hoeve. On Japan's (limited) encouragement of Islam during the war years.

   1965. "Decolonization in Indonesia: The Problem of Continuity and Change." *American Historical Review* 70:1058–73. Emphasizes continuity, focusing on the Javanese bureaucratic aristocracy.

Brackman, Arnold C. 1969. *The Communist Collapse in Indonesia*. New York: Norton. A standard account of the events of 1965.

Cribb, Robert. 1988. "Opium and the Indonesian Revolution." *Modern Asian Studies* 28:701–22. Emphasizes the fiscal constraints and dilemmas of the revolutionaries.

   1991. *Gangsters and Revolutionaries: The Jakarta People's Militia and the Indonesian Revolution 1945–1949*. Honolulu: University of Hawaii Press. A fascinating study of the revolution in Jakarta, emphasizing the improbable coalition of young radical nationalists and the Jakarta underworld.

II. Southeast Asia

Crouch, Harold. 1988. *The Army and Politics in Indonesia*. Revised edition. Ithaca, NY: Cornell University Press. Focuses on the army's growing political power since independence, which has its roots in the postwar struggle against the Dutch.

Dahm, Bernhard. 1969. *Sukarno and the Struggle for Indonesian Independence*. Translated by Mary F. Somers Heidhues. Ithaca, NY: Cornell University Press. Still helpful.

Frederick, William H. 1983. "Hidden Change in Late Colonial Urban Society in Indonesia." *Journal of Southeast Asian Studies* 14:354–71. A social history of prewar Surabaya.

———. 1989. *Visions and Heat: The Making of the Indonesian Revolution*. Athens, OH: Ohio University Press. An excellent study of Surabaya, the principal port city of East Java; includes a close analysis of the events of 1945.

Furnivall, J. S. 1939. *Netherlands India: A Study of Plural Economy*. Cambridge, UK: Cambridge University Press. A classic study.

Geertz, Clifford. 1963. *Agricultural Involution: The Processes of Ecological Change in Indonesia*. Berkeley, CA, and Los Angeles: University of California Press. The author's classic account of agricultural change during the colonial period, although now widely contested, remains indispensable.

Groen, Petra M. H. 1993. "Militant Response: The Dutch Use of Military Force and the Decolonization of the Dutch East Indies, 1945–50." *Journal of Imperial and Commonwealth History* 21:30–44. Why force failed.

Hanna, Willard A. 1963. "Nationalist Revolution and Revolutionary Nationalism: Indonesia." Pp. 129–77 in *Expectant Peoples: Nationalism and Development*, edited by K. H. Silvert. New York: Vintage Books. Includes an overview of the period from 1942 to 1949.

Ingleson, John. 1979. *Road to Exile: The Indonesian Nationalist Movement, 1927–1934*. Singapore: Heinemann Educational Books. Focuses on Sukarno's Indonesian Nationalist Party (PNI).

———. 1981. "Worker Consciousness and Labour Unions in Colonial Java." *Pacific Affairs* 54:485–501. Includes an interesting discussion of why workers were more likely to develop a racial as opposed to class consciousness.

Kahin, Audrey R. 1985. "Introduction." Pp. 1–20 in *Regional Dynamics of the Indonesian Revolution: Unity From Diversity*, edited by Audrey R. Kahin. Honolulu: University of Hawaii Press. A helpful overview of several important regional histories.

Kahin, Audrey R. and George McT. Kahin. 1995. *Subversion as Foreign Policy: The Secret Eisenhower and Dulles Debacle in Indonesia*. New York: The New Press. Chronicles the Eisenhower Administration's growing fear of Communist influence in Indonesia, culminating in a massive, yet ultimately abortive and counterproductive, covert military intervention.

Kahin, George McT. 1952. *Nationalism and Revolution in Indonesia*. Ithaca, NY: Cornell University Press. The classic (and still very helpful) account by the dean of Indonesia specialists. Kahin was the only American in Indonesia's revolutionary capital of Yogyakarta in 1948–9.

1963. "Indonesia." Pp. 535–700 in *Major Governments of Asia*, edited by George McT. Kahin. Second edition. Ithaca, NY: Cornell University Press. An excellent book-length overview.

Larson, George D. 1987. *Prelude to Revolution: Palaces and Politics in Surakarta, 1912–1942*. Dordrecht, Netherlands: Foris Publications. The background to "social revolution" in Central Java.

Legge, J. D. 1972. *Sukarno: A Political Biography*. New York: Praeger. The most reliable biography of Sukarno; a sober and informative account by a knowledgeable Indonesianist.

Maddison, Angus. 1990. "Dutch Colonialism in Indonesia: A Comparative Perspective." Pp. 322–35 in *Indonesian Economic History in the Dutch Colonial Era*, edited by Anne Booth, W. J. O'Malley, and Anna Weidemann. New Haven, CT: Yale University Southeast Asia Studies. An excellent short introduction to the subject; includes some very interesting comparative data.

McMahon, Robert J. 1981. *Colonialism and Cold War: The United States and the Struggle for Indonesian Independence, 1945–1949*. Ithaca, NY: Cornell University Press. The best work on the subject.

McVey, Ruth T. 1965. *The Rise of Indonesian Communism*. Ithaca, NY: Cornell University Press. The authoritative study of the PKI up to the events of 1926–7.

Mortimer, Rex. 1974. "Traditional Modes and Communist Movements: Change and Protest in Indonesia." Pp. 99–123 in *Peasant Rebellion and Communist Revolution in Asia*, edited by John Wilson Lewis. Stanford, CA: Stanford University Press. An excellent analytic treatment.

Palmier, L. 1972. "Indonesia Since Independence." Pp. 225–64 in *Reform and Revolution in Asia*, edited by G. F. Hudson. London: George Allen and Unwin. An overview of the revolution and its aftermath.

Reid, Anthony. 1974. *The Indonesian National Revolution, 1945–1950*. Hawthorn, Australia: Longman. The best short history.

1975. "The Japanese Occupation and Rival Indonesian Elites: Northern Sumatra in 1942." *Journal of Asian Studies* 35:49–61. Examines the violence precipitated by the Japanese occupation, a harbinger of the postwar "social revolution."

1979. *The Blood of the People: Revolution and the End of Traditional Rule in Northern Sumatra*. Kuala Lumpur: Oxford University Press. A richly detailed local study, from colonialism to the postwar "social revolution."

1981. "Indonesia: Revolution Without Socialism." Pp. 113–57 in *Asia – The Winning of Independence*, edited by Robin Jeffrey. London: Macmillan. Reid's title nicely encapsulates precisely what needs to be explained; an excellent short overview.

1986. "The Revolution in Regional Perspective." *Utrechtse Historische Cahiers* 7 (2/3):183–99. A useful overview of recent regional studies of the revolution, emphasizing how diverse regions shared similar experiences.

Ricklefs, M. C. 1993. *A History of Modern Indonesia Since c. 1300*. Second edition. Stanford, CA: Stanford University Press. An excellent general history.

Stoler, Ann Laura. 1985a. *Capitalism and Confrontation in Sumatra's Plantation Belt, 1870–1979*. New Haven, CT: Yale University Press. Includes a discussion of the role of plantation workers in the revolution.

1985b. "Perceptions of Protest: Defining the Dangerous in Colonial Sumatra." *American Ethnologist* 12:642–58. How Dutch planters came to fear a "Communist threat," even after it was smashed.

1986. "Plantation Politics and Protest on Sumatra's East Coast." *Journal of Peasant Studies* 13:124–43. Labor control "from above" versus popular resistance "from below" over the long haul.

1988. "Working the Revolution: Plantation Laborers and the People's Militia in North Sumatra." *Journal of Asian Studies* 47:227–47. On popular participation in the revolution in one region.

Sutherland, Heather. 1979. *The Making of a Bureaucratic Elite: The Colonial Transformation of the Javanese Priyayi*. Singapore: Heinemann. How the Dutch (largely) coopted Java's elite.

Swift, Ann. 1989. *The Road to Madiun: The Indonesia Communist Uprising of 1948*. Ithaca, NY: Cornell University Modern Indonesia Project. Unfortunately, this short study, which draws on contemporary newspaper reports, does not resolve any of the mysteries surrounding the Madiun affair.

Tornquist, Olle. 1984. *Dilemmas of Third World Communism: The Destruction of the PKI in Indonesia*. London: Zed Books. Focuses primarily on the events leading up to 1965, but includes some discussion of the 1920–50 period.

van der Eng, Pierre. 1988. "Marshall Aid as a Catalyst in the Decolonization of Indonesia, 1947–49." *Journal of Southeast Asian Studies* 19:335–52. Emphasizes the economic rationality of Indonesian independence for the Netherlands; Marshall aid was a catalyst, not a cause, of the Dutch decision to decolonize.

Wertheim, W. F. 1964. *Indonesian Society in Transition*. Second revised edition. The Hague: W. van Hoeve. An important study of the impact of colonial rule.

Wertheim, W. F. and The Siauw Giap. 1962. "Social Change in Java, 1900–1930." *Pacific Affairs* 35:223–47. A rich, seminal analysis.

Williams, Michael C. 1980. "Sneevliet and the Birth of Asian Communism." *New Left Review* 123:81–90. Includes a short discussion of the founding of the PKI.

1990. *Communism, Religion, and Revolt in Banten*. Athens, OH: Center for International Studies, Ohio University. How the Communist revolt of 1926 became mixed up with Islam in West Java.

Wright, Richard. 1994 (1956). *The Color Curtain: A Report on the Bandung Conference*. Jackson, MS: Banner Books, University Press of Mississippi. A journalistic account by the noted writer.

D. *Malaya*

Allen, J. de Vere. 1970. "Malayan Civil Service, 1874–941: Colonial Bureaucracy/Malayan Elite." *Comparative Studies in Society and History* 12:149–78. How the British (largely) coopted the ethnic Malay elite.

Andaya, Barbara Watson and Leonard Y. Andaya. 1982. *A History of Malaysia*. London: Macmillan. A good general history.

Caldwell, Malcolm. 1977a. "The British 'Forward Movement', 1874–1914." Pp. 13–37 in *Malaya: The Making of a Neo-Colony*, edited by Mohamed Amin and

Malcolm Caldwell. Nottingham, UK: Spokesman. A Marxist analysis of British colonialism.

1977b. "From 'Emergency' to 'Independence', 1948–1957." Pp. 216–65 in *Malaya: The Making of a Neo-Colony*, edited by Mohamed Amin and Malcolm Caldwell. Nottingham, UK: Spokesman. A Marxist analysis of the insurgency and its suppression.

Cham, B. N. 1977. "Colonialism and Communalism in Malaysia." *Journal of Contemporary Asia* 7:178–99. A radical analysis that emphasizes the colonial origins and class character of communalism.

Cheah Boon Kheng. 1977. "Some Aspects of the Interregnum in Malaya (14 August–3 September 1945)." *Journal of Southeast Asian Studies* 8:48–74. A close analysis of an important period; helps to explain why there was no "August Revolution" in Malaya.

1987. *Red Star Over Malaya: Resistance and Social Conflict During and After the Japanese Occupation, 1941–1946*. Second edition. Singapore: Singapore University Press. One of the best studies of the MCP/MPAJA during this period.

1988. "The Erosion of Ideological Hegemony and Royal Power and the Rise of Postwar Malay Nationalism, 1945–1946." *Journal of Southeast Asian Studies* 19:1–26. Emphasizes how the British Malayan Union scheme led to a surge of Malay nationalism.

Clutterbuck, Richard. 1985. *Conflict and Violence in Singapore and Malaysia, 1945–1983*. Boulder, CO: Westview Press. Includes a political-military account of the "Emergency."

Greene, Graham. 1951. "Malaya, the Forgotten War." *Life* 31 (July 30):51–65. An interesting period piece; no trace of the novelist's alleged Communist sympathies here.

Heng Pek Koon. 1988. *Chinese Politics in Malaysia: A History of the Malaysian Chinese Association*. Singapore: Oxford University Press. Focuses on the period 1949–57, when the MCA was the Communist Party's principal rival within the so-called Chinese community.

Hua Wu Yin. 1983. *Class and Communalism in Malaysia: Politics in a Dependent Capitalist State*. London: Zed Books. A Marxist analysis of communalism from the colonial period through independence.

Jomo Kwame Sundaram. 1988. *A Question of Class: Capital, the State, and Uneven Development in Malaya*. Manila: Journal of Contemporary Asia Publishers; New York: Monthly Review Press. A sophisticated and detailed Marxist economic history.

Jomo Kwame Sundaram and Patricia Todd. 1994. *Trade Unions and the State in Peninsular Malaysia*. Kuala Lumpur: Oxford University Press. An excellent overview; emphasizes the role of the state.

Kratoska, Paul H. 1982. "Rice Cultivation and the Ethnic Division of Labor in British Malaya." *Comparative Studies in Society and History* 24:280–314. Challenges the "divide-and-conquer" perspective on British communal policies.

1985. "The Peripatetic Peasant and Land Tenure in British Malaya." *Journal of Southeast Asian Studies* 16:16–45. Explains why the British goal of creating a conservative class of Malay peasant proprietors was only imperfectly realized.

340

Lau, Albert. 1991. *The Malayan Union Controversy, 1942–1948*. Singapore: Oxford University Press. An extraordinarily well-researched study of the controversy over a unified versus federated state.

Leary, John D. 1995. *Violence and the Dream People: The Orang Asli in the Malayan Emergency, 1948–1960*. Athens, OH: Ohio University Center for International Studies. The most comprehensive study of indigenous people during the Emergency.

Lee Kam Hing. 1981. "Malaya: New State and Old Elites." Pp. 213–57 in *Asia – The Winning of Independence*, edited by Robin Jeffrey. London: Macmillan. A very helpful overview; the title says it all.

Lee Tong Foong. 1977. "The MPAJA and the Revolutionary Struggle, 1939–1945." Pp. 95–119 in *Malaya: The Making of a Neo-Colony*, edited by Mohamed Amin and Malcolm Caldwell. Nottingham, UK: Spokesman. A short overview of the anti-Japanese resistance.

Leong Yee Fong. 1992. "The Impact of the Cold War on the Development of Trade Unionism in Malaya (1948–57)." *Journal of Southeast Asian Studies* 23:60–73. Discusses Britain's sponsorship of non-Communist unions as part of its counterinsurgency strategy.

Lim Teck Ghee. 1977. *Peasants and Their Agricultural Economy in Colonial Malaya, 1874–1941*. Kuala Lumpur: Oxford University Press. Emphasizes how British policies impoverished the Malay peasantry.

Milne, R. S. and Diane K. Mauzy. 1986. *Malaysia: Tradition, Modernity, and Islam*. Boulder, CO: Westview Press. A solid introduction.

Nonini, Donald M. 1992. *British Colonial Rule and the Resistance of the Malay Peasantry, 1900–1957*. New Haven, CT: Yale University Southeast Asia Studies. The best study of this subject.

O'Ballance, Edgar. 1966. *Malaya: The Communist Insurgent War, 1948–1960*. Hamden, CT: Archon Books. A Cold-Warish, but still useful overview by a long-time student of Communist insurgencies.

Purcell, Victor. 1954. *Malaya: Communist or Free?* Stanford, CA: Stanford University Press. Interesting reflections by a long-time observer.

Pye, Lucian W. 1956. *Guerrilla Communism in Malaya: Its Social and Political Meaning*. Princeton, NJ: Princeton University Press. Pye mainly examines, in a rather psychologistic fashion, supporters of the Communist insurgency who later surrendered to government authorities.

Ramasamy, P. 1992. "Labour Control and Labour Resistance in the Plantations of Colonial Malaya." *Journal of Peasant Studies* 19:87–105. Exploitation and resistance in British plantations.

Renick, Roderick Dhu, Jr. 1965. "The Emergency Regulations of Malaya: Causes and Effect." *Southeast Asian History* 6:1–39. Examines the "new villages," collective punishment, and, more generally, how the British counterinsurgency entailed "detailed intrusion into the daily lives of the people" (p. 35).

Roff, William R. 1967. *The Origins of Malay Nationalism*. New Haven, CT: Yale University Press. The best book on the subject for the period up to the Second World War.

341

Said, Muhammad Ikmal. 1992. "Ethnic Perspectives of the Left in Malaysia." Pp. 254–81 in *Fragmented Vision: Culture and Politics in Contemporary Malaysia*, edited by Joel S. Kahn and Francis Loh Kok Wah. Honolulu: University of Hawaii Press. A useful discussion of the historic ethnic division of the Malaysian left.

Sarkesian, Sam C. 1975. "The Malayan Emergency – Roots of Insurgency." Pp. 375–92 in *Revolutionary Guerrilla Warfare*, edited by Sam C. Sarkesian. Chicago: Precedent Publishing. How Malayan society produced a revolutionary movement, albeit one that was fated to fail.

Scott, James C. 1985. *Weapons of the Weak: Everyday Forms of Peasant Resistance*. New Haven, CT: Yale University Press. Focuses on the postindependence period, but includes some material relevant to the colonial era.

Short, Anthony. 1970a. "Communism, Race and Politics in Malaysia." *Asian Survey* 10:1081–9. Emphasizes the essentially Chinese character of Malayan Communism, although Short discusses the Tenth Regiment, an ethnic Malay guerrilla unit.

1970b. "Nationalism and the Emergency in Malaya." Pp. 43–58 in *Nationalism, Revolution, and Evolution in South-East Asia*, edited by Michael Leifer. Centre for South-East Asian Studies, University of Hull. London: Inter-Documentation Co. A helpful overview.

1975. *The Communist Insurrection in Malaya, 1948–1960*. London: Frederick Muller Ltd. The most detailed history of the insurgency. Short was given access to confidential government papers, although the Malayan government branded the manuscript "subversive" and refused to publish it.

Smith, Simon C. 1994. "The Rise, Decline and Survival of the Malay Rulers During the Colonial Period, 1874–1957." *Journal of Imperial and Commonwealth History* 22:84–108. On the making of a neocolonial elite.

Soenarno, Radin. 1960. "Malay Nationalism, 1896–1941." *Southeast Asian History* 1:1–28. Includes an interesting comparison of conservative Malay nationalism with the revolutionary nationalism of Indonesia.

Stenson, Michael. 1970. *Industrial Conflict in Malaya: Prelude to the Communist Revolt of 1948*. London: Oxford University Press. An important examination of organized labor in Malaya from the depression to 1948 as well as of the immediate background to the Communist Party's decision to take up armed struggle.

1974. "The Ethnic and Urban Bases of Communist Revolt in Malaya." Pp. 125–50 and 330–5 (endnotes) in *Peasant Rebellion and Communist Revolution in Asia*, edited by John Wilson Lewis. Stanford, CA: Stanford University Press. An excellent short analysis of the limitations of the Communist insurgency.

1980. *Class, Race and Colonialism in West Malaysia: The Indian Case*. St. Lucia, Queensland: University of Queensland Press. The best account of the role of ethnic Indians in the Communist revolt.

Stockwell, A. J. 1977. "The Formation and First Years of the United Malays National Organization (U.M.N.O.), 1946–1948." *Modern Asian Studies* 11:481–513. An excellent, well-researched study of a period when the

Western-educated Malay elite was quickly politicized, but then just as quickly returned to collaboration with the British against the Communists.

1987. "Insurgency and Decolonisation During the Malayan Emergency." *Journal of Commonwealth and Comparative Politics* 25:71–81. Emphasizes the counterinsurgent effects of decolonization.

1993. "'A Widespread and Long-Concocted Plot to Overthrow Government in Malaya'? The Origins of the Malayan Emergency." *Journal of Imperial and Commonwealth History* 21:66–88. Argues that the British banned the Malayan Communist Party in July 1948 on the basis of rather flimsy evidence; also rejects the counterclaim (see Furedi 1989, 1993) that the Emergency was a "colonial conspiracy" aimed at provoking a Communist insurgency.

Stubbs, Richard. 1979. "The United Malays National Organization, the Malayan Chinese Association, and the Early Years of the Malayan Emergency, 1948–1955." *Journal of Southeast Asian Studies* 10:77–88. How conservative nationalists stole some of the Communists' fire.

1989. *Hearts and Minds in Guerrilla Warfare: The Malayan Emergency, 1948–1960*. Singapore: Oxford University Press. One of the very best monographs on the Emergency, emphasizing the broadly political as well as military aspects of the counterinsurgency after 1952.

1997. "The Malayan Emergency and the Development of the Malaysian State." Pp. 50–71 in *The Counter-Insurgent State: Guerrilla Warfare and State Building in the Twentieth Century*, edited by Paul B. Rich and Richard Stubbs. London: Macmillan. How the Emergency produced a strong state; a short, helpful overview.

Tilman, Robert O. 1966. "The Non-Lessons of the Malayan Emergency." *Asian Survey* 6:407–19. Explains why the "New Villages" were not and could not be successfully copied in South Vietnam.

White, Nicholas J. 1994. "Government and Business Divided: Malaya, 1945–57." *Journal of Imperial and Commonwealth History* 22:251–74. Describes tensions between (and among) British officials and businessmen in Malaya during the postwar period.

Yeo Kim Wah. 1980. "The Grooming of an Elite: Malay Administrators in the Federated Malay States, 1903–1941." *Journal of Southeast Asian Studies* 11:287–319. The origins and evolution of the inheritors of state power from the British; emphasizes the conservatizing and communal character of the Malay Administrative Service (MAS).

Yong, C. F. 1991. "Origins and Development of the Malayan Communist Movement, 1919–1930." *Modern Asian Studies* 25:625–48. Emphasizes the primarily Chinese sources of Malayan Communism.

E. The Philippines

Abaya, Hernando H. 1946. *Betrayal in the Philippines*. New York: A.A. Wyn. An important nationalist study of the postwar oligarchic restoration.

Abueva, Jose V. 1971. *Ramon Magsaysay: A Political Biography*. Manila: Solidaridad Publishing House. The most detailed biography, although Magsaysay's American connection is underplayed.

Allen, James S. [Sol Auerbach]. 1938. "Agrarian Tendencies in the Philippines." *Pacific Affairs* 11:52–65. Based in part on a 1935 government report to President Quezon.

    1985. *The Radical Left on the Eve of War: A Political Memoir*. Quezon City: Foundation for Nationalist Studies. A short memoir by a North American Communist who helped to arrange the merger of the Socialist and Communist parties in the Philippines in 1938.

Anderson, Benedict. 1988. "Cacique Democracy in the Philippines: Origins and Dreams." *New Left Review* 169:3–31. A provocative analysis of oligarchic rule, from colonialism to Aquino.

Anonymous. 1958 (1946). "The Peasant War in the Philippines: A Study of the Causes of Social Unrest in the Philippines – An Analysis of Philippine Political Economy." *Philippine Social Sciences and Humanities Review* 23:373–436. A fascinating and informative document from the immediate postwar period; examines the reimposition of oligarchic and (neo)colonial domination.

Committee on Un-Filipino Activities (CUFA), House of Representatives, Republic of the Philippines. 1949. *General Report on Communism and the Communist Party*. Manila: Bureau of Printing. This fascinating document argues that Communism is an ideological cancer that must be primarily attacked, accordingly, on an ideological level.

Constantino, Renato. 1975. *The Philippines: A Past Revisited*. Manila: Renato Constantino. A radical-nationalist history, from the pre-Spanish period to 1941.

Constantino, Renato and Letizia R. Constantino. 1978. *The Philippines: The Continuing Past*. Quezon City: Foundation for Nationalist Studies. A continuation of the preceding work; covers the period from 1941 to 1965.

Crippen, Harlan R. 1946. "Philippine Agrarian Unrest: Historical Backgrounds." *Science and Society* 10:337–60. Analyzes the plight of Central Luzon's tenant farmers.

Doty, Roxanne Lynn. 1993. "Foreign Policy as Social Construction: A Post-Positivist Analysis of U.S. Counterinsurgency Policy in the Philippines." *International Studies Quarterly* 37:297–320. Includes an interesting analysis of official U.S. documents on the Philippines circa 1950, albeit one that lapses into a sort of linguistic determinism.

Fast, Jonathan. 1973. "Imperialism and Bourgeois Dictatorship in the Philippines." *New Left Review* 78:69–96. A Marxist analysis, from colonialism to Marcos.

Friend, Theodore. 1963. "The Philippine Sugar Industry and the Politics of Independence, 1929–1935." *Journal of Asian Studies* 22:179–92. Examines the struggle between U.S. sugar cane and beet producers, who favored Philippine independence, and Filipino producers, who opposed it so long as it threatened access to the North American market.

    1965. *Between Two Empires: The Ordeal of the Philippines, 1929–1946*. New Haven, CT: Yale University Press. A good political and diplomatic history of the period.

II. Southeast Asia

Goodwin, Jeff. 1997. "The Libidinal Constitution of a High-Risk Social Movement: Affectual Ties and Solidarity in the Huk Rebellion, 1946 to 1954." *American Sociological Review* 62:53–69. Employs a "libidinal economy" as opposed to the state-centered perspective of this volume.

Greenberg, Maj. Lawrence M. 1987. *The Hukbalahap Insurrection: A Case Study of a Successful Anti-Insurgency Operation in the Philippines, 1946–1955.* Washington, DC: Analysis Branch, U.S. Army Center of Military History. Attributes the defeat of the insurrection to Magsaysay and his U.S. backers; the author notes that General Edward Landsdale, the famous (or infamous) counterinsurgency specialist, "validated my assumptions and conclusions" (p. vii).

Jones, Gregg R. 1989. *Red Revolution: Inside the Philippine Guerrilla Movement.* Boulder, CO: Westview Press. An excellent study of the post-1969 insurgency.

Jose, F. Sionil. 1985. "The Huks in Retrospect: A Failed Bid for Power" (interview with Casto Alejandrino, Jesus B. Lava, Alfredo B. Saulo, and Luis Taruc). *Solidarity* [Manila], 102:64–103. A fascinating and lively interview of four leading Huks by a noted Filipino writer.

Karnow, Stanley. 1989. *In Our Image: America's Empire in the Philippines.* New York: Random House. Like the author's popular book on Vietnam (1983), this volume is not highly regarded by many country specialists and critics of U.S. foreign policy. It does bring together, however, an impressive array of factual material.

Kerkvliet, Benedict J. 1977. *The Huk Rebellion: A Study of Peasant Revolt in the Philippines.* Berkeley, CA, and Los Angeles: University of California Press. By far the single best study of the rebellion, although one that polemically underplays the role of the Communist Party.

1990. *Everyday Politics in the Philippines: Class and Status Relations in a Central Luzon Village.* Berkeley, CA, and Los Angeles: University of California Press. Central Luzon in the 1980s.

Lachica, Eduardo. 1971. *Huk: Philippine Agrarian Society in Revolt.* Manila: Solidaridad Publishing House. A journalistic overview.

Lava, Jesus. 1979. "The Huk Rebellion." *Journal of Contemporary Asia* 9:75–81. A short critique of Kerkvliet (1977) – similar to Pomeroy's (1978) – by a leader of the Communist Party.

Leighton, Richard M., Ralph Sanders, and Jose N. Tinio. 1964. *The Huk Rebellion: A Case Study in the Social Dynamics of Insurrection.* Washington, DC: Industrial College of the Armed Forces. Includes some interesting tidbits on Huk efforts to expand outside of Central Luzon.

Li Yuk-Wai. 1992. "The Chinese Resistance Movement in the Philippines During the Japanese Occupation." *Journal of Southeast Asian Studies* 23:308–21. Discusses a number of movements, actually, from left to right.

Lieberman, Victor. 1966. "Why the Hukbalahap Movement Failed." *Solidarity* [Manila] 1:22–30. Emphasizes the movement's regional roots and isolation.

McCoy, Alfred W. 1981. "The Philippines: Independence Without Decolonisation." Pp. 23–65 in *Asia – The Winning of Independence,* edited by Robin Jeffrey. London: Macmillan. An excellent overview; the title says it all.

1992. "Sugar Barons: Formation of a Native Planter Class in the Colonial Philippines." *Journal of Peasant Studies* 19:106–41. Elite-formation under American hegemony.

Maravilla, Jorge [William J. Pomeroy]. 1968. "The Postwar Huk in the Philippines." Pp. 237–42 in *Guerrilla Warfare and Marxism*, edited by William J. Pomeroy. New York: International Publishers. A short but provocative summary.

Miller, Stuart Creighton. 1994. *Benevolent Assimilation: The American Conquest of the Philippines, 1899–1902*. New Haven, CT: Yale University Press. A superb account of an especially brutal conquest.

Milne, R. S. 1963. "The Uniqueness of Philippine Nationalism." *Southeast Asian History* 4:82–96. Attributes the conservative character of Filipino nationalism to the mildness of North American colonialism; largely neglects the Huk rebellion.

Morris, Stephen J. 1994. "The Soviet Union and the Philippine Communist Movement." *Communist and Post-Communist Studies* 27:77–93. A historical overview; notes the lack of Soviet material aid to the Huk rebellion.

Nemenzo, Francisco. 1984. "Rectification Process in the Philippine Communist Movement." Pp. 71–101 in *Armed Communist Movements in Southeast Asia*, edited by Lim Joo-Jock. Singapore: Institute of Southeast Asian Studies. Charts the rise of Maoism in the Philippine Communist movement; includes a discussion of the Maoist critique of the Huk leadership ("Lavaism").

Pomeroy, William J. 1963a. *The Forest: A Personal Record of the Huk Guerrilla Struggle in the Philippines*. New York: International Publishers. An unsentimental memoir by a North American Communist who participated in the rebellion.

1963b. "Lessons of the Philippine Guerrilla War." *Monthly Review* 15 (5):246–51. A very brief, but interesting, summation.

1974. "The Philippines: A Case History of Neocolonialism." Pp. 157–99 in *Remaking Asia: Essays on American Uses of Power*, edited by Mark Selden. New York: Pantheon. A short but informative radical analysis.

1978. "The Philippine Peasantry and the Huk Revolt." *Journal of Peasant Studies* 5:497–517. An informative critique of Kerkvliet (1977).

1992. *The Philippines: Colonialism, Collaboration, and Resistance!* New York: International Publishers. A radical analysis of the period from 1898 to the post-Marcos era.

Ramsay, Ansil. 1965. "Ramon Magsaysay and the Philippine Peasantry." *Philippine Social Sciences and Humanities Review* 30:65–86. Focuses on the 1953 presidential election; demonstrates that Magsaysay did not do particularly well among farmers and tenants.

Saulo, Alfredo B. 1990. *Communism in the Philippines: An Introduction*. Enlarged edition. Quezon City: Ateneo de Manila University Press. A journalistic account by a former Huk; includes an extensive, detailed chronology.

Scaff, Alvin H. 1955. *The Philippine Answer to Communism*. Stanford, CA: Stanford University Press. An old Cold War tract, albeit one not without a few interesting nuggets; the author's data from interviews with about a hundred former Huks must be used very cautiously, but are still informative.

Schirmer, Daniel B. and Stephen Rosskamm Shalom. 1987. "Colonialization: Introduction." Pp. 35–44 in *The Philippines Reader: A History of Colonialism, Neocolonialism, Dictatorship, and Resistance*, edited by Daniel B. Schirmer and Stephen Rosskamm Shalom. Boston: South End Press. A radical analysis of American colonialism and neocolonialism.

Shalom, Stephen Rosskamm. 1977. "Counter-Insurgency in the Philippines." *Journal of Contemporary Asia* 7:153–77. Emphasizes the U.S. role.

1986 (1981). *The United States and the Philippines: A Study of Neocolonialism*. Quezon City: New Day Publishers. An important, meticulously researched study; includes important details on the postwar restoration and on the U.S.-backed counterinsurgency against the Huks.

Steinberg, David Joel. 1966. "The Philippine 'Collaborators': Survival of an Oligarchy." Pp. 67–86 in *Southeast Asia in World War II: Four Essays*, edited by Josef Silverstein. New Haven, CT: Southeast Asia Studies Monograph Series No. 7, Yale University. A good short account of Filipino collaboration with the Japanese; the subtitle tells the tale.

1967. *Philippine Collaboration in World War II*. Ann Arbor, MI: University of Michigan Press. The best account of the subject.

1972. "An Ambiguous Legacy: Years at War in the Philippines." *Pacific Affairs* 45:165–90. Further reflections on the impact of World War II on the Philippines.

Sturtevant, David R. 1962. "Sakdalism and Philippine Radicalism." *Journal of Asian Studies* 21:199–213. Sakdalism as the first "sophisticated" peasant movement in the Philippines.

1976. *Popular Uprisings in the Philippines, 1840–1940*. Ithaca, NY, and London: Cornell University Press. Charts a path from mysticism to sophistication; indispensable background to the Huk rebellion.

Taruc, Luis. 1953. *Born of the People*. New York: International Publishers. The Huk leader's genuinely gripping life story (as of 1950), ghostwritten by William J. Pomeroy and edited by James S. Allen.

1967. *He Who Rides the Tiger: The Story of an Asian Guerrilla Leader*. London: Geoffrey Chapman. Focuses on Taruc's adventures after 1950; written after his break from the Communist Party.

U.S. Department of State. 1987 (1950). "The Hukbalahaps." Pp. 70–7 in *The Philippines Reader*, edited by Daniel B. Schirmer and Stephen Rosskamm Shalom. Boston: South End Press. A fascinating and anxious State Department analysis of the Huks.

Welch, Richard E., Jr. 1984. "America's Philippine Policy in the Quirino Years (1948–1953): A Study in Patron-Client Diplomacy." Pp. 285–306 and 388–93 (endnotes) in *Reappraising an Empire: New Perspectives on Philippine-American History*, edited by Peter W. Stanley. Cambridge, MA: Harvard Studies in American-East Asian Relations, Harvard University Press. Emphasizes U.S. interventionism; Shalom (1977), however, provides much more detail about the U.S. role in the counterinsurgency against the Huks.

Wurfel, David. 1958. "Philippine Agrarian Reform Under Magsaysay." *Far Eastern Survey* 27:7–15, 23–30. Examines the results of Magsaysay's unprecedented, but extremely modest, land reform efforts after 1954.

1959. "Foreign Aid and Social Reform in Political Development: A Philippine Case Study." *American Political Science Review* 53:456–82. An analysis of U.S. aid during the Magsaysay era.

1988. *Filipino Politics: Development and Decay.* Quezon City: Ateneo de Manila University. An excellent general analysis; focuses primarily on the rise and fall of Marcos, but includes the 1946–72 background to that story.

III. Central America

A. General Studies (Including Latin America)

Abugattas, Luis A. 1987. "Populism and After: The Peruvian Experience." Pp. 121–43 in *Authoritarians and Democrats: Regime Transition in Latin America*, edited by James M. Malloy and Mitchell A. Seligson. Pittsburgh, PA: University of Pittsburgh Press. Background to the 1980s.

Adams, Jan S. 1992. *A Foreign Policy in Transition: Moscow's Retreat from Central America and the Caribbean, 1985–1992.* Durham, NC, and London: Duke University Press. The best work on the subject.

Aguero, Felipe. 1990. "The Military and Democracy in Venezuela." Pp. 257–75 in *The Military and Democracy: The Future of Civil-Military Relations in Latin America*, edited by Louis W. Goodman, Johanna S. R. Mendelson, and Juan Rial. Lexington, MA: Lexington Books. A useful overview.

Americas Watch [AW]. 1992. *Peru Under Fire: Human Rights Since the Return to Democracy.* New Haven, CT, and London: Yale University Press. This and the following report document the extreme abuses in Peru through the 1980s.

Amnesty International [AI]. 1990. *Peru: Continuing Human Rights Violations, 1989–90.* London: Amnesty International.

Anderson, Thomas P. 1988. *Politics in Central America: Guatemala, El Salvador, Honduras, and Nicaragua.* Revised edition. New York: Praeger. A basic introduction to the region.

Arango Z., Manuel. 1984. *FARC: Veinte años.* Bogota: Ediciones Aurora. A standard source on the Colombian insurgency, though now dated.

Arnson, Cynthia J. 1993. *Crossroads: Congress, the President, and Central America, 1976–1993.* Second edition. University Park, PA: Pennsylvania State University Press. A thorough study of U.S.-Central American relations for the period covered; see also LeoGrande 1998.

Arnson, Cynthia J. and Robin Kirk. 1993. *State of War: Political Violence and Counterinsurgency in Colombia.* New York: Human Rights Watch. Thorough documentation of army and paramilitary violence.

Baloyra-Herp, Enrique A. 1983a. "Reactionary Despotism in Central America." *Journal of Latin American Studies* 15:295–319. An influential conceptualization of the region, albeit one that applies best to El Salvador and Guatemala.

III. Central America

Barraclough, Solon L. and Michael F. Scott. 1987. *"The Rich Have Already Eaten . . .": Roots of Catastrophe in Central America*. Amsterdam: Transnational Institute. An astute analysis of the problem of food security, focusing mainly on El Salvador and Nicaragua.

Barry, Deborah, Raul Vergara, and Rodolfo Castro. 1987. "La guerra total: la nueva ideología contrainsurgente norteamericana." Pp. 187–237 in Raul Vergara Meneses et al., *Centroamérica: la guerra de baja intensidad*. San Jose, Costa Rica: Editorial DEI. An excellent overview of U.S. counterinsurgency strategy in Central America during the 1980s.

Barry, Tom. 1987. *Roots of Rebellion: Land and Hunger in Central America*. Boston: South End Press. The rural "roots" of rebellion. But would they have nurtured armed rebellion except in a garden of violent repression?

Barry, Tom and Deb Preusch. 1986. *The Central America Fact Book*. New York: Grove Press. A treasure trove of information, including extensive details on U.S. corporations in the region.

1988. *The Soft War: The Uses and Abuses of U.S. Economic Aid in Central America*. New York: Grove Press. Explores the counterinsurgent uses of economic and "humanitarian" aid.

Benjamin, Jules R. 1990. *The United States and the Origins of the Cuban Revolution: An Empire of Liberty in an Age of National Liberation*. Princeton, NJ: Princeton University Press. Extremely thoughtful and well researched. Perhaps the best book on U.S.-Cuban relations through the early years of the revolution.

Bermúdez, Lilia. 1987. *Guerra de baja intensidad: Reagan contra Centroamérica*. Mexico City: Siglo Veintiuno Editores. Explores how the U.S. applied the doctrine of "low-intensity war" in the region.

Berryman, Phillip. 1984. *The Religious Roots of Rebellion: Christians in Central American Revolutions*. Maryknoll, NY: Orbis Books. An outstanding, exhaustive study of liberation theology – theory and practice – in the region.

1994. *Stubborn Hope: Religion, Politics, and Revolution in Central America*. Maryknoll, NY: Orbis Books. Includes chapters on Nicaragua, El Salvador, and Guatemala in the 1980s.

Black, George. 1982. "Central America: Crisis in the Backyard." *New Left Review* 135:5–34. A short but perceptive overview.

Blank, David Eugene. 1973. *Politics in Venezuela*. Boston: Little, Brown. One of the best analyses of events through the 1960s.

Bonachea, Ramón L. and Marta San Martín. 1974. *The Cuban Insurrection, 1952–1959*. New Brunswick, NJ: Transaction. How Castro came to power. An excellent study.

Booth, John A. and Thomas W. Walker. 1993. *Understanding Central America*. Second edition. Boulder, CO, and London: Westview Press. An invaluable short introduction by two leading area experts. Includes a very astute analysis of the rebellions in the region.

Boudon, Lawrence. 1996. "Guerrillas and the State: The Role of the State in the Colombian Peace Process." *Journal of Latin American Studies* 28:279–97. Emphasizes how Colombia's historically weak state has allowed revolutionary groups to survive and even flourish in isolated areas.

Brockett, Charles D. 1998. *Land, Power, and Poverty: Agrarian Transformation and Political Conflict in Central America*. Second edition. Boulder, CO: Westview Press. An outstanding comparative study.

1991a. "The Structure of Political Opportunities and Peasant Mobilization in Central America." *Comparative Politics* 23:253–74. Social-movement theory visits Latin America. A perceptive piece.

1991b. "Sources of State Terrorism in Rural Central America." Pp. 59–76 in *State Organized Terror: The Case of Violent Internal Repression*, edited by P. Timothy Bushnell, Vladimir Shlapentokh, Christopher K. Vanderpool, and Jeyaratnam Sundram. Boulder, CO: Westview Press. One of the very best short analyses of political violence in the region.

1992. "Measuring Political Violence and Land Inequality in Central America." *American Political Science Review* 86:169–76. Emphasizes how politics mediates land inequality and political violence.

1995. "A Protest-Cycle Resolution of the Repression/Popular-Protest Paradox." Pp. 117–44 in *Repertoires and Cycles of Collective Action*, edited by Mark Traugott. Durham, NC, and London: Duke University Press. Contains some important insights, although the "resolution" is arguable; the author exaggerates the waning of protest in Guatemala and especially El Salvador after the early 1980s.

Brooke, James. 1993. "The Rebels Lose Leaders, But Give Peru No Peace." *The New York Times*, February 5, p. A3. Sendero after Gúzman's capture.

Bulmer-Thomas, Victor. 1983. "Economic Development Over the Long Run – Central America Since 1920." *Journal of Latin American Studies* 15:269–94. The condensed version of Bulmer-Thomas (1987).

1987. *The Political Economy of Central America Since 1920*. Cambridge, UK: Cambridge University Press. A detailed comparative treatment, with chapters on the origins and implications of the "crisis of 1979."

Burbach, Roger. 1984. "Introduction: Revolution and Reaction." Pp. 9–28 in *The Politics of Intervention: The United States in Central America*, edited by Roger Burbach and Patricia Flynn. New York: Monthly Review Press, Center for the Study of the Americas. A radical analysis of the region up through the early 1980s.

Burt, Jo-Marie and José López Ricci. 1994. "Shining Path After Guzmán." *NACLA Report on the Americas* 28 (3):6–9. Discusses the regroupment of Shining Path following Guzmán's arrest.

Cala, Andrés. 2000. The Enigmatic Guerrilla: FARC's Manuel Marulanda." *Current History* (February) 99:56–9. On the main Colombian guerrilla group and its long-time leader.

Camacho, Daniel and Rafael Menjívar. 1985. "El movimiento popular en Centroamérica (1970–1983): Síntesis y perspectivas." Pp. 9–61 in *Movimientos populares en Centroamérica*, edited by Daniel Camacho and Rafael Menjívar. San José, Costa Rica: Editorial Universitaria Centroamericana (EDUCA). Charts the emergence of a Central American "civil society."

Castañeda, Jorge G. 1993. *Utopia Unarmed: The Latin American Left After the Cold*

III. Central America

War. New York: Alfred A. Knopf. A sweeping history and analysis, with prescriptions for a revitalized left.

CEPAL [Comisión Económica para América Latina y el Caribe]. 1982. *Notas sobre la evolución del desarrollo social del istmo centroamericano hasta 1980*. Mexico City: CEPAL. Some important statistics.

Chernick, Marc. 1999. "Negotiating Peace amid Multiple Forms of Violence: The Protracted Search for a Settlement to the Armed Conflicts in Colombia." Pp. 159–99 in *Comparative Peace Processes in Latin America*, edited by Cynthia J. Arnson. Washington, DC: Woodrow Wilson Center Press; Stanford, CA: Stanford University Press. The elusive search for peace in Colombia; includes an appendix on Colombia's main guerrilla groups.

Coatsworth, John H. 1994. *Central America and the United States: The Clients and the Colossus*. New York: Twayne. An extremely valuable study of the postwar period, although the author draws some rather overgeneralized conclusions about the effects of the region's dependency on the United States.

Cohen, Youssef. 1994. *Radicals, Reformers, and Reactionaries: The Prisoner's Dilemma and the Collapse of Democracy in Latin America*. Chicago: University of Chicago Press. Game theory in Latin America.

Cotler, Julio. 1986. "Military Interventions and 'Transfer of Power to Civilians' in Peru." Pp. 148–172 in *Transitions from Authoritarian Rule: Latin America*, edited by Guillermo O'Donnell, Philippe C. Schmitter, and Laurence Whitehead. Baltimore and London: Johns Hopkins University Press. Military-civilian relations in Peru, by a noted Peruvian analyst.

Davis, Shelton H. 1985. "Agrarian Structure and Ethnic Resistance in Guatemalan and Salvadoran National Politics." Pp. 78–106 in *Ethnicities and Nations*, edited by Remo Guidieri, Francesco Pellizzi, and Stanley J. Tambiah. Houston, TX: Rothko Chapel. An interesting discussion of the ethnic question.

Deere, Carmen Diana. 1984. "Agrarian Reform as Revolution and Counter-Revolution: Nicaragua and El Salvador." Pp. 163–88 in *The Politics of Intervention: The United States in Central America*, edited by Roger Burbach and Patricia Flynn. New York: Monthly Review Press. Emphasizes the failures of the Salvadoran reform.

Degregori, Carlos Iván. 1990. *El surgimiento de Sendero Luminoso: Ayacucho 1969–1979*. Lima: Instituto de Estudios Peruanos. An excellent study of the origins of the Shining Path insurgency.

———. 1994. "Shining Path and Counterinsurgency Strategy Since the Arrest of Abimael Guzmán." Pp. 81–100 in *Peru in Crisis: Dictatorship or Democracy?*, edited by Joseph S. Tulchin and Gary Bland. Boulder, CO, and London: Lynne Rienner Publishers. An important overview.

———. 1999. "Reflections." Pp. 251–6 in *Comparative Peace Processes in Latin America*, edited by Cynthia J. Arnson. Washington, DC: Woodrow Wilson Center Press; Stanford, CA: Stanford University Press. Provocative thoughts on the demise of the Shining Path movement.

DESCO [Centro de Estudios y Promocion del Desarrollo]. 1989. *Violencia política en el Peru*. Two volumes. Lima: DESCO. Contains a wealth of information.

351

Dix, Robert H. 1984. "Why Revolutions Succeed and Fail." *Polity* 16:423–46. The first of a number of studies to emphasize the vulnerability of personalist dictators to overthrow by broad "negative" coalitions.

Domínguez, Jorge I. and Marc Lindenberg. 1984. *Central America: Current Crisis and Future Prospects*. New York: Foreign Policy Association. A short introduction, focusing mainly on Nicaragua and El Salvador.

Dore, Elizabeth and John Weeks. 1992. "Up from Feudalism." *NACLA Report on the Americas* 26 (3):38–45. An interesting retrospective on the crisis years, albeit one with a rather reductionistic view of politics.

Dunkerley, James. 1985. "Central America: The Collapse of the Military System." Pp. 171–200 in *The Political Dilemmas of Military Regimes*, edited by Christopher Clapham and George Philip. London: Croom Helm. An astute analysis of military regimes under pressure.

1988. *Power in the Isthmus: A Political History of Modern Central America*. London and New York: Verso. The most extensive historical treatment of the region; focuses mainly on the post–World War II period.

1994. *The Pacification of Central America: Political Change in the Isthmus, 1987–1993*. London and New York: Verso. A short study of the period; includes a detailed chronology and helpful statistical appendices.

Ellner, Steve. 1988. *Venezuela's Movimiento al Socialismo: From Guerrilla Defeat to Innovative Politics*. Durham, NC: Duke University Press. How former guerrillas have worked above-ground in Venezuela.

Fagen, Richard. 1987. *Forging Peace: The Challenge of Central America*. New York: Basil Blackwell. A short, policy-oriented introduction to the regional crisis.

Flora, Jan L. and Edelberto Torres-Rivas. 1989. "Sociology of Developing Societies: Historical Bases of Insurgency in Latin America." Pp. 32–55 in *Sociology of "Developing Societies": Central America*, edited by Jan L. Flora and Edelberto Torres-Rivas. New York: Monthly Review Press. An interesting interpretive essay that links the regional insurgencies to the development of oligarchic states that excluded popular classes.

Flynn, Patricia. 1984. "Central America: The Roots of Revolt." Pp. 29–64 in *The Politics of Intervention: The United States in Central America*, edited by Roger Burbach and Patricia Flynn. New York: Monthly Review Press. A useful short introduction from a radical perspective.

Fogel, D. 1985. *Revolution in Central America*. San Francisco, CA: Ism Press. A Marxist perspective on El Salvador, Nicaragua, and Guatemala.

Foran, John. 1994. "The Causes of Latin American Social Revolutions: Searching for Patterns in Mexico, Cuba, and Nicaragua." Pp. 209–44 in *World Society Studies, Vol. 3: Conflicts and New Departures in World Society*, edited by Peter Lengyel and Volker Bornschier. New Brunswick, NJ: Transaction. See also Foran 1992, 1997b.

Foran, John, Linda Klouzal, and Jean-Pierre Rivera. 1997. "Who Makes Revolutions? Class, Gender, and Race in the Mexican, Cuban, and Nicaraguan Revolutions." *Research in Social Movements, Conflict and Change* 20:1–60. An exhaustive study of the protagonists of revolution in three Latin American cases.

III. Central America

Gallardo, María Eugenia and José Roberto Lopez. 1986. *Centroamérica: La crisis en cifras*. San José, Costa Rica: Instituto Interamericano de Cooperacion para la Agricultura (IICA) and Facultad Latinoamericana de Ciencias Sociales (FLACSO). A wealth of statistical data on the region.

Giraldo, Javier. 1996. *Colombia: The Genocidal Democracy*. Monroe, ME: Common Courage Press. Documents the horrendous human rights abuses of the Colombian state – "the state which devours the country."

Gleijeses, Piero. 1986. "The Reagan Doctrine and Central America." *Current History* 85:401–4, 435–7. A perceptive overview of U.S. policy.

Goldfrank, Walter L. 1979. "Theories of Revolution and Revolution Without Theory: The Case of Mexico." *Theory and Society* 7:135–65. One of the best short analyses of the Mexican revolution.

Gonzalez, José E. 1992. "Guerrillas and Coca in the Upper Huallaga Valley." Pp. 105–25 in *The Shining Path of Peru*, edited by David Scott Palmer. New York: St. Martin's Press. A regional study of peasant support for the Shining Path.

González Casanova, Pablo. 1984. *La hegemonia del pueblo y la lucha centroamericana*. San José, Costa Rica: Editorial Universitaria Centroamericana (EDUCA). A short Gramscian interpretation by a well-known Mexican scholar.

Gorriti, Gustavo. 1999. *The Shining Path: A History of the Millenarian War in Peru*. Translated by Robin Kirk. Chapel Hill, NC: University of North Carolina Press. One of the best interpretive histories of the Shining Path through the 1980s.

Gott, Richard. 1970. *Guerrilla Movements in Latin America*. Garden City, NY: Doubleday. One of the best comparative treatments of the guerrilla movements of the 1960s. (Also published as *Rural Guerrillas in Latin America* [Harmondsworth, UK: Penguin Books, 1973].)

Gross, Liza. 1995. *Handbook of Leftist Guerrilla Movements in Latin America and the Caribbean*. Boulder, CO: Westview Press. Includes short descriptions of revolutionary groups throughout the region; a very useful reference work.

Gude, Edward W. 1975. "Batista and Betancourt: Alternative Responses to Violence." Pp. 569–85 in *Revolutionary Guerrilla Warfare*, edited by Sam C. Sarkesian. Chicago: Precedent Publishing, Inc. An interesting comparison of a failed (Cuba) and successful (Venezuela) counterinsurgency.

Gudmundson, Lowell. 1986. *Costa Rica Before Coffee: Society and Economy on the Eve of the Export Boom*. Baton Rouge, LA: Louisiana State University Press. Interesting reflections on the origins of democracy in Costa Rica.

Guevara, Che. 1985 (1960). *Guerrilla Warfare*, with an Introduction and Case Studies by Brian Loveman and Thomas M. Davies, Jr. Lincoln, NE: University of Nebraska Press. Guevara's how-to manual, with warnings about the futility of armed struggle in democracies (a view Che later abandoned).

Halloran, Richard. 1987. "Latin Guerrillas Joining Forces, U.S. Officers Say." *The New York Times* (March 3). Wishful thinking.

Harnecker, Marta. 1984. *Pueblos en armas*. Mexico City: Ediciones Era. Important and sometimes fascinating interviews with guerrilla leaders in Nicaragua, El Salvador, and Guatemala.

Hellinger, Daniel C. 1991. *Venezuela: Tarnished Democracy*. Boulder, CO: Westview Press. A short but helpful overview.

Human Rights Watch. 1996. *Colombia's Killer Networks: The Military-Paramilitary Partnership and the United States*. New York: Human Rights Watch. A chilling follow-up to Arnson and Kirk 1993.

———. 2000. *The Ties That Bind: Colombia and Military-Paramilitary Links*. New York: Human Rights Watch. Notes that military support for and collusion with paramilitary groups are national in scope.

Jamail, Milton and Margo Gutierrez. 1987. "Getting Down to Business." *NACLA Report on the Americas* 21 (2):25–30. Discusses how Israel filled the gap when the United States suspended military aid to brutal regimes.

Karl, Terry. 1994. "Central America in the Twenty-First Century: The Prospects for a Democratic Region." Paper presented at workshop on "Democracy in the Americas: Approaching the Year 2000," Kellogg Institute, Notre Dame, April–May 1994. Sober reflections.

———. 1995. "The Hybrid Regimes of Central America." *Journal of Democracy* 6:72–86. Between democracy and authoritarianism.

Kenworthy, Eldon. 1973. "The Function of the Little-Known Case in Theory Formation, or What Peronism Wasn't." *Comparative Politics* 6:1–35. How big theories sometimes rest (and crumble) on little-known cases.

Kirk, Robin. 1991. *The Decade of Chaqwa: Peru's Internal Refugees*. Washington, DC: U.S. Committee for Refugees. A legacy of the revolutionary conflict.

Krauss, Clifford. 1991. *Inside Central America: Its People, Politics, and History*. New York: Simon & Schuster. A journalistic overview.

———. 2000. "Colombia's Rebels Keep the Marxist Faith." *The New York Times*, July 25, p. A1. A report from the front lines.

Krumwiede, Heinrich-W. 1984. "Regimes and Revolution in Central America." Pp. 9–36 in *Political Change in Central America: Internal and External Dimensions*, edited by Wolf Grabendorff, Heinrich-W. Krumweide, and Jörg Todt. Boulder, CO: Westview Press. A very helpful sketch of the subject.

LaFeber, Walter. 1993. *Inevitable Revolutions: The United States in Central America*. Second edition. New York: Norton. One of the best and better-known historical overviews, with special emphasis on the perverse consequences of U.S. policy toward the region. The book's provocative title, however, is quite misleading.

Landau, Saul. 1993. *The Guerrilla Wars of Central America: Nicaragua, El Salvador, Guatemala*. New York: St. Martin's Press. A short but useful overview by a sympathetic observer.

LeoGrande, William M. 1984. "Through the Looking Glass: The Kissinger Report on Central America." *World Policy Journal* 1:251–84. The author demolishes a now- (and best) forgotten semiofficial report.

LeoGrande, William M. 1998. *Our Own Backyard: The United States in Central America, 1977–1992*. Chapel Hill, NC: University of North Carolina Press. A monumental survey of U.S. policy by an author with intimate knowledge of the region.

III. Central America

Lindenberg, Marc. 1990. "World Economic Cycles and Central American Political Instability." *World Politics* 42:397–421. Argues that world economic crises "have been a more important determinant of political instability [in Central America] than any other factor, such as density of population or ethnic composition, with the exception of initial regime type" (p. 419).

Liss, Sheldon B. 1991. *Radical Thought in Central America.* Boulder, CO: Westview Press. Short summaries of the ideas of leading radical intellectuals in each country.

Loveman, Brian and Thomas M. Davies, Jr. 1997. "Venezuela." Pp. 209–31 in Che Guevara, *Guerrilla Warfare,* with an Introduction and Case Studies by Brian Loveman and Thomas M. Davies, Jr. Third edition. Lincoln, NE: University of Nebraska Press. A short overview of the guerrilla insurgency of the 1960s.

McAuley, Christopher. 1997. "Race and the Process of the American Revolutions." Pp. 168–202 in *Theorizing Revolutions,* edited by John Foran. London: Routledge. A path-breaking effort to "bring race back in" to theories of revolution.

McClintock, Cynthia. 1984. "Why Peasants Rebel: The Case of Peru's Sendero Luminoso." *World Politics* 37:48–84. An early analysis of peasant support for the Shining Path.

    1994. "Theories of Revolution and the Case of Peru." Pp. 243–58 in *The Shining Path of Peru,* edited by David Scott Palmer. Second edition. New York: St. Martin's Press. Theorizing the insurgency.

    1998. *Revolutionary Movements in Latin America: El Salvador's FMLN and Peru's Shining Path.* Washington, DC: United States Institute of Peace Press. An extremely well-researched and theoretically sophisticated analysis of two important insurgencies, although the author's theory (unlike her data) still underplays the importance of the state for generating broad revolutionary movements.

    1999. "The Decimation of Peru's Sendero Luminoso." Pp. 223–49 in *Comparative Peace Processes in Latin America,* edited by Cynthia J. Arnson. Washington, DC: Woodrow Wilson Center Press; Stanford, CA: Stanford University Press. An excellent overview of the question.

Mainwaring, Scott. 1999. "The Surprising Resilience of Elected Governments." *Journal of Democracy* 10:101–14. On the spread of democratic and semi-democratic regimes in Latin America during a time of economic crisis.

Maira, Luis. 1986. "Authoritarianism in Central America: A Comparative Perspective." Pp. 14–29 in *The Central American Impasse,* edited by Giuseppe Di Palma and Laurence Whitehead. New York: St. Martin's Press. See also Krumweide (1984).

Manwaring, Max G., ed. 1991. *Uncomfortable Wars: Toward a New Paradigm of Low Intensity Conflict.* Boulder, CO: Westview Press. Essays on counterinsurgency.

Manwaring, Max G., Courtney E. Prisk, and John T. Fishel. 1991. "Other Actions That Make a Difference: The Case of Peru." Pp. 93–101 in *Uncomfortable Wars: Toward a New Paradigm of Low Intensity Conflict,* edited by Max G. Manwaring. Boulder, CO: Westview Press. On the failures of counterinsurgency in Peru during the 1980s.

355

Mauceri, Philip. 1991. "Military Politics and Counter-Insurgency in Peru." *Journal of Interamerican Studies and World Affairs* 33:83–109. A useful overview of the Peruvian counterinsurgency through the 1980s.

1997. "State Development and Counter-Insurgency in Peru." Pp. 152–74 in *The Counter-Insurgent State: Guerrilla Warfare and State Building in the Twentieth Century*, edited by Paul B. Rich and Richard Stubbs. London: Macmillan. Traces the evolution of Peru's counterinsurgency (1980–92), emphasizing the historic weakness of the state in the Andean highlands.

Meeks, Brian. 1993. *Caribbean Revolutions and Revolutionary Theory: An Assessment of Cuba, Nicaragua and Grenada*. London: Macmillan. Argues that these were "post-colonial revolutions from the middle," a theory which underplays their widespread popular support.

Menjívar, Rafael and Juan Diego Trejos. 1992. *La pobreza en América Central*. Second edition. San José, Costa Rica: Facultad Latinoamericana de Ciencias Sociales (FLACSO). A short analysis of poverty in the region, replete with useful statistics.

Midlarsky, Manus I. and Kenneth Roberts. 1985. "Class, State, and Revolution in Central America: Nicaragua and El Salvador Compared." *Journal of Conflict Resolution* 29:163–93. Stresses the difference between the "instrumentalist state" in El Salvador and the "autonomous personalist state" in prerevolutionary Nicaragua.

Millet, Richard. 1984. "Praetorians or Patriots? The Central American Military." Pp. 69–91 in *Central America: Anatomy of Conflict*, edited by Robert S. Leiken. New York: Pergamon. Not a tough question to answer.

1992. "Politicized Warriors: The Military and Central American Politics." Pp. 53–75 in *Political Parties and Democracy in Central America*, edited by Louis W. Goodman, William M. LeoGrande, and Johanna Mendelson Forman. Boulder, CO: Westview Press. An introductory overview.

Needler, Martin C. 1987. *The Problem of Democracy in Latin America*. Lexington, MA: Lexington Books. Chapter 7 ("The Politics of Coffee") discusses Guatemala, El Salvador, Costa Rica, and Colombia; an interesting counterpoint to Paige (1987).

Obando, Enrique. 1998. "Civil-Military Relations in Peru, 1980–1996: How to Control and Coop the Military (and the Consequences of Doing So)." Pp. 385–410 in *Shining and Other Paths: War and Society in Peru, 1980–1995*, edited by Steve J. Stern. Durham, NC: Duke University Press. A provocative overview.

O'Donnell, Guillermo A. 1973. *Modernization and Bureaucratic-Authoritarianism: Studies in South American Politics*. Berkeley, CA: Institute of International Studies, University of California. The classic study of bureaucratic authoritarianism.

Paige, Jeffery M. 1987. "Coffee and Politics in Central America." Pp. 141–90 in *Crises in the Caribbean Basin*, edited by Richard Tardanico. Newbury Park, CA: Sage Publications. A very important analysis of the coffee-growing elites in the region.

1997. *Coffee and Power: Revolution and the Rise of Democracy in Central America*. Cambridge, MA: Harvard University Press. An important study, although for the post-1979 period it focuses less on revolution and more on elite views of democracy.

Palmer, David Scott. 1986. "Rebellion in Rural Peru: The Origins and Evolution of Sendero Luminoso." *Comparative Politics* 18:127–146. An early attempt to make sense of it all.

——— ed. 1994a. *The Shining Path of Peru*. Second edition. New York: St. Martin's Press. The essays in this collection provide perhaps the best introduction to the subject. See also Stern 1998.

——— 1994b. "Conclusion: The View from the Windows." Pp. 259–73 in *The Shining Path of Peru*, edited by David Scott Palmer. Second edition. New York: St. Martin's Press. Interesting general reflections on the insurgency.

——— 1996. "'Fujipopulism' and Peru's Progress." *Current History* (February), 70–5. A report on the surprising popularity of an authoritarian president.

Pardo, Rafael. 2000. "Columbia's Two-Front War." *Foreign Affairs* (July/August) 79:64–73. On guerrillas and drug traffickers.

Pérez, Luis A., Jr. 1988. *Cuba: Between Reform and Revolution*. New York: Oxford University Press. The best general history of modern Cuba.

Pérez Brignoli, Hector. 1985. *Breve historia de Centroamérica*. Madrid: Alianza Editorial. Includes two short but useful chapters on the post–World War II period. (This book was published in English in 1989 by the University of California Press.)

Pérez Brignoli, Héctor and Yolanda Baires Martínez. 1983. "Growth and Crisis in the Central American Economies, 1950–1980." *Journal of Latin American Studies* 15:365–98. Brings together some interesting statistical data.

Pérez-Stable, Marifeli. 1993. *The Cuban Revolution: Origins, Course, and Legacy*. New York: Oxford University Press. An excellent, nonpolemical overview; see my discussion in Chapter 2.

——— 1999. "Caught in a Contradiction: Cuban Socialism between Mobilization and Normalization." *Comparative Politics* 32:63–82. How Cuban Communism has persisted, drawing from "the virtually inexhaustible fount of nationalism" (p. 63).

Petras, James F. and Morris H. Morley. 1983. "Imperialism and Intervention in the Third World: U.S. Foreign Policy and Central America." Pp. 219–38 in *The Socialist Register 1983*, edited by Ralph Miliband and John Saville. London: Merlin Press. An overview of U.S. policy in the region through the 1970s.

——— 1990. *U.S. Hegemony Under Siege: Class, Politics, and Development in Latin America*. London: Verso. Interesting essays by two well-known radical analysts.

Pizarro, Eduardo. 1992. "Revolutionary Guerrilla Groups in Colombia." Pp. 217–39 in *Violence in Colombia: The Contemporary Crisis in Historical Perspective*, edited by Charles Bergquist, Ricardo Peñaranda, and Gonzalo Sánchez. Wilmington, DE: Scholarly Resources Inc. An excellent introduction.

Poole, Deborah and Gerardo Renique. 1991. "The New Chroniclers of Peru: U.S. Scholars and their 'Shining Path' of Peasant Rebellion." *Bulletin of Latin*

American Research 10:133–91. A very harsh assessment of some U.S. scholarship on Shining Path.

1992. *Peru: Time of Fear*. London: Latin America Bureau. One of the very best books on Peru and the 1980s in particular.

Powell, John Duncan. 1971. *Political Mobilization of the Venezuelan Peasant*. Cambridge, MA: Harvard University Press. Excellent source on the postwar period.

Reyna Izaguirre, Carlos. 1996. "Shining Path in the 21st Century: Actors in Search of a New Script." *NACLA Report on the Americas* 30 (1):37–8. "Shining Path poses few risks to Peru's stablility in the short term, but the risks may grow as time marches on" (p. 38).

Rivera Urrutia, Eugenio, Ana Sojo, and José Roberto López. 1986. *Centroamérica: Politica economica y crisis*. San José, Costa Rica: Editorial Departamento Ecuménico de Investigaciones (DEI). Essays on the economic origins of the regional crisis and its various ramifications during the 1980s.

Rohter, Larry. 2000. "Colombians Tell of Massacre, as Army Stood By." *The New York Times*, July 14: A1. On a paramilitary massacre of as many as seventy-one villagers.

Selbin, Eric. 1993. *Modern Latin American Revolutions*. Boulder, CO: Westview Press. Focuses mainly on the outcomes of revolutions in Bolivia, Cuba, Grenada, and (especially) Nicaragua, emphasizing the role of revolutionary leaders and popular beliefs.

1997b. "Magical Revolutions: The Future of Revolution in the Land of Magical Realism." Paper presented at the Twentieth International Congress of the Latin American Studies Association (LASA), Guadalajara, Mexico. Argues that there are revolutions yet to come in Latin America.

Shugart, Matthew Soberg. 1987. "States, Revolutionary Conflict and Democracy: El Salvador and Nicaragua in Comparative Perspective." *Government and Opposition* 22:13–32. An important comparative analysis of rebellion and democratization.

Sims, Calvin. 1996a. "Blasts Propel Peru's Rebels from Defunct to Dangerous." *The New York Times*, August 5: A6. On the Shining Path, still active into the late 1990s. See also the following two articles.

1996b. "On the Trail of Peru's Maoist Rebels." *The New York Times*, August 8: A12.

1997. "Family Pays Price of a Rebel's Fervor." *The New York Times*, February 24: A4.

Smith, Carol A. and Jeff Boyer. 1987. "Central America Since 1979: Part 1." *Annual Review of Anthropology* 16:197–221. This and Smith, Boyer, and Diskin (1988) provide a helpful review of the rapidly growing literature.

Smith, Carol A., Jefferson Boyer, and Martin Diskin. 1988. "Central America Since 1979, Part II." *Annual Review of Anthropology* 17:331–64.

Smith, Wayne S. 1992. "The Soviet Union and Cuba in Central America: Guardians Against Democracy?" Pp. 287–306 in *Political Parties and Democracy in Central America*, edited by Louis W. Goodman, William M. LeoGrande, and Johanna Mendelson Forman. Boulder, CO: Westview Press.

Concludes that the Soviet Union and Cuba were actors of decidedly secondary importance in the region.

Starn, Orin. 1992. "'I Dreamed of Foxes and Hawks': Reflections on Peasant Protest, New Social Movements, and the *Rondas Campesinas* of Northern Peru." Pp. 89–111 in *The Making of Social Movements in Latin America: Identity, Strategy, and Democracy*, edited by Arturo Escobar and Sonia E. Alvarez. Boulder, CO: Westview Press. An important analysis of the rondas.

——— 1998. "Villagers at Arms: War and Counterrevolution in the Central-South Andes." Pp. 224–57 in *Shining and Other Paths: War and Society in Peru, 1980–1995*, edited by Steve J. Stern. Durham, NC: Duke University Press. An important study of peasants at war with revolutionaries.

——— 1999. *Nightwatch: The Politics of Protest in the Andes*. Durham, NC: Duke University Press. The best study of Peru's rondas, which helped defeat Sendero Luminoso, although Sendero was not strong where the author conducted fieldwork.

Stepan, Alfred. 1988. *Rethinking Military Politics: Brazil and the Southern Cone*. Princeton, NJ: Princeton University Press. An important analysis of "military prerogatives" as an impediment to democratization.

Stern, Steve J., ed. 1998. *Shining and Other Paths: War and Society in Peru, 1980–1995*. Durham, NC: Duke University Press. Excellent essays on the rise and fall of Shining Path.

Stone, Samuel Z. 1990. *The Heritage of the Conquistadors: Ruling Classes in Central America from the Conquest to the Sandinistas*. Lincoln, NE, and London: University of Nebraska Press. Demonstrates the common ancestry of the region's elite families.

Taylor, Lewis. 1998. "Counter-Insurgency Strategy, the PCP-Sendero Luminoso and the Civil War in Peru, 1980–1996." *Bulletin of Latin American Research* 17:35–58. How the Shining Path insurgency was (eventually) defeated.

Toriello Garrido, Guillermo. 1985. *A Popular History of Two Revolutions: Guatemala and Nicaragua*. Translated by Rebecca Schwaner. San Francisco, CA: Synthesis Publications. A short analysis of the similarities and differences between the Guatemalan "revolution" of 1944–54 and the Nicaraguan Revolution.

Torres Rivas, Edelberto. 1983a. *Crisis del poder en Centroamérica*. San José, Costa Rica: Editorial Universitaria Centroamericana (EDUCA). An interesting collection of essays on the regional crisis, the Nicaraguan Revolution, and Guatemala.

——— 1983b. "Central America Today: A Study in Regional Dependency." Pp. 1–33 in *Trouble in Our Backyard: Central America and the United States in the Eighties*, edited by Martin Diskin. New York: Pantheon Books. A short socio-economic profile.

——— 1987. *Centroamérica: La democracia posible*. San José, Costa Rica: Editorial Universitaria Centroamericana (EDUCA) and Facultad Latinoamericana de Ciencias Sociales (FLACSO). Interesting and wide-ranging essays.

——— 1989. *Repression and Resistance: The Struggle for Democracy in Central America*. Translated by Jeff Sluyter. Boulder, CO: Westview Press. Translations of selected essays in Torres Rivas 1983, 1987.

1991. "Crisis and Conflict, 1930 to the Present." Translated by Elizabeth Ladd. Pp. 69–118 in *Central America Since Independence*, edited by Leslie Bethell. Cambridge, UK: Cambridge University Press. A concise overview.

1993. *History and Society in Central America*. Translated by Douglass Sullivan-González. Austin, TX: University of Texas Press. A classic study, originally published in 1969, belatedly translated into English; includes disappointingly brief reflections on the recent upheavals in the region.

Torres Rivas, Edelberto and María Eugenia Gallardo. 1987. *Para entender Centroamérica: Resumen bibliografico, 1960–1984*. San José, Costa Rica: Instituto Centroamericano de Documentacion e Investigacion Social (ICADIS). An extensive bibliography of Spanish-language sources on the region.

Vilas, Carlos M. 1988. "Popular Insurgency and Social Revolution in Central America." *Latin American Perspectives* 56 (1):55–77. Provocative reflections on the topic.

1989. "Revolutionary Unevenness in Central America." *New Left Review* 175:111–25. Short but smart; an extended review of Dunkerley 1988.

1995. *Between Earthquakes and Volcanoes: Market, State, and the Revolutions in Central America*. Translated by Ted Kuster. New York: Monthly Review Press. An interesting overview by a knowledgeable observer, sensitive to local particularities. See also Vilas's (1986) important study of the Nicaraguan Revolution.

Weaver, Frederick Stirton. 1994. *Inside the Volcano: The History and Political Economy of Central America*. Boulder, CO: Westview Press. A broad historical overview, from colonial times to the present; includes a chapter on the recent revolutionary upheavals.

Weeks, John. 1985. *The Economies of Central America*. New York and London: Holmes and Meier. An excellent thematic overview.

1986a. "An Interpretation of the Central American Crisis." *Latin American Research Review* 21:31–53. An important if somewhat overgeneralized analysis. See also Dore and Weeks (1992) for an update.

1986b. "Land, Labour and Despotism in Central America." Pp. 111–29 in *The Central American Impasse*, edited by Giuseppe Di Palma and Laurence Whitehead. New York: St. Martin's Press. Exploitation backed by repression.

White, Richard Alan. 1984. *The Morass: United States Intervention in Central America*. New York: Harper and Row. An analysis of U.S. counterinsurgency doctrine and practice.

Wickham-Crowley, Timothy P. 1987. "The Rise (and Sometimes Fall) of Guerrilla Governments in Latin America." *Sociological Forum* 2:473–99.

1989a. "Winners, Losers, and Also-Rans: Toward a Comparative Sociology of Latin American Guerrilla Movements." Pp. 132–81 in *Power and Popular Protest: Latin American Social Movements*, edited by Susan Eckstein. Berkeley, CA, and Los Angeles: University of California Press. This important chapter and the preceding article anticipate the findings in the following book.

1992. *Guerrillas and Revolution in Latin America: A Comparative Study of Insurgents and Regimes Since 1956*. Princeton, NJ: Princeton University Press. The best available comparative study of guerrilla-based revolutionary movements in Latin America (or anywhere else, for that matter); theoretically nimble and extraordinarily well researched.

Williams, Robert G. 1986. *Export Agriculture and the Crisis in Central America.* Chapel Hill, NC, and London: University of North Carolina Press. An excellent comparative analysis; one of the best.

1994. *States and Social Evolution: Coffee and the Rise of National Governments in Central America.* Chapel Hill, NC, and London: University of North Carolina Press. Although the author's focus is primarily on the nineteenth century, this study reveals a great deal about contemporary differences among Central American states.

Winson, Anthony. 1978. "Class Structure and Agrarian Transition in Central America." *Latin American Perspectives* 5 (4):27–48. A rare analysis before the storm.

WOLA [Washington Office on Latin America]. 1989. *Colombia Besieged: Political Violence and State Responsibility.* Washington, DC: Washington Office on Latin America. Human rights abuses through the 1980s.

Woodward, Ralph Lee, Jr. 1984. "The Rise and Decline of Liberalism in Central America: Historical Perspective on the Contemporary Crisis." *Journal of Interamerican Studies and World Affairs* 26:291–312. An important analysis by one of the deans of Central American studies.

1985. *Central America: A Nation Divided.* Second edition. New York and Oxford, UK: Oxford University Press. An outstanding history; includes a chronology and a very extensive bibliographical essay (see also the following bibliographical overview).

1987. "The Historiography of Modern Central America Since 1960." *Hispanic American Historical Review* 67:461–96.

Woy-Hazleton, Sandra and William A. Hazleton. 1994. "Shining Path and the Marxist Left." Pp. 225–42 in *The Shining Path of Peru*, edited by David Scott Palmer. Second edition. New York: St. Martin's Press. On the bitter relationship among revolutionary groups in Peru.

Yashar, Deborah J. 1997. *Demanding Democracy: Reform and Reaction in Costa Rica and Guatemala, 1870s–1950s.* Stanford, CA: Stanford University Press. An outstanding study of the coalitional origins of democracy.

B. *Nicaragua*

Agudelo, William, ed. 1982. *El asalto a San Carlos: Testimonios de Solentiname.* Managua: Editorial La Ocarina, Ministerio de Cultura. Interesting interviews with survivors of the Sandinista attack on the National Guard barracks in San Carlos in October 1977.

Arias, Pilar. 1980. *Nicaragua: Revolución – Relatos de combatientes del Frente Sandinista.* Mexico City: Siglo Veintiuno. An interesting collection of interviews with Sandinista leaders and combatants.

Baumeister, Eduardo. 1985. "The Structure of Nicaraguan Agriculture and the Sandinista Agrarian Reform." Pp. 10–35 in *Nicaragua: A Revolution Under Siege*, edited by Richard Harris and Carlos M. Vilas. London: Zed Books.

361

Emphasizes the distinctiveness, compared to other Central American countries, of Nicaragua's substantial sector of medium-sized farms.

Benjamin, Alan. 1989. *Nicaragua: Dynamics of an Unfinished Revolution*. San
Francisco, CA: Walnut Publishing. A Trotskyist critique of the revolution,
focusing mainly on the postinsurrectionary period.

Bermann, Karl. 1986. *Under the Big Stick: Nicaragua and the United States Since
1848*. Covers much the same period, and from much the same perspective, as
Selser (1984).

Biderman, Jaime. 1983. "The Development of Capitalism in Nicaragua: A Political Economic History." *Latin American Perspectives* 10 (1):7–32. Summarizes
the author's Berkeley dissertation.

Black, George. 1981. *Triumph of the People: The Sandinista Revolution in Nicaragua*.
London: Zed Press. A sympathetic general account.

Booth, John A. 1985. *The End and the Beginning: The Nicaraguan Revolution*. Second
edition. Boulder, CO, and London: Westview Press. A solid overview by a
leading scholar of Central America; includes a good discussion of the opposition to Somoza Debayle and of the insurrection.

Bulmer-Thomas, Victor. 1991. "Nicaragua Since 1930." Pp. 227–76 in *Central
America Since Independence*, edited by Leslie Bethell. Cambridge, UK: Cambridge University Press. A brief historical overview.

Chavarría, Ricardo E. 1994 (1982). "The Revolutionary Insurrection." Pp. 159–65
in *Revolutions: Theoretical, Comparative, and Historical Studies*, edited by Jack A.
Goldstone. Second edition. Fort Worth, TX: Harcourt Brace. An important
and informative analysis of the insurrection.

Christian, Shirley. 1986. *Nicaragua: Revolution in the Family*. New York: Random
House. An often tendentious journalistic account, most of which focuses on
the early 1980s.

Close, David. 1988. *Nicaragua: Politics, Economics and Society*. London and New
York: Pinter Publishers. A broad, workmanlike overview, similar to Walker
(1985a).

Cuzán, Alfred G. 1991. "Resource Mobilization and Political Opportunity in the
Nicaraguan Revolution: The Praxis." *American Journal of Economics and Sociology* 50:71–83. The revolution through the lens of social-movement theory.

Dickey, Christopher. 1987. *With the Contras: A Reporter in the Wilds of Nicaragua*. New York: Simon and Schuster. A journalistic account of the counterrevolution.

Diederich, Bernard. 1981. *Somoza and the Legacy of U.S. Involvement in Central
America*. Maplewood, NJ: Waterfront Press. An interesting first-hand account
of the Somoza dynasty by the long-time *Time* correspondent.

Enriquez, Laura J. 1991. *Harvesting Change: Labor and Agrarian Reform in
Nicaragua, 1979–1990*. Chapel Hill, NC, and London: University of North
Carolina Press. Includes a fine discussion of dependent development in
Nicaragua prior to the revolution.

Everingham, Mark. 1996. *Revolution and the Multiclass Coalition in Nicaragua*. Pittsburgh, PA: University of Pittsburgh Press. An important study of how sectors
of the Nicaraguan bourgeoisie came to cooperate with revolutionaries.

III. Central America

Gilbert, Dennis. 1986. "Nicaragua." Pp. 88–124 and 385–90 (endnotes) in *Confronting Revolution: Security Through Diplomacy in Central America*, edited by Morris J. Blachman, William M. LeoGrande, and Kenneth E. Sharpe. New York: Pantheon Books. Focuses mainly on the postinsurrectionary period.

——. 1988. *Sandinistas: The Party and the Revolution*. New York: Basil Blackwell. A finely balanced overview.

Gonzalez, Mike. 1990. *Nicaragua: What Went Wrong?* London: Bookmarks. Another critique of the revolution from the left, rather similar in perspective to Benjamin (1989).

Goodsell, James Nelson. 1982. "Nicaragua." Pp. 52–60 in *Communism in Central America and the Caribbean*, edited by Robert Wesson. Stanford, CA: Stanford University, Hoover Institution Press.

Gorman, Stephen M. 1984. "Social Change and Political Revolution: The Case of Nicaragua." Pp. 33–66 in *Central America: Crisis and Adaptation*, edited by Steve C. Ropp and James A. Morris. Albuquerque, NM: University of New Mexico Press.

Gould, Jeffrey L. 1990. *To Lead as Equals: Rural Protest and Political Consciousness in Chinandega, Nicaragua, 1912–1979*. Chapel Hill, NC, and London: University of North Carolina Press. A marvelous oral history. Although the revolution itself receives relatively little attention, Gould helps us understand how it could occur.

Gutiérrez Mayorga, Gustavo. 1985. "Historia del movimiento obrero de Nicaragua (1900–1976)." Pp. 196–252 in *Historia del movimiento obrero en américa latina*, vol. 2, edited by Pablo González Casanova. Mexico City: Siglo Veintiuno Editores. Emphasizes the limited influence of trade unions under the Somozas.

Hodges, Donald C. 1986. *Intellectual Foundations of the Nicaraguan Revolution*. Austin, TX: University of Texas Press. Discusses the ideology and strategy of both Sandino and the Sandinistas.

Horton, Lynn. 1998. *Peasants in Arms: War and Peace in the Mountains of Nicaragua, 1979–1994*. Athens, OH: Ohio University Center for International Studies. Focuses mainly on the erosion of peasant support for the revolution in Quilalí during the 1980s.

Ignatiev, O. and G. Borovik. 1980. *The Agony of a Dictatorship*. Translated by Arthur Shkarovsky. Moscow: Progress Publishers. A sketchy journalistic account of the events of 1978–9 by two Moscow correspondents.

Invernizzi, Gabriele, Francis Pisani, and Jesus Ceberio. 1986. *Sandinistas: Entrevistas a Humberto Ortega Saavedra, Jaime Wheelock Roman y Bayardo Arce Castano*. Managua: Editorial Vanguardia. These interviews with leading Sandinistas provide an important window on the Front's ideology and strategy.

Lake, Anthony. 1989. *Somoza Falling*. Boston: Houghton Mifflin. An insider's account of the making of U.S. policy toward Nicaragua during 1978–9; the author was then director of policy planning in the State Department.

Lozano, Lucrecia. 1985. *De Sandino al triunfo de la revolución*. Mexico City: Siglo Veintiuno Editores. Includes an excellent discussion of the insurrectionary period; similar in focus and perspective to Black (1981).

Millet, Richard. 1977. *Guardians of the Dynasty*. Maryknoll, NY: Orbis Books. The standard history of the National Guard.

Nolan, David. 1984. *The Ideology of the Sandinistas and the Nicaraguan Revolution*. Coral Gables, FL: Institute of Interamerican Studies, Graduate School of International Studies, University of Miami. A rather unsubtle, Cold War-ish analysis, much inferior, for example, to Hodges (1986); the book is most useful for its appendices, which include important biographical information and an extensive chronology.

Nuñez Soto, Orlando. 1985. "Los campesinos y la política en Nicaragua." Pp. 116–32 in *Historia politica de los campesinos latinoamericanos*, vol. 2, edited by Pablo González Casanova. Mexico City: Siglo Veintiuno Editores. Disappointingly sketchy.

Nuñez Téllez, Carlos. 1986 (1980). *Un pueblo en armas*. Second edition. Managua: Editorial Vanguardia. An interesting account of the insurrection by a leading Sandinista.

Ortega, Humberto. 1982 (1980). "Nicaragua – The Strategy of Victory." (Interview with Marta Harnecker.) Pp. 53–84 in Tomás Borge et al., *Sandinistas Speak*, edited by Bruce Marcus. New York: Pathfinder Press. An important interview with one of the masterminds of the insurrection; the original Spanish version is in Harnecker (1984).

Paige, Jeffery M. 1989. "Revolution and the Agrarian Bourgeoisie in Nicaragua." Pp. 99–128 in *Revolution in the World-System*, edited by Terry Boswell. New York: Greenwood Press. Why part of the elite supported the revolution.

Pastor, Robert A. 1987. *Condemned to Repetition: The United States and Nicaragua*. Princeton, NJ: Princeton University Press. Draws some interesting parallels between the Cuban and Nicaraguan revolutions and how the United States responded to both. The author was a member of the National Security Council during the Carter Administration.

Pezzullo, Lawrence and Ralph Pezzullo. 1993. *At the Fall of Somoza*. Pittsburgh, PA: University of Pittsburgh Press. An interesting and accessible account of Somoza's last months by the American diplomat and his son.

Ropp, Steve C. 1972. "Goal Orientations of Nicaraguan Cadets: Some Applications for the Problem of Structural/Behavioral Projection in Researching the Latin American Military." *Journal of Comparative Administration* 4:107–16. Emphasizes the National Guard's "internal security fixation."

Ruchwarger, Gary. 1987. *People in Power: Forging a Grassroots Democracy in Nicaragua*. South Hadley, MA: Bergin & Garvey. An analysis of the mass organizations linked but not always subservient to the Sandinista Front; includes a discussion of the emergence of these groups before and during the insurrection.

Ryan, Phil. 2000. "Structure, Agency, and the Nicaragua Revolution." *Theory and Society* 29:187–213. Interesting reflections on the "agential" basis of structural persistence – in this case, how the Sandinistas helped maintain (the better to overthrow) the neopatrimonial Somoza dictatorship.

Seligson, Mitchell A. and William J. Carroll III. 1982. "The Costa Rican Role in the Sandinista Victory." Pp. 331–43 in *Nicaragua in Revolution*, edited by Thomas W. Walker. New York: Praeger. How geopolitics mattered.

Selser, Gregorio. 1984. *Nicaragua de Walker a Somoza*. Mexico City: Mex Sur Editorial. Traces the broad sweep of U.S.-Nicaraguan relations from a critical leftist perspective.

Sierra, Luis. 1985. "Ideology, Religion and Class Struggle in the Nicaraguan Revolution." Pp. 151–74 in *Nicaragua: A Revolution Under Siege*, edited by Richard Harris and Carlos M. Vilas. London: Zed Books. Examines the participation of Christians in both the revolutionary and counterrevolutionary movements.

Spalding, Rose J. 1994. *Capitalists and Revolution in Nicaragua: Opposition and Accomodation, 1979–1993*. Chapel Hill, NC, and London: University of North Carolina Press. Includes an analysis of the development of elite opposition to Somoza. See also Everingham 1996.

Vilas, Carlos M. 1986. *The Sandinista Revolution: National Liberation and Social Transformation in Central America*. Translated by Judy Butler. New York: Monthly Review Press. A sympathetic thematic study by one of the revolution's tireless interpreters; includes an interesting chapter on "Economy and Politics in the Popular Insurrection."

Walker, Thomas W. 1985a. *Nicaragua: The Land of Sandino*. Second edition. Boulder, CO, and London: Westview Press. A short introduction to the history and politics of Nicaragua by a leading country specialist.

1985b. "Nicaragua: From Dynastic Dictatorship to Social Revolution." Pp. 507–27 in *Latin American Politics and Development*, edited by Howard J. Wiarda and Harvey F. Kline. Boulder, CO, and London: Westview Press. A short but helpful overview.

Walter, Knut. 1993. *The Regime of Anastasio Somoza, 1936–1956*. Chapel Hill, NC, and London: University of North Carolina Press. The best analysis of the dictatorship of the elder Somoza.

Weber, Henri. 1981. *Nicaragua: The Sandinist Revolution*. Translated by Patrick Camiller. London: Verso. An early short study, generally sympathetic, from a Marxist perspective.

Wheelock Roman, Jaime. 1975. *Imperialismo y dictadura: crisis de una formación social*. Mexico City: Siglo Veintiuno Editores. An influential study of the Somoza regime and its relations with Nicaraguan capitalists; see also Spalding (1994) and Everingham (1996).

1986. *Vanguardia y revolución en las sociedades periféricas*. (Interview with Marta Harnecker.) Mexico City: Siglo Veintiuno Editores. Analyzes the conditions that made the Sandinista revolution possible.

Whisnant, David E. 1995. *Rascally Signs in Sacred Places: The Politics of Culture in Nicaragua*. Chapel Hill, NC, and London: University of North Carolina Press. This mammoth study includes interesting material on cultural resistance to the Somoza dictatorship.

C. El Salvador

Acevedo, Carlos. 1991. "El Salvador's New Clothes: The Electoral Process (1982–89)." Pp. 19–37 in *A Decade of War: El Salvador Confronts the Future*, edited by Anjali Sundaram and George Gelber. London: Catholic Institute for International Relations; New York: Monthly Review Press, with the Transnational Institute (TNI), the Netherlands. On elections in an authoritarian context.

Alegría, Claribel. 1987. *They Won't Take Me Alive: Salvadorean Women in Struggle for National Liberation*. Translated by Amanda Hopkinson. London: The Women's Press. The story of Commander Eugenia, who was killed during the "general offensive" of January 1981.

Americas Watch Committee [AW]. 1991. *El Salvador's Decade of Terror: Human Rights Since the Assassination of Archbishop Romero*. New Haven, CT: Yale University Press. A comprehensive and even-handed review of human rights violations during the 1980s; see also Betancur et al. (1993).

Amnesty International [AI]. 1988. *El Salvador: "Death Squads" – A Government Strategy*. London: Amnesty International. Argues that death squads were part of the regular security forces in El Salvador.

Baloyra-Herp, Enrique. 1982. *El Salvador in Transition*. Chapel Hill, NC, and London: University of North Carolina Press. A very helpful analysis of "reactionary despotism" in El Salvador, focusing on the late 1970s and early 1980s.

   1983b. "Reactionary Despotism in El Salvador: An Impediment to Democratic Transition." Pp. 101–23 in *Trouble in Our Backyard: Central America and the United States in the Eighties*, edited by Martin Diskin. New York: Pantheon Books. Develops the thesis of Baloyra-Herp 1983a.

   1995. "Elections, Civil War, and Transition in El Salvador, 1982–1994: A Preliminary Evaluation." Pp. 45–65 in *Elections and Democracy in Central America, Revisited*, edited by Mitchell A. Seligson and John A. Booth. Chapel Hill, NC: University of North Carolina Press. How "demonstration elections" (Herman and Brodbead 1984) evolved into the real thing.

Barry, Tom. 1990. *El Salvador: A Country Guide*. Albuquerque, NM: Inter-Hemispheric Education Resource Center. Loaded with important data.

Barry, Tom and Deb Preusch. 1987. "The War in El Salvador: A Reassessment." *Monthly Review* 38 (April):29–44. A helpful overview of a stalemated conflict.

Berryman, Phillip. 1982. "Another View of El Salvador." *Dissent* (Summer):352–7. A response to Zaid (1982).

Betancur, Belisario, Reinaldo Figueredo Planchart, and Thomas Buergenthal. 1993. *From Madness to Hope: The Twelve-Year War in El Salvador; Report of the Commission on the Truth for El Salvador*. New York: United Nations. Attributes most of the violence to the Salvadoran military and allied death squads.

Binford, Leigh. 1996. *The El Mozote Massacre: Anthropology and Human Rights*. Tucson, AZ: University of Arizona Press. A provocative analysis of the massacre and its cultural representations.

366

III. Central America

Blachman, Morris J. and Kenneth E. Sharpe. 1988/89. "Things Fall Apart: Trouble Ahead in El Salvador." *World Policy Journal* 6:107–39. Excellent analysis of the political conjuncture of the late 1980s.

Bonner, Raymond. 1984. *Weakness and Deceit: U.S. Policy and El Salvador*. New York: Times Books. Trenchant criticism of U.S. policy by the journalist who helped to break the story of the massacre at El Mozote – and payed dearly for it (see Danner 1994; Binford 1996).

Brockman, James R. 1982. *The Word Remains: A Life of Oscar Romero*. Maryknoll, NY: Orbis Books. Exceptional biography of the martyred archbishop, from his election in 1977 to his assassination in March 1980.

Browning, David. 1983. "Agrarian Reform in El Salvador." *Journal of Latin American Studies* 15:399–426. A relatively optimistic analysis.

Cabarrús, Carlos Rafael. 1983. *Génesis de una revolución: Analisis del surgimiento y desarrollo de la organizacion campesina en El Salvador*. Mexico City: Ediciones de las Casa Chata. A very important study of the social bases of the insurgency in one region; focuses on the period from 1975 to 1980.

———. 1985. "El Salvador: De movimiento campesino a revolución popular." Pp. 77–115 in *Historia política de los campesinos latinoamericanos*, vol. 2, edited by Pablo González Casanova. Mexico City: Siglo Veintiuno Editores. Nicely summarizes the analysis in Cabarrus 1983.

Cienfuegos, Ferman. 1986. *Veredas de la audacia: Historia del FMLN*. El Salvador: Ediciones Roque Dalton. Short discussion of the formation of the FMLN by an insider.

Clements, Charles. 1984. *Witness to War: An American Doctor in El Salvador*. Toronto: Bantam Books. Memoirs of a pacifist who spent a year in guerrilla-controlled territory in the early 1980s.

Dalton, Roque. 1987. *Miguel Marmol*. Translated by Kathleen Ross and Richard Schaaf. Willimantic, CT: Curbstone Press. The fantastic memoirs of a founding member of the Salvadoran Communist Party, as told to a leading intellectual and guerrilla who was executed by rivals in 1975. Focuses mainly on events of the 1930s and 1940s, including *la matanza* of 1932.

Danner, Mark. 1993. *The Massacre at El Mozote: A Parable of the Cold War*. New York: Vintage. Important and devastating.

Diskin, Martin. 1996. "Distilled Conclusions: The Disappearance of the Agrarian Question in El Salvador." *Latin American Research Review* 31:111–26. A harsh critique of Seligson 1995.

Diskin, Martin and Kenneth E. Sharpe. 1986. "El Salvador." Pp. 50–87 and 375–85 (endnotes) in *Confronting Revolution: Security Through Diplomacy in Central America*, edited by Morris J. Blachman, William M. LeoGrande, and Kenneth E. Sharpe. New York: Pantheon Books. An outstanding interpretive essay that emphasizes the difficulties of ending state repression.

Dunkerley, James. 1983. "Class Structure and Socialist Strategy in El Salvador." Pp. 125–47 in *Crisis in the Caribbean*, edited by Fitzroy Ambursley and Robin Cohen. New York: Monthly Review Press. A Trotskyist critique of the Salvadoran left's alleged adoption of the Nicaraguan model.

1985. *The Long War: Dictatorship and Revolution in El Salvador*. Second edition. London: Verso. One of the best general overviews of events through the early 1980s.

1991. "El Salvador Since 1930." Pp. 159–90 in *Central America Since Independence*, edited by Leslie Bethell. Cambridge, UK: Cambridge University Press. An informative synthesis.

Durham, William H. 1979. *Scarcity and Survival in Central America: Ecological Origins of the Soccer War*. Stanford, CA: Stanford University Press. Demonstrates that land scarcity in El Salvador has been a result of land concentration, not increasing population.

Eguizabal, Cristina. 1992. "Parties, Programs, and Politics in El Salvador." Pp. 135–60 in *Political Parties and Democracy in Central America*, edited by Louis W. Goodman, William M. LeoGrande, and Johanna Mendelson Forman. Boulder, CO: Westview Press. Examines events leading up to the peace accords of 1992.

Las elecciones: Crónica de una derrota. 1989. El Salvador: Editorial Sistema Venceremos. An overview of the FMLN's perspective in the wake of the March 1988 elections.

Envio (Central American Historical Institute). 1991. "The Jesuit Case: Still Plagued by Questions," 10 (December):26–32. On the cover-up of a notorious army massacre.

Estudios Centroamericanos (ECA) Editorial Board. 1984. "El Salvador 1984." *NACLA Report on the Americas* 18 (2):13–47. An exceptional analysis, emphasizing how the goal of the Salvadoran right and the Reagan Administration to defeat the guerrilla insurgency militarily would only prolong the conflict.

Fish, Joe and Cristina Sganga. 1988. *El Salvador: Testament of Terror*. New York: Olive Branch Press. A vivid journalistic portrait of the counterinsurgency.

García, José Z. 1989. "El Salvador: Recent Elections in Historical Perspective." Pp. 60–92 in *Elections and Democracy in Central America*, edited by John A. Booth and Mitchell A. Seligson. Chapel Hill, NC, and London: University of North Carolina Press. Elections as counterinsurgency.

Gettleman, Marvin E., Patrick Lacefield, Louis Menashe, and David Mermelstein, eds. 1986. *El Salvador: Central America in the New Cold War*. Revised and expanded edition. New York: Grove Press. A helpful collection of documents and essays.

Gilly, Adolfo. 1981. *Guerra y política en El Salvador*. Mexico City: Editorial Nueva Imagen. An early interpretive essay by a well-known Mexican leftist; includes Rafael Menjívar's noted 1979 essay, "El Salvador: el eslabon más pequeno."

Gordon R., Sara. 1989. *Crisis política y guerra en El Salvador*. Mexico City: Siglo Veintiuno. An important radical analysis of El Salvador in the 1970s.

Harnecker, Marta. 1983. "From Insurrection to War: An Interview with Joaquín Villalobos." Pp. 69–105 in *Revolution and Intervention in Central America*, edited by Marlene Dixon and Susanne Jonas. San Francisco, CA: Synthesis Publications. Includes a discussion of the failure of the January 1981 general offensive. This important interview is also reprinted, in the original Spanish, in Harnecker 1984, pp. 173–232.

Jung, Harald. 1980. "Class Struggles in El Salvador." *New Left Review* 122:3–25. An early analysis of the emergent civil war.

Karl, Terry Lynn. 1985. "After La Palma: The Prospects for Democratization in El Salvador." *World Policy Journal* 2:305–30. An astute analysis of the hurdles to democratization.

———. 1986. "Imposing Consent? Electoralism vs. Democratization in El Salvador." In *Elections and Democratization in Latin America, 1980–1985*, edited by Paul Drake and Eduardo Silva. San Diego, CA: Center for Iberian and Latin American Studies, University of California, San Diego. Develops the important distinction in the title.

———. 1989. "The Christian Democratic Party and the Prospects for Democratization in El Salvador." Pp. 140–64 in *Sociology of "Developing Societies": Central America*, edited by Jan L. Flora and Edelberto Torres-Rivas. New York: Monthly Review Press. A revised and updated version of Karl 1985.

———. 1992. "El Salvador's Negotiated Revolution." *Foreign Affairs* 71:147–64. An important article, although the author fails to convince that a revolution, negotiated or otherwise, occurred in El Salvador.

Keogh, Dermot. 1985. "The United States and the Coup d'Etat in El Salvador, 15 October 1979: A Case Study in American Foreign Policy Perceptions and Decision-Making." Pp. 21–69 in *Central America: Human Rights and U.S. Foreign Policy*, edited by Dermot Keogh. Cork, Ireland: Cork University Press, 1985. The best study of the subject.

Kincaid, A. Douglas. 1987. "Peasants into Rebels: Community and Class in Rural El Salvador." *Comparative Studies in Society and History* 29:466–94. An outstanding analysis of the social base of the insurgency.

Lawyers Committee for Human Rights. 1989. *Underwriting Injustice: AID and El Salvador's Judicial Reform Program*. New York: Lawyers Committee for Human Rights. A devastating critique of the Salvadoran judicial system and the U.S.-funded "Administration of Justice Program."

Leiken, Robert S. 1984. "The Salvadoran Left." Pp. 111–30 in *Central America: Anatomy of Conflict*, edited by Robert S. Leiken. New York: Pergamon. A helpful road map.

LeMoyne, James. 1987. "After Parades and Promises, Duarte Flounders in Salvador." *The New York Times*, February 16. On the collapsing fortunes of Christian Democracy.

———. 1989. "El Salvador's Forgotten War." *Foreign Affairs* 68:105–25. The author was a *New York Times* correspondent in El Salvador from 1984 to 1988.

LeoGrande, William M. and Carla Anne Robbins. 1980. "Oligarchs and Officers: The Crisis in El Salvador." *Foreign Affairs* 58:1084–103. A useful early analysis.

Lungo Uclés, Mario. 1995. "Building an Alternative: The Formation of a Popular Project." Pp. 153–79 in *The New Politics of Survival: Grassroots Movements in Central America*, edited by Minor Sinclair. New York: Monthly Review

Press/EPICA. On the (unarmed) popular movements that emerged during the 1980s.

1996 (1990). *El Salvador in the Eighties: Counterinsurgency and Revolution.* Translated by Amelia F. Shogan. Philadelphia, PA: Temple University Press. A fascinating leftist analysis, packed with insights; includes an important discussion of the political evolution of the FMLN.

McClintock, Michael. 1985a. *The American Connection, Volume I: State Terror and Popular Resistance in El Salvador.* London: Zed Books. A well-researched account of U.S.-supported state terrorism; focuses on the Kennedy era through the early 1980s. The author has written a companion volume on Guatemala (see McClintock 1985b).

McDonald, Ronald H. 1985. "El Salvador: The Politics of Revolution." Pp. 528–44 in *Latin American Politics and Development*, edited by Howard J. Wiarda and Harvey F. Kline. Second edition. Boulder, CO, and London: Westview Press. A short overview.

Menjívar, Rafael. 1979. *Formación y lucha del proletariado industrial salvadoreño.* San José, Costa Rica: Editorial Universitaria Centroamericana (EDUCA). An interpretive overview of Salvadoran working-class history by a noted radical scholar.

1985. "Notas sobre el movimiento obrero salvadoreño." Pp. 61–127 in *Historia del movimiento obrero en América Latina*, vol. 2, edited by Pablo González Casanova. Mexico City: Siglo Veintiuno Editores. Summarizes Menjívar 1979; discusses developments through 1977.

Metzi, Francisco. 1988. *The People's Remedy: Health Care in El Salvador's War of Liberation.* Translated by Jean Carroll in collaboration with the author and Rhoda Mahler. New York: Monthly Review Press. Short memoirs of a Mozambican-born health-care worker who spent several years with the FMLN guerrillas.

Miles, Sara and Bob Ostertag. 1989. "D'Aubuisson's New ARENA." *NACLA Report on the Americas* 23 (2):14–39. On the evolution of the party of the oligarchy.

1991. "The FMLN: New Thinking." Pp. 216–46 in *A Decade of War: El Salvador Confronts the Future*, edited by Anjali Sundaram and George Gelber. New York: Monthly Review Press, with the Transnational Institute (TNI), the Netherlands. Excellent analysis of the evolution of the FMLN after the collapse of the Soviet bloc.

Millman, Joel. 1989. "A Force unto Itself." *The New York Times Magazine* (December 10), 47, 95, 97. An important analysis of the Salvadoran armed forces.

Montgomery, Tommie Sue. 1983. "The Church in the Salvadoran Revolution." *Latin American Perspectives* 10 (1):62–87. A helpful overview.

1995. *Revolution in El Salvador: From Civil Strife to Civil Peace.* Second edition. Boulder, CO: Westview Press. One of the very best general studies of the subject.

Nairn, Allan. 1984. "Behind the Death Squads." *The Progressive* (May):20–5, 28–9. A journalistic exposé.

III. Central America

North, Liisa. 1985. *Bitter Grounds: Roots of Revolt in El Salvador*. Second edition. Westport, CT: Lawrence Hill. Focuses on the rural economy.

Norton, Chris. 1985. "Build and Destroy." *NACLA Report on the Americas* 19 (6):26–36. How the American Institute for Free Labor Development (AIFLD) turned on a "centrist" labor federation that turned left.

Paige, Jeffery M. 1993. "Coffee and Power in El Salvador." *Latin American Research Review* 28:7–40. A fascinating analysis, based on first-hand interviews, of the world views of the factions within El Salvador's dominant class.

    1996. "Land Reform and Agrarian Revolution in El Salvador: Comment on Seligson and Diskin." *Latin American Research Review* 31:127–39. Suggests that a "semiproletariat" of poor landowners, renters, and sharecroppers was the backbone of the Salvadoran revolutionary movement.

Pearce, Jenny. 1986. *Promised Land: Peasant Rebellion in Chalatenango, El Salvador*. London: Zed Books. An important study, based on the author's sojourns with the guerrillas.

Pelupessy, Wim. 1991. "Agrarian Reform in El Salvador." Pp. 38–57 in *A Decade of War: El Salvador Confronts the Future*, edited by Anjali Sundaram and George Gelber. London: Catholic Institute for International Relations; New York: Monthly Review Press, with the Transnational Institute (TNI), the Netherlands. A highly critical perspective.

    1997. *The Limits of Economic Reform in El Salvador*. New York: St. Martin's Press. Includes an excellent analysis of the deficiencies of the agrarian reforms of the 1980s.

Petras, James. 1986 (1981). "Blots on the White Paper: The Reinvention of the 'Red Menace.'" In *El Salvador: Central America in the New Cold War*, edited by Marvin E. Gettleman et al. Revised and updated edition. New York: Grove Press. A devastating critique of Reagan-Administration propaganda.

Preston, Julia. 1990. "The Battle for San Salvador." *New York Review of Books*, February 1:6–12. On the guerrillas' November 1989 offensive.

Ramos, Carlos. 1987. "El Salvador, un país dividido entre dos poderes enfrentados." *El País* (Madrid), February 16. An interesting analysis of the evolving conflict of the 1980s.

Seligson, Mitchell A. 1995. "Thirty Years of Transformation in the Agrarian Structure of El Salvador, 1961–1991." *Latin American Research Review* 30:43–74. A controversial quantitative analysis.

    1996. "Agrarian Inequality and the Theory of Peasant Rebellion." *Latin American Research Review* 31:140–57. A defense of the author's 1995 article against the criticisms of Diskin (1996) and Paige (1996); includes some interesting reflections on theories of peasant rebellion.

Shaull, Wendy. 1990. *Tortillas, Beans and M-16s: A Year with the Guerrillas in El Salvador*. London: Pluto Press. The diary of a North American photojournalist.

Stahler-Sholk, Richard. 1994. "El Salvador's Negotiated Transition: From Low-Intensity Conflict to Low-Intensity Democracy." *Journal of Interamerican Studies and World Affairs* 36:1–59. Focuses on the 1992 peace accords and the 1994 elections.

Stanley, William. 1996. *The Protection Racket State: Elite Politics, Military Extortion, and Civil War in El Salvador*. Philadelphia: Temple University Press. Argues that the Salvadoran military was more autonomous than it seemed; also contains some interesting comparative analyses. See also Williams and Walter 1997.

Studemeister, Margarita. 1986. *The New El Salvador: Interviews from the Zones of Popular Control*. San Francisco, CA: Solidarity Publications. First-hand accounts of life in guerrilla-controlled territories.

Uhlig, Mark A. 1989. "Plane in Salvador with Soviet Arms Crashes and 4 Die." *The New York Times*, November 26, 1. On efforts to deliver Soviet antiaircraft missiles to the guerrillas.

United Nations. 1995. *The United Nations and El Salvador, 1990–1995*. New York: United Nations, Department of Public Information. A valuable compilation of U.N. documents on El Salvador, including the report by the so-called Commission on the Truth, "From Madness to Hope."

United Nations Security Council. 1992. "Report of the Secretary-General of the United Nations Observer Mission in El Salvador." Document S/24833. 23 November, New York, NY. The U.N. report on El Salvador's peace accords.

Ventura, José. N.d. *El poder popular en El Salvador*. Mexico City: Editorial Mex-Sur. A short analysis of FMLN policies and programs in guerrilla-controlled areas.

Vickers, George. 1992. "El Salvador: A Negotiated Revolution." *NACLA Report on the Americas* 25 (5):4–8. A short but astute analysis of the peace accords.

Vickers, George and Jack Spence. 1994. "Elections in El Salvador: The Right Consolidates Power." *NACLA Report on the Americas* 28 (1):6–11. Argues that the elections of March–April 1994 reflect a still-polarized society.

Vigil, Maria Lopez. 1987. *Marxismo y cristianismo en Morazán: Testimonio del Padre Rogelio*. El Salvador: Editorial Sistema Venceremos. The story of a radicalized priest who threw in with the insurgency.

Villalobos, Joaquín. 1985. *Revolutionary Strategy to Defeat U.S. Intervention*. San Francisco, CA: El Salvador Information System. This pamphlet details the FMLN's strategy of a "war of attrition." The author, probably the best-known surviving FMLN leader, has a controversial past (see, e.g., Dunkerley 1985, 1988) and, currently, relatively moderate politics.

　　1986. *The War in El Salvador: Current Situation and Outlook for the Future*. San Francisco, CA: Solidarity Publications. The author predicts an eventual guerrilla victory, but holds out a negotiated settlement as the best solution to the war.

　　1988. *Una revolución democrática para El Salvador*. El Salvador: Editorial Sistema Venceremos. The insurgency in moderate rhetorical dress; the second half of this short book has been published in English (see Villalobos 1989b).

　　1989a. *El Salvador ingobernable*. (Interview.) El Salvador: Editorial Sistema Venceremos. Villalobos presents a rather optimistic view of the insurgency's potential in the late 1980s, touching upon the possibilities of a "social explosion" and even an outright guerrilla victory.

1989b. "A Democratic Revolution for El Salvador." *Foreign Policy* 74:103–22. See Villalobos 1988. Socialism can wait.

Wickham-Crowley, Timothy P. 1989b. "Understanding Failed Revolution in El Salvador: A Comparative Analysis of Regime Types and Social Structures." *Politics and Society* 17:511–37. Draws on the astute analysis that would appear in Wickham-Crowley 1992.

Williams, Philip J. and Knut Walter. 1997. *Militarization and Demilitarization in El Salvador's Transition to Democracy.* Pittsburgh, PA: University of Pittsburgh Press. Includes extremely informative chapters on the 1970s and 1980s. See also Stanley 1996.

Wood, Elisabeth Jean. 2000b. *Insurgent Collective Action and Civil War: Redrawing Boundaries of Class and Citizenship in Rural El Salvador.* Unpublished book manuscript. A fascinating study based on extensive field research.

Woodward, Ralph Lee. 1988. *El Salvador.* Oxford, UK: Clio. An excellent annotated bibliography by a leading Central Americanist.

Zaid, Gabriel. 1982. "Enemy Colleagues: A Reading of the Salvadoran Tragey." *Dissent* (Winter):13–40. See Berryman's (1982) important response.

D. *Guatemala*

Aguilera Peralta, Gabriel. 1979. "The Massacre at Panzós and Capitalist Development in Guatemala." *Monthly Review* (December) 31:13–23. A short but astute analysis of an important event.

1980. "Terror and Violence as Weapons of Counterinsurgency in Guatemala." *Latin American Perspectives* 7:91–113. Written before elections fully entered the arsenal.

Americas Watch [AW]. 1988. *Closing the Space: Human Rights in Guatemala.* New York: Human Rights Watch. This and the following reports document in chilling detail how the Guatemalan regime abused human rights through the 1980s.

1989. *Persecuting Human Rights Monitors: The CERJ in Guatemala.* New York and Washington, DC: Americas Watch Committee. Documents the armed forces' attacks on the Runujel Junam ("Everybody Is Equal") Council of Ethnic Communities (CERJ), a human rights organization that opposed the civilian patrol system.

1990. *Messengers of Death: Human Rights in Guatemala, November 1988–March 1990.* New York: Human Rights Watch.

Americas Watch and Physicians for Human Rights. 1991. *Guatemala: Getting Away with Murder.* New York: Human Rights Watch.

Amnesty International [AI]. 1987. *Guatemala: The Human Rights Record.* London: Amnesty International Publications. In a word, abominable.

Andersen, Nicolas. 1982. *Guatemala, Escuela revolucionaria de nuevos hombres.* Mexico City: Editorial Nuestro Tiempo. Testimonies collected in 1981–2 from members of the Guerrilla Army of the Poor (EGP).

Anderson, Ken and Jean-Marie Simon. 1987. "Permanent Counterinsurgency in Guatemala." *Telos* 73:9–46. Argues that the armed forces are the equal, not the lackies, of the oligarchy.

Arias, Arturo. 1985. "El movimiento indígena en Guatemala, 1970–1983." Pp. 62–119 in *Movimientos populares en Centroamérica*, edited by Daniel Camacho and Rafael Menjívar. San José, Costa Rica: Editorial Universitaria Centroamericana (EDUCA). An excellent analysis of the participation of Mayans in the revolutionary movement; the author is a noted novelist.

Balcarcel, José Luis. 1985. "El movimiento obrero en Guatemala." Pp. 9–60 in *Historia del movimiento obrero en américa latina*, vol. 2, edited by Pablo González Casanova. Mexico City: Siglo Veintiuno Editores. Includes a short discussion of developments in the 1960s and 1970s.

Barry, Tom. 1986. *Guatemala: The Politics of Counterinsurgency*. Albuquerque, NM: Inter-Hemispheric Education Resource Center. A short, lucid analysis of a "textbook-style counterinsurgency campaign."

1989. *Guatemala: A Country Guide*. Albuquerque, NM: Inter-Hemispheric Education Resource Center. A useful reference work.

Black, George, with Milton Jamail and Norma Stoltz Chinchilla. 1984. *Garrison Guatemala*. New York: Monthly Review Press. One of the very best analyses of events through the early 1980s.

1985. "Under the Gun." *NACLA Report on the Americas* 19 (6):10–25. Argues that the armed forces allowed elections after eviscerating the power of elected officials.

Bran, Antonio. 1985. "Guatemala: Organización popular y lucha de clases en el campo (Notas para su estudio)." Pp. 9–27 in *Historia política de los campesinos latinoamericanos*, vol. 2, edited by Pablo González Casanova. Mexico City: Siglo Veintiuno Editores. Discusses the forces driving peasants to armed struggle.

Carmack, Robert M., ed. 1988. *Harvest of Violence: The Maya Indians and the Guatemalan Crisis*. Norman, OK: University of Oklahoma Press. A collection of studies by anthropologists on the devastation wrought by the counterinsurgency of the early 1980s.

1995. *Rebels of Highland Guatemala: The Quiché-Mayas of Momostenango*. Norman, OK: University of Oklahoma Press. A sweeping regional history, from the prehispanic period through the 1980s.

Carr, Matthew. 1991. "Guatemala: State of Terror." *Race and Class* 33 (1):31–56. An analysis of the continuing repression following the elections of the mid-1980s.

Concerned Guatemala Scholars. 1982. *Guatemala: Dare to Struggle, Dare to Win*. Brooklyn, NY: Concerned Guatemala Scholars. A short, sympathetic introduction to the revolutionary movement.

Davis, Shelton H. 1983. "State Violence and Agrarian Crisis in Guatemala." Pp. 155–72 in *Trouble in Our Backyard*, edited by Martin Diskin. New York: Pantheon. A short but helpful overview.

1988. "Introduction: Sowing the Seeds of Violence." Pp. 3–36 in *Harvest of Violence: The Maya Indians and the Guatemalan Crisis*, edited by Robert

M. Carmack. Norman, OK: University of Oklahoma Press. An excellent introduction to the local studies in Carmack 1988.

Dunkerley, James. 1991. "Guatemala Since 1930." Pp. 119–57 in *Central America Since Independence*, edited by Leslie Bethell. Cambridge, UK: Cambridge University Press. A very general overview.

Falla, Ricardo. 1994. *Massacres in the Jungle: Ixcán, Guatemala, 1975–1982*. Translated by Julia Howland. Boulder, CO: Westview Press. A very important, detailed study of army massacres of indigenous villagers during the early 1980s.

Farnsworth, Elizabeth. 1987. "Voices from Guatemala." *World Policy Journal* 4:527–52. Interesting interviews with then-President Cerezo, an opposition legislator, and a bishop.

Fauriol, Georges A. and Eva Loser. 1988. *Guatemala's Political Puzzle*. New Brunswick, NJ, and Oxford, UK: Transaction Books. A short analysis of Guatemala's "lurch toward democracy" during the 1980s; unsympathetic to the left and leftist scholarship.

Frank, Luisa and Philip Wheaton. 1984. *Indian Guatemala: Path to Liberation; The Role of Christians in the Indian Process*. Washington, DC: EPICA Task Force. Emphasizes the role of Mayans and liberation theology in the resistance movement.

Frundt, Henry. 1987. *Refreshing Pauses: Coca-Cola and Human Rights in Guatemala*. New York: Praeger. On an important labor struggle in the capital.

Goldston, James A. 1989. *Shattered Hope: Guatemalan Workers and the Promise of Democracy*. Boulder, CO: Westview Press. Examines repression of the urban labor movement; see also Levenson-Estrada 1994.

Gruson, Lindsey. 1990. "Guerrilla War in Guatemala Heats Up, Fueling Criticism of Civilian Rule." *The New York Times*, June 3, 4. The guerrillas struggle on.

Guatemalan Church in Exile (IGE). 1989. *Guatemala: Security, Development, Democracy*. N.p.: IGE. Another disturbing account of the counterinsurgency.

Guerra Vilaboy, Sergio. 1985. *Luchas sociales y partidos politicos en Guatemala*. Havana: Departamento de Actividades Culturales, Universidad de Habana. This short analysis concentrates on the post–World War II period.

Handy, Jim. 1984. *Gift of the Devil: A History of Guatemala*. Boston: South End Press. One of the best historical overviews, focusing mainly on the post–World War II period.

——— 1986. "Resurgent Democracy and the Guatemalan Military." *Journal of Latin American Studies* 18:383–408. On military-sponsored democratization.

Harbury, Jennifer. 1994. *Bridge of Courage: Life Stories of the Guatemalan Compañeros and Compañeras*. Monroe, ME: Common Courage Press. Includes interesting testimonies from guerrillas. The author's husband was a guerrilla leader who was apparently captured alive and then tortured and murdered on the orders of a Guatemalan officer who was on the CIA's payroll.

——— 1997. "Army Has Final Say on Justice in Guatemala." (Letter to the editor.) *The New York Times*, January 14, A14. "The real danger to any justice in Guatemala remains the fact that any judge who dares rule against the army can still be shot to death."

Hegstrom, Edward. 1998. "Church Finds Higher Toll of Victims in Guatemala War." *Miami Herald*, April 24. On the Catholic Church's report on human rights abuses during the civil war; see REMHI 1999.

Jamail, Milton and Margo Gutierrez. 1987. "Guatemala: The Paragon." *NACLA Report on the Americas* 21 (2):31–6. Analyzes Israeli support for the counterinsurgency.

Jiménez, Dina. 1985. "El movimiento campesino en Guatemala, 1969–1980." Pp. 293–343 in *Movimientos populares en Centroamérica*, edited by Daniel Camacho and Rafael Menjivar. San José, Costa Rica: Editorial Universitaria Centroamericana (EDUCA). Includes a discussion of the Committee of Peasant Unity (CUC).

Jonas, Susanne. 1991. *The Battle for Guatemala: Rebels, Death Squads, and U.S. Power*. Boulder, CO: Westview Press. One of the very best studies of the civil war.

1995. "Electoral Problems and the Democratic Project in Guatemala." Pp. 25–44 in *Elections and Democracy in Central America, Revisited*, edited by Mitchell A. Seligson and John A. Booth. Chapel Hill, NC: University of North Carolina Press. Argues that democratization requires a just peace settlement.

1997. "The Peace Accords: An End and a Beginning." *NACLA Report on the Americas* 30 (6):6–10. A sober analysis of the gains and limitations of the peace accords in Guatemala.

2000. *Of Centaurs and Doves: Guatemala's Peace Process*. Boulder, CO: Westview Press. An exceptional and thorough study of the topic.

Levenson-Estrada, Deborah. 1994. *Trade Unionists Against Terror: Guatemala City, 1954–1985*. Chapel Hill, NC, and London: University of North Carolina Press. The best study of urban trade unionism in Guatemala.

Lovell, W. George. 1988. "Surviving Conquest: The Maya of Guatemala in Historical Perspective." *Latin American Research Review* 23:25–57. A broad historical perspective.

McCleary, Rachel M. 1996. "Guatemala: Expectations for Peace." *Current History* (February):88–92. A short update on the eve of the peace accords.

McClintock, Michael. 1985b. *The American Connection, Volume II: State Terror and Popular Resistance in Guatemala*. London: Zed Books. On U.S. support for counterinsurgency and generalized terror.

Manz, Beatriz. 1988. *Refugees of a Hidden War: The Aftermath of Counterinsurgency in Guatemala*. Albany, NY: State University of New York Press. Based on extensive fieldwork, this important book documents the brutal human consequences of the counterinsurgency in three regions.

Martínez, Emma G. and David Loeb. 1994. "Who's in Charge Here? Divisions in the Guatemalan Army and the Prospects for Peace." *Report on Guatemala* (Summer):6–11. On the conflict between "institutionalists" and hard-liners. See also Schirmer 1998.

Melville, Thomas and Marjorie Melville. 1971. *Guatemala: The Politics of Land Ownership*. New York: Free Press. Dated, but still a useful resource on Guatemala in the 1950s and 1960s.

Menchú, Rigoberta. 1984. *I, Rigoberta Menchú: An Indian Woman in Guatemala*. Edited by Elisabeth Burgos-Debray. Translated by Ann Wright. London: Verso. A fascinating personal testimony; see also Stoll 1999.

Mondragón, Rafael. 1983. *De indios y cristianos en Guatemala*. Mexico City: COPEC/CECOPE. An excellent study of the role of radicalized Christians in the revolutionary movement.

Montejo, Victor. 1987. *Testimony: Death of a Guatemalan Village*. Translated by Victor Perera. Willimantic, CT: Curbstone Press. A harrowing eyewitness account of the Guatemalan army's attack on a small village in 1982.

Nairn, Allan. 1986. "The Guatemala Connection." *The Progressive* (May):20–2. The connection to the United States.

Nairn, Allan and Jean-Marie Simon. 1986. "Bureaucracy of Death." *The New Republic* (June 30):13–7. On Guatemala's national security state. Harrowing.

Painter, James. 1986. "Guatemala in Civilian Garb." *Third World Quarterly* 8:818–44. Guatemala after the elections of 1985.

1987. *Guatemala: False Hope, False Freedom*. London: Latin America Bureau. A very insightful short overview.

Payeras, Mario. 1983. *Days of the Jungle*. New York: Monthly Review Press. Fascinating account of the early years of the Guerrilla Army of the Poor (EGP).

1986. "The Guatemalan Army and U.S. Policy in Central America." *Monthly Review*, Vol. 37, No. 10, pp. 14–20. Depicts a sort of Frankenstein monster.

1987. *El trueno en la ciudad: Episodios de la lucha armada urbana de 1981 en Guatemala*. Mexico City: Juan Pablos. Describes the perils of urban guerrilla warfare.

Perera, Victor. 1993. *Unfinished Conquest: The Guatemalan Tragedy*. Berkeley, CA, and Los Angeles: University of California Press. An engrossing portrait of contemporary Guatemala, focusing on four regions; full of fascinating vignettes.

REMHI [Recovery of Historical Memory Project]. 1999. *Guatemala: Never Again!* Maryknoll, NY: Orbis Books. An abridged edition of the massive study of human rights abuses conducted by the Human Rights Office of the Archdiocese of Guatemala.

Richards, Michael. 1985. "Cosmopolitan World View and Counterinsurgency in Guatemala." *Anthropological Quarterly* 58:90–107. Includes some interesting material on the racism of Guatemalan officers and soldiers.

Rosada Granados, Héctor. 1992. "Parties, Transitions, and the Political System in Guatemala." Pp. 89–109 in *Political Parties and Democracy in Central America*, edited by Louis W. Goodman, William M. LeoGrande, and Johanna Mendelson Forman. Boulder, CO: Westview Press. A short analysis of a flawed transition.

Schirmer, Jennifer. 1989. "Waging War to Prevent War." *The Nation* (April 10):476–9.

1996. "The Looting of Democratic Discourse by the Guatemalan Military: Implications for Human Rights." Pp. 85–97 in *Constructing Democracy: Human Rights, Citizenship, and Society in Latin America*, edited by Elizabeth Jelin and Eric Hershberg. Boulder, CO: Westview Press. This and the previous piece are based on rare interviews with officers of the Guatemalan armed forces.

1998. *The Guatemalan Military Project: A Violence Called Democracy*. Philadelphia, PA: University of Pennsylvania Press. The best study of the ideology, culture, and practices of the Guatemalan military.

Schoultz, Lars. 1983. "Guatemala: Social Change and Political Conflict." Pp. 173–202 in *Trouble in Our Backyard*, edited by Martin Diskin. New York: Pantheon. A helpful primer on the conflict.

Simon, Jean-Marie. 1987. *Guatemala: Eternal Spring, Eternal Tyranny*. New York: Norton. Brilliant photographs; thoughtful text.

1988. "Government Apathy Toward Human Rights." *Report on Guatemala* 9 (May–June):6–7. An update on the repression.

Smith, Carol A. 1987. "Culture and Community: The Language of Class in Guatemala." Pp. 197–217 in *The Year Left 2*, edited by Mike Davis et al. London: Verso. On the difficult dialectic of class and ethnicity.

1990. "The Militarization of Civil Society in Guatemala: Economic Reorganization as a Continuation of War." *Latin American Perspectives* 17 (4):8–41. On the economic dimension of the counterinsurgency.

1991. "Maya Nationalism." *NACLA Report on the Americas* 25 (3):29–33. Argues that the insurgency's ladino leadership erred by neglecting ethnic as opposed to class oppression in Guatemala.

Solórzano Martínez, Mario. 1986. "Guatemala: Between Authoritarianism and Democracy." Pp. 151–74 in *The Central American Impasse*, edited by Giuseppe Di Palma and Laurence Whitehead. New York: St. Martin's Press. Interesting reflections by a well-known social democrat.

Stoll, David. 1990/91. "Guatemala: Why They Like Ríos Montt." *NACLA Report on the Americas* 24 (4):4–7. Popular support for a former dictator.

1993. *Between Two Armies in the Ixil Towns of Guatemala*. New York: Columbia University Press. An important study, although its findings about the views of Ixil Mayas toward the guerrillas seem more limited than the author sometimes recognizes.

1999. *Rigoberta Menchú and the Story of All Poor Guatemalans*. Boulder, CO: Westview Press. A rather one-sided analysis of the Guatemalan conflict wrapped in a fascinating, if occasionally picayune, account of Menchú's (1984) famous testimony.

Taylor, Ruth. 1997. "The Left in Transition: Moving into the Electoral Arena." *Report on Guatemala* (Winter):2–5, 14. This and the following piece analyze the lead-up to the peace accords and their immediate aftermath.

Taylor, Ruth and John Marshall. 1996. "A Rocky Road to the Final Peace." *Report on Guatemala* (Winter):2–5, 14.

Trudeau, Robert H. 1989. "The Guatemalan Election of 1985: Prospects for Democracy." In *Elections and Democracy in Central America*, edited by John Booth and Mitchell A. Seligson. Chapel Hill, NC: University of North Carolina Press. Why this crucial election hardly meant that Guatemala had become a democracy.

III. Central America

1993. *Guatemalan Politics: The Popular Struggle for Democracy*. Boulder, CO: Lynn Rienner. An excellent analysis of the obstacles to democratization through the 1980s.

Trudeau, Robert and Lars Schoultz. 1986. "Guatemala." Pp. 23–49 in *Confronting Revolution: Security Through Diplomacy in Central America*, edited by Morris J. Blachman, William M. LeoGrande, and Kenneth E. Sharpe. New York: Pantheon. An excellent short overview.

Warren, Kay B. 1993. "Interpreting *La Violencia* in Guatemala: Shapes of Mayan Silence and Resistance." Pp. 25–56 in *The Violence Within: Cultural and Political Opposition in Divided Nations*, edited by Kay B. Warren. Boulder, CO: Westview Press. The effects of the violence on a Mayan town.

E. Honduras

Acker, Alison. 1988. *Honduras: The Making of a Banana Republic*. Boston: South End Press. A solid introduction to Honduran history.

Amnesty International [AI]. 1988. *Honduras: Civilian Authority – Military Power; Human Rights Violations in the 1980s*. London: Amnesty International. Documents violence against popular organizations.

Anderson, Thomas P. 1988. "Politics and the Military in Honduras." *Current History* (December):425–8, 431. An overview of the military's political role during the 1980s.

Arancibia C., Juan. 1984. *Honduras: ¿Un estado nacional?* Tegucigalpa: Editorial Guaymuras. A short, synoptic history, emphasizing the weakness of the national bourgeoisie.

Benjamin, Medea, ed. 1987. *Don't Be Afraid, Gringo: A Honduran Woman Speaks from the Heart; The Story of Elvia Alvarado*. San Francisco, CA: Institute for Food and Development Policy. The moving life history of a peasant organizer for the National Congress of Rural Workers (CNTC).

1988. "Campesinos: Between Carrot and Stick." *NACLA Report on the Americas* 22 (1):22–30. Explains why many Honduran peasants actually prefer the military to civilian politicians.

Brockett, Charles D. 1987. "Public Policy, Peasants, and Rural Development in Honduras." *Journal of Latin American Studies* 19:69–86. Policy effects on the rural population and economy.

Bulmer-Thomas, Victor. 1991. "Honduras Since 1930." Pp. 191–225 in *Central America Since Independence*, edited by Leslie Bethell. Cambridge, UK: Cambridge University Press. Interesting, but rather short and sketchy.

Center for Justice and International Law (CEJIL) and Human Rights Watch/Americas. 1994. *Honduras: The Facts Speak for Themselves: The Preliminary Report of the National Commission for the Protection of Human Rights in Honduras*. New York: Human Rights Watch. A detailed report on the armed forces' violations of human rights through the 1980s.

Danby, Colin and Richard Swedberg. 1984. *Honduras: Bibliography and Research Guide*. Cambridge, MA: CAMINO (Central America Information Office). An excellent bibliography and guide to the literature, although now somewhat dated.

Euraque, Darío A. 1996. *Reinterpreting the Banana Republic: Region and State in Honduras, 1870–1972*. Chapel Hill, NC: University of North Carolina Press. A very important revisionist history; an essential corrective to the "absent oligarchy" thesis in Honduran historiography.

Lapper, Richard and James Painter. 1985. *Honduras: State for Sale*. London: Latin America Bureau. A short, synoptic history, emphasizing Honduran subservience to the United States.

MacCameron, Robert. 1983. *Bananas, Labor, and Politics in Honduras: 1954–1963*. Syracuse, NY: Foreign and Comparative Studies/Latin American Series, No. 5, Maxwell School of Citizenship and Public Affairs, Syracuse University. Perhaps the best general study of the decade in question.

Menjívar, Rafael, Sui Moy Li Kam, and Virginia Portuguez. 1985. "El movimiento campesino en Honduras." Pp. 373–408 in *Movimientos populares en Centroamérica*, edited by Daniel Camacho and Rafael Menjívar. San José, Costa Rica: Editorial Universitaria Centroamericana (EDUCA). Concludes that there is a "certain margin of open and legal 'play' for the [Honduran] peasantry, as distinct from other Central American cases" (p. 408).

Meza, Victor. 1985. "Historia del movimiento obrero en Honduras." Pp. 128–95 in *Historia del movimiento obrero en américa latina*, vol. 2, edited by Pablo Gonzalez Casanova. Mexico City: Siglo Veintiuno Editores. A fine overview.

——— 1988. "The Military: Willing to Deal." *NACLA Report on the Americas* 22 (1):14–21. Suggests that nationalistic officers have been able to maintain considerable autonomy from the United States.

Morris, James A. 1984a. *Honduras: Caudillo Politics and Military Rulers*. Boulder, CO: Westview Press. An introductory analysis by a leading country specialist. The following two pieces develop some of its themes.

——— 1984b. "Honduras: The Burden of Survival in Central America." Pp. 189–225 in *Central America: Crisis and Adaptation*, edited by Steve C. Ropp and James A. Morris. Albuquerque, NM: University of New Mexico Press.

——— 1985. "Honduras: Civil-Military Politics and Democracy." Pp. 562–80 in *Latin American Politics and Development*, edited by Howard J. Wiarda and Harvey F. Kline. Second edition. Boulder, CO, and London: Westview Press.

Morris, James A. and Steve C. Ropp. 1977. "Corporatism and Dependent Development: A Honduran Case Study." *Latin American Research Review* 12:27–68. Informative, although the "corporatism" argument, which was quite popular among Latin Americanists at the time, fails to convince.

Paz Aguilar, Ernesto. 1992. "The Origin and Development of Political Parties in Honduras." Pp. 161–74 in *Political Parties and Democracy in Central America*, edited by Louis W. Goodman, William M. LeoGrande, and Johanna Mendelson Forman. Boulder, CO: Westview Press. Emphasizes the truncated ideological spectrum inhabited by Honduras's major parties.

Pearson, Neale J. 1980. "Peasant Pressure Groups and Agrarian Reform in Honduras, 1962–1977." Pp. 297–320 in *Rural Change and Public Policy: Eastern Europe, Latin America, and Australia*, edited by William P. Avery, Richard

III. Central America

E. Lonsdale, and Ivan Volgyes. New York: Pergamon Press. Short but informative.

Peckenham, Nancy and Annie Street, eds. 1985. *Honduras: Portrait of a Captive Nation*. New York: Praeger. An excellent collection of material on a variety of topics; focuses mainly on the 1980s.

Posas, Mario. 1985. "El movimiento campesino hondureño: Un panorama genderal (Siglo XX)." Pp. 28–76 in *Historia política de los campesinos latinoamericanos, vol. 2*, edited by Pablo González Casanova. Mexico City: Siglo Veintiuno Editores. An excellent overview by a noted expert.

Posas, Mario and Rafael del Cid. 1983. *La construcción del sector publico y del estado nacional en Honduras, 1876–1979*. Second edition. San José, Costa Rica: Editoral Universitaria Centroamericana. The best account of state formation in Honduras, although see also Williams 1994 and Euraque 1996.

Reina, Jorge Arturo. 1981. "Honduras: ¿Revolución pacífica o violenta?" *Nueva Sociedad* 52 (Jan.–Feb.):35–56. Astute observations on Honduran exceptionalism.

Ropp, Steve C. 1974. "The Honduran Army in the Sociopolitical Evolution of the Honduran State." *The Americas* 30:504–28. An important piece, although see also Salamón 1982, Sieder 1995, and Euraque 1996: chs. 4, 7–9.

Rosenberg, Mark B. 1995. "Democracy in Honduras: The Electoral and the Political Reality." Pp. 66–83 in *Elections and Democracy in Central America, Revisited*, edited by Mitchell A. Seligson and John A. Booth. Chapel Hill, NC: University of North Carolina Press. Sanguine observations by a country specialist.

Ruhl, J. Mark. 1984. "Agrarian Structure and Political Stability in Honduras." *Journal of Interamerican Studies and World Affairs* 26:33–68. A very important analysis of Honduras's surprising political stability.

———. 1985. "The Honduran Agrarian Reform Under Suazo Córdova, 1982–1985: An Assessment." *Inter-American Economic Affairs* 39:63–80. A brief analysis of a limited reform.

———. 1996. "Redefining Civil-Military Relations in Honduras." *Journal of Interamerican Studies and World Affairs* 38/1:33–66. Charts the growth of the military's power and autonomy during the 1980s as well as its subsequent decline.

Salamón, Leticia. 1982. *Militarismo y reformismo en Honduras*. Tegucigalpa: Editorial Guaymuras. The best book-length study of the military reformism of the early 1970s. See also Euraque 1996: ch. 9 and Conclusion.

Schulz, Donald E. and Deborah Sundloff Schulz. 1994. *The United States, Honduras, and the Crisis in Central America*. Boulder, CO: Westview Press. One of the best recent analyses; focuses mainly on the 1980s. Especially relevant is Chapter 9, "How Honduras Escaped Revolutionary Violence." But see the critique in Euraque 1996: Conclusion.

Shepherd, Philip L. 1986a. "Honduras Confronts Its Future: Some Closing, But Hardly Final Thoughts." Pp. 229–55 in *Honduras Confronts Its Future: Contending Perspectives on Critical Issues*, edited by Mark B. Rosenberg and Philip L. Shepherd. Boulder, CO: Lynne Rienner. Provocative reflections by a noted country specialist.

1986b. "Honduras." Pp. 125–55 in *Confronting Revolution: Security Through Diplomacy in Central America*, edited by Morris J. Blachman, William M. LeoGrande, and Kenneth E. Sharpe. New York: Pantheon. An excellent overview.

1988. "The Case of Invisible Aid." *NACLA Report on the Americas* 22 (1):31–8. A very astute summary of the historic and contemporary features of Honduras's political economy.

Sieder, Rachel. 1995. "Honduras: The Politics of Exception and Military Reformism (1972–1978)." *Journal of Latin American Studies* 27:99–127. An important analysis of Honduran "exceptionalism," emphasizing how military reformism divided the labor and peasant movement.

Volk, Steven. 1983. "Honduras: On the Border of War." Pp. 203–43 in *Trouble in Our Backyard: Central America and the United States in the Eighties*, edited by Martin Diskin. New York: Pantheon. Discusses U.S. machinations in the early 1980s.

Wheaton, Philip E. 1982. *Inside Honduras: Regional Counterinsurgency Base*. Washington, DC: EPICA Task Force. A short analysis of the projection of U.S. armed forces into the country.

Williams, Robert G. 1989. "Coffee, Class, and the State in Honduras: A Comparative Sketch." Paper presented at the XV International Congress of the Latin American Studies Association, San Juan, Puerto Rico, September. Why Honduras is different. See also Williams 1994.

IV. Eastern Europe (Including the Soviet Union)

Arato, Andrew. 1993. "Interpreting 1989." *Social Research* 60:609–46. Emphasizes the development of "civil society."

Banac, Ivo, ed. 1992. *Eastern Europe in Revolution*. Ithaca, NY, and London: Cornell University Press. One of the best collections on the subject.

Baylis, Thomas A. 1994. "Plus Ça Change? Transformation and Continuity Among East European Elites." *Communist and Post-Communist Studies* 27:315–28. A critical analysis of the non-Communist intellectuals who assumed the most prominent positions in the post-Communist regimes.

Borocz, J. 1992. "Dual Dependency and Property Vacuum: Social Change on the State Socialist Semiperiphery." *Theory and Society* 21:77–104. Interesting reflections on the structural constraints (and opportunities) for radical change.

Brown, J. F. 1991. *Surge to Freedom: The End of Communist Rule in Eastern Europe*. Durham, NC, and London: Duke University Press. A very helpful overview.

Bruszt, László and David Stark. 1992. "Remaking the Political Field in Hungary: From the Politics of Confrontation to the Politics of Competition." Pp. 13–55 in *Eastern Europe in Revolution*, edited by Ivo Banac. Ithaca, NY, and London: Cornell University Press. Hungary's "negotiated revolution" in regional perspective.

Bunce, Valerie. 1985. "The Empire Strikes Back: The Transformation of the Eastern Bloc from a Soviet Asset to a Soviet Liability." *International Organization* 39: 1–46. The backdrop to Gorbachev's abandonment of the Brezhnev Doctrine.

IV. Eastern Europe (Including the Soviet Union)

1989. "Soviet Decline as a Regional Hegemon: Gorbachev and Eastern Europe." *Eastern European Politics and Societies* 3:235–67. Why Gorbachev pulled back.

1999. *Subversive Institutions: The Design and Destruction of Socialism and the State.* Cambridge, UK: Cambridge University Press. One of the sharpest and most important analyses of the fall of Communism.

Bunce, Valerie and Dennis Chong. 1990. "The Party's Over: Mass Protest and the End of Communist Rule in Eastern Europe." Paper presented at the 1990 Annual Meeting of the American Political Science Association, San Francisco, CA. How mass protest occurred with little formal organization; see also Pfaff 1996.

Burawoy, Michael and J. Lukacs. 1992. *The Radiant Past: Ideology and Reality in Hungary's Road to Capitalism.* Chicago and London: University of Chicago Press. Based on a fascinating workplace ethnography.

Campeanu, Pavel. 1991. "National Fervor in Eastern Europe: The Case of Romania." *Social Research* 58:805–28. On an interesting variant of nationalism.

Chilton, Patricia. 1995. "Mechanics of Change: Social Movements, Transnational Coalitions, and the Transformation Processes in Eastern Europe." Pp. 189–226 in *Bringing Transnational Relations Back In: Non-State Actors, Domestic Structures and International Institutions*, edited by Thomas Risse-Kappen. Cambridge, UK: Cambridge University Press. Emphasizes civil society and, less persuasively, transnational coalitions.

Chirot, Daniel. 1991. "What Happened in Eastern Europe in 1989?" Pp. 3–32 in *The Crisis of Leninism and the Decline of the Left: The Revolutions of 1989*, edited by Daniel Chirot. Seattle and London: University of Washington Press. Emphasizes the "utter moral rot" of Communism.

Codrescu, Andrei. 1991. *The Hole in the Flag: A Romanian Exile's Story of Return and Revolution.* New York: William Morrow. An interesting journalistic account by the well-known poet and essayist.

Connor, Walter. 1988. *Socialism's Dilemmas: State and Society in the Soviet Bloc.* New York: Columbia University Press. An excellent interpretive analysis of Communism.

Csanadi, M. 1990. "Beyond the Image: The Case of Hungary." *Social Research* 57:321–46. Why Hungary was different.

1992. "The Diary of Decline: A Case-Study of the Disintegration of the Party in One District in Hungary." *Soviet Studies* 43:1085–99. A fascinating case study.

Dahrendorf, Ralf. 1990. *Reflections on the Revolution in Europe.* New York: Times Books. A liberal interpretation.

de Flers, René. 1984. "Socialism in One Family." *Survey* 28:165–74. On Ceauşescu's Romania, of course.

Dix, Robert H. 1991. "Eastern Europe's Implications for Revolutionary Theory." *Polity* 24:227–42. Some very interesting reflections from a scholar best known for his work on Latin America.

Echikson, W. 1990. *Lighting the Night: Revolution in Eastern Europe.* New York: William Morrow and Company. A journalistic account.

Eisenstadt, S. N. 1992. "The Breakdown of Communist Regimes and the Vicissitudes of Modernity." *Daedalus* 121:21–41. Thoughtful reflections from the well-known sociologist.

Ekiert, Grzegorz. 1990. "Transitions from State-Socialism in East Central Europe." *States and Social Structures Newsletter* (Social Science Research Council) 12:1–7. A crisp, short analysis, emphasizing the posttotalitarian character of the state-socialist regimes.

1996. *The State Against Society: Political Crises and Their Aftermath in East Central Europe.* Princeton, NJ: Princeton University Press. A brilliant account of the crises in Hungary (1956), Czechoslovakia (1968), and Poland (1980), as well as the legacies of these crises for each country and the region as a whole.

Fagan, G. 1991. "Hungary: The Collapse of Kádárism." *Labour Focus on Eastern Europe* (June):23–32. An insightful overview.

Fields, G. 1991. "The Road From Gdansk: How Solidarity Found Haven in the Marketplace." *Monthly Review* 43 (July–August):95–121. On Solidarity's ideological and programmatic evolution.

Fischer, Mary Ellen. 1990. "Totalitarianism, Authoritarianism, and Revolution: The Sultanistic Tendencies of Nicolae Ceauşescu in Romania." Paper presented at the Workshop on Sultanistic Regimes, Center for International Affairs, Harvard University, November 1990. On the "sultanistic" nature of Ceauşescu's regime; see also Linz and Stepan 1996: ch. 18, and Chehabi and Linz 1998.

Fuller, Linda. 1999. *Where Was the Working Class? Revolution in East Germany.* Urbana, IL: University of Illinois Press. Based on extensive field research; the author does recognize (see ch. 6) that a significant minority of workers *were* involved in the revolution.

Garton Ash, Timothy. 1990. *The Magic Lantern: The Revolution of '89 Witnessed in Warsaw, Budapest, Berlin and Prague.* New York: Random House. The best eyewitness account – moving and insightful, although occasionally tendentious. See the commentary by Glenn (2000).

1991. "Poland After Solidarity." *The New York Review of Books* 38 (June 13):46–58. On the new regime.

Gati, Charles. 1990. *The Bloc That Failed: Soviet-East European Relations in Transition.* Bloomington, IN, and Indianapolis: Indiana University Press. One of best analyses of tensions within the bloc.

Georgescu, Vlad. 1988. "Romania in the 1980s: The Legacy of Dynastic Socialism." *Eastern European Politics and Societies* 2:69–93. What Ceauşescu wrought.

Gilberg, Trond. 1990. "Romania: Will History Repeat Itself?" *Current History* 89:409–12, 431–3. Reflections on the "revolution."

Glenn, John K. 2000. "Velvet Opportunities? A Commentary on Timothy Garton Ash's *The Magic Lantern.*" Forthcoming in *Paths to Protest: Political Opportunities in Contemporary Social Movement Studies,* edited by Jeff Goodwin. Unpublished manuscript.

Glenny, Misha. 1990. *The Rebirth of History: Eastern Europe in the Age of Democracy.* London: Penguin Books. Interesting short history of the demise of Communism.

IV. Eastern Europe (Including the Soviet Union)

Goldstone, Jack A. 1993. "Why We Could (and Should) Have Foreseen the Revolutions of 1989–1991 in the U.S.S.R. and Eastern Europe." *Contention* 2:127–52. If only we had used Goldstone's (1991) model.

Goodwin, Jeff and Valerie Bunce. 1991. "Eastern Europe's 'Refolutions' in Comparative and Theoretical Perspective." Paper presented at the 1991 Annual Meeting of the American Political Science Association, Washington, DC. An earlier version of the analysis in Chapter 8 of this book.

Gross, Jan T. 1992. "Poland: From Civil Society to Political Nation." Pp. 56–71 in *Eastern Europe in Revolution*, edited by Ivo Banac. Ithaca, NY: Cornell University Press. A helpful overview of the transition.

Habermas, Jürgen. 1990. "What Does Socialism Mean Today? The Rectifying Revolution and the Need for New Thinking on the Left." *New Left Review* 183:3–21. A provocative interpretation of 1989 by the well-known social theorist.

Hankiss, Elemer. 1990. "What the Hungarians Saw First." Pp. 13–36 in *Spring in Winter: The 1989 Revolutions*, edited by G. Prins. Manchester, UK, and New York: Manchester University Press. An interesting overview of the Hungarian transition.

Heyns, Barbara and Ireneusz Bialecki. 1991. "Solidarnosc: Reluctant Vanguard or Makeshift Coalition?" *American Political Science Review* 85:351–70. Who voted for Solidarity?

Hirschman, Albert O. 1993. "Exit, Voice, and the Fate of the German Democratic Republic: An Essay in Conceptual History." *World Politics* 45:173–202. An application of the author's well-known scheme to the fall of the GDR.

Holmes, Leslie. 1993. *The End of Communist Power: Anti-Corruption Campaigns and Legitimation Crisis*. New York: Oxford University Press. An interesting account of anticorruption campaigns that provides only a partial window on the end of Communism.

James, Harold. 1997. "The Landscape That Didn't Blossom." *Times Literary Supplement* (June 13), No. 4195, pp. 5–6. Discusses recent literature on the GDR and German unification.

Joppke, Christian. 1995. *East German Dissidents and the Revolution of 1989: Social Movement in a Leninist Regime*. New York: New York University Press. An account of East German "cxccptionalism" – that is, the predominance of reform Communists within the opposition movement prior to late 1989.

Jowitt, Kenneth. 1983. "Soviet Neotraditionalism: The Political Corruption of a Leninist Regime." *Soviet Studies* 35:275–97. An astute analysis of corruption under Communism.

Judt, Tony. 1988. "The Dilemmas of Dissidence: The Politics of Opposition in East-Central Europe." *Eastern European Politics and Societies* 2:185–240. An interesting account of dissent *apres le deluge*.

1992. "Metamorphosis: The Democratic Revolution in Czechoslovakia." Pp. 96–116 in *Eastern Europe in Revolution*, edited by Ivo Banac. Ithaca, NY, and London: Cornell University Press. On the "velvet revolution" and its immediate aftermath.

Kamiński, Bartlomiej. 1991. *The Collapse of State Socialism: The Case of Poland.* Princeton, NJ: Princeton University Press. A sophisticated account of the institutional weaknesses of Communism; see also Bunce 1999.

Kinzer, Stephen. 1996. "East German Ex-Activists Continue as a Force in West." *The New York Times*, May 26, 3. Still seeking democratic socialism.

Kolankiewicz, G. 1988. "Poland, and the Politics of Permissible Pluralism." *Eastern European Politics and Society* 2:152–83. Polish civil society in the making.

Konrád, George. 1984. *Antipolitics.* New York: Harcourt Brace Jovanovich. An influential political response to political repression.

——— 1995. *The Melancholy of Rebirth: Essays from Post-Communist Central Europe, 1989–1994.* San Diego, CA: Harcourt Brace. Provocative essays on the transition.

Kopstein, Jeffrey. 1996. "Chipping Away at the State: Workers' Resistance and the Demise of East Germany." *World Politics* 48:391–423. Suggests that workers more than bureaucrats immobilized the old regime by resisting economic "reforms."

Kornai, Janos. 1980. *Economics of Shortage.* Amsterdam: North Holland Press. One of the most influential anatomies of state-socialist economies.

Kuran, Timur. 1991. "Now Out of Never: The Element of Surprise in the East European Revolution of 1989." *World Politics* 44:7–48. How "falsified preferences" disguised an imminent revolution.

Laqueur, Walter. 1994. *The Dream That Failed: Reflections on the Soviet Union.* New York: Oxford University Press. Includes sober chapters on the fall of the Soviet Union and of East Germany.

Lieven, Anatol. 1994. *The Baltic Revolution: Estonia, Latvia, Lithuania and the Path to Independence.* Second edition. New Haven, CT: Yale University Press. The best book on the nationalist movements in this part of the Soviet Union's internal empire.

Linden, Ronald H. 1986. "Socialist Patrimonialism and the Global Economy: The Case of Romania." *International Organization* 40:347–80. One of the best analyses of Ceauşescu's Romania.

Maslovski, Mikhail. 1996. "Max Weber's Concept of Patrimonialism and the Soviet System." *Sociological Review* 44:294–308. A short but helpful discussion of the concept.

Mason, David S. 1989. "Solidarity as a New Social Movement." *Political Science Quarterly* 104:41–58. A theoretical analysis of the emergence and development of Solidarity.

——— 1992. *Revolution in East-Central Europe: The Rise and Fall of Communism and the Cold War.* Boulder, CO: Westview Press. A very helpful overview.

Michnik, Adam. 1985 (1976). "The New Evolutionism." Pp. 135–48 in *Letters From Prison and Other Essays.* Berkeley, CA, and Los Angeles: University of California Press. An influential essay by the Polish dissident.

Naimark, Norman M. 1992a. "Revolution and Counterrevolution in Eastern Europe." Pp. 61–83 in *The Crisis of Socialism in Europe*, edited by C. Lemke and G. Marks. Durham, NC, and London: Duke University Press. A broad interpretive essay.

IV. Eastern Europe (Including the Soviet Union)

1992b. " 'Ich will hier raus': Emigration and the Collapse of the German Democratic Republic." Pp. 72–95 in *Eastern Europe in Revolution*, edited by Ivo Banac. Ithaca, NY: Cornell University Press. A fine short overview of "the turn." See also Hirschman 1993.

Opp, Karl-Dieter and C. Gern. 1993. "Dissident Groups, Personal Networks, and Spontaneous Cooperation: The East German Revolution of 1989." *American Sociological Review* 58:659–80. Rational-choice theory in Leipzig.

Ost, David. 1989. "The Transformation of Solidarity and the Future of Central Europe." *Telos* 79:69–94. How martial law transformed Solidarity. See also Mason 1989.

Pakulski, J. 1986. "Legitimacy and Mass Compliance: Reflections on Max Weber and Soviet-Type Societies." *British Journal of Political Science* 16:35–56. How Communism secured compliance.

Pehe, Jiri. 1989. "An Annotated Survey of Independent Movements in Eastern Europe." Radio Free Europe Research, RAD Background Report/100 (Eastern Europe), June 13, pp. 1–29. Poland had sixty independent movements in June 1989, Hungary twenty-one, the GDR nine, and Romania two.

Pfaff, Steven. 1996. "Collective Identity and Informal Groups in Revolutionary Mobilization: East Germany in 1989." *Social Forces* 75:91–118. A sharp account of mobilization when dense social ties and political opportunities are lacking.

Piekalkiewicz, Jarolaw. 1991. "Poland: Nonviolent Revolution in a Socialist State." Pp. 136–61 in *Revolutions of the Late Twentieth Century*, edited by Jack A. Goldstone, Ted Robert Gurr, and Farrokh Moshiri. Boulder, CO: Westview Press. A helpful overview of the revolution.

Pravda, A. 1981. "East-West Interdependence and the Future of Eastern Europe." Pp. 162–90 in *East-West Relations and the Future of Eastern Europe*, edited by M. Bornstein, Z. Gitelman, and W. Zimmerman. London: Allen and Unwin. How ties to the West mattered.

Prins, G., ed. 1990. *Spring in Winter: The 1989 Revolutions*. Manchester, UK, and New York: Manchester University Press. Interesting essays by activists and intellectuals.

Ramet, Sabrina Petra. 1991. *Social Currents in Eastern Europe: The Sources and Meaning of the Great Transformation*. Durham, NC, and London: Duke University Press. One of the best overviews of recent trends; full of interesting data and reflections.

Ratesh, Nestor. 1991. *Romania: The Entangled Revolution*. New York: Praeger. An attempt to sort it all out.

Reich, Jens. 1990. "Reflections on Becoming an East German Dissident, on Losing the Wall and a Country." Pp. 65–97 in *Spring in Winter: The 1989 Revolutions*, edited by G. Prins. Manchester, UK, and New York: Manchester University Press. Provocative personal reflections.

Roper, Steven D. 1994. "The Romanian Revolution from a Theoretical Perspective." *Communist and Post-Communist Studies* 27:401–10. In the author's words, "a cursory examination of the Romanian revolution and its theoretical basis" (p. 409).

Rosenberg, Tina. 1995. *The Haunted Land: Facing Europe's Ghosts After Communism*. New York: Vintage. An engaging journalistic tour.

Rothschild, Joseph. 1993. *Return to Diversity: A Political History of East Central Europe Since World War II*. Second edition. New York: Oxford University Press. One of the best general histories.

Sampson, S. 1986. "The Second Economy in Eastern Europe and the Soviet Union." *Annals of the American Association of Political and Social Science*, 493:120–36. An interesting overview.

Schöpflin, George. 1991. "Obstacles to Liberalism in Post-Communist Polities." *Eastern European Politics and Societies* 5:189–94. On some of the pernicious legacies of Communism.

——— 1993. *Politics in Eastern Europe, 1945–1992*. Oxford: Blackwell. An excellent political analysis.

Scruton, Roger. 1988a. "The New Right in Central Europe I: Czechoslovakia." *Political Studies* 36:449–62. This and the following piece chart an important intellectual trend.

——— 1988b. "The New Right in Central Europe II: Poland and Hungary." *Political Studies* 36:638–52.

Segal, Gerald and John Phipps. 1990. "Why Communist Armies Defend Their Parties." *Asian Survey* 30:959–76. It's difficult, of course, when their parties are divided.

Simons, Thomas W., Jr. 1993. *Eastern Europe in the Postwar World*. Second edition. New York: St. Martin's Press. Along with Rothschild (1993) and Schöpflin (1993), one of the best general overviews of the postwar era.

Staniszkis, Jadwiga. 1991a. "'Political Capitalism' in Poland." *Eastern European Politics and Societies* 5:127–41. Very interesting reflections by an important Polish scholar.

——— 1991b. *The Dynamics of Breakthrough in Eastern Europe: The Polish Experience*. Berkeley, CA, and Los Angeles: University of California Press. One of the key texts on Poland.

Stark, David. 1996. "Recombinant Property in East European Capitalism." *American Journal of Sociology* 101:993–1027. On the emergence of a distinctively Eastern European capitalism.

Stokes, Gale. 1993. *The Walls Came Tumbling Down: The Collapse of Communism in Eastern Europe*. New York and Oxford: Oxford University Press. An excellent overview.

Suny, Ronald. 1990. "The Revenge of the Past: Socialism and Ethnic Conflict in Transcaucasia." *New Left Review* 184:5–34. National liberation turns nasty.

Szelenyi, Ivan and Balazs Szelenyi. 1994. "Why Socialism Failed: Toward a Theory of System Breakdown – Causes of Disintegration of East European State Socialism." *Theory and Society* 23:211–31. Argues that failure was neither inevitable nor strictly economically determined.

Tismăneanu, Vladimir. 1989. "The Tragicomedy of Romanian Communism." *Eastern European Politics and Societies* 3:329–76. An important and entertaining overview.

IV. Eastern Europe (Including the Soviet Union)

Tökés, Rudolf L. 1996. *Hungary's Negotiated Revolution: Economic Reform, Social Change and Political Succession.* Cambridge, UK: Cambridge University Press. Extremely detailed, with much information on the Kádár era.

Torpey, John C. 1995. *Intellectuals, Socialism, and Dissent: The East German Opposition and Its Legacy.* Minneapolis, MN: University of Minnesota Press. An excellent study of intellectual support for a democratic and reformed socialism in the GDR.

Verdery, Katherine. 1993. "What Was Socialism and Why Did It Fall?" *Contention* 3:1–23. Extremely provocative and important.

Verdery, Katherine and Gail Kligman. 1992. "Romania after Ceausescu: Post-Communist Communism?" Pp. 117–47 in *Eastern Europe in Revolution*, edited by Ivo Banac. Ithaca, NY, and London: Cornell University Press: 117–147. Interesting reflections by two of the most astute commentators on Romania.

Walicki, Andrzej. 1991. "From Stalinism to Post-Communist Pluralism: The Case of Poland." *New Left Review* 185:92–121. A helpful overview of Poland's transition.

Waller, Michael. 1993. *The End of the Communist Power Monopoly.* Manchester, UK, and New York: Manchester University Press. An interesting analytic study; includes a chapter on the events of 1989.

Wheaton, Bernard and Zdeněk Kavan. 1992. *The Velvet Revolution: Czechoslovakia, 1988–1991.* Boulder, CO: Westview Press. A useful historical overview, with several chapters on the "November revolution" of 1989.

Index

Acción Democrática (AD) (Venezuela), 231, 233, 237
Afghanistan, 57, 256–7
Africa, 129–30, 132, 257, 272, 289, 300, 305
agrarian reform. *See* land reform.
agroexporting economies, 22–3, 146
Agüero, Fernando (Nicaragua), 156
Agüero-Somoza pact (Nicaragua), 156
Albania, 281n, 297
Alegrett, José Ivan (Nicaragua), 191
Alejandrino, Casto (Philippines), 99
Algeria, 57, 130, 132, 261, 263, 269, 272, 277, 289, 297, 301
Alliance, the (Malaya), 116–7
Allies (World War II), 86, 92–3, 97, 99
Álvarez Martínez, Gustavo (Honduras), 173
Amenta, Edwin, 14n
Americas Watch (AW), 222, 237–40
Amnesty International (AI), 161, 199
Anderson, Perry, 42
Angola, 132, 257, 261, 269
Aquino, Benigno, Jr. (Philippines), 120
Archer, Margaret, 54
Argentina, 226
armed forces, 144, 148, 157–60, 181, 183, 202, 209, 217–8, 233–4, 237, 246–7, 249, 252, 282, 285–6, 291–2, 296

Armed Forces of National Liberation (FALN) (Venezuela), 220, 231, 233, 237
Armed Forces of National Resistance (FARN) (El Salvador), 164, 167
armed struggle, 47–8, 50, 60, 62, 74, 76–7, 79, 81–2, 89, 91–2, 94–6, 99–102, 115, 122–8, 149, 155, 162–6, 168, 171, 176–8, 186, 188, 209, 220–1, 232–3, 235, 237, 245–6, 260, 275–6, 294, 296, 300–2
Army of the Republic of Vietnam (ARVN), 111–2
Ash, Timothy Garton, 260, 271, 273, 279–81
Association of Rural Workers (ATC) (Nicaragua), 163–4
Associated State of Vietnam, 110
Atlacatl Battalion (El Salvador), 197, 238
Australia, 301

banana industry, in Honduras, 170–1, 174
Bandung conference (Indonesia), 89
Bao Dai (Vietnam), 93, 110–2, 114
Barquín, Ramón (Cuba), 61
base communities, Christian, 159–60
Batista, Fulgencio (Cuba), 50, 60, 186, 212, 263

391

Index

China, 75, 77, 91–3, 112, 114, 116, 122–4, 186, 228, 257, 277, 279, 289, 296–7
Chinese (in Malaya), 84, 94–7, 115–7, 121, 125–7, 225, 232, 236
Chinese Communists, 47, 49, 77, 82, 96, 110, 116, 122–3
Chinese Nationalists (Kuomintang), 93, 96, 124
Ching Peng (Malaya), 95, 117–8
Chorley, Katharine, 283
Christian Democratic Party (DCG) (Guatemala), 158
Christian Democratic Party (PDC) (El Salvador), 196
Christian Democrats, in Central America, 148, 157–8, 162, 164–5, 167, 200, 202, 208, 233
Christian Federation of Salvadoran Peasants (FECCAS) (El Salvador), 160, 167
Cienfuegos (Cuba), naval uprising at, 61
Civic Forum (Czechoslovakia), 276, 280
Civil Defense Patrols (PACs) (Guatemala), 199, 202, 239
civil rights movement (U.S.), 295
civil society, 33, 35–7, 46, 51, 55–6, 63, 185, 248, 257–8, 262–3, 265, 273, 276–8, 285, 287–8, 290–2, 302
civilian guards (Philippines), 119, 235
Clark Air Base (Philippines), 100
class, analysis, 51, 59–60, 75, 101–2, 225; oppression, 90; structure, 30, 55, 63, 75, 143–4, 213, 262, 288, 290; struggle or conflict, 20, 36, 42–3, 45n, 62, 75, 81, 88, 109, 144, 150, 168, 274, 293, 301. *See also* economic grievances and exploitation; Marxists, Marxist theory.
coffee, 174–5, 202, 229–30, 246
Cold War, Cold War era, 3, 5–6, 8, 16, 88–9, 95, 107, 148, 252, 289–91, 298–300, 304

Collins, Randall, 44n
Colom Argueta, Manuel (Guatemala), 158
Colombia, 217–8, 220, 241–3, 250, 289, 294, 297, 305
Colombian Communist Party, 241
colonialism, colonialists, 32, 74–82, 84–5, 87, 89–90, 101–2, 104–6, 109–10, 114–5, 121, 124–5, 127, 129–31, 142, 262, 269, 272, 289, 291–2, 296; direct, 80n; exclusionary, 80, 88–9, 104, 124, 128, 132, 212, 225, 261, 265–6, 269, 274, 291, 300; inclusionary, 80, 104, 126–8, 131, 291; indirect, 80n, 104n, 126; settler, 82; variations of, 109, 128–30, 133. *See also* regimes, colonial or neocolonial; states, colonial.
Cominform (Communist Information Bureau), 95
Committee of Peasant Unity (CUC) (Guatemala), 161, 168
Communism, Communists, 17–8, 21, 31–3, 47, 72, 75–81, 84, 86–7, 89–91, 95–6, 100–3, 105–7, 109, 111, 120, 122, 125, 130–1, 148, 157, 162, 178, 220, 256–7, 260, 262, 268, 291, 297–8, 301, 304. *See also* socialism.
Communist Party of Peru (Maoist). *See* Shining Path.
Communist Party of the Philippines (PKP), 77, 98–100, 118, 120–1, 128, 235
Communist Party of Venezuela (PCV), 233, 237
Communities of People in Resistance (CPR) (Guatemala), 199
comparative-historical analysis, xvi, 3, 5–8. *See also* qualitative comparative analysis.
Confucian scholar-gentry (Vietnam), 84
Conservative Party (Nicaragua), 156

Index

204, 209, 211–3, 235, 291, 303;
chronology, 140–1
Honecker, Erich (East Germany), 276
Huk rebellion (Philippines), xvi, 77,
83, 97–101, 118–20, 127–8, 219,
223, 225, 227, 231–2, 235–6, 250
Hukbalahap (Philippines), 77, 98,
100–1
Hukbong Bayan Laban sa Hapon
(Philippines). *See* Hukbalahap.
Hukbong Mapagpalaya ng Bayan
(HMB) (Philippines), 77, 100
human rights abuses, 173, 198, 200,
202–3, 222, 237–9, 241, 243, 247–8.
See also repression.
Hungary, 256, 260–1, 263, 266, 267n,
271, 273, 276–8, 282–3, 286, 288,
292
Huntington, Samuel, 17–9, 278
Hussein, Saddam (Iraq), 185–6, 304
Huynh Kim Khanh, 91

identity, collective, 47, 55, 57, 133,
145; national or ethnic, 122, 130,
132. *See also* nationalism.
ideology, 26, 53, 57, 263–4, 267,
270–1, 273, 276, 282, 288, 290, 296,
304
imperial overextension, 39, 258
imperialism, 74, 75n, 90, 95, 101,
103–4, 123, 129, 133, 144, 148, 168,
259, 272, 287, 300. *See also*
colonialism, colonialists.
impunity, military, 202, 207, 238,
248
independence, political, 81–2, 86–8,
94, 96, 98–100, 110, 116, 118, 123,
125–7, 130. *See also* national
liberation.
Independent Liberal Party (PLI)
(Nicaragua), 167
Independent Movement of
Professionals and Technicians of El
Salvador (MIPTES), 168
India, 129, 295. *See also* South Asia.
Indian Independence League, 94

Indian National Army, 94
Indians (in Malaya), 84, 94, 96–7, 126
indigenous people, in El Salvador,
225; in Guatemala, 166, 199, 207,
224, 239; in Peru, 224
Indochina, French Indochina, 76,
81–2, 85, 91, 105, 107n, 111. *See
also* Cambodia; Laos; Vietnam.
Indochinese Communist Party (ICP),
78, 81, 84, 91, 109, 111, 121. *See
also* Vietnam, Vietnamese
Revolution.
Indonesia, Indonesian National
Revolution, 31–2, 72, 77–9, 80n,
81–91, 99, 101–4, 123, 131, 177,
211, 220n, 291, 296–8; chronology,
70–1
Indonesian Communist Party (PKI),
32, 77, 81–2, 86–7, 89, 124; "Illegal
PKI," 85
Indonesian Nationalist Party (PNI),
85
Inevitable Revolutions (LaFeber), 149
infrastructural power (or weakness),
11, 28–30, 41–3, 49, 51, 143, 148,
163, 166, 168, 180, 195, 204, 212–3,
217, 235, 241, 243, 245, 250–3, 262,
267, 275, 284, 290–2, 296–7;
defined, 38. *See also* state power.
insurgencies. *See* guerrillas;
revolutionary movements.
intellectuals, intelligentsia, 267, 273,
303
International Monetary Fund (IMF),
268n
international state system. *See* state,
international system.
Iran, Iranian Revolution, 47, 185, 212,
256–7, 261, 263, 269, 277n, 278,
284, 294–5, 301, 304
Iraq, 186, 296–7, 304
Islam, 85–6; "fundamentalism," 58
Israel, 203, 224, 226. *See also* West
Bank and Gaza.
Italy, 300n
Ixils, ethnic (Guatemala), 161, 163

Index

resource-mobilization theory, 57, 132, 293

resources, material, 55–8, 63, 122, 128, 132, 182

Revolutionary Armed Forces of Colombia (FARC), 220, 241

revolutionary movements, 12, 16, 18, 23, 25–7, 29–33, 40, 42–3, 51, 55–6, 72–5, 78–9, 81–2, 84, 102–3, 105–6, 108, 143–4, 146, 149, 171, 177–8, 219, 223, 260, 303; defeated or failed, 219–20, 223, 225–9, 231, 243, 247, 249–50, 297, 299, 304; defined, 10; in Eastern Europe, 267–2; formation of (generally), 44–50, 290–3; formation of (Central America), 150–69; formation of (Southeast Asia), 89–101; nationalist, 83; nonviolent, 260–1, 275, 295; radical, 10–1, 16, 72, 80, 122, 133, 155, 176; size of, 223–4; socialist, 23, 83; successful, 219; trajectories of (Central America), chap. 6 *passim*; trajectories of (Southeast Asia), 120–8, 130–2; use of violence by, 48, 242–3, 275. *See also* guerrillas; mass or popular mobilization; nationalism; persistent insurgencies; popular insurrection.

Revolutionary Organization of People in Arms (ORPA) (Guatemala), 165–6, 207

Revolutionary Party of Central American Workers (PRTC) (El Salvador), 164, 168

revolutionary situation, 49, 80, 100, 172, 182, 220–1; defined, 12

revolutionary wave, 6, 165

revolutions, anticolonial, 78; anti-imperialist, 258; bourgeois, 21, 261; conservative or reformist, 11; defined, 8–10, 260; "Eastern," 278; failed, 7, 217–8; from above, 9; future of, 297–306; Marxist, 301; morality of, xvii; nationalist, 259; negotiated, 218, 273; outcomes,

36n, 80; peripheral, 290; permanent, 21; political, 9, 81; radical, 10; social, 9, 11, 81, 149, 259–60, 298; socialist, 20, 23; successful, 6–7, 217–8; theories of, 16–24, 132–3, 146, 176; "total," 47–8, 266–7; "velvet," 287–8; "Western," 278

Ríos Montt, Efraín (Guatemala), 158, 196–7, 199

riots, 302

rising expectations, 18

Robelo Callejas, Alfonso (Nicaragua), 187, 189

Romania, 50, 212, 258, 260–1, 263, 273, 275, 278–80, 284–7, 292, 299

Romanian Communist Party (RCP), 284–6

Romero, Carlos Humberto (El Salvador), 160, 196

Romero, Oscar (El Salvador), 197, 245, 247

rondas campesinas (Peru), 242–3

Roosevelt, Franklin D. (U.S.), 130

Rosenberg, Tina, 270

Rostow, Walter, 17

Roxas, Manuel (Philippines), 100

Ruhl, Mark, 172–4

ruling or dominant class, 45, 49, 51, 54, 144, 167, 182, 184, 274, 283

Russian Revolution, 93, 296

Ryan, Phil, 194

Saigon (Vietnam), 93, 109

Salvadoran Communist Party (PCS), 162, 164, 168

Samayoa, Salvador (El Salvador), 142

San Salvador (El Salvador), 160–1, 197, 204–5, 227, 238

Sandinista National Liberation Front (FSLN) (Nicaragua), 33, 143–5, 159–60, 163–4, 166–7, 169, 178, 180, 182, 186, 188–95, 203, 210–1, 218, 246

Schulz, Deborah Sundloff, 169

Schulz, Donald E., 169

Scott, James C., 45n

Index

Wheelock, Jaime (Nicaragua), 187n
Wickham-Crowley, Timothy, 212–3, 233
Williams, Robert, 209
Wolf, Eric, 22–3, 75, 263
Wood, Elisabeth, 163
workers, working class, wage-earners, 7, 20–1, 23, 27, 32, 46, 83–4, 95–6, 115, 121, 125–6, 146, 148n, 160, 163–7, 171, 177, 201–2, 205, 207, 209, 230, 232–3, 265, 267, 270, 273, 301
world-historical context, 149
world region, 5, 7; defined, 14. *See also* regional approach.

world-systems, world-systems theory, 16n, 74–5, 132, 272
World War II, 5, 21, 31, 72, 75–6, 79–80, 82, 84, 87, 89–90, 94, 101, 103–4, 106–9, 123, 125–6, 129–32, 243, 259, 291–2, 296
Wuthnow, Robert, 53

Yen Bay (Vietnam), 124
Yugoslavia, 297

Zaire, 185, 212, 297–8
Zamora, Rubén (El Salvador), 168, 201
Zimbabwe, 132, 289

Yossi Shain and Juan Linz, eds., *Between States: Interim Governments and Democratic Transitions*

Theda Skocpol, *Social Revolutions in the Modern World*

David Stark and László Bruszt, *Postsocialist Pathways: Transforming Politics and Property in East Central Europe*

Sven Steinmo, Kathleen Thelan, and Frank Longstreth, eds., *Structuring Politics: Historical Institutionalism in Comparative Analysis*

Sidney Tarrow, *Power in Movement: Social Movements and Contentious Politics*

Ashutosh Varshney, *Democracy, Development, and the Countryside*

Elisabeth J. Wood, *Forging Democracy from Below: Insurgent Transitions in South Africa and El Salvador*